Innovations in International Business

Also by Peter J. Buckley

FOREIGN DIRECT INVESTMENT, CHINA AND THE WORLD ECONOMY

THE MULTINATIONAL ENTERPRISE REVISITED (*with Mark Casson*)

THE MULTINATIONAL ENTERPRISE AND THE GLOBALIZATION OF KNOWLEDGE

THE CHALLENGE OF INTERNATIONAL BUSINESS

CANADA-UK BILATERAL TRADE AND INVESTMENT RELATIONS (*with Christopher L. Paes and Kate Prescott*)

THE CHANGING GLOBAL CONTEXT OF INTERNATIONAL BUSINESS

FOREIGN DIRECT INVESTMENT AND MULTINATIONAL ENTERPRISES

INTERNATIONAL STRATEGIC MANAGEMENT AND GOVERNMENT POLICY

THE FUTURE OF MULTINATIONAL ENTERPRISE (*with Mark Casson*)

INTERNATIONAL TECHNOLOGY TRANSFER BY SMALL AND MEDIUM-SIZED ENTERPISES (*co-edited with Jaime Campos and Eduardo White*)

MULTINATIONAL ENTERPRISES IN LESS DEVELOPED COUNTRIES (*co-edited with Jeremy Clegg*)

MULTINATIONAL FIRMS, COOPERATION AND COMPETITION IN THE WORLD ECONOMY

THE STRATEGY AND ORGANIZATION OF INTERNATIONAL BUSINESS (*co-edited with Fred Burton and Hafiz Mirza*)

STUDIES IN INTERNATIONAL BUSINESS

INTERNATIONAL BUSINESS: Economics and Anthropology, Theory and Method

Innovations in International Business

Peter J. Buckley
Professor of International Business, University of Leeds, UK

Selection and editorial content © Peter J. Buckley 2012
Foreword © Donald Lessard 2012
Individual chapters © the contributors 2012

All rights reserved. No reproduction, copy or transmission of this publication may be made without written permission.

No portion of this publication may be reproduced, copied or transmitted save with written permission or in accordance with the provisions of the Copyright, Designs and Patents Act 1988, or under the terms of any licence permitting limited copying issued by the Copyright Licensing Agency, Saffron House, 6–10 Kirby Street, London EC1N 8TS.

Any person who does any unauthorized act in relation to this publication may be liable to criminal prosecution and civil claims for damages.

The authors have asserted their rights to be identified as the authors of this work in accordance with the Copyright, Designs and Patents Act 1988.

First published 2012 by
PALGRAVE MACMILLAN

Palgrave Macmillan in the UK is an imprint of Macmillan Publishers Limited, registered in England, company number 785998, of Houndmills, Basingstoke, Hampshire RG21 6XS.

Palgrave Macmillan in the US is a division of St Martin's Press LLC, 175 Fifth Avenue, New York, NY 10010.

Palgrave Macmillan is the global academic imprint of the above companies and has companies and representatives throughout the world.

Palgrave® and Macmillan® are registered trademarks in the United States, the United Kingdom, Europe and other countries

ISBN: 978–0–230–28966–6

This book is printed on paper suitable for recycling and made from fully managed and sustained forest sources. Logging, pulping and manufacturing processes are expected to conform to the environmental regulations of the country of origin.

A catalogue record for this book is available from the British Library.

Library of Congress Cataloging-in-Publication Data

    Innovations in international business / edited by Peter J. Buckley.
      pages cm
    Includes bibliographical references.
    ISBN 978–0–230–28966–6
    1. International business enterprises – Management. I. Buckley, Peter J., 1949–
HD62.4.I524 2012
658'.049—dc23   2012016696

10 9 8 7 6 5 4 3 2 1
21 20 19 18 17 16 15 14 13 12

For Janet Wood

With thanks for all the hard work and for putting up with me!

Contents

List of Figures	ix
List of Tables	xi
Acknowledgements	xiii
Foreword by Donald Lessard	xv
Notes on Contributors	xix

1 Introduction   1

Part I   Theory and Modelling the MNE

2 Business History and International Business   7

3 Internalisation Thinking: From the Multinational
Enterprise to the Global Factory   39

4 The Theory of International Business Pre-Hymer   60

5 The Governance of the Multinational Enterprise:
Insights from Internalization Theory   94
Co-authored with Roger Strange

6 Formalizing Internationalization in the Eclectic Paradigm   107
Co-authored with Niron Hashai

7 The Impact of the Global Factory on Economic Development   129

Part II   Knowledge, Innovation and Management

8 Under What Conditions Do Firms Benefit from the
Research Efforts of Other Organizations?   157
Co-authored with Mario I. Kafouros

9 The Role of Internationalization in Explaining
Innovation Performance   183
*Co-authored with Mario I. Kafouros,
John A. Sharp, and Chengqi Wang*

viii *Contents*

10 Knowledge Accession and Knowledge Acquisition
in Strategic Alliances: The Impact of Supplementary and
Complementary Dimensions 206
Co-authored with Keith W. Glaister, Elko Klijn, and Hui Tan

11 Do Managers Behave the Way Theory Suggests?
A Choice-Theoretic Examination of Foreign Direct Investment
Location Decision-Making 224
Co-authored with Timothy M. Devinney and Jordan J. Louviere

12 The Role of Headquarters in the Global Factory 266

Part III   Cultural Distance and Asian Business

13 Close Neighbours and Distant Friends – Perceptions of
Cultural Distance 291
Co-authored with Malcolm Chapman,
Hanna Gajewska-De Mattos, and Jeremy Clegg

14 Doing Business in Developing and Transitional Countries: An
Empirical Example of the Dominant Logic and Its Alternative 318
Co-authored with Malcolm Chapman, Jeremy Clegg, and Hanna
Gajewska-De Mattos

15 The Rise of the Japanese Multinational Enterprise:
Then and Now 343

16 Japanese Multinational Enterprises in China:
Successful Adaptation of Marketing Strategies 358
Co-authored with Sierk A. Horn

Index 387

Figures

3.1	Information flows in the multinational firm	43
3.2	The timing of a foreign direct investment	45
3.3	Diagrammatic solution of the entry strategy under uncertainty	46
3.4	Strategy for information gathering	47
3.5	Globally distributed operations	48
3.6	Interaction of location and ownership strategies	49
3.7	A typical offshore production process	50
3.8	The standardization-differentiation continuum	50
3.9	The information structure of the global factory	52
5.1	The choice of governance structure	102
7.1	Internationalisation of firms – conflict of markets	130
7.2	The global factory – globally distributed operations	135
7.3	'Hub and spoke' strategies: an example	136
7.4	The information structure of the global factory	138
7.5	Original equipment manufacturer	144
7.6	Original design manufacturer	145
7.7	Original brand manufacture	145
8.1	Transformation of the weighting matrix	168
9.1	The main implications of internationalization	186
10.1	Knowledge accession	208
10.2	Knowledge acquisition	211
10.3	Supplementary versus complementary knowledge acquisition	212
10.4	Supplementary and complementary knowledge transfer modes	213
11.1	Example of an investment choice option	234
11.2	Example of the best–worst experiment	237
11.3	Aggregate best–worst experiment results	247
12.1	The global factory	267
12.2	'Hub and spoke' strategies: an example	268
12.3	The information structure of the global factory	269
12.4	Phases of the external integration process	270
12.5	Information flows in the multinational firm	272
12.6	Frecknall's sequential affiliate business models	280
13.1	German–Polish cultural distance, as perceived by the Germans	302
13.2	German–Polish cultural distance, as perceived by the Poles	304

x *List of Figures*

13.3	British–Polish cultural distance, as perceived by the British	307
13.4	British–Polish cultural distance, as perceived by the Poles	308
15.1	Globally distributed production: 'the global factory'	345
15.2	'Hub and spoke' strategies: an example	346
15.3	The information structure of the global factory	347

Tables

2.1	Contents of this special issue analysed	29
3.1	Two possible errors in strategic choice under uncertainty	47
3.2	Benefits and costs of different types of network configuration	51
3.3	Motivation, information and coordination losses and costs in the firm	53
6.1	Production characteristics in different operation modes	113
8.1	Sectoral analysis of the sample	163
8.2	Descriptive statistics	164
8.3	Intra-industry spillovers	165
8.4	Inter-industry spillovers	167
8.5	The role of firm size and technological opportunities	169
8.6	The role of competition	174
9.1	Sectoral analysis	194
9.2	Descriptive statistics and correlations	195
9.3	Regression results for firm performance	196
9.4	Regression results for firms with lower and higher degree of internationalization	198
10.1	Relative cost and trust implications of inter-firm knowledge transfer	217
11.1	Sample and respondent characteristics	231
11.2	Investment features and levels used in the choice experiment	232
11.3	Environment and investment level conditions	234
11.4	Characteristics of last investment made	235
11.5	Propensity to choose any investment	238
11.6	Aggregate consider and invest models	240
11.7	Consider and invest models split by manager's FDI experience	243
11.8	Consider and invest models split by market stability	245
11.9	Differences in individual BW scores split by manager's FDI experience	248
11.10	Comparison between BW and individual level DCM estimates of preference ordering	249
11.A1	Recent literature on FDI location decisions	255
13.1	Summary of Hofstede's culture scores for Germany, UK and Poland	310
14.1	Characteristics of the respondents	328
14.2	Summary of the German characterization of the German/Polish Oppositions	333

xii *List of Tables*

14.3	Summary of the Polish characterization of the German/Polish oppositions	334
15.1	Japanese multinationals in world's top 100 non-financial transnational corporations 2004	350
15.2	Japanese non-financial transnational corporations 2004	350
15.3	Japanese firms in top 50 financial transnational corporations 2004	351
15.4	Models of multinational firms	352
15.5	The global factory and the hybrid Japanese ideal type	352
16.1	Japanese marketing as portrayed in the extant literature	360
16.2	Comparative analysis of case studies	370

Acknowledgements

This volume is a collection of published materials, for which permissions are acknowledged as follows:

Chapter 2: Peter J. Buckley (May 2009) "Business History and International Business" *Business History*, vol. 51, no. 3, pp. 307–333.

Chapter 3: Peter J. Buckley (2009) "Internalisation Thinking – from the Multinational Enterprise to the Global Factory" *International Business Review*, vol. 18, no. 3, pp. 224–235.

Chapter 4: Peter J. Buckley (2011) "The Theory of International Business Pre-Hymer" *Journal of World Business*, vol. 46, no. 1, pp. 61–73.

Chapter 5: Peter J. Buckley and Roger Strange (March 2011) "The Governance of the Multinational Enterprise: Insights from Internalization Theory" *Journal of Management Studies*, vol. 48, no. 2, pp. 460–470.

Chapter 6: Peter J. Buckley and Niron Hashai (January 2009) "Formalizing Internationalization in the Eclectic Paradigm" *Journal of International Business Studies*, vol. 40, no. 1, pp. 58–70.

Chapter 7: Peter J. Buckley (2009) "The Impact of the Global Factory on Economic Development" *Journal of World Business*, vol. 44, no. 2, pp. 131–143.

Chapter 8: Mario I. Kafouros and Peter J. Buckley (2008) "Under What Conditions do Firms Benefit from the Research Efforts of Other Organizations?" *Research Policy*, vol. 37, no. 2, pp. 225–239.

Chapter 9: Mario I. Kafouros, Peter J. Buckley, John A. Sharpb and Chengqi Wang (2008) "The Role of Internationalization in Explaining Innovation Performance" *Technovation*, vol. 28, no. 1–2, pp. 63–74.

Chapter 10: Peter J. Buckley, Keith W. Glaister, Elko Klijn and Hui Tan (December 2009) "Knowledge Accession and Knowledge Acquisition in Strategic Alliances: The Impact of Supplementary and Complementary Dimensions" *British Journal of Management*, vol. 20, no. 4, pp. 598–609.

Chapter 11: Peter J. Buckley, Timothy M. Devinney and Jordan J. Louviere (2007) "Do Managers Behave the Way Theory Suggests? A Choice Theoretic Examination of Foreign Direct Investment Location Decision Making" *Journal of International Business Studies*, vol. 38, no. 7, pp. 1069–1094.

Chapter 12: Peter J. Buckley (2010) "The Role of Headquarters in the Global Factory" in Ulf Andersson and Ulf Holm (eds) *Managing the Contemporary Multinational*, Cheltenham: Edward Elgar, pp. 60–84.

Chapter 13: Malcolm Chapman, Hanna Gajewska-De Mattos, Jeremy Clegg and Peter J. Buckley (June 2008) "Close Neighbours and Distant Friends – Perceptions of Cultural Distance" *International Business Review*, vol. 17, no. 3, pp. 217–234.

xiv *Acknowledgements*

Chapter 14: Peter J. Buckley, Malcolm Chapman, Jeremy Clegg and Hanna Gajewska-De Mattos (Summer 2011) "Doing Business in Developing and Transitional Countries, an Empirical Example of the Dominant Logic and Its Alternative" *International Studies of Management and Organisation*, vol. 41, no. 1, pp. 26–54.

Chapter 15: Peter J. Buckley (July 2009) "The Rise of the Japanese Multinational Enterprise: Then and Now" *Asia Pacific Business Review*, vol. 15, no. 3, pp. 309–321.

Chapter 16: Peter J. Buckley and Sierk A. Horn (August 2009) "Japanese Multinational Enterprises in China: Successful Adaptation of Marketing Strategies" *Long Range Planning*, vol. 42, no. 4, special issue, pp. 495–517.

Foreword

International business (IB) has undergone three significant transformations in the roughly 50 years since it has become a recognized field of study – in its context, in its core phenomenon, and in the disciplinary and methodological lenses that are applied to characterize it.

Of the three, the context for IB probably has undergone the greatest transformation with substantially increased "institutional" integration resulting from a number of large countries coming into the world economy, the rapid growth of these economies as a result, and a bumpy but nevertheless cumulative reduction in barriers to international trade and investment. This institutional transformation has been accompanied by two major transformations in the infrastructure of business – shipping with containerization and air freight and, most importantly, the information and communications technology (ICT) revolution that has made possible deep connectivity – one might even say hyper connectivity – among economic activities in different countries. While institutional integration was perhaps equally high in the pre-WWI era, albeit in many cases though imperialism, there is no question that we are now in a markedly different era – even from that of the 1980s and 1990s – in terms of both the interconnectedness of economic activity and the geographic dispersion of important markets and the associated potential for innovation.

The phenomenon of IB has changed substantially as well, from the predominant role of the multinational firm (MNC) that projected itself internationally largely on the basis of capabilities developed in its home market, to the MNC as orchestrator of a global factory but still exploiting technologies largely developed at its core, and in some cases to the MNC as a globally distributed (re)combinatorial innovation system and supply-chain orchestrator. Also, while early protagonists were European, American, and then Japanese in origin, firms from other countries are now significant players as well.

The IB literature, which has been strongly influenced by the economic models of Dunning, Vernon, Buckley and Casson, Hennart, Rugman and others, has changed as well, albeit more slowly and unevenly. Perspectives have opened to include sociology/organizations and political economy, but the economic model remains dominant. It also has lagged the phenomenon with a continued emphasis on the MNC as a firm made up of geographically bound units, despite the fact that in many cases these elements are now virtual. Further, while all recognize that these firms operate in local and global ecosystems, the focus in the literature remains largely on the focal

xvi *Foreword*

MNC rather than the system it orchestrates. This is in contrast to the origins of the field 50 years ago, where the need to explain a new phenomenon (the MNC) drove the development of new theory and insights.

Buckley is an exception. A leading IB theorist and writer for more than 30 of the 50 years of the field, he treats us in this volume to his writing over the last five years. As a key developer of the internationalization/transaction cost approach to explaining the existence of the MNC, he has been consistent in the approach he takes, but extends it to address two aspects of the MNC that have become much more salient in recent years – the MNC as a distributed factory and as a knowledge system. He also recognizes Japan and China as major drivers of the phenomenon, and provides some tantalizing clues regarding how the shifting geographic focus of MNC activity is changing his perspective on its global impact.

The articles in the first section (plus 9) provide a theoretical "travelling companion" to the evolution of the MNC that has taken place over the last half century seen through the internalization lens. *Business History* provides a sweeping prior history of the theory of the multinational firms and its interaction with business history in general, showing not only the richness of knowledge regarding the phenomenon at the time, but also the lack of a coherent framework. *Internalization Thinking* takes the now classic PJB (Peter J. Buckley) bundle – a cost minimizing rational solution to the total system – and relates it to changes in the context and form of the MNC over time. Buckley's focus remains largely on the positive questions of "what is a MNC?" and "when is MNC the dominant form of international production, knowledge development and deployment?" However, with his recognition of the emergence of the global factory, he focuses on the broader chain of international production of which MNC is only part, albeit an important integrating part. This justifies the title *Innovations in International Business* rather than "innovation in (the theory) of the MNC," and provides a clear example to IB scholars of how working from a theory of the firm need not imply a focus on the MNC alone.

In *The Theory of International Business Pre-Hymer*, Buckley could be writing about his own work:

A great deal of previous theorizing has been ignored because of its lack of conceptual clarity and its non-cumulative nature. However, pre-Hymer theorising has several virtues. First, it is deeply empirically grounded. Second, it integrates international business theorising on FDI and the MNE with international management concepts such as cultural differences and methods of operating in foreign environments. Third, it provides avenues for the reconsideration of theoretical advances such as the relationship between FDI and trade ... and the external consequences and effects of FDI. One of the underestimated advances of modern international business theory is to integrate macro perspectives (the country, balance of payments flows, national assets and liabilities) and micro elements (the multinational firm). This is done by the device of attributing a single nationality to "the firm". ... to give the theory of the multinational enterprise a clear analytical core.

Buckley's singular theoretical focus is powerful, even if at times limiting. The *Governance* of the multinational firm, for example, remains concerned with how well internalization theory explains the existence of the MNC, but it says little about how to construct it. *Formalizing Internationalization*, however, formally models the various ways that different types of transaction costs enter into a firm's optimization and provides a basis for parameterizing these costs along with scale, scope, and locational cost differentials to determine the sensitivity of MNC design to these variables. *Global Factory* applies the internalization perspective to elucidate this phenomenon where, as the result of ICT, activities are increasingly fine sliced, dispersed, and often orchestrated rather than owned by the MNC. Together with *Theorizing*, it provides a more general view of firms that perform and orchestrate the various elements of design, production and sales in an international context. *The Rise of the Japanese Multinational*, which appears in Part III, also fits in this section as it shows how Japanese MNCs have moved from projector to global factory, and how they have become more similar to and yet remain different in important ways from western MNCs.

In Part II, we see Buckley in exploration mode, extending his focus beyond internalization theory to empirically examine knowledge, innovation, and managerial behaviour in the international firm. *The Role of Internationalization* argues that the degree of internationalization should increase payoffs to R&D due both to greater capacity to produce innovation and greater capacity to exploit it. *Knowledge Accession and Knowledge Acquisition* applies the distinction to create a typology of a number of current learning alliances. *Do Managers Behave* seeks to test the single point rationality model against a more locally bounded incremental model of the international firm and finds that decision-making is neither totally local or incremental nor totally single point rational. *The Role of Headquarters* establishes that coordination functions typically performed by HQ are likely to be even more important in the global factory MNC than the multiple-replica MNC.

In Part III, Buckley steps further out of the confines of internalization theory to delve into some of the "international management concepts such as cultural differences and methods of operating in foreign environments." *Close Neighbors* and *Doing Business* both demonstrate that "distance" is not symmetric, especially where there has been substantial interaction. While *The Rise of the Japanese Multinational* is largely an examination of the changing Japanese MNC through the internalization lens, it also reveals a re-examination on Buckley's part of the efficiency he typically attributes to

xviii *Foreword*

the MNC. First, he worries that with the greater distance between HQ, its dispersed activities, and customers, negative externalities are likely to be out of sight and out of control. He also expresses the concern that although the global factory provides emerging economies with a way to participate in the global economy, it may also present a barrier to their entry to higher value-added activities.

This is the thoughtful, theoretically based analysis we would expect from Buckley, with a significant extension to the case of the global factory. It also shows Buckley in exploration mode, digging into aspects of learning and knowledge transfer that expand the boundaries of internalization theory, and looking beyond the first order efficiency effects of the international firm. All students of the MNC should read it, whether their primary interest is with the MNC as a key instance of theory of the firm or with normative strategic and managerial issues that are illuminated by this perspective. Buckley clearly shows not only how a consistent point of view can provide a dynamic understanding of a constantly changing phenomenon, but also how staying in touch with the phenomenon can alter one's perspective.

Donald Lessard
MIT

Contributors

Malcolm Chapman is Senior Lecturer in International Business at the University of Leeds, UK. His research interests at the moment are cultural issues in management; anthropological concepts as applied to consumer behaviour; anthropological analysis of corporate life; anthropology and transaction cost economics; the pharmaceutical industry.

Jeremy Clegg is Jean Monnet Professor of European Integration and International Business Management at the University of Leeds, UK. His research interests include the determinants of foreign direct investment (FDI) into the European Union, particularly the relationship between market integration and FDI by US and Japanese multinational firms.

Tim Devinney is Professor of Strategy at the University of Technology, Sydney, Australia. Previously he was a Professor and Professorial Research Fellow at the Australian Graduate School of Management (AGSM) and Director of the Centre for Corporate Change and the AGSM Executive MBA.

Hanna Gajewska-De Mattos is Lecturer in Business Development in Emerging Markets at the University of Leeds, UK. She graduated in European Studies from the University of Economics in Poznan and in Translation and Interpreting from the University of Adam Mickiewicz in Poznan. She was also a European Union Phare ACE Scholar at the University of Leeds from which she obtained her doctorate.

Keith Glaister is Professor of International Strategic Management and Dean of the Management School, University of Sheffield, UK. To this role he brings a wide range of research, teaching and practical experience. As a leading researcher in the field of international strategic management, he has published five books and over 80 articles and book chapters. As a teacher he has taught undergraduate and postgraduate students, both in the UK and overseas, and has supervised several PhD students to successful completion.

Niron Hashai is Senior Lecturer at the School of Business Administration, The Hebrew University of Jerusalem, Israel. His research areas include the theory of the multinational corporation, the impact of knowledge intensity and firm size on internationalization patterns and entry modes, the relationship between geographic diversification, product diversification and performance, technological Innovation and internationalization, knowledge xx *Notes on Contributors*

transfer costs, R&D internationalization and growth patterns of small high technology firms.

Mario I. Kafouros is Professor of International Business and Innovation at the Centre for International Business, University of Leeds, UK. He is a member of the Centre for International Business University of Leeds (CIBUL), and an Advanced Institute of Management (AIM) Scholar. Kafouros is an Electronic Engineer by first degree, and holds a degree in Business and Economics, and a PhD in Innovation.

Elko Klijn is Assistant Professor of Strategic Management in the Department of Strategic Management and Business Environment, Rotterdam School of Management, Erasmus University, the Netherlands. He earned his PhD from Leeds University Business School, University of Leeds, UK. His research interests lie in the field of international strategic alliance activity and knowledge transfer.

Donald Lessard is the Epoch Foundation Professor of International Management and Engineering Systems at the MIT Sloan School of Management, Cambridge, Massachusetts. His research interests are in global strategic management and project management, particularly in the face of uncertainty and risk and in the energy sector. His project, "Global dynamics of energy technology development, production, and deployment," brings together these themes. He has published extensively on these topics in academic and professional journals, and is co-author of *Strategic Management of Large Engineering Projects: Shaping Institutions, Risks, and Governance* (2001, with Roger Miller). A leader in international management education, Donald is a past President of the Academy of International Business and Dean of the Fellows of the Academy. He is also a Senior Fellow of the Fung Global Institute, a Hong-Kong based think tank.

Jordan Louviere is Professor of Marketing at the University of Technology, Sydney, Australia. His research interests include marketing research/ research methods quantitative analysis of consumer behaviour, quantitative methods, especially multivariate statistics, experimental design and marketing models, and consumer judgment, decision making and choice behaviour.

John Sharp is Professor of Management at the Canterbury Business School, University of Kent, UK. His research interests include information systems strategy and design, investment decision making, manufacturing strategy and business implications of e-commerce.

Roger Strange is Professor of International Business at the School of Business, Management and Economics, University of Sussex, UK. Before joining the University of Sussex, he was a professor of International Business at King's

College London, where he was formerly the head of the department. He is Treasurer and a member of the Executive Committee of the UK and Ireland Chapter of the Academy of International Business (AIB-UKI), and the President-elect and UK Representative of the European International Business Academy (EIBA).

Hui Tan is Reader in Strategy at the School of Management, Royal Holloway, University of London, UK. His research focuses on knowledge transfer and organizational learning with special reference to emerging markets. He has published in journals such as *Journal of World Business*, *Management International Review*, *Transnational Corporations*, *International Studies on Management and Organization* and *Multinational Business Review*.

Chengqi Wang is Associate Professor and Reader in International Business at Nottingham University Business School, University of Nottingham, UK. His research interests include determinants and spillover effects of foreign direct investment, antecedents and performance implications of internationalization by emerging market enterprises, antecedents and performance implications of R&D internationalization, and China's integration into the world economy through inward and outward foreign direct investment.

1
Introduction

This volume is a collection of my published papers, with a set of excellent co-authors, between 2008 and 2011. It focuses particularly on the development and modelling of the development of the multinational enterprise (MNE), its role in knowledge creation and dissemination and the role of cultural distance in international business, particularly with respect to Asian business.

International business has a long tradition – longer than most people acknowledge – and this is developed in Chapter 4. It is conventional to date the genesis of international business theory to Hymer's 1960 dissertation (Hymer 1960, published 1976) or to John Dunning's seminal book on US investment in the UK (Dunning 1958), however there was a rich and vibrant body of literature already extant when Hymer wrote his dissertation. Hymer chose to ignore most of this literature and, in many ways, his thesis was all the stronger for this (Buckley 2006) but a re-reading of this largely ignored body of knowledge pays dividends and illuminates the current concerns of international business theorists and practitioners. Chapter 2 is a wide ranging review of international business theory drawing parallels with the cognate area of business history. Chapter 3 traces the evolution of internalisation thinking from its origins in Coase's key article of 1937 to its application to the MNE, by Buckley and Casson (1976) and others, to its current role of a crucial underpinning of the conceptual structure of "the global factory". The insights this approach provides for governance issues are examined in Chapter 5. Chapter 6 develops the formal modelling of the MNE, in this instance with an application to internationalisation. Chapter 7 ends Part I by revisiting "the global factory" as a network of firms driven by a central MNE and examining the impact of this development on economic development.

The role of the MNE as creator, developer and disseminator of knowledge is well known. The centrality of "intangible assets" as the key source of profitability is also well understood in the international business literature. The Part II of the book re-examines several facets of these important

2 *Peter J. Buckley*

issues. Chapter 8 and 9 raise two interesting questions – when and how do MNEs benefit from the research of others and how far does internationalisation play a role in innovation performance? Chapter 10 looks at knowledge within international alliances of MNEs and investigates the dual role of knowledge accession version acquisition with the additional dimension of what we call supplementary and complementary knowledge combination. Chapter 11 confronts theory with actual managerial decision making in MNEs by examining the way in which managers make foreign direct investment location decisions. The management of knowledge throughout the dispersed and diverse global factory by the headquarters of MNEs ties together some of the themes of Part II.

I have maintained an interest in the role of cultural distance and business cultures right from the beginning of my career in international business. It is evident to all that business practice follows different rules in different locations and that these rules are fundamentally determined by deep rooted, although constantly changing, local cultures. These cultural boundaries do not align perfectly with national boundaries as we know (Buckley 2004) but national differences provide an approximation (very imperfect in some cases) to groups with similar cultures. They are often taken to represent homogeneous cultural groups which is often a massive anthropological mistake, but careful analysts note this and work around it. (This is often because the only available aggregate data is at national level.) Chapter 13 examines those "close neighbours" (Germany and Poland) and "distant friends" (Poland and Britain) to tease out the role of cultural distance perceptions in a limited, but telling population of cross border co-operators. Chapter 14 is a critique of "the dominant logic" that is often unthinkingly brought to analyses of international operations, particularly those between "advanced" and "developing and transitional countries". (The categorisation is interesting in itself). The final two chapters are the first two pieces that I have written on Japanese business since Buckley and Mirza (1985). My most recent research focus has been China (see Buckley, 2009) and the final chapter links Japan and China by investigating the adaptation strategy of Japanese MNEs in marketing in China. Chapter 15 is a comparison in time of the appraisal of Japanese MNEs in the days when they were perceived as all-powerful and competitively unstoppable with the 21st century where they are seen as staid and solid but undynamic. It is intriguing to see the parallels between writings on Japan in the 1980s and writing on "Chinese dominance" now. It will be fascinating to track this in the future.

Finally, I would like to thank all my co-authors for their hard work and for inspiring me – and Don Lessard for his support over the years and for the excellent Foreword – which has given me at least one idea for a future paper!

References

Buckley, Peter J., April 2004. "Cartography and International Business". *International Business Review*, Vol. 13, No. 2, pp. 239–255.

Buckley, Peter J., 2006. "Stephen Hymer: Three Phases, One Approach?" *International Business Review*, Vol. 15, No. 2, pp. 140–147.

Buckley, Peter J and Mark Casson, 1976. *The Future of the Multinational Enterprise*, London: Macmillan.

Buckley, Peter J., 2009. *Foreign Direct Investment, China and the World Economy*, Basingstoke: Palgrave Macmillan, p. 311.

Buckley, Peter J. and Hafiz Mirza, 1985. "The Wit and Wisdom of Japanese Management: An Iconoclastic Analysis". *Management International Review*, Vol. 25, No. 3, pp. 16–32.

R.H. Coase, 1937. "The Nature of the Firm". *Economica*, Vol. 4, pp. 386–405.

Dunning, J. H., 1958. *American Investment in British Manufacturing Industry*. London: George Allen & Unwin.

Hymer, S., 1976. *The International Operations of National Firms: A Study of Direct Foreign Investment*. Cambridge, Mass: MIT Press.

Part I
Theory and Modelling the MNE

2
Business History and International Business

Business history and international business are cognate subjects. There are few, if any, studies of international business that do not require a proper study of context. International business decision making must be made relevant by a considered evaluation of the circumstances surrounding that decision. This often means putting it into its historical context. The contributions that the study of international business can make to business history are the input of appropriate theory and appropriate research methods. The best international business theory can illuminate the seemingly disparate strategies of firms in given historical circumstances and can provide an integrated, overarching conceptual structure of the study of business history. The research methods used in international business are also worthy of scrutiny by business historians. As David Cannadine (2008, p. 29) says,

> as most historians recognise, analysis without narrative loses any sense of the sequencing (and unpredictability) of events through time, while narrative without analysis fails to convey the structural constraints within which events actually take place... there is in practice a long continuum extending from 'pure' narrative to 'pure' analysis, which means that the best history is situated somewhere between these extremes, seeking simultaneously to animate structure and contextualise narrative.

A critical assessment of business history by Hannah (1983, p. 166, quoted by Wilson, 1995, p. 2) centres on its narrative qualities: 'Most business historians have clung to a tradition which, at its best, is a triumph of narrative skill, honest to the facts of the individual case, but at its worst is narrow, insular and antiquarian.' The proposition of this piece (and the demonstration effect of this special issue) is that international business theory and method can complement business history and avoid the worst-case scenario described by Hannah. This cross-fertilisation has been occurring with increasing regularity over the past few decades and this special issue of *Business History* brings together some of the fruits of this conjunction of intellectual domains.

Business history

Business history is clearly a subset of history, which Burrow (2007, p. 1) defines as follows: 'History – the elaborated, secular, prose narrative (all these qualifications are necessary) of public events, based on enquiry.' History (or at least 'Western' history) began with Herodotus in the fifth century BC (Herodotus, 2003). Herodotus – the father of history (or the 'father of lies', according to taste (Evans, 1968)) used narrative history but also clear conceptual analysis and geographical knowledge (Bury, 2006). Explanation, not description, became the true hallmark of a successful historian. Thucydides (1972) 'analysed politics and ethics, and applied logic to everything in the world' (Bury, 2006, p. 47) in his analysis of the Peloponnesian War. The humanist historians, including Machiavelli, sought to explain diplomacy, war and conflict in terms of a historically grounded analysis in which the motives of man, not blind fate, guided action (Machiavelli, 1979). The early eighteenth-century-Neapolitan thinker Giambattista Vico suggested that culture was a collective product of a whole people (Burrow, 2007, p. 391) and 'decided that it ought to be possible to apply to the study of human history methods similar to those proposed by Bacon for the study of the natural world' (Wilson, 1972, p. 9). The tradition of providing a 'summary – not a narrative – of general European history' dates back at least as far as James Harrington's *Oceana* (1656) (Burrow, 2007, p. 318). This tradition laid the basis for the 'philosophic history' epitomised by David Hume. Indeed, the 'Scottish Enlightenment' whose key project was to address the problem of reconciling economic growth, based on entrepreneurial individualism, with virtue – moral behaviour (Herman, 2001) relied greatly on reflections from history – including those of Adam Ferguson, William Robertson and Adam Smith (Burrow, 2007; Smith, 1759, 1776). The growth of positivist analyses of history and the structuralist approach of the *Annales* school both bring theory to bear on historical processes as does 'the grand narrative' of Marxist and Whig historians (Butterfield, 1965).[1]

An interesting bridge between history and business history was attempted by John Hicks' (1969) *a Theory of Economic History*. This is essentially a theory of how market institutions evolved and builds on the Scottish economists (particularly Smith's refined theory of the evolution of society through distinct 'stages' (Smith, 1776). The purpose remains to identify the underlying causes of economic growth (and development) and to provide a basis for useful generalisation.

Business history has a more confined remit. It has been defined as follows:

> The main aim of business history is to study and explain the behaviour of the firm over long periods of time, and to place the conclusions in a broader framework composed of the markets and institutions in which

that behaviour occurs. On a more general level, business history can also provide a dynamic insight into the evolution of capitalism, bringing a comparative element to the field which can draw on material from firms, industries, or national groupings of businessmen. (Wilson, 1995, pp. 1–2)

Nor should we forget George Orwell's dictum that those who control the past, control the future. The logic of historical writing has been a major influence on the organisation of knowledge across many cultures and time periods. This has particularly influenced methods of formulating problems, presenting arguments and drawing conclusions.[2] There are many business histories – notably those of Alfred Chandler (1962, 1977) that have influenced business strategy and therefore the policies and actions of major multinational companies. Business history matters both as record keeping and as a guide to future action.

Jones and Khanna (2006) advanced four arguments on the way that 'history matters' to international business research:

(1) history as a source of time series variation ('augmenting the sources of variation');
(2) dynamics matter ('things change');
(3) illuminating path dependence;
(4) FDI and development in the really long run ('expanding the domain of inquiry').

All of these contributions feature in this article and in the special issue generally. The fourth argument is taken up in the section on long-run theories below.

International business theory[3]

Until the 1960s, mainstream economic theorists treated multinational enterprises (MNEs) simply as 'arbitrageurs' of capital, moving equity from countries where returns were low to those where they were higher (Jones, 1996, 2005). A major theoretical breakthrough came in 1960, when Stephen Hymer expressed his dissatisfaction with the theory of portfolio capital transfers to explain the international operations of firms. Hymer stated that many of the predictions became invalidated once risk and uncertainty, volatile exchange rates and the cost of acquiring information and making transactions were incorporated into classical portfolio theory. This was because market imperfections altered the performance of firms and their strategy in servicing foreign markets (Dunning, 1993). Although Hymer had written his thesis in 1960, it was published only in 1976, when sponsored by his supervisor Charles Kindleberger. Follow-up developments to refine and test the 'Hymer–Kindleberger hypotheses' were carried out only in the early 1970s.

Hymer was also the first to recognise that FDI involved the transfer of a package of resources, such as technology, management skills, entrepreneurship, and not just capital. The most fundamental characteristic of FDI was that it involved no change in the ownership of resources, whereas indirect investment was transacted through the market. Hymer's identification of the international firm as a firm that internalises and supersedes the market provided a useful prologue to the theory of internalisation as a means for transferring knowledge, business techniques, and skilled personnel (Hymer, 1960).

However, Hymer's work is best known for its application of an industrial organisation approach to the theory of international production. In foreign markets, local firms were assumed to possess superior knowledge about the markets, resources, legal and political system, language and culture, and the many other things which distinguish one country from another. As far as this is true, foreign firms would have no incentive to locate in that market or have the ability to survive in it without an advantage. Hymer used Bain's classic treatise on the barriers to competition in domestic markets (Bain, 1956). In extending this analysis to explain the cross-border activities of firms, he argued that such firms had to possess some kind of proprietary advantage. This reasoning led to the view that a foreign firm required competitive advantages over its local rivals to overcome the liability of foreignness (Hymer, 1960). These firm-specific advantages, or ownership advantages, because they are exclusive to the firm owning them, imply the existence of some kind of structural market failure. Multinationals could not only exploit perceived market imperfections, but could use their ownership advantages to create market imperfections themselves (Caves, 1971).

Hymer examined the kind of ownership advantages that firms might possess or acquire, as well as the kind of industrial sectors and market structures in which foreign production was likely to be concentrated. Firms can possess any number of ownership advantages when they operate in a foreign market. The type of ownership advantage will differ considerably according to the products and industries. Within manufacturing, superior technology and innovative capacity are especially important in the case of production goods, while product differentiation will often be more relevant for consumer goods. Ownership advantages can be generated internally within the firm, or acquired by licensing a technology from a foreign competitor or buying an entire foreign firm. Hymer was also interested in the international expansion of firms as a means of fostering their monopoly power, rather than of reducing costs, improving product quality or fostering innovations. In his later publications, Hymer (1968, 1970) did appear to acknowledge that MNEs might help to improve international resource allocation by circumventing market failure. As such, Hymer's work was a point of departure for the more rigorous work of the internalisation economists in the following decade.

Despite the invaluable contributions of Hymer, Kindleberger, and Caves, the credit for transforming internalisation into a theory of international production is usually attributed to Buckley and Casson (1976). They placed the work of Coase (1937) on the multi-plant firm in an international context. Parallel to internalisation theory, Oliver Williamson (1975, 1979, 1985) developed transaction cost analysis, which was later applied in an international context by Teece (1981, 1982, 1985) and Hennart (1982). While traditional economic reasoning concentrates on the operative consequences of changes in sales revenues and production costs, transaction cost economics calls attention to factors that influence the choice of foreign operation methods – which are mainly regarded as a question of the degree of control the firm should have over a foreign operation (Anderson & Gatignon, 1986). The underlying logic and analysis of the two approaches is characterised more by similarity than any substantial differences (Rugman, 1980).

Transaction cost theory provided a different perspective on the reasons for the growth of MNEs. The fundamental insight is derived from the pioneering article by Coase (1937), which sought to explain the boundaries of the firm. Coase's focus was on the multi-plant domestic firm rather than on the international operations of firms. He argued that firms and markets represent alternative methods of organising production. This theory suggested that the market is costly and inefficient for undertaking certain types of transactions. The transaction costs of the market include the costs of discovering relevant prices and in arranging contracts for each market transaction. The existence of such costs means that whenever transactions can be organised and carried out at a lower cost within the firm than through the market, they will be internalised and undertaken by the firm itself. Firms will internalise transactions until the marginal cost of doing so exceeds the marginal revenue.

This theory attracted little attention from economists until the 1970s, when it was extended and refined by Oliver Williamson (1975, 1979, 1985). Williamson suggested that transaction costs could be examined systematically in relation to three factors, namely bounded rationality, opportunism and asset-specificity. Bounded rationality refers to the impossibility of anyone knowing all possible information, which means that people invariably make less than fully rational decisions. Opportunism refers to the tendency of some people to cheat or engage in misrepresentations. Asset-specificity reflects the extent to which certain types of transactions, in order to be carried out, necessitate investments in material and intangible assets (such as knowledge), which are dedicated to particular uses, and how much their value will be diminished if used in alternative ways. If it is difficult to measure the value of goods and services, and if the opportunities for bargaining and dishonesty are therefore high, there is an incentive to replace the market by hierarchy. The combination of bounded rationality, opportunism, and asset specificity produces the strongest incentive to internalise a transaction rather than to use contracts in the market.

Internalisation is concerned with imperfections in the markets for intermediate products, including technology, organisational know-how and marketing skills. Intermediate products embrace all the different types of goods or services that are transferred between one activity and another within the production process. The theory proposes that firms expand across borders because the transaction costs incurred in international intermediate product markets can be reduced by internalising these markets within the firm. Internalisation theory can be used to explain patterns of both vertical and horizontal integration across borders (Casson, 1987b). The internalisation of tangible intermediate product flows between upstream and downstream production explains vertical integration between mining and manufacture, agriculture and food processing, component production and final assembly. Vertical backward integration – for example, by steel firms into iron ore or rubber manufacturers into natural rubber plantations – can be seen as arising from small number conditions, when the number of parties to the exchange is small, which can often arise from the presence of physical asset specificity, and from information asymmetry, which can cause problems of quality control because of opportunistic behaviour (Hennart, 1991). The internalisation of intangibles such as knowledge and reputation can explain patterns of cross-border horizontal integration. Internalisation also avoids the difficulties of determining market prices and the proprietary problems associated with arm's length transactions. Moreover, internalisation may allow the company to circumvent government-created market imperfections including trade barriers, differences in tax systems and levels, and restrictions on capital movements.

Although internalisation is a deviation from perfect markets, the internalisation of firm-specific advantages constitutes an internal transfer of intangible assets that might not take place otherwise. By replacing inefficient or non-existent external markets with internal ones, or by overcoming government-created market distortions such as tariffs, taxes, or exchange rates, MNEs produce a more efficient allocation of resources globally (Casson, 1987a). Thus, in internalisation theory, MNEs represent an integrating and welfare-enhancing force in the world economy rather than a source of collusion, monopoly, and extortion.

One of the most frequently cited intangible competencies transferred through FDI is technology (Blomström & Kokko, 1996b; Blomström, Kokko, & Zejan, 1994). Technology transfer can trigger and speed up economic development, for instance, by facilitating the production of goods with higher value added content, by increasing exports and improving efficiency. MNEs possess the bulk of all patents worldwide, much of the world's R&D takes place within MNEs, and MNEs possess many of the technologies that are pivotal to economic and industrial development. Often these technological competencies cannot be obtained in the marketplace (e.g. via licensing) and FDI may therefore be the fastest, most efficient, and sometimes the only way for developing countries to get access to these competencies. MNEs can also play a central role in the transfer of know-how, knowledge, and experience to the local workforce through its employment of indigenous professionals and managers (Blomström, et al., 1994).

MNEs provide highly efficient organisations that are characterised by a high degree of managerial efficiency arising from training, higher standards of recruitment, effective communication with the parent company and other subsidiaries, and a more global outlook. By virtue of these characteristics, they are able to think strategically on a global scale and to organise complex integrated production networks. The integration into this transnational production network can give developing countries advantages (Blomström, Kokko, & Zejan, 2000). MNEs bring with them improvements in storage, transport and marketing arrangements leading to cheaper delivery, better quality of products, and better information about products to consumers. More importantly, developing countries will be able to use the worldwide marketing outlets of MNEs, selling products where huge marketing investments would otherwise have been required. Hence, the presence of MNEs may assist developing countries in penetrating foreign markets.

At the macro level, the internalisation logic would imply that FDI by MNEs may encourage governments to adopt more rational and competitiveness-oriented economic policies (Dunning & Narula, 1996). At the micro level, MNEs may produce various spillovers on the host economy. Two types of spillovers from MNE activity in developing countries have been identified, namely intra-industry spillovers and inter-industry spillovers (Blomström & Kokko, 1996a). Intra-industry spillovers are effects such as those that improve the competitiveness of national industries by forcing inefficient companies to adopt more efficient methods and invest in improvements of their assets. The presence of MNEs may force local companies to become more efficient and introduce new technologies earlier than they would otherwise have done (Kokko, 1994). They diffuse competencies when trained employees move to local companies where those skills are in short supply, and speed up technology transfer by forcing local companies to get hold of those technologies. Inter-industry spillovers are effects on suppliers and customers, as the growing use of subcontractors and suppliers by MNEs encourage backward spillovers in terms of diffusion of the standards, know-how and technology of MNEs. The entrance of MNEs may improve the technology and productivity of local firms, as they demonstrate new technologies; provide technical assistance to their local suppliers and customers; and train managers and workers.

Stephen Magee (1977a, 1977b), in a more detailed examination of technology as a valuable intangible asset, was primarily interested in the question of why the incentive of firms to internalise the market for technology varied over time. Magee coined the concept of the industry technology cycle, which built upon the Vernon hypothesis that the competitive advantages of firms were likely to change over the life of the product. According to Magee, MNEs distinguish themselves as specialists in the production of advanced and complex products and are better equipped to appropriate the revenues of sophisticated information and knowledge (Calvet, 1981). Magee argued that the incentive for firms to internalise the market for technology varies over time. As such, firms were unlikely to sell their rights to new and idiosyncratic technology because the buying firm was unlikely to pay the selling firm a price that would yield at least as much economic rent as it could earn using the technology itself, and because the licensee might use the technology to the disadvantage of the licensor, and even become a competitor. As the technology matured, however, and lost some of its uniqueness, the need to internalise (or appropriate in Magee's parlance) its use decreased and the firm would consider switching its modality of transfer from FDI to licensing.

In a similar yet contradictory vein, the process of gradually increasing involvement in foreign markets has been a widely noted phenomenon especially in Scandinavian (mostly Swedish) studies (Johanson & Vahlne, 1977; Johanson & Wiedersheim-Paul, 1975; Luostarinen, 1979; Welch & Luostarinen, 1988). Two types of increasing involvement are often implied: an increasing involvement in any one foreign market through an orderly process of exporting, agency establishment, sales subsidiary, and finally production subsidiary with the possible intervention of a licensing or other contractual form also being included. Second, orderly stepwise penetration of different foreign markets beginning with the closest market in terms of psychic distance (Hallen & Wiedersheim-Paul, 1993) and often physical distance, gradually extending to more distant and therefore more difficult markets. The proponents of the model hypothesise that commitment to internationalisation increases with each further step into the international arena. There is a feedback relationship between the level of internationalisation and commitment to further internationalisation. Many longitudinal, cross-sectional, case studies show that a growing international awareness in managers is a major motivating force in overcoming barriers to internationalisation. Psychic barriers are perceived to be lower as internationalisation proceeds. These stages are often tied to hypotheses on the learning of firms. At each stage, the firm acquires knowledge of the market, or it can transfer lessons learned in one foreign market to another one (Newbould, Buckley, & Thurwell, 1978). This orderly process and the gradualism and risk aversion it implies have been criticised (Hedlund & Kverneland, 1983; Turnbull, 1987). The gradual learning theory can be criticised on methodological grounds and in terms of its applicability. First, when looking back in time over the development process of foreign production subsidiaries, other ventures may have failed before reaching this stage and consequently will no longer be extant. Thus, a bias is induced toward success in longer establishment patterns (Hedlund & Kverneland, 1983). Second, the so-called Scandinavian model may apply more to inexperienced first-time foreign investors than to experienced companies. This is acknowledged by its proponents, who expect jumps in the establishment chain in firms with extensive experience in other foreign markets.

Despite these controversies, it is obvious that internationalisation patterns are influenced by the previous stages in the internationalisation of the company. The key barriers identified in stage models are the lack of knowledge and of resources. Their applicability to smaller firms is thus likely to be stronger. As such, barriers to internationalisation as seen by a small, inexperienced firm will be easily overcome by a well-established multinational (Vermeulen & Barkema, 2002). This means that different firms enter a market in different ways and at different moments in time.

The stages approach finds an echo in models of foreign market servicing because such models attempt to establish the conditions under which a firm will service a foreign market by a particular method (Contractor, 1981; Telesio, 1979). The generic methods are exporting, licensing and foreign direct investment. Each of these methods has a variety of subtypes, and the interactions between the methods are, in practice, very important. However, although the scholars who subscribe to this view began to identify the circumstances in which firms might wish to control the use of the technological assets they possessed, they did not really come to grips with the more fundamental issue of the organisation of transactional relationships as part of a general paradigm of market failure. This task was left to another group of scholars, i.e. transaction cost economists, who had a positive influence on these market-servicing models.

Exporting is separated from the other two main forms of foreign market servicing by the location factor in that the bulk of the value-adding activities takes place in the home and not in the foreign market. International licensing appears to combine the best of both worlds, i.e. the advantage in technology and skills of the licensing multinational plus the local knowledge of the licensee. However, the same might be said of an international joint venture. The choice between licensing and direct investment is crucial in illustrating the choice between licensing, an external market solution, and direct investment, an internal solution (Buckley & Casson, 1976, 1981). Foreign investment is a decisive step in internationalisation. Just as there are many forms of contractual arrangements for conducting international business, so there are several forms of foreign direct investment. The major motives for conducting foreign direct investment are market oriented, cost oriented, and for control of key inputs, either low-end (e.g. raw materials) or high-end (e.g. strategic assets).

Buckley and Casson (1976) used a cost–benefit analysis to suggest an internationalisation path. Their claim was that, in normal conditions, the

16   *Peter J. Buckley*

fixed costs associated with licensing are lower than those resulting from FDI. They are, however, higher than exports because of the need to guarantee that the licensing agreements are respected by the licensees. Since the opposite happens with variable costs, market servicing tends to follow the sequence: exporting, licensing, FDI. Buckley & Casson (1981) added that the switch in modes of market servicing is also affected by the life cycle of the product, the firm's familiarity with the foreign market, and the firm's degree of internationalisation.

Vernon and his followers at Harvard were the first to acknowledge the relevance of trade theories to help explain MNE activity. In a seminal article published in 1966, Vernon used the product life cycle to explain the foreign activities of MNEs. His starting point was that in addition to immobile natural endowments and human resources, the propensity of countries to engage in trade also depended on their capability to upgrade these assets or to create new ones, notably technological capacity (Dunning, 1992). In order to introduce the dynamics of technological change into the Heckscher–Ohlin model, the product life cycle theory was applied to international capital flows. It was argued that firms based in high wage countries had a greater propensity to develop new products because of high per capita incomes and high unit labour costs in their home economy. The model suggested that when a new product was developed, a firm normally chose a domestic production location, because of the need for close contact with customers and suppliers, because of uncertainties concerning the production and because of low price elasticity of the product. As a product matures and as the technology becomes more difficult to protect and as price elasticity grows, long-run production runs based on established technology become possible. The firm will begin to look for lower cost production locations in other industrialised countries with bigger market opportunities and the firm grows from an inward-oriented domestic firm to an outward-oriented firm investing abroad. The decision to invest is thus seen as a strategy to sustain technological and managerial advantages before they become diffused in overseas markets. Vernon's original article (1966), for instance, focused on post-war US investment in Europe. When it became economic for US companies to invest abroad, Western Europe was the preferred choice of location since demand patterns were close to the US and labour costs were relatively low at that time. When the product enters its standardised phase, the lowest cost supply point becomes a priority, and production can be transferred to developing countries, replacing exports from the parent company or even exporting back to the country of origin (Vernon, 1966). The third stage of evolution is referred to as the standardised product stage. Both the product and the production process are now completely standardised. Competition is extremely intense in both the local and developed countries' markets. There is pressure to be price competitive in the face of this increased competition. In order to decrease the product's price, production costs must be reduced, particularly if the process is labour intensive. Because the product and the production process are standardised, the company can now relocate manufacturing operations to a low labour cost county. The strategy is to serve both the home and developed countries' markets from these developing countries.

The product life cycle theory of FDI introduced dynamics to the theory of comparative advantage, arguing that developing countries will enjoy comparative advantages with regard to mature and especially standardised products. Consequently, technology transfer through FDI will mainly take place where the products that the technologies are associated with are in the mature stages of the product cycle. This process favours developing countries in that they would get access to technologies without experiencing the mistakes and costs associated with the introduction of new products, or what is called the advantage of being backward. Moreover, the product cycle theory predicts that MNEs might assist developing countries in getting access to international markets. Mature products are subject to significant barriers to entry, especially at the marketing stage, and MNEs can help developing economies overcome these barriers. The influence of Vernon's original model goes way beyond its original application to the development of US direct investment in Europe and in the cheap labour countries, and beyond Vernon's own Mark II appraisal of its usefulness (1979) in response to critics (Giddy, 1978). The dynamics of the model lies in the interaction of the evolving forces of demand patterns and production possibilities. The twin rationales of cost imperatives and market pull are simply explained in Vernon's model. In some ways, its simple, yet powerful, dynamic, resting on the interaction of demand and supply over time, has never been improved (Buckley, 1993; Buckley & Casson, 1981).

A group of Vernon's doctoral students, notably Knickerbocker (1973), Graham (1978) and Flowers (1976), argued that it was not just locational variables that determined the spatial distribution of the economic activity of firms but their strategic response to these variables and to the anticipated behaviour of their competitors. Nowhere is this more clearly seen than in an oligopolistic market situation. Economists, for more than a century, have acknowledged that output and price equilibrium depends on the assumptions made by one firm about how its own behaviour will affect that of its competitors, and how, in turn, this latter behaviour will impinge upon its own position. Knickerbocker (1973) argued that oligopolists, wishing to avoid destructive competition, would normally follow each other into new and foreign markets to safeguard their own commercial interests. This so-called bandwagon effect can be triggered not only by decisions of competitors but also of customers deciding to establish themselves in a certain market. Empirical evidence supports the follow-the-leader idea that FDI is subject to bunching. For instance, an analysis of FDI by US MNEs in European manufacturing industry in the 1960s seemed to support the

18   *Peter J. Buckley*

hypotheses (Flowers, 1976). There has also been a stampede of Japanese MNEs in the US and European auto and consumer electronics industries (De Beule & Van Den Bulcke, 1998). Graham's (1978) tit-for-tat hypothesis is that an MNE which found its home territory invaded by a foreign MNE would retaliate by penetrating the invader's home turf. Examples of the so-called exchange of threats hypothesis abound in sectors such as tyre, automobile, colour television, advertising, banking and hotel sectors.

An organising framework – incorporating different theoretical approaches – has been put forward by Dunning (1979, 1993, 2001) in his eclectic paradigm in which he attempts to explain all forms of international investment. The eclectic paradigm maintains that firms will engage in international production if they possess ownership advantages in a particular market to overcome the liability of foreignness; if the enterprises perceive it to be in its best interest to add value to these ownership advantages rather than to sell them to foreign firms; and if locational advantages make it more profitable to exploit theses assets in a particular foreign location rather than at home.

In explaining the growth of international production, several strands of economic and business theory assert that this is dependent on the investing firms possessing some kind of unique and sustainable competitive advantage (or set of advantages), relative to that (or those) possessed by their foreign competitors. Since the 1960s, the extant literature has come to identify three main kinds of firm- or ownership-specific competitive advantages. A first set are those competitive advantages relating to the possession and exploitation of monopoly power, as initially identified by Hymer (1960) and Bain (1956), and the industrial organisation scholars (Caves, 1971; Porter, 1980, 1985). These advantages stem from some kind of barrier to entry in final product markets to (potential) competitors.

A second set of ownership advantages are related to the possession of a bundle of scarce, unique and sustainable resources and capabilities, which essentially reflect the superior technical efficiency of a particular firm relative to those of its competitors. The identification and evaluation of these advantages has been one of the main contributions of the resource-based view (Barney, 1991; Conner, 1991; Conner & Prahalad, 1996; Dierickx & Cool, 1989; Montgomery, 1995; Wernerfelt, 1984) and evolutionary theories of the firm (Cantwell, 1989, 1994; Dosi, Freeman, Nelson, & Soete, 1988; Dosi, Nelson, & Winter, 2002; Nelson & Winter, 1984; Saviotti & Metcalfe, 1991; Teece, Pisano, & Shuen, 1997).

The basis of the resource-based view of the firm is that it is the heterogeneity, not the homogeneity, of the productive services available from its resources that give each firm its unique character. As such, resource-based views of the firms tend to see differences across companies as the result of differences in efficiency, rather than differences in market power (Montgomery, 1995). In explaining these differences, resource-based theorists tend to focus on resources and capabilities that are long-lived and

Business History and International Business 19

difficult to imitate (Conner, 1991). In the resource-based view history matters, profits are persistent, and change most often occurs slowly and incrementally (Peteraf, 1993).

The evolutionary theory of the firm – while accepting much of the content of resource-based theory – pays more attention to the process or path by which the specific ownership advantages of firms evolve and are accumulated over time (Dunning, 2000). In contrast, or in addition to internalisation theory, it tends to regard the firm as innovator and organiser of a repository of knowledge to promote its long term prosperity, rather than a nexus of treaties designed to optimise the efficiency of existing resource usage. Evolutionary theory is, by its very nature, a dynamic theory, which, like the resource-based theory, not only accepts but also seeks to explain the diversity of firms. However, unlike the latter, it concentrates on the firm's long term strategy towards asset protection and augmentation, and the implications for its routines and the development of their dynamic capabilities (Nelson & Winter, 1984; Teece, et al., 1997).

A third set of firm specific advantages relate to relating to the competencies of the managers of firms to identify, evaluate and harness resources and capabilities from all over the world, and to coordinate these with the existing resources and capabilities under their jurisdiction in a way which best advances the long term interests of the firm. These advantages – stressed by organisational scholars (Bartlett & Ghoshal, 1989; Prahalad & Doz, 1987) – tend to be management specific and are an acknowledgement of the fact that, even within the same corporation, managerial competencies may vary widely. While the focus of interest is similar to that of the resource and evolutionary theories, the emphasis of organisational related theories is on the capabilities of management to orchestrate and integrate the resources it can internally upgrade or innovate, or externally acquire, rather than on the resources themselves. But, as with the resource-based and evolutionary theories, the objective of the decision taker is assumed to be as much directed to growth of assets as to optimising the income stream from a given set of assets (Dunning, 1998).

The eclectic paradigm has also included location advantages of countries as a key determinant of the foreign investment of multinational corporations. Location advantages include the spatial distribution of natural and created resource endowments and markets, input prices, quality and productivity (e.g. labour, energy, materials, components, semi-finished goods), economic system and strategies of government, such as commercial, legal, educational, transport and communication provisions, as well as ideological, language, cultural, business and political differences (Dunning, 1981, 1988, 1992; Ghoshal, 1987).

While the observation that location-specific characteristics matter to firms is hardly novel (Marshall, 1890; Smith, 1776; von Thünen, 1826), for the most part, neither the economics nor the business literature has given much attention to how the emergence and growth of the cross-border activities of firms might be explained by the kind of location related theories which were initially designed to explain the siting of production within a nation state, nor to how the spatial dimension of FDI might affect the competitiveness of the investing companies.

There have been numerous context-specific theories of the siting of particular value added activities of firms and of geographical distribution of FDI. They include the location component of Vernon's (1966) product cycle theory, Knickerbocker's (1973) 'follow-my-leader' theory, which was one of the earliest approaches to analysing the clustering or bunching effect of FDI, and Rugman's (1975, 1979) risk diversification theory, which suggested that MNEs normally prefer a geographical spread of FDI to having all their eggs in the same geographic basket. However, researchers extended, rather than replaced standard theories of location to encompass cross-border value added activities. In particular, they embraced new location advantages, such as exchange rates, political risks, inter-country cultural differences, and placed a different value on a variety of variables common to both domestic and international location choices, such as wage levels, demand patterns, policy related variables, supply capacity and infrastructure. These add-on or revalued variables could be easily accommodated within the existing analytical theories (Dicken, 1998). This marks off older explanations of the location specific advantage of nations from those of the ownership specific advantages of firms.

The emergence of the knowledge-based global economy and asset-augmenting FDI is compelling scholars to take a more dynamic approach to both the logistics of the siting of corporate activities, and to the competitive advantages of nations and regions (Dunning, 1998). Firms need to take account not only of the presence and cost of traditional factor endowments, of transport costs, of current demand levels and patterns, and of Marshallian types of agglomerative economies, but also of distance related transaction costs (Storper & Scott, 1987), of dynamic externalities, knowledge accumulation and interactive learning (Enright, 1990, 1998, 2000; Florida, 1995; Malmberg, Sölvell, & Zander, 1996), of spatially related innovation and technological standards (Antonelli, 1998; Frost, 1998; Sölvell & Zander, 1998), of the increasing dispersion of created assets, and of the need to conclude cross-border augmenting and asset exploiting alliances (Dunning, 1995, 1998). As such, since 1990, location has been taken up in explaining the stickiness of certain locations in an increasingly slippery world (Markusen, 1994). Theories suggest that firms may be drawn to the same locations because proximity generates positive externalities or agglomeration effects. Economists have proposed agglomeration effects in the form of both static (pecuniary) and dynamic (technological) externalities to explain industry localisation (Baptista, 1998). Theoretical attempts to formalise agglomeration effects have focused on three mechanisms that would yield such positive feedback loops: inter-firm technological spillovers, specialised labour, and intermediate inputs (Marshall, 1890).

Research methods[4]

International business theory has therefore been analytic, diagnostic and programmatic. There has been considerable debate as to the extent to which it has succeeded in being dynamic. The corpus of academic work on international business has been divided between quantitative studies and qualitative ones. Quantitative research has been largely cross-sectional in method, often using large scale datasets. Qualitative research is more normally single firm (or single industry) focused and longitudinal.

Historical research has been described as research driven versus theory driven. 'Research driven' refers to the study of archives or text filtered through the historian's imagination to see its possibilities (see Burrow, 2007, p. 510). This is contrasted with (usually long term, overarching) studies inspired by theoretical conceptions of key drivers of events (Marxist theory being the epitome of such structuring).

Both international business and business history struggle with causality versus correspondence (or correlation). The role of chance – risk and uncertainty in business, fortune or fate in history is often underrated in a search for determinism. Both areas have attempted large scale comparisons and forensic studies in efforts to discern the real drivers of change.

There are however differences in approach. The use of archives and primary data continues to be a distinctive feature of business history (paralleled perhaps by participant observation and case study methods in international business research). The foundation of business history is longitudinal study although methods of comparative statics have to be perforce employed regularly because of data deficiencies. Complementarities between the two intellectual domains therefore exist. The importation of 'mid level theory' from international business (internalisation theory, the eclectic paradigm, transaction cost theory, the resource-based view of the firm) enhances generalisation, explanatory power and classification of business historical data. Business history provides sources of testing for international business theory and like extension to 'new' sources of foreign direct investment (like China, e.g. see Buckley et al., 2007) provides some severe tests for generalisability of these theories.

The impact of Japan as the first important 'non-Western' (non-Judaeo-Christian) economic power gave a powerful impetus to comparative studies in international business research. There has been a long and fruitful tradition of 'comparative management' which has, in particular, drawn attention to the conceptual and empirical pitfalls in comparative work. Much of the difficulty and excitement of comparative research lies in the area of research methods (see Lonner & Berry, 1986). An illustration of the difficulties and

22 *Peter J. Buckley*

frustrations of comparative analysis was given by Adler, Campbell, and Laurent (1989). The comparative perspective is particularly challenging because, as Etzioni and Dubow (1970, p. viii) point out, 'the comparative perspective is more than a scientific technique – it provides a basic intellectual outlook.' There can be few of us who do not believe that we have something to learn from other cultures and societies but the issues of how real differences are to be identified and how they relate to other elements in society are of crucial analytical importance. An illustration of this was the controversy over the transferability or otherwise of Japanese management practices. Are these practices rooted in unique Japanese cultural traits? Or can they be extracted, transferred and transplanted on a piecemeal basis? Such controversies are not new. In 1953 Arnold Toynbee opined that fragments of a culture, such as its technological advances, were much more likely to have an impact on another culture than an attempt to introduce a way of life en bloc (Toynbee, 1953). Social anthropologists would typically look sceptically at this idea, wedded as they are to holistic and contextual analyses; a fragment of one culture when transferred to another takes on a new contextual meaning. Toynbee concedes this contextual point, however, going on to note that the piecemeal absorption which he describes may have profound long term effects, pulling in related elements from the exported culture. How often have we observed developing countries' desire to obtain advanced technology without the associated cultural dominance? Lest this be thought far removed from international business practice, note the increase in non-equity technology deals under pressure from this demand.

The basic problem in comparative research arises from the monumental nature of the task. The great strength of comparative research is that it provides a carefully specified 'counterfactual' – the situation existing in the country with which comparisons are being drawn. However difficulties arise from abstracting from the investigator's own cultural bias which is likely to impinge on objectivity (Campbell, 1970). The method of comparative research can be very precise. Indeed it is analytically more rigorous than single country studies as it provides measurable counterfactuals. However the difficulty of carrying it out arises from the large amount of information necessary. Because of this a focus on 'the local, the concrete, the specific' (Rokkan, 1970) is more likely to lead to immediate, short term results than the careful design of comparative work. A further obvious, but important difficulty exists. This is language difference in comparative research. Even the most expert translations and retranslations can produce differences of meaning (Brislin, 1986; Phillips, 1970). The underlying difficulty arises in the nuances of meaning as expressed through language. Cultural biases in language are not easy to exclude.

Of crucial importance to the comparative method in research is choosing the right comparator. There are three basic possibilities (Buckley, Pass, & Prescott, 1988, p. 195). First, there is the historical comparison – the situation relative to a different point of time. Second, there is the spatial comparison – relative to a different locational, national, cultural or regional point. Third, there is the counterfactual comparison – what might have been had not a particular action been taken or event occurred (this method has been used to good effect by cliometricians). Of great importance in this type of research method is to ensure that as many factors as possible are held constant other than the research object which is being comparatively analysed. International business lends itself to this type of analysis and it is relatively well developed. Analyses of firms and nations over time are well established. National comparisons are the stock-in-trade of the international business research community which often takes advantage of the uniqueness of the multinational enterprise – the same firm operating in different national environments. Paired groups of firms (e.g. of different national ownerships within the same market) are also utilised. Counterfactual comparisons are also frequent, particularly in the analysis of foreign direct investment outcomes. The actual situation is often contrasted with 'the alternative position' – what would have happened if the investment under scrutiny had not taken place. The difficulty, of course, lies in specifying the feasible (or most likely) alternative position.

For our purposes it is clearly the historical comparator that is prominent. Changes over time represent 'in-case' comparisons and of course it is the stock-in-trade of business historians to compare their main focus of analysis (the firm or firms being analysed) with other cases from similar times or other eras. Where the modern era is the comparator, we can allude to 'the lessons of history' but most business historians would treat such notions with massive 'health warnings'! It is only under very tightly specified control of conditions that the forward projection of understandings ('lessons') from a past era can enlighten the present, tempting as such allusions are.

It is instructive that business historians use not only historical comparators but also geographical ones and counterfactual constructions.

A long-run theory of international business?

It is true that international business theory is either atemporal or, by implication, short run in its conception. Theories with a time dimension potentially include the product cycle hypothesis of Vernon (1966), the Uppsala approach (Johanson & Vahlne, 1977; Johanson & Wiedersheim-Paul, 1975) and, casting the net a little wider, evolutionary theories of firm (Nelson & Winter, 1984). In all of these theories the role of time and particularly of the timing of strategic changes is vague. Vernon's approach has been termed 'programmatic not dynamic' (Buckley & Casson, 1976, p. 77) because it does not specify the timing of changes from exporting to direct foreign investment nor the temporal aspect of trigger variables that change the firm's foreign market servicing decision. The Uppsala 'stages' approach is descriptive in terms of the sequential development of the firm's internationalisation (in both its choice of foreign markets and the deepening involvement in each of them) and its coherence is much disputed.

In order to produce, and to test, a long run theory of sufficient power, it needs to be confronted with appropriate set of historical facts.

> In general, the historical record does not present an orderly set of facts that point to a single conclusion. In some cases, there is too much information, leading either to redundancy or to contradiction. Some standard must be used to choose the 'useful facts' from among the whole body of evidence.... Thus historians must use some organising principle, or even several principles, in order to make sense of their evidence. (Robertson, 1996, p. 132)

Buckley and Casson (1976, p. 31) took a set of stylised facts as 'phenomena which require explanation'. For our purposes, these included: 'the dating of the "take-off" of the multinationalisation of business to the immediate postwar world' and 'postwar international direct investments apparently do not conform to the theory that capital moves from capital-abundant countries to capital-scarce countries: the problem is not only that in certain cases capital flows in the "wrong" direction, but that in several cases substantial amounts of capital in fact flow between two countries in both directions at once' (Buckley & Casson, 1976, p. 31). In fact part of the explanation for the latter point resides in other phenomena requiring explanation, the industrial structure of FDI and vertical diversification.

It is probably the case that many business historians would dispute the first proposition, that multinationalisation began post-World War II, but the context of this assertion is that FDI is being examined rather than international trade. Nevertheless it is possible to look at FDI and different types of international capital flows over the long run and to attempt a theoretical explanation. Many early post-World War II manufacturing multinationals conformed to product cycle type strategies, first developing skills, knowledge, brands and economies of scale in the home (largely US) market. Growth of rival metropolitan centres of FDI led to international oligopoly of the Knickerbocker (1973) type with Europe and Japan challenging US hegemony in several leading industries such as automobiles, electronics and machinery. In FDI statistics, this was overlaid on top of an earlier and continuing use of FDI to achieve control of key inputs, particularly raw materials.

A key shift occurred with the development of skills in multinational firms that allowed greater degrees of 'fine-slicing' of activities over time such that each sliver of activity could be optimally located and controlled (Buckley, 2007). This allowed a 'global factory' type of organisation to emerge which involves a combination of directly owned and controlled activities with outsourced and offshored facilities (Buckley & Ghauri, 2004).

These secular shifts of dominant types (or are they really ideal types) from extractive MNEs to integrated multinational manufacturers to more flexibly organised global factories can be considered as aspects within a single paradigm (as the OLI [ownership, location and internalisation] theory of Dunning would explain them (Dunning, 1979, 2000, 2001)) or as a response to changing imperfect external markets (as the internalisation theory would suggest (Buckley & Casson, 1976)) or as evolutionary adaptation (or more recently co-evolution (Murmann, 2003)) of the firm (Nelson & Winter, 1984).

Historical 'facts' which might present challenges to long run theories of international business include not only changes in the strategy organisation and existence of multinationals but also in their nationality of ownership and sector. The relationship between sector and internationalisation was a key issue in the product cycle explanation, taking new product, maturing product and standardised product (Vernon, 1966) or innovation-based oligopoly, mature oligopoly, senescent oligopoly (Vernon, 1974) as stages of development. The challenge here is to specify carefully what is exogenous. In Vernon's case, exogenous valuable were changing tastes, dependent on income, communication costs that increase with distance and an imperfect market in knowledge. The dynamic is given by *predictable* changes in technology and marketing. Perhaps here lies the key to a truly dynamic 'historical' or long run theory of international business – theorising on technological, marketing and wider types of *knowledge*. Knowledge-based theories of the firm (Conner, 1991; Conner and Prahalad, 1996; Montgomery, 1995) and the multinational firm (Buckley & Carter, 2002, 2003, 2004; Magee, 1977a, 1977b; Vermeulen & Barkema, 2002) do not confront the exogeneity or endogeneity of knowledge in a complete fashion. However, theories of the firm that focus on the accumulation, acquisition, creation and retention of knowledge have promise for business historical theorising (Kogut & Zander, 1992; Nelson, 1991). A more grounded theoretical approach to dynamic capabilities (Teece, Pisano, & Shuen 1997), correctly specifying exogeneity, has the potential to be a key element in a long run theory of the development of firms over time (Langlois, 1991). Long run theories combining the need for flexibility (Buckley & Casson, 1998; Carlsson, 1989) with coherence (Teece, Rumelt, Dosi, & Winter, 1994) are a major challenge (see Hausman, Hertner, & Wilkins, 2008).

A second challenge comes from the rise of MNEs from emerging economies. International business theory has met this in one of two ways – either by asserting that these multinationals are entirely explicable by the judicious application of extant theories (Dunning (2006) and Narula (2006) using the eclectic or OLI approach, for instance) or by claiming that completely new theories are required (Mathews' (2002, 2006a, 2006b) LLL (Learning, Leverage and Linkage) approach for instance). An intermediate stance is taken by Buckley et al. (2007) which argues that the emergence of Chinese multinationals can be explained as a special application of the general theory of the growth of the firm by internalisation of imperfect markets – the special application arising because of the peculiar imperfections in the Chinese capital market. In fact, emerging country multinationals are the latest in a long line of 'unconventional multinationals' that are frequently presented as challenges to established theory – a perfectly respectable means of attempting to refute orthodoxy.

There are, of course, exemplars of business historians which have influenced business theory. The prime example is Alfred Chandler (1962, 1977), who produced a series of hypotheses on the way in which business enterprises change their internal deployment of resources in response to changes in scope and in their external environment. Chandler unashamedly used theoretical categories to drive his case study material (see Chandler, 1962, p. vii, Acknowledgements). Indeed, Chandler's theoretical innovations influenced in turn Thompson (1967) and Williamson (1985) and these adaptations were adopted in Chandler's 1990 book. Cross-fertilisation with organisational sociology and organisational economics produced an improved synthesis (Robertson, 1996, p. 112). Since Chandler, 'organisation theory has provided a battleground between advocates of "the one best way" and contingency theorists, accompanied by disputes within each group over which way is best or what contingencies are relevant' (Loasby, 1996, p. 112). It is precisely this interface that business history theorising can illuminate.

The monumental works of Mira Wilkins (1970, 1974b, 1989; Wilkins & Hill, 1964) are exemplars of international business history. In the epilogue to *The Maturing of Multinational Enterprise*, Wilkins (1974b, p. 414) provides a commentary on the then extant international business theory that 'brings her squarely in agreement with those theorists who look at the dynamics of direct foreign investments and view such investments as part of a process – a process developing over time out of the requirements of the innovative business enterprise.' This is, in effect, an Uppsala model *avant le temps*. Despite the usual historian's caveat – 'no inevitability is implied by the growth pattern that the author is about to describe' (Wilkins, 1974b, p. 415), she produces a three stage model of the development of American multinational enterprise. Stage one is a 'monocentric' approach with little coordination or complexity in the organisation. In stage two the 'monocentric relationship is shattered' (Wilkins, 1974b, p. 417) and foreign units develop their own satellite activities. In stage three, 'the parent company comes to have a number of foreign multifunctional centres, servicing overlapping geographical areas with various products' (Wilkins, 1974b, p. 419). Wilkins explicitly describes this evolutionary approach as 'a model' and analyses the extent to which the model fits (and predicts) various sectors. These theoretical innovations draw on Hymer (1960), Kindleberger (1969) and Aharoni (1966), anticipate the Uppsala model and have a great deal in common with Buckley and Casson's (2007) elaboration of Penrose's *Theory of the Growth of the Firm* (1959).

Cross-fertilisation between business history and intuitionalist economics is also a feature of Lazonick (1983, 1991, 1993), whose work on the role of technological and knowledge-based discontinuities moving systems into new equilibrium is the basis for a long run theory of international business. The notions of 'atomistic economic organisation', 'institutional rigidities' and stages of the evolution of industrial capitalism are important building blocks for (comparative) theories of international business. Lazonick's focus on the role of the changing knowledge basis of societies is a valuable link to knowledge-based theories of the multinational firm. Strong theoretical links can be made between this tradition, the fundamental work of Schumpeter (1928, 1934, 1943) on innovation and its disruptive consequences and with the theory of the growth of the firm following Penrose (1959; and see Buckley & Casson, 2007).

The work of Piore and Sabel (1984) points in a different direction. If the tradition above suggests global firms are the future, 'flexible specialisation' points firmly in direction of theories of localisation. This is pertinent because international business theories have long tried to reconcile pressures for globalisation versus tendencies to localisation (Buckley, 2007). In times of extreme pressure of the environment (as with the current, 2009, 'credit crunch'), firms are torn between maintaining their global networks and securing local strengths. The historical record on this balance ('glocalisation') is crucial and possibly predictive of future events (Buckley, 2007; Lazonick, 1993).

International business theory can therefore benefit from the work of business historians by the constant reminder that time, with all its implications, is a key variable in any analysis of MNEs and that a test of a good theory is how well it can account for time. (It may also serve as a reminder of the time-bounded nature of some theories.) This requires theorists to give careful thought to what exactly is exogenous in their theorising. When exogenous variables change (e.g. over time), the system's response has to be explained. Perhaps this is the easy part. Specifying changes in exogenous variables is more difficult. This section has attempted, in an extremely cursory and preliminary fashion, to provide steps towards a long run business historical theory of international business.

This special issue of *Business History*

The international status of business history is reflected here in papers from researchers in USA, Spain, Norway, England and Scotland.

In 1974 *Business History Review* published a special issue on 'Multinational Enterprise', including a piece on 'Multinational oil companies in South America in the 1920s' by Mira Wilkins (1974a). Another piece by Charles Kindleberger on the 'Origins of United States direct investment in France' opens with the sentence 'Most analysis of American direct investment abroad

28 *Peter J. Buckley*

focus on the post-World War II era, and on manufacturing' (Kindleberger, 1974, p. 382). Kindleberger's paper examines pre-1950 developments with special attention to services (finance, insurance, trade, marketing). The focus of papers in this special issue of *Business History* is largely on foreign investors from Europe and the USA – the exception is Hang and Godley on overseas Chinese investors. The sectoral focus is predominately on service industries – insurance, general services, banking, the film industry, shipping and railways are included. The historical period covered is not uniformly post-World War II, with papers examining the pre-World War I period and analyses beginning in the mid-nineteenth century (see Table 2.1).

The richness of this special issue is brought out in Table 2.1. As well as the variety in host countries, source countries and industry or sector, the authors use both primary and secondary data, ranging from private papers to extensive data sets (some compiled *ab initio* for the purposes of analysis). The theory drawn up ranges from 'traditional' theories of foreign direct investment and international business to theories of economic integration, internationalisation, international management theory and theoretical concepts that have arisen from business history such as the 'free standing company'. A wide time span is covered too, ranging from the mid-nineteenth century to the present. It is interesting that a number of innovative key concepts can be identified in each paper giving a unique take on the subject matter – these are internationalisation at the level of the (insurance) industry (Wilkins), capital market integration and its relationship with economic integration (Ferguson), the psychic distance paradox (Hang and Godley), subsidiary evolution (Dimitratos, Liouka, Ross, and Young), the liability of foreignness (Miskell), the internationalisation process (Amdam), internationalisation as applied to family firms (Puig and Fernández Perez) and the free standing company[5] (Boughey). All of the authors have combined theory with empirical analysis and enriched their material.

As Casson (1997, p. 151) has pointed out, 'The institutional theory of the firm, derived from Coase and developed by Williamson and others, has only partly fulfilled its early promise. ... It has succeeded in explaining where the boundaries of the firm are drawn, but has failed to relate these boundaries to what goes on inside the firm.' The articles in this special issue go some way to answering the crucial, and difficult, issue of the relationship between the management and strategy within the firm and relating this to the firm's boundaries and geographical extent. There is much more work to do in this area and business history research has a great deal to offer in further empirical findings and improved conceptualisation of the issue.

Conclusion

It is conventional to suggest that empirically based subjects like business history can be used to test theories. This has been true and remains true.

Table 2.1   Contents of this special issue analysed

	Wilkins	Ferguson	Hang and Godley	Dimitratos et al.	Miskell	Amdam	Puig and Fernández Pérez	Boughey
Home (source) country	US, Europe and Canada	UK	Overseas Chinese; more recent foreign investors	US main investor, global sources	US	Norway	Spain	UK
Host countries	World	Europe	China	Scotland	Britain	World, mainly Europe	World	Mainly North and South America and India
Industry/ sector	Insurance	Financial services, banking	Retailing	Manufacturing	Film Industry	Mainly manufacturing and shipping	Manufacturing and services	Railways
Data	Primary firm level and industry data	Private papers, secondary data	Primary and secondary (firm level) data	Secondary data, case studies at firm level	Primary and secondary data. Firm and industry level	Database of contemporary surveys of firms	Database of family owned firms	Company reports secondary data industry level data
Theory	Theory of the MNE and FDI	Theory of economic integration	Theory of MNE and FDI, internationalisation theory	Theory of MNE and FDI, 'Global Factory' international management theory	Theory of MNE, international management theory	Internationalisation theory	Theory of FDI, internationalisation theory	International new ventures, free-standing company
Era	Pre-World War I to date	1960s	1840–2005	1945 to date	1930s and 1940s	1945–1980	Mid-nineteenth century to date	1900–1915
Key concepts	Internationalisation at industry level	Capital market internationalisation and economic integration	Psychic distance (paradox)	Subsidiary evolution	Liability of foreignness	Internationalisation process	Internationalisation of family firms	Free-standing company

30 *Peter J. Buckley*

However, there is an opportunity to do more than that. In concert with international business theory and method, business historians have the potential to develop and extend existing theory and to produce new or improved theory. The comparative method is part of the contribution that the study of international business can make. Business historians are skilled at historical (over time) comparisons and international business historians have two key comparators (time and space) at their disposal. Given the imaginative conjectures of analysts, the third comparator – the counterfactual – is ready to be deployed. From careful use of new primary (archival) data, the construction of stylised facts is just a step away. The explication of these styled facts leads to new hypotheses and generalised structuring of hypotheses to new theory. Business history has long been a fruitful test bed of (international business) theory. The new business history could become a powerful generator of theory.

Acknowledgements

I am grateful for comments on earlier drafts of this piece by Mira Wilkins, Thomas Buckley, John Wilson, Paloma Fernández Pérez and especially to Andrew Godley for a thought-provoking response that led to substantial changes.

Notes

1. I owe the genesis of this paragraph to Paloma Fernández Pérez.
2. See 'Historical knowledge in/on East and South East Asia' Conference at Tallinn University, 13–15 September 2009.
3. This section is largely derived from Buckley and De Beule (2005). See also Buckley and Casson (1976, chapter 3, 1998), Buckley (2002, 2004) and Buckley and Lessard (2005). For a recent overview, see Forsgren (2008). For a superb overview of the whole corpus of international business, see Dunning and Lundan (2008).
4. For a fuller exposition, see Buckley and Chapman (1996).
5. The notion of the 'free standing company' is a theoretical innovation that has emerged from business history (Wilkins, 1988; Wilkins & Schroter, 1998). Its status and significance are not uncontested however (Casson, 1998; Corley, 1998) and it promises to be an interesting concept for the further refinement and testing of theory.

References

Adler, N.J., Campbell, N., & Laurent, A. (1989). In search of appropriate methodology: From outside the People's Republic of China looking in. *Journal of International Business Studies, 20*(1), 61–74.

Aharoni, Y. (1966). *The foreign investment decision process.* Boston, MA: Division of Research, Graduate School of Business Administration, Harvard University.

Anderson, E., & Gatignon, H. (1986). Modes of foreign entry: Transaction costs and propositions. *Journal of International Business Studies, 17*(3), 1–26.

Antonelli, C. (1998). The dynamics of localized technological changes: The interaction between factor costs inducement, demand pull and Schumpeterian rivalry. *Economics of Innovation and New Technology, 6*(2–3), 97–120.

Bain, J.S. (1956). *Barriers to new competition.* Cambridge, MA: Harvard University Press.

Baptista, R. (1998). Clusters, innovation, and growth. In P. Swann, M. Prevezer, & D. Stout (Eds.), *The dynamics of industrial clustering: International comparisons in computing and biotechnology* (pp. 13–51). Oxford: Oxford University Press.

Barney, J. (1991). Firm resources and sustained competitive advantage. *Journal of Manangement, 17*(1), 99–120.

Bartlett, C.A., & Ghoshal, S. (1989). *Managing across borders: The transnational solution.* Boston, MA: Harvard Business School Press.

Blomström, M., & Kokko, A. (1996a). *The impact of foreign investment on host countries: A review of the empirical evidence.* Washington, DC: World Bank.

Blomström, M., & Kokko, A. (1996b). *Multinational corporations and spillovers.* London: Centre for Economic Policy Research.

Blomström, M., Kokko, A., & Zejan, M. (1994). Host country competition, labor skills, and technology transfer by multinationals. *Weltwirtschaftliches Archiv, 130*(3), 521–533.

Blomström, M., Kokko, A., & Zejan, M. (2000). *Foreign direct investment: Firm and host country strategies.* Houndmills: Macmillan.

Blomström, M., Zejan, M., & Kokko, A. (1992). *Host country competition and technology transfer by multinationals.* Cambridge, MA: National Bureau of Economic Research.

Brislin, R.W. (1986). The wording and translation of research instruments. In J.W. Lonner & J.W. Berry (Eds.), *Field methods in cross cultural research* (pp. 137–164). Beverly Hills, CA: Sage.

Buckley, P.J. (1993). Contemporary theories of international direct investment. *Revue Economique, 44*(4), 725–736.

Buckley, P.J. (2002). Is the international business research agenda running out of steam? *Journal of International Business Studies, 33*(2), 365–373.

Buckley, P.J. (Ed.). (2004). *What is international business?* Basingstoke: Palgrave Macmillan.

Buckley, P.J. (2007). The strategy of multinational enterprises in the light of the rise of China. *Scandinavian Journal of Management, 23*(2), 107–126.

Buckley, P.J., & Carter, M.J. (2002). Process and structure in knowledge management practices of British and US multinational enterprises. *Journal of International Management, 8*(1), 29–48.

Buckley, P.J., & Carter, M.J. (2003). Governing knowledge sharing in multinational enterprises. *Management International Review.* Special issue, *43*(3), 7–25.

Buckley, P.J., & Carter, M.J. (2004). A formal analysis of knowledge combination in multinational enterprises. *Journal of International Business Studies, 35*(5), 371–384.

Buckley, P.J., & Casson, M. (1976). *The future of the multinational enterprise.* London: Macmillan.

Buckley, P.J., & Casson, M. (1981). The optimal timing of a foreign direct investment. *Economic Journal, 91*(361), 75–87.

Buckley, P.J., & Casson, M. (1988). A theory of co-operation in international business. In F.J. Contractor & P. Lorange (Eds.), *Co-operative strategies in international business* (pp. 31–33). Lexington, MA: Lexington Books.

Buckley, P.J., & Casson, M. (1998). Models of the multinational enterprise. *Journal of International Business Studies, 29*(1), 21–44.

Buckley, P.J., & Casson, M. (2007). Edith Penrose's theory of the growth of the firm and the strategic management of multinational enterprises. *Management International Review, 47*(2), 151–173.

Buckley, P.J., & Chapman, M. (1996). Theory and method in international business research. *International Business Review, 5*(3), 233–245.

Buckley, P.J., Clegg, J., Cross, A., Zheng, P., Voss, H., & Liu, X. (2007). The determinants of Chinese outward foreign direct investment. *Journal of International Business Studies, 38*(4), 499–518.

Buckley, P.J., & De Beule, F. (2005). The research agenda in international business: Past, present and future. In L. Cuyvers & F. De Beule (Eds.), *Transnational corporations and economic development: From internationalisation to globalisation* (pp. 200–221). London: Palgrave Macmillan.

Buckley, P.J., & Ghauri, P.N. (2004). Globalisation, economic geography and the strategy of multinational enterprises. *Journal of International Business Studies, 35*(2), 81–98.

Buckley, P.J., & Lessard, D.R. (2005). Regaining the edge for international business research. *Journal of International Business Studies, 36*(6), 595–599.

Buckley, P.J., Pass, C.L., & Prescott, K. (1988). Measures of international competitiveness: A critical survey. *Journal of Marketing Management, 4*(2), 175–200.

Burrow, J. (2007). *A history of histories.* London: Allen Lane.

Bury, J.B. (2006). *The Ancient Greek historians.* New York: Barnes & Noble (originally published 1909).

—— *Business History Review.* (1974). Special issue: Multinational enterprise, *48*(3).

Butterfield, H. (1965). *The Whig interpretation of history.* New York: W.W. Norton & Company, Inc.

Calvet, A.L. (1981). A synthesis of foreign direct investment theories and theories of the multinational firm. *Journal of International Business Studies, 12*(1), 43–59.

Campbell, D.T. (1970). Techniques for determining cultural biases in comparative research. In A. Etzioni & F.L. DuBow (Eds.), *Comparative perspectives: Theories and methods* (pp. 407–410). Boston, MA: Little, Brown and Co.

Cannadine, D. (2008). *Making history: Now and then.* Basingstoke: Palgrave Macmillan.

Cantwell, J. (1989). *Technological innovation and multinational corporations.* Oxford: Basil Blackwell.

Cantwell, J. (Ed.). (1994). *Transnational corporations and innovatory activities.* United Nations Library on Transnational Corporations. London: Routledge.

Carlsson, B. (1989). Flexibility and the theory of the firm. *International Journal of Industrial Organization, 7*(2), 179–203.

Casson, M. (1987a). Transaction costs and the theory of the multinational enterprise. In P.J. Buckley & M. Casson (Eds.), *The economic theory of the multinational enterprise* (pp. 113–143). London: Macmillan.

Casson, M. (1987b). *The firm and the market: Studies on multinational enterprise and the scope of the firm.* Oxford: Basil Blackwell.

Casson, M. (1997). Institutional economics and business history: A way forward? *Business History.* Special issue: Institutions and the evolution of modern business, *39*(4), 151–171.

Casson, M. (1998). An economic theory of the free-standing company. In M. Wilkins & H. Schroter (Eds.), *The free standing company in the world economy 1930–1996* (pp. 99–129). Oxford: Oxford University Press.

Caves, R.E. (1971). International corporations: The industrial economics of foreign investment. *Economica, 38*(149), 1–27.

Business History and International Business   33

Chandler, A.D. (1962). *Strategy and structure: Chapters in the history of American industrial enterprise*. Cambridge, MA: MIT Press.

Chandler, A.D. (1977). *The visible hand: The managerial revolution in American business*. Cambridge, MA: The Belknap Press of Harvard University Press.

Chandler, A.D. (1990). *Scale and scope: The dynamics of industrial capitalism*. Cambridge, MA: The Belknap Press of Harvard University Press.

Coase, R. (1937). The nature of the firm. *Economica, 4*(November), 386–405.

Conner, K.R. (1991). A historical comparison of resource-based theory and five schools of thought within industrial organizational economics. *Journal of Management, 17*(1), 121–154.

Conner, K.R., & Prahalad, C.K. (1996). A resource-based theory of the firm: Knowledge versus opportunism. *Organisation Science, 7*(5), 477–501.

Contractor, F.J. (1981). *International technology licensing compensation, costs and negotiation*. Lexington, MA: Lexington Books.

Corley, T.A.B. (1998). The free-standing company in theory and practice. In M. Wilkins & H. Schroter (Eds.), *The free standing company in the world economy 1930–1996* (pp. 129–151). Oxford: Oxford University Press.

De Beule, F., & Van Den Bulcke, D. (1998). *Japanese subsidiaries in the Belgian manufacturing industry: Changing characteristics*. Antwerp: Centre for International Management and Development (CIMDA).

Dicken, P. (1998). *Global shift: Transforming the world economy*. London: Paul Chapman.

Dierickx, I., & Cool, K. (1989). Asset stock accumulation and sustainability of competitive advantage. *Management Science, 35*(12), 1504–1511.

Dosi, G., Freeman, C., Nelson, R.R., & Soete, L. (1988). *Technical change and economic theory*. London: Pinter Publishers.

Dosi, G., Nelson, R.R., & Winter, S. (2002). *The nature and dynamics of organizational capabilities*. Oxford: Oxford University Press.

Dunning, J.H. (1979). Explaining changing patterns of international production: In defence of the eclectic theory. *Oxford Bulletin of Economics and Statistics, 41*(4), 269–295.

Dunning, J.H. (1981). *International production and the multinational enterprise*. London: Allen & Unwin.

Dunning, J.H. (1988). *Explaining international production*. London: Unwin Hyman.

Dunning, J.H. (1992). Governments, markets, and multinational enterprises: Some emerging issues. *International Trade Journal, 7*(1), 1–14.

Dunning, J.H. (1993). *Multinational enterprises and the global economy*. Wokingham: Addison Wesley.

Dunning, J.H. (1995). The role of foreign direct investment in a globalizing economy. *Banca Nazionale del Lavoro Quarterly Review, 48*(193), 125–144.

Dunning, J.H. (1998). Globalization, technological change and the spatial organization of economic activity. In A.D. Chandler, Jr., P. Hagström, & Ö. Sölvell (Eds.), *The dynamic firm: The role of technology, strategy, organization and regions*. Oxford: Oxford University Press.

Dunning, J.H. (2000). The eclectic paradigm as an envelope for economic and business theories of the MNE. *International Business Review, 9*, 163–190.

Dunning, J.H. (2001). The eclectic (OLI) paradigm of international production: Past, present and future. *International Journal of the Economics of Business, 8*(2), 173–190.

Dunning, J.H. (2006). Comment on dragon multinationals: New players in 21st century globalisation. *Asia Pacific Journal of Management, 23*, 139–141.

34 *Peter J. Buckley*

Dunning, J.H., & Lundan, S. (2008). *Multinational enterprises and the global economy* (2nd ed.). Cheltenham: Edward Elgar.

Dunning, J.H., & Narula, R. (1996). *Foreign direct investment and governments: Catalysts for economic restructuring.* London and New York: Routledge.

Elbaum, B., & Lazonick, W. (1986). An institutional perspective on British decline. In B. Elbaum & W. Lazonick (Eds.), *The decline of the British economy* (pp. 1–17). Oxford: Oxford University Press.

Elbaum, B. & Lazonick, W. (Eds.). (1986). *The decline of the British economy.* Oxford: Oxford University Press.

Enright, M. (1990). *Geographic concentration and industrial organization.* Cambridge, MA: Harvard University Press.

Enright, M.J. (1998). Regional clusters and firm strategy. In A.D. Chandler, Jr., P. Hagström, & Ö. Sölvell (Eds.), *The dynamic firm: The role of technology, strategy, organization and regions* (pp. 315–343). Oxford: Oxford University Press.

Enright, M.J. (2000). The globalization of competition and the localization of competitive advantage: Policies towards regional clustering. In N. Hood & S. Young (Eds.), *The globalization of multinational enterprise activity and economic development* (pp. 303–331). London: Macmillan.

Etzioni, A. & DuBow, F.L. (Eds.). (1970). *Comparative perspectives: Theories and methods.* Boston, MA: Little, Brown & Co.

Evans, J.A.S. (1968). Father of history or father of lives: The reputation of Herodotus. *The Classical Journal, 64*(1), 11–17.

Florida, R. (1995). Toward the learning region. *Futures, 27*(5), 527–536.

Flowers, E.B. (1976). Oligopolistic reactions in European and Canadian direct investment in the United States. *Journal of International Business Studies, 7*(2), 43–55.

Forsgren, M. (2008). *Theories of the multinational firm.* Cheltenham: Edward Elgar.

Frost, T.S. (1998). The geographic sources of innovation in the multinational enterprise: US subsidiaries and host country spillovers: 1980–1990. Working paper. Sloan School of Management. Cambridge, MA: Massachusetts Institute of Technology.

Ghoshal, S. (1987). Global strategy: An organising framework. *Strategic Management Journal, 8*(5), 425–440.

Giddy, I.H. (1978). The demise of the product cycle model in international business theory. *Columbia Journal of World Business, 13*(Spring), 90–97.

Graham, E.M. (1978). Transatlantic investment by multinational firms: A rivalistic phenomenon. *Journal of Post Keynesian Economics,* (1), 82–99.

Hallen, L., & Wiedersheim-Paul, F. (1993). Psychic distance and buyer-seller interaction. In P.J. Buckley & P. Ghauri (Eds.), *The internationalisation of the firm* (pp. 244–260). London: Dryden Press.

Hannah, L. (1983). *The rise of the corporate economy* (2nd edn). London: Methuen.

Hausman, W.J., Hertner, P., & Wilkins, M. (2008). *Global electrification: Multinational enterprise and international finance in the history of light and power.* Cambridge: Cambridge University Press.

Hedlund, G., & Kverneland, A. (1983). Are entry strategies for foreign markets changing? The case of Swedish investments in Japan. In P.J. Buckley & P. Ghauri (Eds.), *The internationalisation of the firm: A reader* (pp. 106–123). London: Dryden Press.

Hennart, J.F. (1982). *A theory of multinational enterprise.* Ann Arbor, MI: University of Michigan Press.

Hennart, J.F. (1991). The transaction cost theory of the multinational enterprise. In C.-N. Pitelis & R. Sugden (Eds.), *The nature of the transnational firm* (pp. 81–116). London and New York: Routledge.

Herman, H. (2001). *The Scottish enlightenment*. London: Simon & Schuster.

Herodotus (2003). *Histories*. Harmondsworth: Penguin Books.

Hicks, J. (1969). *A theory of economic history*. Oxford: Oxford University Press.

Hymer, S. (1960). *The international operations of national firms: A study of direct investment*. Cambridge, MA: MIT.

Hymer, S. (1968). La grande corporation multinationale: Analyse de certaines raisons qui poussent à l'intégration internationale des affaires. *Revue Economique, 14*(b), 949–973.

Hymer, S. (1970). The efficiency (contradictions) of multinational corporations. *American Economic Review, 60*(2), 441–448.

Johanson, J., & Vahlne, J.E. (1977). The internationalization process of the firm: A model of knowledge development and increasing foreign market commitments. *Journal of International Business Studies, 8*(1), 23–32.

Johanson, J., & Wiedersheim-Paul, F. (1975). The internationalisation process of the firm: Four Swedish cases. *Journal of Management Studies, 12*(3), 305–322.

Jones, G. (1996). *The evolution of international business*. London: Routledge.

Jones, G. (2005). *Multinationals and global capitalism: From the nineteenth to the twenty-first century*. Oxford: Oxford University Press.

Jones, G., & Khanna, T. (2006). Bringing history (back) into international business. *Journal of International Business Studies, 37*(4), 453–468.

Kindleberger, C.P. (1969). *American business abroad*. New Haven, CT: Yale University Press.

Kindleberger, C.P. (1974). Origins of United States direct investment in France. *Business History Review*. Special issue: Multinational enterprise, *48*(3), 414–447.

Knickerbocker, F.T. (1973). *Oligopolistic reaction and the multinational enterprise*. Cambridge, MA: Harvard University Press.

Kogut, B., & Zander, U. (1992). Knowledge of the firm, combinative capabilities and the replication of technology. *Organization Science, 3*(3), 383–397.

Kokko, A. (1994). Technology, market characteristics, and spillovers. *Journal of Development Economics, 43*(2), 279–293.

Langlois, R.N. (1991). Transaction cost economics in real time. *Industrial and Corporate Change, 1*(1), 99–127.

Lazonick, W. (1983). Industrial organization and technological change: The decline of the British cotton industry. *Business History Review, 107*, 195–236.

Lazonick, W. (1991). *Business organization and the myth of the market economy*. Cambridge: Cambridge University Press.

Lazonick, W. (1992). Controlling the market for corporate control: The historical significance of managerial capitalism. *Industrial and Corporate Change, 1*, 445–488.

Lazonick, W. (1993). Industry clusters versus global webs: Organizational capabilities in the American economy. *Industrial and Corporate Change, 2*, 1–24.

Loasby, B.J. (1996). Organisation and innovation at DuPont 1902–1980. In P.E. Earl (Ed.), *Management, marketing and the competitive process* (pp. 112–148). Cheltenham: Edward Elgar.

Lonner, W.J., & Berry, J.W. (1986). *Field methods in cross-cultural research*. Beverly Hills, CA: Sage.

Luostarinen, R. (1979). *Internationalisation of the firm*. Helsinki: Acta Acadamie Oeconomicae, Helsinki School of Economics.

Machiavelli, N. (1979). *The portable Machiavelli* (P. Bondanella & M. Musa, Eds.). Harmondsworth: Viking Penguin.

36   *Peter J. Buckley*

Magee, S.P. (1977a). Information and the multinational corporation. An appropriability theory of foreign direct investment. In J.N. Bhagwati (Ed.), *The new international economic order* (pp. 57–81). Cambridge, MA: MIT Press.

Magee, S.P. (1977b). Multinational corporations, the industry technology cycle and development. *Journal of World Trade Law, 11*(4), 297–321.

Malmberg, A., Sölvell, Ö., & Zander, I. (1996). Spatial clustering, local accumulation of knowledge and firm competitiveness. *Geografiska Annaler, 78*(2), 85–97.

Markusen, A. (1994). Studying regions by studying firms. *The Professional Geographer, 46*, 477–490.

Marshall, A. (1890). *Principles of economics.* London: Macmillan.

Mathews, J.A. (2002). *Dragon multinational: A new model for global growth.* New York: Oxford University Press.

Mathews, J.A. (2006a). Dragon multinationals: New players in 21st century globalisation. *Asia Pacific Journal of Management, 23*(1), 5–27.

Mathews, J.A. (2006b). Response to Professor Dunning and Narula. *Asia Pacific Journal of Management, 23*(2), 153–155.

Montgomery, C.A. (1995). *Resource-based and evolutionary theories of the firm: Towards a synthesis.* Dordrecht: Kluwer Academic Publishers.

Murmann, J.P. (2003). *Knowledge and competitive advantage: The coevolution of firms, technology and national institutions.* Cambridge: Cambridge University Press.

Narula, R. (2006). Globalization, new ecologies, new zoologies, and the purported death of the eclectic paradigm. *Asia Pacific Journal of Management, 23*(2), 143–151.

Nelson, R.R. (1991). Why do firms differ, and how does it matter? *Strategic Management Journal, 12*(S2), 61–74.

Nelson, R., & Winter, S. (1984). *An evolutionary theory of economic change.* Cambridge, MA: Harvard University Press.

Newbould, G.D., Buckley, P.J., & Thurwell, J.C. (1978). *Going international: The experience of smaller companies overseas.* New York: John Wiley & Sons, Inc.

Penrose, E.T. (1959). *The theory of the growth of the firm.* London: George Allen & Unwin.

Peteraf, M.A. (1993). The cornerstones of competitive advantage: A resource-based view. *Strategic Management Journal, 14*(3), 179–191.

Phillips, H.P. (1970). Problems of translation and meaning in field work. In A. Etzioni & F.L. DuBow (Eds.), *Comparative perspectives: Theories and methods* (pp. 387–406). Boston, MA: Little, Brown & Co.

Piore, M.J., & Sabel, C.F. (1984). *The second industrial divide.* New York: Basic Book.

Porter, M.E. (1980). *Competitive strategy.* New York: Free Press.

Porter, M.E. (1985). *Competitive advantage: Creating and sustaining superior performance.* New York: Free Press.

Prahalad, C.K., & Doz, Y.L. (1987). *The multinational mission: Balancing local demands and global vision.* New York: Free Press.

Robertson, P.L. (1996). Business history: Lessons for the future of business? In P.E. Earl (Ed.), *Management, marketing and the competitive process* (pp. 130–148). Cheltenham: Edward Elgar.

Rokkan, S. (1970). Recent developments in cross-national research. In A. Etzioni & F.L. DuBow (Eds.), *Comparative perspectives: Theories and methods* (pp. 79–93). Boston, MA: Little, Brown & Co.

Rugman, A.M. (1975). Motives for foreign investment: The market imperfections and risk diversification hypothesis. *Journal of World Trade Law, 9*(September–October), 567–573.

Rugman, A.M. (1979). *International diversification and the multinational enterprise*. Lexington, MA: Lexington Books.

Rugman, A.M. (1980). Internalization as a general theory of foreign direct investment: A reappraisal of the literature. *Weltwirtschaftliches Archiv, 116*(2), 365–379.

Saviotti, P.P., & Metcalfe, J.S. (1991). *Evolutionary theories of economic and technological change: Present status and future prospects*. London: Harwood.

Schumpeter, J.A. (1928). The instability of capitalism. *Economic Journal, 38*(251), 385–386.

Schumpeter, J.A. (1934). *The theory of economic development*. Cambridge, MA: Harvard University Press.

Schumpeter, J.A. (1943). *Capitalism, socialism and democracy*. London: George Allen & Unwin.

Smith, A. (1759). *The theory of moral sentiments* (D.D. Raphael & A.L. Macfie, Eds.). Indianapolis: Liberty Fund.

Smith, A. (1776). *An inquiry into the nature and causes of the wealth of nations*. Chicago: University of Chicago Press.

Sölvell, Ö., & Zander, I. (1998). International diffusion of knowledge: Isolating mechanisms and the role of the MNE. In A.D. Chandler, Jr., P. Hagström, & Ö. Sölvell (Eds.), *The dynamic firm: The role of technology, strategy, organization and regions* (pp. 402–416). Oxford: Oxford University Press.

Storper, M., & Scott, A. (1987). The wealth of regions: Market forces and policy imperatives in local and global context. *Futures, 27*(5), 505–526.

Teece, D.J. (1981). The multinational enterprise: Market failure and market power considerations. *Sloan Management Review, 22*(3), 3–17.

Teece, D.J. (1982). Towards an economic theory of the multiproduct firm. *Journal of Economic Behavior and Organization, 3*(1), 39–63.

Teece, D.J. (1985). Multinational enterprise, internal governance, and industrial organization. *American Economic Review, 75*(2), 233–238.

Teece, D.J., Pisano, G., & Shuen, A. (1997). Dynamic capabilities and strategic management. *Strategic Management Journal, 18*(7), 509–533.

Teece, D.J., Rumelt, R., Dosi, G., & Winter, S. (1994). Understanding corporate coherence: Theory and evidence. *Journal of Economic Behaviour and Organization, 23*, 1–30.

Telesio, P. (1979). *Technology licensing and multinational enterprise*. New York: Praeger.

Thompson, J.D. (1967). *Organizations in action*. New York: McGraw-Hill.

Thucydides (1972). *History of the Peloponnesian War*. Harmondsworth: Penguin Books.

Toynbee, F.L. (1953). *The world and the West: BBC Reith Lectures 1952*. Oxford: Oxford University Press.

Turnbull, P.W. (1987). A challenge to the stages theory of the internationalization process. In P.J. Rosson & S.D. Reed (Eds.), *Managing export entry and expansion* (pp. 21–38). New York: Praeger.

Vermeulen, G.A.M., & Barkema, H.G. (2002). Pace, rhythm and scope: Process dependence in building a profitable multinational corporation. *Strategic Management Journal, 23*(7), 637–653.

Vernon, R. (1966). International investment and international trade in the product cycle. *Quarterly Journal of Economics, 80*(2), 190–207.

Vernon, R. (1974). The location of economic activity. In J.M. Dunning (Ed.), *Economic analysis and the multinational enterprise* (pp. 89–114). London: Allen & Unwin.

38   Peter J. Buckley

Vernon, R. (1979). The product cycle hypothesis in a new international environment. *Oxford Bulletin of Economics and Statistics, 41*(4), 255–267.

von Thünen, J.H. (1826). *Der isolierte Staat in Beziehung auf Landwirtschaft und Nationalökonomie.* Jena: G. Fischer.

Welch, L., & Luostarinen, R. (1988). Internationalization: Evolution of a concept. *Journal of General Management, 14*(2), 34–55.

Wernerfelt, B. (1984). A resource-based view of the firm. *Strategic Management Journal, 5*(2), 171–180.

Wilkins, M. (1970). *The emergence of multinational enterprise: American business abroad from the colonial era to 1914.* Cambridge, MA: Harvard University Press.

Wilkins, M. (1974a). Multinational oil companies in South America in the 1920s. *Business History Review.* Special issue: Multinational enterprise, *48*(3), 414–446.

Wilkins, M. (1974b). *The maturing of multinational enterprise: American business abroad from 1914–1970.* Cambridge, MA: Harvard University Press.

Wilkins, M. (1988). The free-standing company 1870–1914: An important type of British foreign direct investment. *Economic History Review* (Second series), *41*(May), 259–282.

Wilkins, M. (1989). *The history of foreign investment in the United States to 1914.* Cambridge, MA: Harvard University Press.

Wilkins, M., & Hill, F.E. (1964). *American business abroad: Ford on six continents.* Detroit: Wayne State University Press.

Wilkins, M. & Schroter, H., (Eds.). (1998). *The free standing company in the world economy 1930–1996.* Oxford: Oxford University Press.

Williamson, O.E. (1975). *Markets and hierarchies: Analysis and antitrust implications.* New York: Free Press.

Williamson, O.E. (1979). Transaction cost economics: The governance of contractual relations. *Journal of Law and Economics, 22,* 223–261.

Williamson, O.E. (1985). *The economic institutions of capitalism: Firms, markets, relational contracting.* New York: Free Press.

Wilson, E. (1972). *To the Finland Station: A study in the writing and acting of history.* London: Macmillan.

Wilson, J.F. (1995). *British business history 1720–1994.* Manchester: Manchester University Press.

3
Internalisation Thinking: From the Multinational Enterprise to the Global Factory

1. Introduction

In *The Future of the Multinational Enterprise* (Buckley & Casson, 1976) set up a research agenda that is still being worked out. The principles of internalising a market and least cost location of activities are part of a wider research agenda whose key elements are: (1) information costs (knowledge management); (2) systems theory (networks); (3) innovation (entrepreneurship); and (4) differences in social interaction across the world (psychic distance).

The intellectual journey traced here is the transition from the theory of the multinational enterprise to "the global factory". (Buckley, 2004a, 2007, 2009; Buckley & Ghauri, 2004).

2. Internalisation–externalisation

The key issue is that the underlying theory does not change but the actions of firms respond to changing circumstances. The balance between externalisation and internalisation has shifted but the principles underlying the decisions determining the boundaries of the firm have remained. These may be listed as advantages and disadvantages of internalisation (or conversely the costs and benefits of using the market). These shifts over time are traced below.

3. The advantages of internalising a market

The general advantages of internalising an imperfect or missing external market can be listed as follows:

1. Coordination of multistage process in which time lags exist but futures markets are lacking.

40 *Peter J. Buckley*

2. Discriminatory pricing in internal markets allows efficient exploitation of market power.
3. Bilateral concentration of market power – internalisation eliminates instability.
4. Inequalities of knowledge between buyer and seller ("Buyer uncertainty") removed.
5. Internal transfer pricing reduces tax liability on international transactions (Buckley & Casson, 1976, pp. 37–39).

These factors drive the consolidation of firms and account for both large uni-national and multinational firms.

4. The costs of internalising a market

In every case the advantages of internalising a market must be compared to the costs.

1. Higher resource costs when a single external market becomes several internal markets (can be reduced by partial internalisation).
2. Communication costs in internal markets rise (vary with psychic distance).
3. Political problems of foreignness.
4. Management costs in running complex multiplant multicurrency operations (Buckley & Casson, 1976, pp. 41–44).

The costs of internalisation are often underemphasised, or even ignored leading to an unbalanced view of the theory. Where costs exceed benefits, markets will not be internalised and market solutions (external licensing, outsourcing) will be sought. The (changing) choices of foreign market entry and development are key features of the internalisation approach (Buckley & Casson, 1981, 1996, 1998a, 2001).

5. The future of the multinational enterprise: broad-based intellectual framework of Coase

The future of the multinational enterprise analysed the multinational enterprise within a broad-based intellectual framework based on the pioneering work of Coase (1937). It demonstrated how seemingly unrelated aspects of multinational operations, such as technology transfer and international trade in semi-processed products, can be understood using a single concept – the internalisation of imperfect markets. The idea of applying Coase to multinationals occurred to a number of other authors at about the same time. (Hennart, 1982; Hymer, 1968; McManus, 1972; Swedenborg, 1979). The distinguishing feature of this book was that it provided a particularly compact and parsimonious explanation of the evidence (Buckley & De Beule, 2005).

Parsimony was achieved by invoking the principle of rational action modelling, which not only lies at the heart of economics, but provides a basis for rigorous research in other social sciences too. Rational action modelling applies to a wide range of international business issues, including dynamic market entry (Buckley & Casson, 1981, 1998a, 1998b), international joint ventures (Buckley & Casson, 1996), international entrepreneurship (Casson, 2000), business culture (Buckley & Casson, 1991; Casson, 1991) and strategic complexity in international business (Buckley & Casson, 2001).

The general approach embodied in The future of the multinational enterprise sheds light on the internal mechanisms of the firm by opening up the "black box" to analyse the relationships between production, marketing and R&D, whilst leaving a "single rational mind" to configure the boundaries of the firm. Here, the role of information costs is crucial when examining the costs of monitoring employees (agency costs) and the costs of inefficiencies and mistakes (which may be worth bearing if the expenditure that would be incurred for correction is great). Organisations thus have an economic logic to their design (Buckley & Carter, 1996, 1997). When the rational action approach is taken, many of the precepts of system theory are found to apply in the appropriate context. For instance, rule-driven behaviour is shown to be rational in certain types of environment but in others entrepreneurial improvisation is correct. Economy of co-ordination calls for a division of labour in information processing and this in turn calls for co-operative behaviour of a social nature (Buckley & Casson, 1988). Because the environment of the firm differs in different (national) locations, there will be differences between locations in the kinds of decision making rules that are used. In other words, social interactions will follow different rules in different places. ("Psychic distance")

6. The future of the multinational enterprise: not so much an ending as a beginning for a research agenda

The future of the multinational enterprise presented not a complete theory but the core of a general approach to MNEs and their near relations (Buckley, 2002; Buckley & Lessard, 2005). It is not the system of concepts and the particular insights that are crucial but an appropriate method of analysis. The theory can analyse alternative contractual arrangements "externalisation theory of the firm" and disintegration is raised as a possibility. Overall the future of the multinational enterprise is not unorthodox. It retains profit maximisation and marginal calculus as its key analytical elements. Imperfections are made explicitly (observable and systematic) so direction of growth is predictable. The methods used were to compile stylised facts in a testable fashion to derive predictions. An important innovation was the

42　*Peter J. Buckley*

modelling of dynamics especially R&D and innovation. It was suggested that the dominant force for internalisation was undergoing change. "The advantages of internalising specialised technical know-how are diminishing relative to the advantages of internalising general marketing expertise". (Buckley & Casson, 1976, original preface (xxi))

7. The future of the multinational enterprise: general and special theories

Within the general theory of internalisation of imperfect markets and least cost location there are a number of special theories where the principles apply with particular force. Examples of special theories within the general theory were:

- Internalising markets in knowledge: Section 2.4 (pp. 56–59) Internalisation of knowledge, its implications for the growth and profitability of the MNE.
- Multi stage production processes (vertical integration) (p. 34).
- Perishable agricultural products (p. 40).
- Intermediate production in intensive manufacturing processes (p. 40).
- Raw materials where deposits are geographically concentrated (pp. 40–41).

These special theories have since been extended to, for instance, Chinese multinationals as an example of emerging country multinationals (Buckley, Clegg, et al., 2007). If the theory is robust enough to explain Chinese, largely state-owned, naïve foreign investors then it has indeed stood the test of time.

8. The future of the multinational enterprise: focus on innovation

"The main dynamic in the post war growth of the MNE has been a structural shift in favour of technology based goods, which has significantly increased investment in R&D" (p 102). The book focused firmly on innovation (broadly defined) as the key factor driving the development of MNEs. The dynamic is given by an analysis of innovation at firm level – contrasting with Hymer's analysis based on monopoly power (Buckley, 2006).

The approach to innovation in the 1976 book is very much on the power of internal markets to integrate knowledge flows and so to create dynamic efficiencies in the firm by linking R&D with production and marketing (Figure 3.1). Later emphasis on accessing external markets in knowledge are a major factor leading to a more dispersed "global factory" configuration in markets for knowledge (Buckley & Carter, 1996, 1997, 1999, 2000, 2002, 2004).

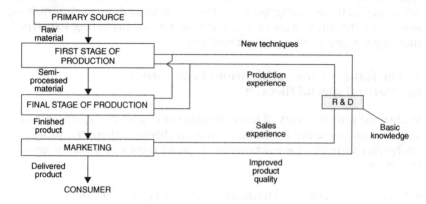

Figure 3.1 Information flows in the multinational firm

Notes: Successive stages of production are linked by flows of semi-process materials. Production and marketing are linked by a flow of finished goods ready for distribution. Production and marketing on the one hand are linked to R&D on the other hand by two-way flows of information and expertise.

Source: Reproduced from Buckley and Casson (1976), p 34.

9. The future of the multinational enterprise: predictions

The book predicted more externalisation (licensing) and outsourcing by multinationals and greater use of IJVs as means of "harmonising objectives of foreign investors with the social policies of host governments". There would be more adaptation of existing products and processes to new environments in particular in less developed (emerging) markets. The book ends with a prediction of increasing substitution of licensing for FDI! (p. 113)

10. Dynamics: transaction costs and entrepreneurship

The original objective of Buckley and Casson (1976) to use the concept of internalisation to develop a model of the growth of the firm. This was abandoned by later writers who take technological capability and marketing and management skills as given (Buckley, 1983).

The dynamics of the theory are given not only by a focus on innovation but also on entrepreneurship. The links between the (multinational) firm, entrepreneurship and transaction costs are strong. Why do entrepreneurs hire assets rather than asset owners hire entrepreneurs? The answer lies in non-contractibility. The key function of the entrepreneur is to exercise judgement in the face of uncertainty (Knight, 1921; Casson, 1982). Incomplete contracts have a positive effect on the exercise of

44   *Peter J. Buckley*

entrepreneurship – they allow sequential adaptation to changing circumstances in an uncertain world. The firm is thus the agency by which the entrepreneur (whose services are the most difficult to measure or evaluate) combines his assets (judgement) with physical assets. The firm enables previously segmented areas of judgement and skills to be blended together and thus individual entrepreneurship becomes collective organisation. Individuals with entrepreneurial judgement can thus coalesce within the organisation and combine their skills. Because of the non-contractibility (or rather the extremely high costs of contracting) of these skills, this coalition becomes embedded in the firm, thus giving a transactions cost rationale for "competencies" residing for a finite period of time in certain companies. "Sticky capabilities" thus emerge. Transaction costs are, of course, not the whole story (again) but they are an indispensable part of the whole story.

11. Uncertainty

The increase in volatility in the global economy has been a major feature in moving MNEs towards a more flexible structure (Buckley & Casson, 1998a). This has an important impact on the foreign market servicing strategies of MNEs. Where MNEs can forecast with certainty what their costs will be of operating in foreign markets, a "deterministic" entry strategy, contingent on the growth of foreign markets can be anticipated and as shown in Figure 3.2 (Buckley & Casson, 1981). This simple model predicates set up costs and variable costs of each mode of foreign operations leading to switches in mode at given market sizes. When uncertainty is introduced, the model can be extended by introducing the probability that foreign unit costs will be below domestic ones, thus introducing a judgement factor into the planning of internationalisation strategies as in Figure 3.3 (Buckley & Casson, 2001). This further allows for a strategy of information gathering on the likelihood that foreign conditions will be as expected (Figure 3.4). Thus we can focus on the ability of the firm to recognise uncertainty and to respond to it either by taking a chance that the probabilities expected will be realised or by investigation – investing in research on costs at home and abroad.

The reaction to uncertainty can be described by different strategies of the firm with probabilities assigned to each potential choice as in Table 3.1. Analytical models of this type can help to reduce uncertainties in international strategies by specifying the conditions under which choices (on foreign market entry, modes of operation) are made.

12. The global factory

There have been significant changes in the organisation and configuration of MNEs since 1976. The balance between internalisation and externalisation

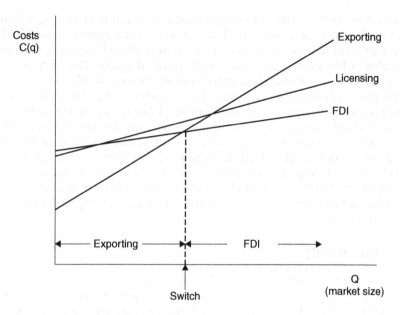

Figure 3.2 The timing of a foreign direct investment
N.B. In this example, licensing is never the preferred alternative.
Reproduced from Buckley and Casson (1981), p 80.

has shifted partly because of reactions to increased volatility and opposition to monopoly (Buckley & Casson, 1998a) partly because of management learning and improved techniques of managing through contracts.

The recent comments of a senior manager in Caterpillar are appropriate here. The key issues are: "What we want to make and where we want to make it" although this is "Simple in concept, difficult in execution". This mirrors precisely the two key decisions that managers of firms are faced with – internalisation and location.

Managers compare external (transactions) costs – the costs of using the market – with internal (agency) costs – the costs of carrying out operations under their own managerial control. The balance of these two sets of costs determines the scope of the firm at any given point of time. Managers endeavour to reduce agency costs. It is only when agency costs are falling relative to transaction costs that the scope of managerial control and therefore the size of the firm will increase (Buckley, 1997). Transaction costs exist in assembling the business processes of the firm (collections of activities that are technologically or managerially linked) so that they jointly contribute to value added. The overall costs of organisation are determined by losses due to the imperfect motivation of process members, imperfect information and co-ordination losses resulting from the architecture of

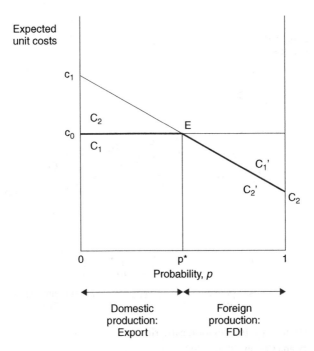

Figure 3.3 Diagrammatic solution of the entry strategy under uncertainty
Source: Buckley and Casson (2001), p 97.

the firm (the allocation of responsibilities amongst individuals and groups and the communication between them), and the resource costs associated with incentives and organisation. Identifying transactional links within "the black box" of the firm enables us to trace the costs and benefits of combining activities within the firm. Further, it is possible to specify losses from imperfections in motivation, information and coordination and to balance these against the costs of correcting them (Buckley & Carter, 1996). Action within the firm on improving business processes and agency costs may entail expansion or contraction of the firm as individual elements of each business process are compared against external provision of the same sub-process. This "fine-slicing" of activities (Buckley, 2004a) means that every element of the firm can be evaluated by comparison with the market alternative and can be externalised if it is profitable to do so (outsourcing) or can be relocated if this reduces overall costs (offshoring). These two decisions – the first on internalisation/externalisation control choice and the second a location decision – have led to the creation of the "global factory" (Buckley, 2004a, 2004b, 2007, 2009; Buckley & Ghauri, 2004).

The opening up of the global factory has provided new opportunities for new locations to enter international business. Emerging countries such as

Internalisation Thinking 47

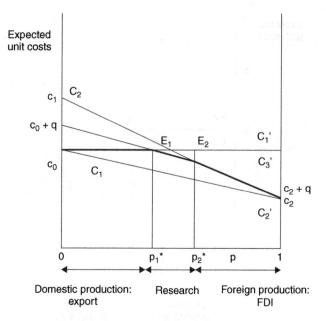

Figure 3.4 Strategy for information gathering
Source: Buckley and Casson (2001), p 100.

Table 3.1 Two possible errors in strategic choice under uncertainty

	State 1: Foreign cost conditions bad	State 2: Foreign cost conditions good
Strategy 1 Produce at home: Exporting	0	Type II errorc $0-c_2$
Strategy 2 Produce abroad: FDI	Type I error c_1-c_0	0

Source: Buckley and Casson (2001), p 99.

India and China are subcontracting production and service activities from the brand-owning MNEs. The use of the market by MNEs enables new firms to compete for business against the internalised activities of the MNE. This not only subjects every internalised activity to "the market test"; it also results in a differentiated network (as presented in Figure 3.5) which we term "the global factory".

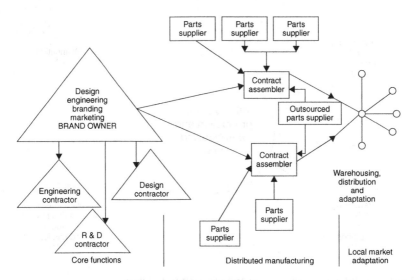

Figure 3.5 Globally distributed operations
Source: Buckley (2007), p 116.

13. Components of the global factory

The global supply chain is divided into three parts. The original equipment manufacturers (OEMs) control the brand and undertake design, engineering and R&D for the product (although there may be outsourced (see Figure 3.5). They are customers for contract manufacturers (CMs) who perform manufacturing (and perhaps logistics) services for OEMs. In this so-called modular production network, CMs need to possess capabilities such as mix, product and new product flexibilities while at the same time carrying out manufacturing activities at low costs with mass production processes. Flexibility is necessary to fulfill consumers' product differentiation needs (local requirements) and low cost for global efficiency imperatives (see Wilson & Guzman, 2005). The third part of the chain is warehousing, distribution and adaptation carried out on a "hub and spoke" principle in order to achieve local market adaptation through a mix of ownership and location policies. As Figure 3.6 shows, ownership strategies are used to involve local firms with marketing skills and local market intelligence in international joint ventures (IJVs) whilst location strategies are used to differentiate the wholly owned "hub" (centrally located) from the jointly owned "spokes".

Two simple illustrations can be given of the power of the global factory to use location and ownership decisions to create a complex, but efficient,

Internalisation Thinking 49

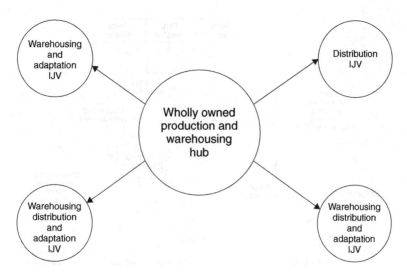

Figure 3.6 Interaction of location and ownership strategies
Source: Buckley (2007), p 114.

response to global economic conditions and to respond to changes in those conditions. First, a complex offshoring and outsourcing strategy can reduce location and transaction costs. Figure 3.7 shows a simple offshoring decision where (in this example) early stages of processing are relocated to a lower-cost foreign country. Intermediate inputs are exported to this foreign-located facility and serve finished goods transported from it. Local inputs are supplied to the offshore unit (thus providing linkage and spillover effects to the local economy (Buckley, Clegg, & Wang, 2002, 2004, 2006, 2007a, 2007b). This location decision can be combined with an ownership/internalisation decision because the offshore plant can be "captive" (owned, internalised) or non-captive-controlled through the market by contract. If we envisage the full panoply of such decisions in a global factory, we can see the complexity, sophistication and difficulty of these ever-changing strategies in a volatile world economy.

Multinational firms have to reconcile pressures to be globally efficient with the need to be locally responsive. The efficiency imperative dictates standardisation, economies of scale and uniformity of product and process. The localisation motive mandates adaptation, differentiation and close liaison with customers. Those pressures have to be accommodated and the global factory is the ideal structure with which to do so. Figure 3.8 shows how a mixed "glocal" strategy can steer an optimal path between rigid standardisation versus differentiation strategies for the

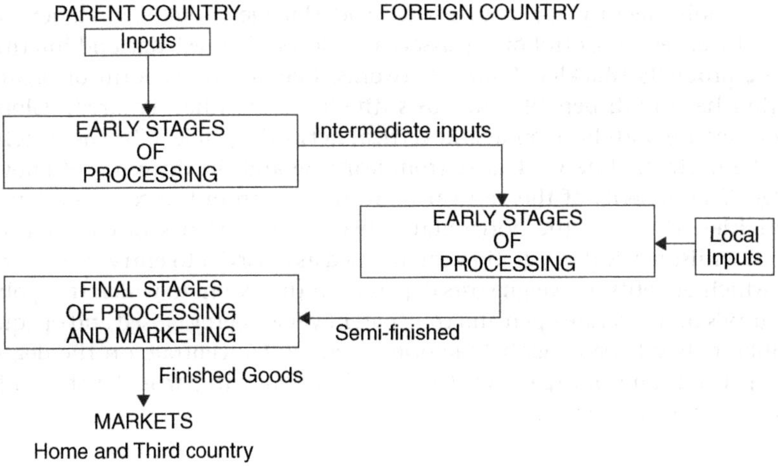

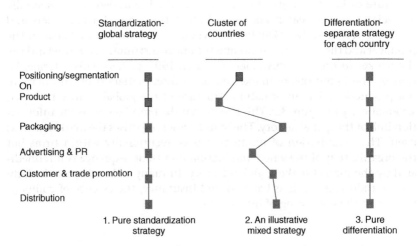

Figure 3.7 A typical offshore production process
Source: Buckley (2004a), p 23.

Figure 3.8 The standardization-differentiation continuum
Source: Buckley (2007), p 22.

example of marketing. The "glocal" strategy seeks the best compromise for each element of the marketing strategy as the balance of global and local pressures dictates across different national markets. This glocalised strategy is well suited to being combined with the "fine-slicing" of activities across the complex set of processes in the whole network of the global factory.

Internalisation Thinking 51

The global factory is, of course, a network (Buckley, 2004b). It is a network held together by control of key assets and flows of knowledge and intermediate products (Buckley, 2007). Networks, like any other form of organisation have both benefits and costs (the latter are often ignored). Global factories are both horizontal and vertical networks (Table 3.2). The benefits of the horizontal network arise from learning and the diffusion of knowledge. The benefits of the vertical network arise from the coordination of activities. However, the horizontal network runs the risk of collusion on price whilst vertical integration can be used as a barrier to entry. The degree to which benefits outweigh costs depends on the extent to which the global factory's networks are open and transparent versus being closed and opaque. Public policy towards global factories needs to concentrate on the degree of openness and transparency. Competition policy in particular should be addressed to these ends.

14. The information structure of the global factory

Casson (1997) highlights the importance of information costs in the structure of business organisation. He sees the brand owner as essentially a specialist in the search and specification functions (for customers and products, respectively). "The brand owner, by intermediating between the producer and the retailer, coordinates the entire distribution channel linking the worker to the final customer" (Casson, 1997, p. 159). This intermediation by the brand owner/market maker is intermediation of information, not production. The information structure of the global factory is shown schematically in Figure 3.9. This shows that the brand owner is the information hub of the global factory. The brand owner organises the market process itself. The organisation of production is conventionally within firms but the organisation of the whole production and trade sequence is intermediated by the market making global factory. In many industries, particularly service industries, such as banking and insurance, the essence of competitiveness is the processing of information.

Table 3.2 Benefits and costs of different types of network configuration

	Benefit of open, and transparent	Cost of closed and opaque
Horizontal	Learning/diffusion	Collusion on price
Vertical	Co-ordination of intermediate product markets and upstream/downstream Investments	Vertical integration as barrier to entry

Source: Buckley (2004b), p. 260.

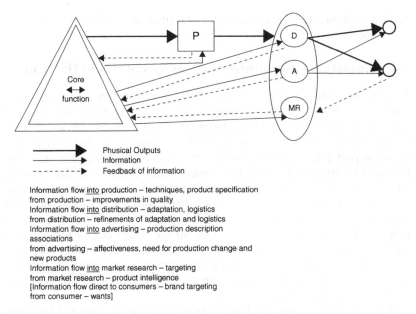

Figure 3.9 The information structure of the global factory
Source: Buckley (2009).

15. Key elements of the global factory

A key attribute of a successful global factory is flexibility. Flexibility is the ability to reallocate resources quickly and smoothly in response to change. This will never be costless and the costs of flexibility need to be borne in mind (Buckley & Casson, 1998a). Flexibility is a response to increasing volatility arising from globalisation and from opposition to monopoly, including internal monopoly. The idea that global factories avoid internal monopoly, in order to escape "hold-up" problems from crucial single activities underperforming, is borne out by the extent of internal (and quasi internal) competition throughout the system leading to dualities and multiplicities of supply sources and to the use of the market to put competitive pressure on internal activities.

A key purpose of flexible structures is to provide resilience. Systems are resilient if they can absorb shocks. Resilient firms can thus survive downturns, crises and panics (like the "credit crunch" of 2009). In a globalised world, shocks from any part of the global economy are rapidly transmitted around the world (the "sub-prime" crises of 2008–2009). Competition with the global factory, multiple alternative sources of supply of key inputs, access to many national markets and supply sources, intelligent use of forecasting and internal transfer of knowledge are all sources of built-in resilience of the global factory.

16. Transaction costs minimising configurations in the firm

Transaction costs exist in assembling the business processes of firms – collections of activities which are technologically or managerially linked so that they jointly affect value added. The overall costs of organisation are determined by losses due to the imperfect motivation of process members (which result, in part at least, from the incentive structure) and imperfect information and coordination which flow from the architecture of the firm (the allocation of responsibilities amongst individuals and groups and communication between them), together with the resource costs associated with incentives and architecture (Buckley & Carter, 1996). Thus transactional links within the firm enable us to split up the "black box" and trace costs and benefits of combining activities within intra-firm processes. Further, it is possible to specify losses from imperfections in motivation, information and coordination and to balance these against the costs necessary to correct these imperfections, as in Table 3.3.

Views about the nature of human behaviour and actions will influence how an outsider might feel about the likelihood of these costs being significant; for example, motivation loss (and the cost of correcting it) will be greater, the greater is the degree of opportunism ("self-seeking with guile"). However, if we believe that individuals naturally seek and appreciate teamworking, then motivation costs will be low.

Table 3.3 Motivation, information and coordination losses and costs in the firm

	Loss	Cost
Motivation	The reduction in the payoff to the firm caused by members pursuing their own objectives	The cost of incentive measures taken by the firm
Information	The reduction in payoff to the firm caused by members not having the best available information	The cost of acquiring and transmitting information
Coordination	The reduction in payoff to the firm arising when complementary actions are not chosen jointly	The cost of communication about complementary actions or of providing for them to be combined

Source: Derived from Buckley and Carter (1996).

54   *Peter J. Buckley*

Buckley and Casson (1988) applied internalisation theory to international joint ventures (IJVs). IJVs are conceptualised as arising from three key factors: internalisation economies in one or more intermediate goods markets, indivisibilities and barriers to merger. Under certain environmental conditions, IJVs can be an optimal organisational solution (Buckley & Casson, 1996). In joint ventures, mutual trust can be a substitute for expensive legalism. Joint ventures provide an ideal institution for the exercise of mutual forbearance, leading to a commitment to cooperation and to the creation of reputation effects where a reputation for cooperative behaviour can lead to further coordination benefits. These effects can be good substitutes for ownership. Skills in joint venturing and the learning effects that arise can lead to a widespread for non-ownership forms of cooperation as in many global factories.

17. New management skills

The rise of the global factory has been paralleled by the growth of new management skills. These include the ability of managers to "fine-slice" activities–to cut the constituent elements of processes into finer and finer slivers. The virtue of this strategy is that is allows each element to be optimally located and controlled. The advantages of the choice of location and the choice of mode of governance can then be forensically applied to each component of the global factory by management.

Together with fine-slicing goes control of information. The information structure of the global factory (Figure 3.9) is a major source of its strength, allowing information to be obtained and to be disseminated to those decision takers best placed to use it. It is the control of this complex flow of information on external conditions and internal competences that is far more important than control of physical assets, the use of which can be increasingly outsourced. The general adage that "you don't have to own something to control it" applies increasingly to physical assets but emphatically not to intangible assets such as brands and to knowledge.

The use of increasingly complex structures involving both internalised and externalised activities requires that externalised activities be carefully monitored (for quality control reasons for example) and integrated with those activities under the ownership of the global factory. "Interface competence"–the ability to coordinate external organisations into the strategy of the focal firm, to liaise with external bodies and governments and to cohere these activities into a grand strategy–are at the heart of the skills necessary to organise a successful global factory. This has implications for the style of management that is needed. A new, more subtle cooperative mode of operation is increasingly necessary. Management needs to be "hard nosed" in requiring adherence to targets (on quality and reliability) but in managing outside the boundaries of the firm, with subcontractors and alliance partners, skills beyond "command and control" are vital.

18. Role of headquarters

It is something of an irony that the spatial distribution strategies – ownership and location – make the role of Headquarters more important in global factories than in conventional vertically and horizontally integrated firms. The authority and choice of Headquarters has expanded. The development of "fine-slicing" means that the determination of ownership and control of each specialised sliver of activity expands Headquarters' area of choice. Evidence of the increased power of Headquarters might be the level of salaries there compared to elsewhere (even in other units in the home country). Remuneration in Headquarters is also likely to increase over time relative to other locations. The control of information in global factories is crucial and the mechanisms determining strategy are more subtle. The doctrine that "you don't have to own an activity to control it" requires new skills of Headquarters functions in global factories. There are important dynamics in this process as Headquarters learn how to manage spatially dispersed and organisationally diffuse units within the global factory. This is not a one-way process. Units within the global factory also learn how to manage Headquarters (Buckley, Glaister & Husan, 2002). The management style that new configurations require is vastly different from conventional "command and control" methods and the full implications of this are yet to be explored. Headquarters as a "controlling intelligence" or orchestrator of activities emerge as the best metaphors for their role in the global factory.

In emphasising extra degrees of autonomy given to subsidiaries and other units within the global factory, we should not forget the big picture. The key issue is competition to be the marketing and distribution platform of the big products of the future. That is the key question for Headquarters. Other units must operate within this framework set by Headquarters, while they may well have crucial areas of decision making and discretion given to them; it is within this overall paradigm that they operate.

19. Unresolved issues

Two issues of considerable importance may be considered unresolved. The first is the spatial element in internalisation. The advantages and disadvantages of internalisation are assumed to be invariant to distance. This issue is resolved by the addition of the location factor which is then combined with internalisation to give a satisfactory explanation of the growth and development of MNEs. The investigation of spatial elements in the internalisation decision itself may be a fruitful avenue for further research.

56   *Peter J. Buckley*

Second, there is an unresolved (unresolvable?) conflict in modelling MNEs between the role of human agency and the result of impersonal forces. How far is human agency (management decision making) the determinant of outcomes? Much of economics assumes that impersonal forces determine the configuration of the world economy. The strategy literature sometimes reads as if all managers had to do it to change the world is to exercise will and decide. Work around entrepreneurship (Casson, 2000) decision making under uncertainty (Buckley & Casson, 2001) and investigations of "how managers decide" (from Aharoni, 1966, onwards, including Buckley, Clegg, et al., 2007; Buckley, Devinney, et al. 2007) are attempting to clarify this issue in the international business area but the philosophical problems run deep (and long, back to Smith, 1759, 1776).

20. Conclusion

"It has long been thought that a theorist is considered great because his theories are true, but this is false. A theorist is considered great, not because his theories are true, but because they are interesting. In fact the truth of a theory has very little to do with its impact, for a theory can continue to be found interesting even though its truth is disputed–even refuted!" (Davis, 1971, pp. 309–310).

It is contended here that internalisation thinking was from its inception, and remains, interesting. As pointed out by Buckley and Casson (2003) *The Future of the Multinational Enterprise* challenged certain assumptions of its audience (the definition of an interesting theory according to Davis (1971)). At the time (1976) multinationals were considered to be exploitative monopolists and the book shifted the emphasis away from market power towards innovation.

Internalisation thinking remains interesting because it challenges its audience to think of the forces that hold global factories together in the face of changing market imperfections, the spread of competition and volatile regulation.

Acknowledgements

I would like to thank Mark Casson, Alain Verbeke, Niron Hashai, DannyVan den Bulcke and Jeremy Clegg for comments on earlier versions of this paper. Participants at the 2006 EIBA Conference in Fribourg, Switzerland, especially Philippe Gugler, are also thanked for their comments.

References

Aharoni, Ya ir (1966). *The foreign investment decision process.* Cambridge, MA: Harvard Business School Press.

Buckley, P. J. (1983). New theories of international business: Some unresolved issues. In M. Casson (Ed.), *The growth of international business*. London: George Allen and Unwin.

Buckley, P. J. (1997). Managers on the high wire. *New Economy, 4*(3), 152–154.

Buckley, P. J. (2002). Is the international business research agenda running out of steam? *Journal of International Business Studies, 33*(2), 365–373.

Buckley, P. J. (2004a). The role of China in the global strategy of multinational enterprises. *Journal of Chinese Economic and Business Studies, 2*(1), 1–25.

Buckley, P. J. (2004b). Asian network firms: An analytical framework. *Asia Pacific Business Review, 10*(3–4), 254–271.

Buckley, P. J. (2006). Stephen Hymer: Three phases, one approach? *International Business Review, 15*(2), 140–147.

Buckley, P. J. (2007). The strategy of multinational enterprises in the light of the rise of China. *Scandinavian Journal of Management, 23*(2), 107–126.

Buckley, P. J. (2009). The impact of the global factory on economic development. *Journal of World Business, 44*(2), 131–143.

Buckley, P. J., & Carter, M. C. (1996). The economics of business process design. *International Journal of the Economics of Business, 3*(1), 5–25.

Buckley, P. J., & Carter, M. C. (1997). The economics of business process design in multinational firms. In M. Ricketts & R. Mudambi (Eds.), *The organisation of the firm: International business perspectives*. London: Routledge.

Buckley, P. J., & Carter, M. C. (1999). Managing cross-border complementary knowledge: Conceptual developments in the business process approach to knowledge management in multinational firms. *International Studies of Management and Organisation, 29*(1), 80–104.

Buckley, P. J., & Carter, M. C. (2000). Knowledge management in global technology markets: Applying theory to practice. *Long Range Planning, 33*(1), 55–71.

Buckley, P. J., & Carter, M. C. (2002). Process and structure in knowledge management practices of British and US multinational enterprises. *Journal of International Management, 8*(1), 29–48.

Buckley, P. J., & Carter, M. C. (2004). A formal analysis of knowledge combination in multinational enterprises. *Journal of International Business Studies, 35*(5), 371–384.

Buckley, P. J., & Casson, M. C. (1976). *The future of the multinational enterprise*. London: Macmillan.

Buckley, P. J., & Casson, M. C. (1981). The optimal timing of a foreign direct investment. *Economic Journal, 92*(361), 75–87.

Buckley, P. J., & Casson, M. C. (1988). A theory of co-operation in international business. In F. J. Contractor & P. Lorange (Eds.), *Co-operative strategies in international business*. Lexington, MA: Lexington Books.

Buckley, P. J., & Casson, M. C. (1991). Multinationals in less developed countries: Cultural and economic interactions. In P. J. Buckley & J. Clegg (Eds.), *Multinational enterprises in less developed countries*. London: Macmillan.

Buckley, P. J., & Casson, M. C. (1996). An economic model of international joint ventures. *Journal of International Business Studies, 27*(5), 849–876.

Buckley, P. J., & Casson, M. C. (1998a). Models of the multinational enterprise. *Journal of International Business Studies, 29*(1), 21–44.

Buckley, P. J., & Casson, M. C. (1998b). Analysing foreign market entry strategies: Extending the internalisation approach. *Journal of International Business Studies, 29*(3), 539–561.

58 Peter J. Buckley

Buckley, P. J., & Casson, M. C. (2001). Strategic complexity and international business. In A. M. Rugman & T. L. Brewer (Eds.), *The Oxford handbook of international business*. Oxford: Oxford University Press.

Buckley, P. J., & Casson, M. C. (2003). The future of the multinational enterprise in retrospect and in prospect. *Journal of International Business Studies, 34*(2), 219–222 [special issue of JIBS on "The Future of the Multinational Enterprise after 25 years"].

Buckley, P. J., Clegg, J., Cross, A., Zheng, P., Voss, H., & Liu, X. (2007c). The determinants of Chinese outward foreign direct investment. *Journal of International Business Studies, 38*(4), 499–518.

Buckley, P. J., Clegg, J., & Wang, C. (2002a). The impact of inward FDI on the performance of Chinese manufacturing firms. *Journal of International Business Studies, 33*(4), 637–655.

Buckley, P. J., Clegg, J., & Wang, C. (2004). The relationship between inward foreign direct investment and the performance of domestically-owned Chinese manufacturing industry. *Multinational Business Review, 12*(3), 23–40.

Buckley, P. J., Clegg, J., & Wang, C. (2006). Inward foreign direct investment and host country productivity: evidence from China's electronics industry. *Transnational Corporations, 15*(1), 13–37 (special issue in honour of V.N. Balasubramanyam edited by Peter J. Buckley).

Buckley, P. J., Clegg, J., & Wang, C. (2007a). Is the relationship between inward FDI and spillover effects linear? An empirical examination of the case of China. *Journal of International Business Studies, 38*(3), 447–459.

Buckley, P. J., Clegg, J., & Wang, C. (2007b). The impact of foreign ownership, local ownership and industry characteristics on spillover benefits from foreign direct investment in China. *International Business Review, 16*(2), 142–158.

Buckley, P. J., & De Beule, F. (2005). The research agenda in international business: Past, present and future. In L. Cuyvers & F. De Beule (Eds.), *Transnational corporations and economic development: From internationalisation to globalisation*. London: Palgrave Macmillan.

Buckley, P. J., Devinney, T. M., & Louviere, J. J. (2007d). Do managers behave the way theory suggests? A choice theoretic examination of foreign direct investment location decision making. *Journal of International Business Studies, 38*(7), 1069–1094.

Buckley, P. J., & Ghauri, P. N. (2004). Globalisation, economic geography and the strategy of multinational enterprises. *Journal of International Business Studies, 35*(2), 81–98.

Buckley, P. J., Glaister, K., & Husan, R. (2002). International joint ventures: Partnering skills and cross-cultural issues. *Long Range Planning, 35*(2), 113–134 (coauthors, Keith Glaister and Rumy Husan).

Buckley, P. J., & Lessard, D. R. (2005). Regaining the edge for international business research. *Journal of International Business Studies, 36*(6), 595–599.

Casson, M. C. (1982). *The entrepreneur*. Oxford: Martin Robertson.

Casson, M. C. (1991). *The economics of business culture*. Oxford: Clarendon Press.

Casson, M. C. (1997). Entrepreneurial networks in international business. *Business and Economic History, 26*(2), 3–17.

Casson, M. C. (2000). *Enterprise and leadership: Studies on firms*. Networks and institutions, Cheltenham: Edward Elgar.

Coase, R. H. (1937). The nature of the firm. *Economica (n.s.), 4*, 386–405.

Davis, M. S. (1971). That's interesting! Towards a phenomenology of sociology and sociology of phenomenology *Philosophy of Social Science, 1*, 309–344.

Hennart, J. F. (1982). *A theory of multinational enterprise*. Ann Arbor, MI: University of Michigan Press.

Hymer, S. H. (1968). The multinational corporation: An analysis of some motives for international business integration. *Revue Economique, 19*(6), 949–973.

Knight, F. (1921). In G. J. Stigler (Ed.), *Risk, uncertainty and profit*. Chicago: University of Chicago Press.

McManus, J. C. (1972). The theory of the international firm. In G. Paquet (Ed.), *The multinational firm and the nation state*. Toronto: Collier Macmillan.

Smith, A. (1759). *The Theory of Moral Sentiments* Eds., D. D. Raphael and A. L. Macfie. (the Glasgow Edition, Oxford University Press, published by the Liberty Fund, Indianapolis 1984).

Smith, A. (1776). *An Inquiry into the Nature and Causes of the Wealth of Nations*. Ed. Edwin Cannan, Chicago: University of Chicago Press.

Swedenborg, B. (1979). *Multinational operations of Swedish firms*. Stockholm: Almquist & Wilksell.

Wilson, John, & Guzman A. C. G. (2005). *Organisational knowledge transfer in modular production networks: the case of Brazil*. Paper presented to AIB World conference, Quebec, July.

4
The Theory of International Business Pre-Hymer[1]

1. Introduction

It is conventional to date the genesis of international business theory to the PhD dissertation of Stephen Hymer (1960, eventually published in 1976) The International Operations of National Firms (Buckley, 2006). It would be fairer to date the start point to John Dunning's 1958 book American Investment in UK Manufacturing, on which Hymer relied for empirical data, but taking a 1960 date for the beginnings of a widely accepted theory of international business provides a useful cut-off point.

There was, in fact, a great deal of international business theorising before 1960 but it simply did not have the required labelling. It existed in fragments, not in a unified and packaged form.[2] Hymer and Dunning provided synoptic views of the multinational firm which have been refined and improved upon since 1960. This article suggests that useful insights and partial theories were extant before our conventional starting date. Indeed, it is further argued that many theoretical advances have been ignored, or forgotten, largely because of the terminology in which they were expressed or because they were embedded in empirical, descriptive or wide ranging writings.

Intellectual history is written backwards. It is arguable that insights and fragments of theory only become relevant once the tide of theorising has passed them by, and in the light of these advances, they then look relevant. Alternatively, there may be insights and advances that have been overlooked in the light of general theoretical advance. David Teece believes that "Hymer could write on an almost clean sheet of paper" (2006, p. 138). Teece (2006, p. 126) says "Hymer's insights laid the foundation for a new paradigm of the multinational enterprise. Admittedly, there was not much in place at the time that might be characterized as a theory of MNE. He touched upon many important ideas; the weakness of his analysis is that he did a poor job of sorting amongst them, and elaborating the more promising". This paper examines the truth of this claim and attempts to evaluate writings on the multinational enterprise and foreign direct investment before 1960.

The Theory of International Business Pre-Hymer 61

There is a profound and important interaction between theorising and empirical work in the social sciences. Theories are necessary to define areas of interest, to group similar and divide dissimilar phenomena and to track changes in important social and economic categories. Theory and definition interact by gradually, repeatedly and continually redefining concepts. This interaction between theory, empirical investigation and conceptual refinement is also reflected in the collection of social "facts" – in our case, statistics. International business provides an important case study of the development of these processes. From the time of Dunning (1958) and Hymer (1960), a recognisable subject area grew. Before these seminal works, it seems, there was little conceptualisation and theorising in international business. This article will show that important, if fragmentary, work had been completed before 1960. Some of it suffered from a concentration on issues of management and business strategy rather than on theorising (plus ça change!) In other cases there was a confusion, or a lack of recognition, of levels of analysis. In international business the choice of level of analysis (manager, firm, network, nation, world economy) is often difficult. It is also difficult to control for the impact of the other levels whilst concentrating on one–ceteris paribus is difficult to maintain in a dynamic situation (Buckley & Lessard, 2005). Careful distinctions were often not made in the pre-1960 literature – between direct versus portfolio investment, between different forms of foreign market servicing, between ownership (internalised) and non-ownership (arms length, contractual) international modes of doing business and between different forms of internal foreign operation (branch, subsidiary, licensee). The nature of the multinational enterprise as an institution was not explored in depth.

The following sections examine the available literature on international business and the multinational enterprise from the standpoints of economics including writings on cartels up to 1960, theories of imperialism and then the literatures extant on international competitiveness, managing foreign operations (international management), foreign direct investment and multinational enterprise are reviewed. The emergence of modern theory is traced from the 1950s up to the time of Hymer's thesis and the conclusion brings together the material both that Hymer did use and literature that he could have used.

2. The heritage of economics

Hymer (1960) wrote his thesis in the tradition of economics, but did not acknowledge many intellectual debts. Bain (1956), Iversen (1935), Arndt (1957), Penrose (1956) and Wu (1946) of Hymer's economist precursors are included in his bibliography. But these are a mere selection of the rich economics literature on foreign direct investment extant in 1960 (e.g. Cairncross, 1953).

62   *Peter J. Buckley*

3. International economics

The difficulties of incorporating capital movements into (international) economics are astutely summarised in the following quote by Nurkse (1933) "The theory of capital movements has not been treated systematically, so far, in the literature of economics. The reason for this neglect may well be found largely in the fact that the classical doctrine of international trade, the theory of comparative costs, rests on the fundamental assumption that while the factors of production, labour and capital, are freely mobile inside a given country, they are lacking external freedom of mobility. This basis premise of the international immobility of capital seems to have prevented the possibility of a theoretical approach to capital movements, at least from the standpoint of international trade theory. It is significant that whenever the so-called problem of transfers comes up in the orthodox theory of international trade, the discussion is always concerned with indemnity payments between governments and matters of this kind, never with spontaneous, economic money transfers, i.e. with capital movements in the strict sense". English translation from Dunning (1972, p. 97).

This difficulty was progressively eased by Nurkse (1933), Jasay (1960), MacDougall (1960), among others, by an analytical device that treated foreign investment as a marginal addition to the host country's capital stock. Progressive removal of restrictions on the restrictive assumptions surrounding this model enabled theoretical deductions about the impact of foreign investment to be made. It is fair to say that by 1960, the model was being stretched to breaking point and no real allowance for the "directness" of FDI was being made. A separate theory of FDI was clearly required.

4. Industrial economics

Industrial economics discusses industrial structure as made up of the size of firms, entry conditions, concentration, vertical integration and diversification. Each of these factors has an international dimension and each had rich discussion in the specialist literature before 1960. For instance, the role of vertical integration in the creation of international companies was extensively analysed in McLean and Haigh (1954) with respect to oil companies. The international dimension of each element of industrial structure had not been brought together and had not been combined with international economics, largely because of the different traditions and starting assumptions from which each evolved. Hymer did rely heavily on Bain (1956), utilising "the types and strength of advantages in connection with his study of the conditions of entry" (Hymer, 1960, p. 42 referring to Bain, 1956).

The period immediately before Hymer's thesis was a rich one in industrial economics. Not only Bain's (1956) classic work on competition, but also Penrose's seminal Theory of the Growth of the Firm (1959) and John

The Theory of International Business Pre-Hymer   63

Dunning's (1958) empirical study had appeared. Hymer quoted Penrose's (1956) article on "Foreign Investment and the growth of the firm" and was therefore influenced by some of Penrose's key insights. It should be noted that Hymer (1960) made the crucial distinction between FDI (internalised transactions) and licensing (externalised transactions). This led to the incorporation of Coasean ideas into international business by Hymer (1968), Buckley and Casson (1976) and by Dunning (1977) (Coase, 1937). For Hymer (1960) the distinction was in terms of control, not ownership.[3] This distinction came to be the basis of much of the foreign entry mode literature (e.g. Sanchez-Peinado & Pla-Barber, 2006). The conceptual and methodological distinctions that Hymer made between different modes of foreign operation and their governance implications (for instance between FDI and licensing) "arguably established Hymer as the founder of the modern theory of the MNE and FDI" (Dunning & Pitelis, 2008, p. 167).

5. Cartels – a neglected body of literature

A considerable body of theory was developed on cartels from the last few decades of the nineteenth century to the post World War II era, reaching a formalised statement in Fellner (1949). Cartels were first seen as primarily a domestic phenomenon in Germany: Hexner (1946, p. 3) writes that "Eugen Richter first used the term cartel publicly on May 5, 1879, in a meeting of the German Reichstag". Then in Britain, France and the USA attention was drawn to the power of cartels. Burns (1936, pp. 456–460) talks of the "territorial integration" of cartels, but by 1946 Hexner's book is entitled International Cartels and Mason's is Controlling World Trade: Cartels and Commodity Agreements (Mason, 1946). Casson (1985a) and Wilkins (1977) both make the point that the growth of (international) enterprises is greatly bound up with cartelization. The parallels between integrated multinational firms and international cartels are instructive. As Casson (1985a) points out, cartels are more likely to be chosen as the favoured institutional form under conditions of product homogeneity, the absence of economies of scale, low capital intensity, static technology, a general absence of innovation and a high risk of appropriation of foreign assets. The absence of these conditions is a set of circumstances favouring the creation of MNEs (Buckley & Casson, 1976). The literature on cartels is therefore useful in examining MNEs and FDI even if from a counterfactual viewpoint (cartels as a substitute for the integrated MNE).

6. International business as the logical intersection of industrial economics, international economics and the theory of the firm

Casson (1985b) argues that "the theory of FDI is a logical intersection of three distinct theories – the theory of international capital markets, the

64   *Peter J. Buckley*

theory of the international firm, and the theory of international trade" (p. 114). His summary following this quote lists very much the same factors as covered here under international and industrial economics and the theory of cartels and contain echoes of another old debate on "overforeignisation" (Überfremdung) (Benaerts, 1933). In 1960 it was much more difficult to see these elements as contributory factors in an overarching theory of FDI. Theories of imperialism were extant and had an overarching element but they did not focus on the level of the firm (the MNE), the key actor in FDI.

7. The literature on imperialism

A parallel tradition of work on which Hymer could have drawn but did not (ironically, since he later became a Marxist) was economic theories of imperialism. J. A. Hobson belonged to the left wing of the British Liberal Party and was an opponent of imperialism. Hobson was an advocate of an active social policy and, in essence, a free trade who believed that, in principle, capitalism was capable of bringing a new and more humane world order (Townshend, 1990). Hobson's Imperialism (1902) argued that the expansion of the British Empire was directly connected to the huge increase in British overseas investment. He suggested that the decisive factor in imperial expansion was the attempt of financial capitalists to find profitable investments overseas in the face of saturation of the home market. Diminishing returns at home were due to under-consumption because of the relative poverty of the lower classes and excessive "over-saving" to accumulate capital by the upper classes. Inadequate purchasing power therefore led to the search for profitable outlets for capital in captive colonial markets. Hobson's copious statistics suggested that British foreign investment was directly linked to the relative stagnation of the domestic economy and the low standard of living (and purchasing power) of the working class. Hobson saw imperialism as a loss from the point of view of society at large. His statistics pointed to the fact that colonial trade was of marginal importance compared to British trade with Europe and there were huge administrative costs in organising the Empire. However, it was not the trader nor the entrepreneur that gained but the investor – the true capitalist. Interests rates in Britain were at an historically low point and overseas returns on capital were high (although they were riskier). Overseas investment doubled between 1880 and 1913 and it was natural to associate this with stagnation and underconsumption (Mommsen, 1980). Hobson's solution was a social programme that would increase the purchasing power of the masses. The way to overcome imperialism was not to do away with capitalism but to remove the monopolistic structures that resulted from an anachronistic social order. Imperialism was a transitional state on the road to an advanced democratic social order.

Schumpeter (1951, written 1918/19) also did not regard imperialism as the highest form of capitalism but as the irrational expansionist tendencies

The Theory of International Business Pre-Hymer   65

of an outmoded social order. Indeed imperialism was alien to a free market capitalist society. The forces of competition and autonomous entrepreneurs would, in the absence of restrictive and protectionist policies implemented by a pre-capitalist aristocratic class, destroy monopolistic structures and with this, imperialism.

Marxist analysis saw imperialism as much more intrinsic to capitalism. Imperialism was seen as staving off the inevitable (to Marxists) stagnation brought about by increasing inequalities. Rudolf Hilferding, an Austrian Marxist who became a leader of the German Social Democratic Party and Finance Minister of Austria (1928–1929) published Das Finanzcapital in 1910. He portrays imperialism as a stage of development beyond free trade. Hilferding describes the emergence of large concerns, trusts, cartels and combines, protectionism and dumping as culminating in the predominance of banks or "finance capital". In contrast to Schumpeter, Hilferding argues that monopoly capitalism and imperialism are a logical stage of development of capitalism. Finance capital is also diametrically opposed to lassez faire capitalism and competition. The absence of earlier capitalist "crises" was due to the opening up of new territories at the turn of the nineteenth century. Finance capital links to the dominance of a tight capitalist oligarchy. The dominance of banks links closely to the particular development trajectory of Germany.

Bukharin (1918) saw imperialism as the intersection of two conflicting trends in the world economy: internationalisation and nationalisation (Radice, 1975). Internationalisation represents the spread of capitalist economic relations throughout the world economy and nationalisation the concentration of capital in larger combinations (trusts and cartels) leading to larger firms and links to the home state. Like Hilferding, Bukharin saw banks as crucial to these processes.

Rosa Luxemberg (1913 translation 1951) proposed that overseas markets were necessary for the continued existence of capitalism, to prevent under consumption and to realise the untapped surplus value of capitalist production in industrial countries by transferring it into foreign investment capital. The corollary of this was that imperialism extended the life of capitalism until, of course the final cataclysm arrived – and Luxemburg drew a link between imperialism and militarism (Frolich, 1940). Luxemburg's arguments were not welcomed in Marxist circles because of the implied longevity of capitalism.

Lenin wrote Imperialism: the Highest Stage of Capitalism in Switzerland in 1916 and drew on the thinking of Hilferding and Hobson. Imperialism involved a temporary postponement of the inevitable capitalist collapse. It predicted the formation of international monopoly capitalist associations that divided the world economy amongst themselves but led to steadily increasing conflict. Lenin also foresaw the "usurer state" relying on rentier income.

66 Peter J. Buckley

The role of firms themselves (and therefore of foreign direct investment) is not specifically addressed in theories of imperialism. Indeed, it can be argued that shareholders of imperialist or colonialist firms were never particularly happy to export capital. Wilson (1954, p. 110) quotes William Lever himself averring that his shareholders were never anxious (in the 1890s) "to put too much money in these associated companies" (Barratt Brown, 1974, p. 201). Theories of imperialism did draw attention to the divergent interests of rentiers, business managers/entrepreneurs and financiers. (Casson (1985b) points out that the development of capital markets makes such functional separation possible.)

Theories of imperialism are pitched at the macro economic level and lump all capital exports into an undifferentiated mass. However, the long term dynamics are worthy of consideration and the institutional setting of both home and host countries are demonstrated to be important. The underlying issue that is unresolved is the role of technological progress. This is both an antidote to stagnation and gives a dynamic to the system as a whole that invalidates the "oversaving" alleged to stall development in these models. Given the current theoretical attention to institutional explanations of FDI, the theories of imperialism are worth consideration. Theories of imperialism also focus attention on (increasing) concentration among large firms and oligopolistic competition.

8. International competitiveness

One of the earliest places to look for international business theory is the work of writers on national competitiveness. This goes back to the concern of mercantilist writers to build the 'national treasure' by ensuring a surplus of exports over imports and thus an inflow of 'specie' (under the gold standard as inflows of gold) (Mun, 1664). Concerns also arose over foreign investment, notably over the efficiency and management of (Chartered) trading companies such as Adam Smith's (1776) criticisms of the governance of the (British) East India Company. Smith's criticism is of joint stock companies in general but he felt that his was especially objectionable when "joint stock" (or chartered) companies ventured into international business. "Negligence and profusion, therefore, must always prevail, more or less, in the management of the affairs of such a company. It is upon this account that joint stock companies for foreign trade have seldom been able to maintain the competition against private adventurers. They have, accordingly, very seldom succeeded without an exclusive privilege, and frequently have not succeeded with one. Without an excusive privilege they have commonly mismanaged the trade. With an exclusive privilege, they have both mismanaged and confined it (Smith, 1776/1976, ii, 264–5). Smith argues that the principal-agent problems of joint stock companies in general become compounded with costs of doing business abroad and

The Theory of International Business Pre-Hymer 67

problems of monopoly, here confined by regulations restricting entry (the "Charter" itself). These are all very modern concerns – governance, "costs of foreigness" and imperfect competition!

The threat to the previously dominant British manufacturing base from Germany, U.S.A. and France in particular led to demands for protection of British industry against foreign competition in the period up to the First World War. A turn-of-the-century example is provided by Williamson's (1894) British Industry and Foreign Competition. This is essentially a polemical case for protection of key industries and for a move away from the traditional (by then) pro-free trade stance of Great Britain. The arguments on foreign investment are confused and not linked to the trade arguments (a common problem that still persists). Distinctions are not made between portfolio and direct investment, the notion that firms can have a strategy (least of all a global strategy) is missing and the argument is cast as a "migration of manufacturing capitalists" issue. The argument is that entrepreneurial skill is scarce and the migration of capitalists reduces domestic capability and strengthens foreign manufacturing locations. The fact that capitalists also take capital with them strengthens the argument.

Williamson makes the tariff–jumping motive for foreign migration of capitalists central. British firms (he alleges) cannot export to the foreign markets therefore capitalists migrate to protected markets. Protection therefore denies British companies access to foreign markets but also induces British capitalists to move there. Interestingly, he implies that British free trade policies do not encourage inward migration of capitalists "While, everywhere, we meet here (Britain) foreign agents, striving to push the sale of their wares, there is not, so far as we know, even one instance of a foreign manufacturer transferring his works to this country. Why should he? By manufacturing abroad, he retains his own market, with its cheaper labour, which did he come here he would lose, while by remaining where he is, he has both markets" (Williamson, p. 205). In this quotation, we can see that Williamson comprehends market-orientated foreign investment as the primary motive and has an efficiency motive for location, based solely on labour costs. Given the conditions of the time, his analysis has some merit.

The lack of analytical distinctions between shifts in location and domicile of manufacturing, and between portfolio foreign investments and direct foreign investments lead to all of these different issues being condemned as migration of manufacturing and therefore as deadweight losses to Britain. The loss of competitiveness of Britain as a manufacturing location for (often) labour intensive production, such as textiles, is mixed with arguments on protectionism and with company strategies as firms seek to find the optimum production locations using a mix of the three different "migration" strategies. Williamson lists close and move transplant strategies (Marshal & Co., flax spinners of Holbeck, Leeds to new mills in Massachusetts) together with the opening of branches (manufacture in Germany including lace, Mudellas

68   *Peter J. Buckley*

hosiery works in Saxony, Titus Salt (Bradford) in America, Wilkinsons lace in U.S.A.) and even foreign takeovers (the purchase of the South Boston Iron works by "an English syndicate"). This illustrates the importance of distinctions between different kinds of migration of industry and the need to integrate the theories of trade and foreign investment.

9. Managing foreign operations

Dudley Maynard Phelps (1936) Migration of Industry to South America is a remarkable book beginning the tradition of what we now call "International Management". Phelps's chapters (8) "Policies of migrating companies", (4) "Difficulties encountered by migrating firms" and (7) "Operating differences and difficulties" are excellent discussions of the management of operations abroad and the familiar tension of local and global pressures on multinational firms.

Phelps saw that "Industrial migration involves not only the exportation of physical products and of capital but also the transfer of managerial abilities and industrial techniques. It may be considered a hybrid of foreign trade and foreign investment, with a greater measure of managerial supervision and control" (1936, p. v). This is a startlingly modern view. Phelps also differentiates earlier migration of industries from the period he is analysing by the fact that "All ties with the parent organisation were cut, and the new industrial enterprise lacked connection with the old" (p. vi). Control from the parent, the distinguishing feature of FDI, was crucial.

Phelps's analysis of motives for migration (FDI) is also modern. He lists "the influence of raw material resources", "production incentives" (relative cost of production abroad compared to home), "the effect of competition", tariff jumping and "marketing inducements to migration". The third and fifth of these motives require expansion. In "The effect of competition", Phelps theorises that market size and the nature of competition (from importers, local firms or other foreign branch plants) will influence the FDI decision. He adduces "first mover advantages" – "securing an early foothold on a manufacturer conceivably might, forestall like action by competitions" (p. 58) and he suggests that local demand might be increased by "the presence effect" (p. 58). The assessments of current and likely future market size and competition are argued from interviews with parent company executives and competitive strategies are analysed. In "marketing inducements to migration", Phelps suggests that with local production, there is less need for forecasting demand, greater flexibility in meeting local demand, lower transportation costs, better adaptation of product to market needs, superior control over distribution and the ability to tap "national sentiment" (p. 83) by playing to the "Buy at Home" attitude. This is a precisely argued and documented list of the marketing advantages of a local presence. In summarising motives, Phelps resist a single cause explanation and gives

The Theory of International Business Pre-Hymer 69

due weight to uncertainty in the investment decision, prefiguring Aharoni (1966).

The modern concerns about the "costs of foreignness" are covered by Phelps. He includes "distance from the Home-office organisation", "prejudice against foreign capital", "race and nationality factors" and "lack of stability in (host) Government" among the key difficulties encountered by migrating companies. He also adds "lack of information on which to base decisions" as a difficulty. Overestimation of market size he pinpoints as the most usual mistake.

It is probably Chapter 8 of Phelps's book "Policies of migrating companies" (reproduced in Buckley, 2003) that makes the greatest contribution to theorising international management. Phelps's recommendation is clearly to "glocalize". "A firm that attempts to stimulate the economic development of a country, which attempts to become as national as possible, which, in a sense, merges its interests in the national economy of which it is a part, is more likely to enjoy successful, long continued operation. It will be considered a part of the national economy, rather than an extraneous element, even though it is of foreign origin. By following these policies, a company strengthens its position against prejudicial action by governmental agencies" (p. 287).

Phelps's conceptual and theoretical work has been largely ignored and then bypassed. An unfortunate bifurcation has occurred latterly between "international business" theory and "international management". This was not evident in the works of Phelps (1936) who, not seeing this separation, ignored it, and managed to integrate management practice with theoretical insight. Hymer cites Phelps as a source of empirical information (Hymer, 1960, p. 109, p. 155 [where Hymer gets the date wrong!], p. 156) but not as a source of theoretical insight.

J. Fred Rippy's Latin America and the Industrial Age (1944, second edition 1947) assumes that foreign investment in Latin America will be temporary, economic nationalism requiring disinvestment after a time. "Latin American leaders are convinced that political independence has little meaning without a large measure of economic independence, and foreign investors will continue to feel the pressure of this conviction. In the use of new processes and techniques to produce new commodities or improve the quality of old ones, however, opportunities for foreign pioneers will always be found, and no serious grievances need arise provided the pioneers can reconcile themselves to the transitory nature of their operations. The future seems to promise no abatement of economic nationalism in the retarded countries" (1947, p. 240). This strong version of the "obsolescing bargain" was a stark prediction.

10. Foreign direct investment – the concept

Until the development of statistics that separated "direct" from "portfolio" foreign investment (see Brecher & Reisman, 1957) the conceptual isolation

70   *Peter J. Buckley*

of direct foreign investment was not complete (see for instance Jenks, 1927). Lewis (1948, pp. 25–27) explained foreign investment largely in respect of the "capacity to invest abroad", an analogue of the excess of exports over imports rather than as a reflection of the relative competitive ability of different national firms. This macro, impersonal approach fitted with an interest rate driven model of flows of funds. The inter-war period saw a gradual process of conceptual clarification.

Staley (1935) is clear that direct investments are dependent on the transfer of management as well as capital. "In the case of direct investment, management, as well as capital, migrates across national boundaries. The foreign investor is a proprietor, not merely a lender", (p. 22). Staley attributes the distinction between portfolio and direct investment to the U.S. Department of Commerce in its estimates of American holdings abroad from 1930 onwards (p. 23) [see U.S. Department of Commerce (1931)].

Cleona Lewis (1938, 1948) provides pre and post World War II inventories of the USA's international credit and debit position. The national accounting purpose of these important books is evident but for our needs they provide fascinating insights into the conceptualisation of foreign direct investment (FDI).

In the first book (1938) the definition of FDI is implicit. In an analytical narrative of "America's Foreign Liabilities" (Part I of the volume), Lewis traces the predominant liabilities through loans, to the financing of railroads, to government bonds sold abroad, foreign funds in American industry (portfolio foreign investment) and finally to "foreign-controlled enterprise in the United States" (FDI) (Chapter V). This is followed by a similar narrative of "America's Foreign Investments" beginning with trade and banking ventures abroad, prospecting and mining, oil minerals and agriculture and (Chapter XIV) "America Factories Abroad" FDI is nowhere explicitly defined. The central issue dividing portfolio from direct foreign investment, the issue of control, is implicit. Foreign controlled enterprises "in which the role of entrepreneur or majority stockholder has been taken by foreigners" (p. 78) is equated with FDI in Appendix C: The "Direct" Investments of Foreigners". Note the quotation marks. In the consideration of "America Factories Abroad" (Chapter XIV beginning p. 292) the term "Branch factories abroad" is introduced without explicit definition. It is also noted (p. 293) that "The American factory was scarcely established at home before it appeared in foreign countries". An early appearance of the "born global" concept, it seems!

Far from allowing the concept of FDI to emerge implicitly, Lewis's 1948 volume goes to great length to define concepts overtly. Chapter III "The Character of Foreign Investments" separates out portfolio and direct foreign investment definitionally. Lewis's definition follows (1948, pp. 17–18) "The direct investments of a given country include (1) the foreign subsidiaries, branches and other foreign properties owned and controlled by its domestic enterprises; (2) companies controlled by its nationals but organised to operate exclusively abroad – whether such companies are incorporated (or registered) at home or abroad; (3) holdings by individual and groups of individuals of important equity interests in foreign corporations; and (4) real property owned by nationals of the country, such as mines, timber lands and plantations. The authority Lewis gives for this definition is Sammonds and Abelson (1942), US Department of Commerce.

The discussion of the status of foreign companies in law had been a point of contention from the beginning of the 20th century. Hilton Young (1912) analyses the position of "foreign companies and other corporations in English law". This issue had become salient following "the important case of Risdon Iron and Locomotive Works in Furness" (p. 185) when a company formed under the Company Acts to acquire and work mines in California became insolvent. The defendant, a shareholder in the company, was sued by suppliers of machinery for his proportion of the price of the machines. The company was held to be under English law and no foreign legislation was deemed valid. The issues of international jurisdictions and local versus source country laws have thus been at issue for over a century.

11. Foreign direct investment and development

C. F. Remer (1933) produced a formidable survey of foreign investments in China. He adopted the heuristic definition of "direct investment" that became familiar in pre-1960s writing. "The methods by which foreign capital has actually come are, then, business investments and government borrowings. The first of these I call direct, since the property remains under foreign control and management. The directness lies in the fact that no-one stands between the foreign investor and the business risk involved in his investment. To avoid any possible misunderstanding it should be added that in the few cases in which foreigners have invested in the obligations of a Chinese corporation we have a business investment which is indirect since capital equipment is not in the legal possession of the foreigner who has in his hands the obligation of a Chinese company" (pp. 65–66). In a footnote (14) Remer says "The terms "direct" and indirect and used here in a way which is consistent with their use by others in this new field of business investments. Paul D. Dickens of the Bureau of Foreign and Domestic Commerce uses direct investments, without specifically saying so, to mean investments in which the business risk and, usually, the legal ownership remain with the investor. See the introduction to his "American Direct Investments in Foreign Countries" Washington, 1930, Trade Information Bulletin No. 731". If we allow bearing of business risk to equate to ultimate control then we have a viable distinction between direct and portfolio foreign investment.

The fact that practically no foreign capital had entered China through the Chinese corporation means that the capital which "has come through the

72   *Peter J. Buckley*

foreign "colony" and it has remained under the control and management of the foreigner" (1933, pp. 115–116). "In this sense direct investments may be said to be connected with extraterritoriality. Extraterritoriality is inconsistent with the development of Chinese nationalism and will, no doubt, come to an end" (p. 116). This prescient prediction was based on the enclave nature of foreign investment in the 1930s and the dualistic nature of the Chinese economy, with linkages to the domestic sector limited, foretold its demise.

As with many early studies of FDI, Remer (1933) is concerned with the "capacity to receive" – what we would now call the absorptive capacity of the Chinese economy. "The checks and hindrances to the flow of capital lie in China rather than in the capital exporting countries. The effective limitations are on the demand rather than the supply side" (Remer, p. 231). Remer identifies "the ineffectiveness of the Chinese government in the economic field (p. 233), "the failure of the Chinese economic and social organisation to develop the concepts, in various fields, which are required for the importation and effective use of foreign capital" (p. 234) and the instability (and rapaciousness) of the Chinese government which raises uncertainty as key obstacles to inward FDI. These are all institutional factors related to the host economy. In addition, Remer identifies "the political difficulties created by the ambition and jealousy of the foreign powers" leading to "fear and distrust of the Chinese people" (p. 233) as a constraint on inward investment. He specifically mentions Manchuria: "the Chinese people have been in the greatest danger of losing the very region in which direct business investment have been greatest" (p. 233). In the introduction to the 1968 reprint, Remer says "When I left China in June, 1931 I was of the opinion that the greatest threat to the success of the new nationalist government lay in Japanese policy, and I believe it to have been a prime factor in the defeat of that government" (Remer, 1968, p. xxiv). Ironically, "On September 18th, 1931, I reached Ann Arbour, Michigan, after more than a year of field work ... That was the very day on which Japanese troops marched into Manchuria" (Remer, 1968 p. xxiii). Remer's study highlights the importance of (global) political circumstances that influence flows of FDI. The study of international business theory must have a political element. Remer's meticulous fieldwork with individual studies of American, British, Japanese, Russian, French, German and other (Belgian, Dutch, Italian and "Scandinavian") investments in China was rendered of historical interest only by the cataclysm that the Japanese invasion precipitated.

Hubbard (1935) also examines foreign investment in China. No definition is provided but the terms "foreign factories" and "foreign owned classes of factories" (p. 222) imply that manufacturing facilities are being examined. "The explanation of the large foreign element in China's modern industrial development lies in the opportunity afforded of uniting foreign enterprise, experience, and efficiency with abnormally cheap labour in conditions which assure entrepreneurs the special advantages attached to the Treaty Port system, including, hitherto, low rates of taxation" (p. 222) "In more or less recent years a further inducement to found foreign factories in China has come from the rise in import duties and the consequences of "getting inside the tariff wall" (p. 222). Thus, both efficiency and market motives are identified. Financing of foreign companies is found to be largely from local banks, and Hong Kong banks. A short case study of the textile industry finds that foreign (Japanese) textile companies pay higher wages, the workers have shorter working days and suffer less from Government interference than do domestically owned cotton mills. Japanese investments in China's textile industry are described as classic offshore operations – "The Japanese mills mostly belong to powerful combines with manufacturing interests in Japan to which they act as 'feeders'" (Hubbard, p. 226). (Note the parallels with modern Japanese investment in China, including locational aspects (see Ma & Delios, 2007).

Frankel's (1938) study of Capital investment in Africa is one of several works on foreign investment in less developed areas that is rich in data gathering but is hampered by the lack of clear conceptual distinctions between types of foreign investment. Frankel is strong on uncovering the problems of increasing the absorptive capacity of the host countries but struggles to gain tractable definitions to enable a fruitful classification of foreign capital. He uses "long term foreign investment owned by residents of the capital exporting countries" as his object of investigation but notes that it is difficult to arrive at the amount of international capital investment. "The task bristles with difficulties due to differences of classification and method, paucity of statistical data, diversity in the purposes for which the calculations were made, and extreme variation in the reliability and objectivity of those making them" (1938, p. 18).

Allen and Donnithorne (1957) examine firms of foreign business in "Instruments of Western Enterprise" (Chapter II, p. 49–66). Given the diverse nature of sectors into which foreign capital has migrated – including, plantations, other agriculture, rubber, banking, shipping, public utilities and commerce as well as manufacturing – their focus is wide and does not emphasise the 'direct' versus 'portfolio' status of FDI until they reach manufacturing. Their typology encompasses managing agencies, joint public–private partnerships with Government, various forms of rentier or portfolio investment and "In the mining and manufacturing industries, apart from the large concerns with widely dispersed interests, direct management by owning companies that specialise in a relatively narrow range of industries is common" (p. 64). Control is mentioned as a key feature and in the statistical Appendix (pp. 288 and 290) "Business (or Direct) Investments" are distinguished from "Rentier Investments, mainly in Government Securities". The authors note that they have followed Callis's (1942) practice in using the term "rentier investments" instead of the usual "portfolio investments".

74   *Peter J. Buckley*

Allen and Donnithorne take a comparative approach, finding Dutch influence on Indonesia contrasts with British in Malaysia. Unfortunately the disparities in organisation of the sectors that they examine rather obscures any firm conclusion on direct investment.

These studies are testimony to the need for sound theory to reinforce important analytical distinctions that can be translated into statistics so that these "social facts" can lead to a new round of theorising. Although insightful, lack of precision on phenomena and lack of clarity and focus on the organisation of firm and foreign investment mode limited their inputs into future theorising.

12. Foreign direct investment – early theorising

C. K. Hobson's The Export of Capital, published in the fateful year of 1914 is, well described in Harrod's introduction to the reissue of 1963: "Its classic combination of very fine analysis of the many theoretical issues relating to foreign investment, extensive historical learning and pioneering ventures in statistical calculation entitle it to be regarded as a classic" (1963, p. v). For our purposes however, although it comes extremely close to identifying the distinction between direct and portfolio foreign investment, it never makes that distinction and so remains a classic analysis of the effects of indirect foreign investment largely on the source economy with particular attention to interest rate effects, exports, the balance of trade and emigration. Hobson notes (pp. 28–9) the different methods of investing British and American capital in Canada, but attributes this to proximity, not explicitly to the directness of control. He emphasises knowledge barriers as key determinants to (direct) foreign investment in addition to risk and cultural/political distance. The nascent nature of "international companies" is illustrated by the loose nature of Hobson's discussion. "Foreign individuals are in most cases accommodated through the means of joint-stock enterprises such as banks and finance companies, which have grown up apace. Such organisations are often international in character; they are companies incorporated according to the law of one particular country, but carry on business in other countries as well" (Hobson, 1914, p. 123). However, the emerging multinational firm is well captured by Hobson (pp. 123–4). "The organisation of business on a large scale has made it more and more difficult to cramp a concern within political boundaries. The desire of investors to secure a higher return by investing in businesses abroad, while retaining substantial control over the management, was probably the dominant motive marking for international companies in other cases". This was written (also in a doctoral thesis) nearly 50 years before Hymer's thesis. Hobson is well aware of distance and communication problems that restricted the directness of foreign investment before World War I: ".cheaper quicker, and more regular communication has diminished the obstacles and assisted the development of such international companies; though even now they are at a disadvantage compared with companies which are controlled on the spot, in those industries in which flexibility and quick adaptability are required in the management" (Hobson, 1914, p. 124). Mining, land improvement and mortgage companies and railways are deemed to be industries where "the difficulties of management from a distance were comparatively small" (pp. 124–5) and thus Hobson provides a sector specific explanation of pre-First World War foreign investment. "The international company has even extended to manufacturing, but therein it is still somewhat rare, showing that the difficulties of management have not yet been fully overcome" (p. 125). This, and the lack of equal treatment by host countries of foreign owned companies, restricts the growth of international companies.

In the inter-war years, much of the concern about private economic power in the global economy was expressed with regard to cartels or "international combines" (Plummer, 1934, 1938, 1951). As noted previously, it is with respect to cartels that much inter-war theory on international operations was developed. However, the strategies of international firms became salient between the two world wars and U.S. foreign direct investment was noted as being significant especially in Canada but also in Europe and Latin America.

Southard's (1931) empirical study is strikingly modern in conception. Its first chapter examines modes of doing foreign business ("external form") and covers agent or representative, branch (house), majority control of subsidiary company (divided into (a) organised by American company (b) purchased), minority interests and contractual firms ("working agreements", "concession and contract", licensing agreement). The directness of investment is defined not by control but by directness of means, such as buying stock directly, lending money directly, building a factory (p. 190).

Southard's book examines the extent of American industry in Europe, organising and operating European subsidiaries and general problems arising including fears of the "industrial Americanization of Europe". The chapter on "Why American Industry Migrates to Europe" is an excellent checklist of elements of the theory of FDI. Staley lists these as follows: (1) Cost Factors: high tariffs, transportation, raw materials and fuel, wages, and taxation; (2) Supplement to home activities: raw materials, intercontinental services; (3) Servicing: catering to national peculiarities; (4) Expansion: patent exploitation; market control and (5) Nationalism (the desire of European countries to purchase local services and products). A little rearrangement gives us our familiar categories of motive: efficiency seeking, resource and asset seeking, market seeking. It is perhaps surprising in retrospect that Southard's book did not supply the basis of the theory of FDI nearly thirty years before Hymer as all the ingredients are present. Except, perhaps, that the theory is too far hidden behind empirical details.

Canadian-American Industry (1936) by Marshall, Southard, and Taylor explicitly analyses two way flows of foreign direct investment. The extent of "American Industry in Canada" is mapped as is Canadian industry in the United States. There is no explicit discussion of "direct" investment. The book opens with a chapter on the historical background of each country's investment in the other. Chapter II on American industry in Canada begins by referring to the "establishment of American subsidiaries across the Border" (p. 19) but the term "subsidiaries" is left undefined. In the opening paragraph on Canadian industry in the U.S. (where it is pointed out that as a proportion of Canada's wealth her direct investment in the U.S. is larger than the U.S.'s in Canada), the term "direct investment" is undefined (p. 175). In contrast to the looseness of definition of (what are now regarded as) key terms, the discussion of motives for undertaking FDI is precise and is generalised from the evidence. The establishment of "branch factories" is attributed largely to tariffs, segmenting a markets which would otherwise be served by exports (p. 199). Differential consumer preferences also play a role, importing a local element of varying categories to differentiating the market. However, the tariff jumping motive is crucial. "In the absence of tariffs the remaining barriers would be insufficient to explain the establishment of many – probably the majority of the plants now in existence" (1936, p. 209). The analysis of tariff jumping ends with an analysis of the dynamics of the FDI decision – a balancing of costs and benefits that echoes Kindleberger's (1988) analysis of "close cases". The efficiency seeking motive is largely dismissed on the grounds that cost differentials, including wages are too similar – very few of the companies answering the questionnaire cited wage differentials as an important motive for entry. There were some areas (e.g. bulky goods) where lower costs of transportation in Canada improved the choice of FDI versus exporting. However the abilities of sales subsidiaries to have "Better control over the sales force, better adjustment to the market, close association with the customer, and quicker delivery of goods are all more surely obtainable through the medium of a local subsidiary" (p. 209). For the sector of "mines, forests and fisheries" Marshall et al. invoke a resource-seeking explanation. For services, a straightforward market seeking explanation is given (p. 215). A final rather unclear motive is given for "auxiliary subsidiaries" (pp. 207–8). This appears to be a network of firms type argument as these companies "owe their existence to a contribution they make to the main product of an associated company" (p. 207). This is related diversification abroad – supplying parts or semi-fabricated materials from the foreign country or companies being pulled into the foreign market to supply "familiar customers" (p. 208). The authors simply do not have the language and concepts to describe these more complex relationships. In summary, two paramount motives are the search for raw materials and market seeking. It will be noted that efficiency seeking is investigated and dismissed as unimportant and wider influences such as network effects and pull factors from powerful stakeholders are also discussed.

The Theory of International Business Pre-Hymer 77

In terms of the operations (international management) of the foreign direct investments, Marshall et al. set up a "typical" (idealtype) branch factory and contrast this with the findings from their questionnaire. The idealtype (of American plant in Canada) is "a limited company, (wholly) owned by the parent company, financed by it and closely controlled by it. It is a factory, not an assembly plant" (p. 219). The issues of joint ventures and of cross-continent coordination largely do not arise, the latter because of tariffs. Location strategy is discussed by comparison with Canadian industry in general. There is found to be a higher concentration of U.S. plants in the larger industrial centres in Canada (p. 222). In the form of organisation, most branch plants are incorporated under the laws of the host country although a few operate as "direct and unincorporated branches" because of the "simplicity" of that form of organisation. They can operate on the same basis as their American branches (p. 223). Acquisition and greenfield methods of entry are described, but in a non-analytical fashion. Financing is overwhelmingly from the parent company, although some funds (perhaps 10%) are raised in the local capital market. On "policy determination" (p. 229) or company strategy, the authors set up a continuum with at one end complete independence and at the other the "factory branch" completely controlled by the parent. Most situations are in between, of course, but only examples from the questionnaire, are given. Interestingly, "There is much evidence that Canada has been considered more a division of the domestic market than part of the foreign market" (p. 231) because where separate "International" companies have been formed by many American companies, they do not control Canadian affairs. This is early evidence of regional strategies forming – although crudely (North America and the rest of the world). Levels of integrated strategy, too, are considered on a continuum a completely self contained factory versus a packaging and assembly plant. From the questionnaire, the authors conclude that increased localisation of activities occurs over time. In generalising, they find a market size explanation best fit the empirical facts. "Where the market is reasonably large and no insuperable costs exist or hindrances the branch factory is more likely to turn out a complete product. If a factory for independent production is too large for the market, some, or all, of the parts will be imported" (1936, p. 236) (Tariffs permitting of course). On costs (unsurprisingly) the evidence they are able to adduce suggests higher costs (in Canada), "sheltered by a tariff, they pass those costs on to the customer" (p. 239). Wages were at the going rate, or slightly higher.

In the final chapter (VII Consequences and Problems) the authors allow themselves wider generalisations. Canadian investment in the U.S.A. "can be accounted for under two heads – economic necessity and individual personalities" (p. 203). This need for a wide market and entrepreneurial abilities are the drivers. For U.S. companies in Canada, "certain types of production" are critical (p. 204). First "industries for which the United States

78 *Peter J. Buckley*

has become particularly noted" (p. 246) i.e. where U.S. firms have built ownership-specific advantages. Second where US firms need to "maintain and develop the sales in Canada of well-known, well advertised, branded or patented articles, the demand for which has been fostered and extended by their familiarity to the Canadian customer through travel, magazines, radio and motion pictures" (p. 265). Market motivation is here combined with the internalisation of activities based on firm specific advantages. "A third class of American companies has entered Canada to obtain control of necessary raw materials or other industrial requirements" (p. 265). The authors then examine why other areas of industry and services are not colonised by FDI (banking, railways, textiles, animal products and flour and cereal products, iron and steel). They find regulation, lack of competitive advantage, high levels of domestic competition and lack of established distribution networks to explain the various cases. Their puzzlement arises of course from the lack of a complete theory of FDI and of foreign market servicing. Their list of low FDI industries looks remarkably similar to the 'stylised facts' adduced in Buckley and Casson's (1976) list of what a theory of FDI and the MNC needs to explain!

Finally, Marshall et al. look at the relationship of investment flows and trade flows. They reflect concern that FDI weakens the capital exporting industry and they exonive export-inducing versus export substituting effects of FDI. This is linked with the balance of payments problems that Canada (along with many other countries) experienced 1929–1935. The effect of tariffs is of course overwhelming at this time but the resultant tariff jumping FDI began to concern Canadians because of lack of control of domestic industry leading to the ultra protectionist "Watkins Report" and to the Canadian Stephen Hymer's theorising.

The Marshall et al. volume is an empirical piece of great quality. It was based on a questionnaire sent to 1200 American corporations "believed to be operating in Canada" (p. 331) and to 900 companies in Canada "believed to be American controlled" (p. 232). The text (p. 26) gives a figure of "1100 American companies which have Canadian subsidiaries". "Each of these questionnaires yielded about 170 usable replies. Allowing for duplications, they provide us with the experience of more than 300 companies that are directly a part of the "Canadian-American industry" (p. 26). Reporting of questionnaire results is not as rigorous as today, but the full questionnaires are reproduced as Appendix IV. It will be noted that only U.S. firms in Canada are surveyed but that results were obtained from both parent and subsidiary (or "branch plant"). The excellent empirical and descriptive work is constrained by the lack of a theoretical framework and of precision in conceptualisation. Nevertheless Marshall et al. may be considered to have advanced "theory". The notion of examining two-way flows of FDI, the crucial importance for explanation of understanding why FDI does not exist in certain sectors and circumstances, the relationship of flows of FDI

The Theory of International Business Pre-Hymer   79

and trade, the analysis of clear generalisations on motives for FDI, alternatives to FDI (largely exports), the preliminary establishment of a "typical" branch factory as an idealtype (and the understanding of deviation from the stereotype) and the groping towards the conceptualisation of regional (and global) strategies are key steps forward. Hymer took from Marshall et al. (1936) variations in the share of Canadian industries under American control. This formed part of the empirical evidence supporting an industrial organisation theory of FDI following Bain (1956).

Before the mid-1950s, foreign direct investment was largely studied separately from the institution directing the investment – the multinational enterprise. It was as if FDI had to be first proven to be salient before MNEs could be conceptualised as more than "national companies with international operations" as Hymer's (1960) title has it. Several studies of individual industries pointed to the growth of integrated (cross-national) companies such and McLean and Haigh (1954) in the oil industry, but recognition of the MNE as an institution did not emerge in the literature until the 1960s. Staley's (1939) World Economy in Transition examined "The Future of International Investments". Interestingly in a Chapter (17) on the "Spread of Capital and Techniques," he predicts that "direct investment will loom large in future foreign investment" (Page 277). "Direct investment, consisting of branch factories or commercial facilities operated directly, and "equity" investment in general, have important advantages over international loans that bear a fixed rate of interest in the conditions of the modern world. The service payments on such investments are less likely to raise exchange difficulties, for their yield is likely to fall in times of depression, thus automatically decreasing the burden of external payments that has to be carried by the economies of borrowing countries. Direct investments also have the advantage of being undertaken, in most cases, by those who have a specialised knowledge of some branch of industry, and this knowledge goes along with the investment, making it more productive" Staley takes this point further in a prescient discussion that places foreign direct investment firmly in the context of international knowledge transfer. "The internationalization of science is notorious" (p. 280).

An "early and insightful piece of FDI thinking" (Pedersen & Strandskov, 2006) was the 1944 article in Danish by Arne Lund. Lund (1915–1995) was at the University of Aarhus, Denmark from 1946 to 1951, was managing director of the Association of Danish Employers 1959–1979 and was a member of Parliament for the Conservative Party 1984–1989 as well as a columnist for a social-liberal newspaper. His 1944 piece identifies FDI as different from other foreign investments because of the element of managerial control. FDI is seen as an entrepreneurial activity and the crucial aspect of FDI is the combination of ideas and capital together. International mobility of capital and ideas give the conditions for an explanatory sequence of the business decisions to go abroad. First is the "why" – spotting business opportunities.

80 *Peter J. Buckley*

Second is "how" – mobilising international entrepreneurship and finally an investment calculus gives the "where" when opportunities abroad are compared to rank their relative return. Lund is particularly astute in picking up the interaction between entrepreneurial vision and monopolistic advantages arising from proprietary know how and technology. This is directly linked to exploitation via FDI. "Entrepreneurs in industrialised countries acquire power and monopoly advantages that can be capitalised and as such represent a value. This relates not only to monopolistic advantages based on the (increasing) concentration in industries, but in addition to specialised know-how and technology. This tendency is not clearly observed when innovations are patented or acquire a trade mark, but idiosyncratic technical or commercial insight will in its own right and even without protection give advantages when applied in a nation which is technical and commercially less developed. The initial investment may in such cases by quite limited, but the advantage guarantees an income which is accumulated and capitalised and thus contributes to financing the further expansion of the foreign business unit" (Lund, 1944, pp. 41–42, translation Pedersen & Standskov (2006, pp. 8–9). It will be noted that this passage not only anticipates "ownership advantages", it also contains suggestions on dynamics not dissimilar to Vernon's (1966) product cycle hypothesis and on "the Gambler's Earnings Hypothesis" (Barlow & Wender, 1955; Penrose, 1956) and Penrosian views of the autonomous expansion of foreign subsidiaries. Lund (1944) had identified an anomaly in received theory (the dichotomy between FDI and portfolio foreign investment). He identified an explanation based on managerial control, entrepreneurial insights and uncertainty revolving round the international exploitation of the firm's competitive advantages (Pedersen & Strandskov, 2006, p. 13).

13. Foreign direct investment and the control of domestic industry

Concern with the preponderance of U.S. activities in Canadian economic relationships led to a Royal Commission Report (Brecher & Reisman, 1957). The Report covers business cycle transmission, "non resident ownership and control of Canadian industry with special reference to United States investment" (Part II), commercial relations, trade union links and dimensions of economic growth in Canada and the U.S. (see also Blyth & Carty, 1956 and Knox, 1957).

Brecher and Reisman (1957) analyse non-resident ownership and control of Canadian industries in three chapters, covering Canada's international investment position, the determinants of foreign financing in Canada and the meaning and effects of nonresident ownership and control of Canadian industry, followed by a conclusion. There is a clear division between direct and portfolio foreign investment. "In particular, the definition of direct

The Theory of International Business Pre-Hymer 81

investment and the statistical concept of control should be carefully noted" (p. 90). They then go on to quote from Dominion Board of Statistics Canada's International Investment Position. "The category of direct investments shown here generally includes all concerns in Canada which are known to have 50% or more of their voting stock held in one country outside Canada. In addition, a few instances of concerns are included where it is known that effective control is held by a parent firm with less than 50% of the stock. In effect, this category includes all known cases of unincorporated branches of foreign companies in Canada and all wholly-owned subsidiaries, together with a number of concerns with a parent company outside of Canada which holds less than all of the capital stock. In addition, there are a relatively small number of Canadian companies included in cases where more than one-half of their capital stock is owned in a single country outside of Canada where there is no parent concern. These exceptional cases are confined to instances where control is believed to rest with non-residents" (quoted by Brecher and Reisman p. 90). The authors note that this statistical concept of control is necessarily a formal one indicating the existence of potential control of the firm by nonresidents, rather than the extent to which managerial control is in fact exercised. "Portfolio investments, by contrast, are typically scattered minority holdings of stocks and bonds which do not carry with them control of the enterprises" (Brecher & Reisman, 1957, p. 90). The rise in U.S. investment in Canada is noted to be due to the establishment or acquisition of enterprises in Canada and to the expansion of existing enterprises – the latter being the dominant factor.

Brecher and Reisman note that both direct and portfolio investment are made up of debt as well as equity holdings. "For some purposes, it is useful to look at foreign investment in terms of the fixed monetary claims represented by debt and the variable real claims relating to equity financing" (p. 93). This neatly summarises a measurement and conceptual problem that is with us today. It also influences the host country's debt servicing problem – an issue taken up by Barlow and Wender (1955) and Penrose (1956) almost contemporaneously. Brecher and Reisman go on to examine changes in both ownership and control (noting that the two are not co-terminus) across sectors of Canadian industry, including the issue of concentration of foreign control (examining for instance large firms).

The capacity of a host country to attract foreign capital is described as the "investment climate" by Brecher and Reisman (1957, p. 114). "This embraces the broad economic, political, and social framework of institutions and attitudes, which have a profound impact on the confidence of foreign investors". Similarity of institutions with major capital exporting nations, the U.S. and UK has favoured Canada they argue as well as cultural factors – "language and social customs" (p. 114). Proximity to the U.S.A. also helps.

In examining the motives for direct investment, Brecher and Reisman (1957, p. 116) identify two broad types. "Much direct investment in Canada,

82 Peter J. Buckley

particularly from the United States, has been undertaken basically to supply parent companies and other non-residents with raw or semi-processed materials. A second general type of direct investment is undertaken mainly to supply the Canadian market, and also certain export markets overseas..." The first motive "the "resource" type of investment usually resolves about the desire to develop and guarantee sources of supply for materials. In most instances, cost considerations have been dominant" (p. 115). "The second broad motive for direct investment is that of bringing a commodity or service into the Canadian market as an extension of the parent company's United States operations.... Export markets may also be involves...in the case of United States controlled companies the export interests have usually been confined to Commonwealth markets" (p. 117). Market driven investment is related to tariff protection and Brecher and Reisman consider market servicing alternatives – "given Canadian tariffs, the non-resident finds direct investment in Canada a convenient and profitable alternative to servicing the Canadian market through exports" (p. 117).

Brecher and Reisman (1957) include a fascinating section on capital requirements where they consider Canadian attitudes to risk taking. They speculate that Canadians (in contrast to U.S. citizens) and Canadian institutions prefer to purchase debt securities rather than equities which reflects risk-aversion (pp. 121–122). Institutions reinforce this preference and they speculate that Canadian taxation legislation also is culpable (pp. 126–128). They say (p. 122) "it would have been very difficult, and sometimes impossible, for Canadians to undertake many of Canada's larger investment projects. The basic proposition here is that risk is a relative concept: investment undertakings which entail a considerable element of risk for Canadians are often a routine operation for large non-resident corporations. The Canadian venture, large though it may be by Canadian standards, is typically only a small part of the non-resident's global operation. Furthermore, the nonresident corporation usually has the ancillary facilities – such as technology, skills and markets – in the abundant quantities necessary to minimise risk". This leads to a discussion of the wider advantages of belonging to a multinational enterprise. Brecher and Reisman have developed the 'package of advantages' view of multinational enterprises well ahead of Kindleberger (1969). "For the fact is that connections with a parent or affiliated company abroad often involve advantages which either cannot be duplicated by a purely Canadian enterprise, or can be duplicated only at greater cost to the firm and the public at large. These advantages to do not flow exclusively from the availability of capital in the form and amounts required. Availability of capital is extremely important, but so too are technology, research, product development, technical and managerial personnel, training facilities, market and supply contacts and accumulated experience over the whole range of business activity" (Brecher & Reisman, 1957, p. 138). A comprehensive listing of firm-specific advantages!

The Theory of International Business Pre-Hymer 83

Chapter 8 of Brecher and Reisman's (1957) book is a superb analysis of the meaning and effects of non-resident ownership and control of Canadian industry. It sets out to answer three questions – "to what extent does statistical or potential nonresident control of a Canadian corporation constitute control in practice?" "does a corporation so controlled behave differently than a resident controlled company?" and "what are the consequences for the Canadian economy?" (p. 131). On the first question, a nuanced view is taken; "the concept of control is highly elusive and differs from case to case because of factors which are not measurable. For these reasons, it is useful to adopt a functional approach to this concept by asking what the effects of such control have been in specific areas of company operations" (p. 133). It is necessary to examine the composition of boards of directors and senior executives and the relationship between parent and subsidiary board to begin to answer this question. The extent of decentralisation is also important. This may be determined by motive of the subsidiary's operation and the nature and sources of financing. On the second question, Brecher and Reisman state "the key to an evaluation of the effects of foreign direct investment (as of investment generally) is the overriding consideration of maximising profits…. Companies operating in more than one country may be expected, in the long run, so to respond to market demands and cost considerations as to maximise their global profits" (1957, p. 137). In general, the results for Canada are benign. "The search for profits through direct investment has led to advantages for Canada which permeate every aspect of its development, including the rate of economic growth, standards of living and industrial diversification. The development of Canadian resources, of facilities for processing them, and of Canadian manufacturing industries has been stimulated by the activities of non-resident corporations in their energetic search for supplies and pursuit of markets" (p. 138). However, adverse effects may occur in "the development and expansion of competitive facilities in Canada where similar facilities – owned by the parent exist in the United States and elsewhere; marketing and purchasing policies; price policy and economic stability" (p. 138). The first such "competitive facilities" argument analysed is research facilities – where nascent concern for Canada's research base are expressed. Branch-plant concerns are expressed together with concerns that tariff-jumping motives may not out last the tariff, purchasing policy may be biased towards the parent plant rather than local suppliers and there is a concern that rate of resource development may be slower under foreign ownership (see Byé, 1958a). Finally, non-economic factors may cause foreign firms to differ in their decision making from locally-owned ones – personal preference arising from national biases and foreign governmental policy such as (U.S.) anti-trust policy are mentioned by Brecher and Reisman.

Overall, Brecher and Reisman's (1957) account of foreign direct investment is precise and prescient. Many of the concerns – the nature and meaning of

84   *Peter J. Buckley*

control in direct foreign investment, financing issues, risk-taking behaviour, motives and effects of FDI, the impact on the local economy and the question of the difference made by foreign ownership – are a comprehensive catalogue of the international business research agenda from the time of writing onwards. The close contextualisation of the analysis with the Canadian situation is a major strength, but perhaps obscured the conceptual and theoretical advances within this remarkable work.

14. The emergence of modern theory

Moving into the late 1950s and early 1960s, international business begins to become professionalised as an academic discipline. Key publications begin to appear in journals as well as books. Applied economists, such as Penrose (1956), Byé (1958a) and Dunning (1958), produce empirical works of substance based largely on the economic theory of the firm. Conceptual advances multiply and interact and an academic discipline starts to coalese around a body of work further stimulated by Hymer's conceptual advances in 1960. To a large extent these developments ignored earlier theorising, using the works of Phelps (1936), Lewis (1938, 1948), Southard (1931), Marshall et al. (1936) and Brecher and Reisman (1957) simply as data sources, not as theoretical precursors.

Edith Penrose's (1956) "Foreign investment and the growth of the firm" preceded her work on the growth of the firm (to come to fruition in her classic 1959 book The Theory of the Growth of the Firm). In this article, Penrose evinced a version of the "Gambler's Earnings Hypothesis" (Barlow & Wender, 1955). This phenomena is the large plough-back of profits in foreign owned subsidiaries for an extended period which is then remitted as dividends (the "winnings" from the game). Multinational firms are thus likened to gamblers who, beginning the game with a small stake (the initial investment, usually small) continually ploughed back their "winnings" (profits) into the game until the real "killing" is made. Such behaviour poses adjustment problems for the host country because the eventual large repayment can disrupt its balance of payments stability.

Underlying this hypotheses are three relevant features. First, the subsidiary is assumed to be largely independent of the parent. This may be because of (physical or psychic) distance, because of the need for local judgement or because of the lack of a firm-wide (global) strategy. Second, the differences between establishing a foreign subsidiary rather than a domestic subsidiary are relevant. The rate of return on a foreign subsidiary needs to be higher in order to compensate for the greater risks. Moreover, foreign investment is often in the nature of an exploratory strategy in order to see if further foreign investment is desirable. Therefore, the risk averse firm is likely, initially at least, to under-invest and begin on a small scale. The initial, limited, investment economises on the costs of investment and organisation. Thus, the gambler's earnings hypothesis is a primitive form of the real options analysis of internationalisation (Buckley, Casson, & Gulamhussen, 2002). Third, this process has a dynamic. At the point when the firm has a (small) successful foreign subsidiary, uncertainty is lower and the costs of search for further profits approximate to zero. Rather than scanning the world for further, possibly more profitable opportunities, the firm will re-invest in its safest best – its existing subsidiary. It may well be that the firm will continue to re-invest long after this is justified by a comparison of rates of return with other alternatives, if they are considered at all. In other words, these approaches hypothesise that multinational firms exhibit a bias towards existing, profitable subsidiaries in their investment decisions (Buckley, 1989).

The 'gambler's earnings' hypothesis is not a complete explanation of FDI and especially of FDI by established multinational firms used to monitoring global, or even regional, opportunities. The hypotheses may still have validity for (small) firms where the costs of information and coordination are high. It may apply to first time or naïve foreign investors. In the long run, the behaviour hypothesised results in missed opportunities, declining rates of return and the loss of coordination gains from internationalisation. However, it does prefigure the current real options theorising on internationalisation.

Maurice Byé, drawing on the traditions of French, and English, economics, produced a stimulating but idiosyncratic paper "Self Financed Multi-Territorial Units and their Time Horizon" in 1957, published in English in 1958. Byé describes a "large unit" as "an organised set of resources depending on a single decision centre capable of autonomous action in the market" (p. 148). Thus the "large multiterritorial unit (LMU)" may not be a single firm – an important point given current attention to networks of firms (references) following single strategies or "global factories" (Buckley, 2003; Buckley & Ghauri, 2004). Byé however speaks throughout of large firms and concentrates particularly on the extractive industries. His key point is that "a large firm is one whose plans are to some extent independent of the market and which, by the same token, can choose the length of its planning period" (p. 148). LMU's do not simply react to market stimuli. Following Cournot, the firm is seen as a centre of decision making and planning. The conception is dynamic, because Byé (following Joan Robinson (1953)), wishes to include a theory of expectations. The decision of LMUs therefore depends on prices, the rate of output, the length of the planning period and the rate of investment. The time horizon is seen as a "strategic variable in the behaviour of the large firm" (p. 149). Byé explicitly compares the decisions of LMUs with those of governments "There is nothing absurd in comparing the decisions of such a firm, its optima, its growth, its foreign trade and its internal financing with those of governments responsible for the long-run objectives, optima, growth and control of the foreign trade of nations" (Byé, 1958a, p. 150).

86 *Peter J. Buckley*

Byé (1958a) goes on to provide a model of the LMU in the extractive industries. The model examines the optimum rate of extraction of existing reserves and the tapping of new reserves. The ability of LMUs to self-finance is related to the duration of exploitation – a composite of the time horizon of the firm and the level of uncertainty (including political uncertainty concerning nationalisation). "Uncertainty also encourages geographical diversification" (p. 159). The firm's decisions on keeping resources in reserve, exploiting first its high cost resources or its low cost resources depend on the marginal cost of developing resources and the financing of exploitation. Again, Byé comes back to the length of plan of the LMU as critical in developing and exploiting natural resources. Control over reserves is one source of power of the LMU; the other is control over the market. Byé considers that cartelisation is an attempt to coordinate the length of planning periods under the control of big (American) companies (p. 167). The planning periods of LMUs may conflict with national governments. This will be reflected in the conflict between the LMUs "balance of payments" (its exports, imports, profits and capital movements) versus the host countries' balance of payments. For Byé, this conflict is not ameliorated by the development impact of LMUs in the host country. "Large international units do not really constitute "development poles" in underdeveloped economies, but are merely very rich taxpayers" (Byé, 1958a, p. 174).

For Byé, international capital movements implied an overlapping of "areas of private control" with "areas of public control" (p. 174). He utilises the term "direct investment" when discussing U.S. Department of Commerce Statistics (p. 175). "Direct investment is almost entirely financed out of the firm's own profits and there are practically no transfers at all between one industry and another" (Byé, 1958a, p. 175). The intra-industry nature of FDI is forcefully noted – "There could be no other explanation for a situation in which capital returns are 17 per cent in the petroleum industry and 6 per cent in manufacturing industry" (p. 175). This is a point worthy of Hymer himself – the industrial organisation explanation of FDI is latent in Byés 1958aByé's 1958 paper. The world capital market clearly has strong, definite barriers to movement between industries. Byé also notes two way movement of capital within industries and the dualistic nature of development in poor countries caused by the enclaves of LMUs. LMUs are however a currency area phenomenon. "No LMU could cut itself loose from its currency area without modifying one of the fundamental data of its plans, namely its financing conditions" (Byé, 1958a, p. 177). This anticipates the "home currency advantage" theory of Aliber (1970, 1971).

Byé's final synthesis anticipates the later work of Hymer (1970, 1971) in suggesting an increasing concentration of the oil (or extractive) industries – "If it is true that self-financing implies that only the most powerful firms can engage in international ventures; if these firms try to optimize their planning periods by maintaining high reserves/output rates; and if long

The Theory of International Business Pre-Hymer 87

plans can be profitable only in connection with a very large capital market and a very large consumption market – then the firms satisfying all these conditions must tend to acquire a growing part of world reserves" (1958, p. 177). Byé's (1958) analysis focuses on (internal) finance and its relation to the time horizon of large firms as a key explanation for FDI, particularly in extractive industries. In this it parallels Penrose's (1956) piece. It is perhaps international financial movements, and their salience that brought the MNE to the forefront of theorising (together with issues on the foreign control of domestic industry, particularly in Canada). Byé's work puts MNEs firmly in the industrial organisation mode of analysis but also emphasises currency area advantages. The solid differentiation between the LMU and its external markets (for finance, for resources) makes this rather curious paper fit well within the Coasean internalisation tradition. Its inferences for competition and more particularly for restriction of competition anticipate Hymer's emphasis on oligopoly and of the increasing power of autonomous MNEs.

Byé's paper is not referred to in Hymer (1960) (although Hymer later contributed a paper to a symposium of Byé's (1958b)) and, as a generalisation, Byé's paper did not have a large impact on theorising FDI. In this sense, Byé 1958aByé's 1958 paper became a neglected contribution, largely because of its unorthodox approach.

15. Conclusion

Hymer's thesis drew on a restricted range of then current economic theory. He eschewed works on imperialism to which he turned in a later phase of his career. He also ignored a rich vein of work on cartels that could have shed light on the competitive and anti-competitive behaviour of large firms.

It is untrue to say that there was no international business theory before Hymer (1960) and Dunning (1958). However, the theory that existed was uncodified, unsystematic, fragmented and not institutionalised in an academic discipline. Both "international management", superbly exemplified by Phelps (1936) and "international business" (Lewis, 1938, 1948) had generated testable hypotheses derived from data and had progressed to generalisation, the former from qualitative information collected from (largely) unstructured interviews, the latter from substantial datasets. The incorporation of their insights into theorising such as Dunning's eclectic theory (Dunning, 1977) has not been influential in subsequent theoretical development because more academic foundations were sought – notably Bain (1956) for Hymer (1960) and Coase (1937) for Buckley and Casson (1976). This is to some degree an opportunity missed, but perhaps not irretrievably.

Considered as a book of theory, Hymer drew on few sources – Bain (1956) in particular, Coase (1937) unwittingly and perhaps Penrose (1956, 1959). In giving a clear conceptual lead, Hymer was successful. The addition of Coasean concepts by Buckley and Casson (1976) and the parallel development of location theory provided further key theoretical building blocks. The neglect of (Schumpeterian) innovation as a driver has been corrected in more recent works (Schumpeter, 1934, 1942). However, much previous theoretical innovation was buried in largely empirical works such as Phelps (1934), Marshall et al. (1936) and Dunning (1958). A great deal of previous theorising has been ignored because of its lack of conceptual clarity and its non-cumulative nature. However, pre-Hymer theorising has several virtues. First, it is deeply empirically grounded. Second, it integrates international business theorising on FDI and the MNE with international management concepts such as cultural differences and methods of operating in foreign environments. Third, it provides avenues for the reconsideration of theoretical advances such as the relationship between FDI and trade at all levels (firm, region, industry, nation), the interaction between inflows and outflows of FDI and two-way investment, and the external consequences and effects of FDI. One of the underestimated advances of modern international business theory is to integrate macro perspectives (the country, balance of payments flows, national assets and liabilities) and micro elements (the multinational firm). This is done by the device of attributing a single nationality to "the firm". This has downsides too, because all the activities of Toyota, for example, are not attributable to Japan and subsidiaries are not simple unthinking appendages of the parent firm. Following Hymer, we are able to achieve a greater degree of synthesis. Hymer drew on a restricted range of sources and his virtue was to give the theory of the multinational enterprise a clear analytical core. The insights of Hymer were perhaps achieved precisely because he did not cast his conceptual net widely.

16. Managerial relevance

Early, pre-Hymer (1960) theorising on international business and the strategy of the multinational enterprise has several insights for current managers. First, it is necessary to have a clear understanding of the role of cultural differences and the impact that these are likely to have on operating strategies in particular host countries both when considering entry and in the operating period. Second, the modes of operating abroad are important and the subtleties of choice go beyond simplistic views of export versus foreign direct investment. Finally, early international business theorising encourages managers to think beyond immediate tactical decisions to the holistic relationship between the firm and its external environments.

Notes

1. I am grateful to Mark Casson, Mira Wilkins and two anonymous referees for comments on earlier drafts.

The Theory of International Business Pre-Hymer 89

2. John Dunning and Sarianna Lundan (2008) sum up their views as follows:"Prior to the 1960s there was no established theory of the MNE or of FDI. Attempts to explain the activities of firms outside their national boundaries represented an amalgam of:
   1. A fairly well-formalised theory of (portfolio) capital movements (Iversen, 1935);
   2. A number of empirical and largely country-specific studies on the factors influencing the location of FDI (Barlow, 1953; Dunning, 1958; Marshall et al., 1936; Southard, 1931);
   3. A recognition by some economists, notably Williams (1929), that the internationalisation of some industries required a modification to neoclassical theories of trade;
   4. An appreciation that the common ownership of the cross-border activities of firms could not only be considered as a substitute for the international cartels and combines (Plummer, 1934), but could also be explained, in part at least, by the perceived gains of vertical or horizontal integration (Penrose, 1956; Byé, 1958a): and
   5. An extension of the extant theory of international capital movements to embrace the role of entrepreneurship and business competence (Lund, 1944). Lund refers to this combination of entrepreneurial ideas and financial capital as an 'international wandering combination'."
3. I owe the emphases of this paragraph to an anonymous referee. For other works on Hymer see special issues of *International Business Review* (2006) and *Contributions to Political Economy* (2002).

References

Aharoni, Y. (1966). *The foreign investment decision process*. Cambridge, Mass: Harvard UP.

Aliber, R. Z. (1970). A theory of foreign direct investment. In C. P. Kindleberger (Ed.), *The international firm*. Cambridge, Mass: MIT Press.

Aliber, R. Z. (1971). The multinational enterprise in a multiple currency world. In *The multinational enterprise* (pp. 49–56). London: George Allen & Unwin.

Allen, G. C., & Donnithorne, A. G. (1957). *Western enterprise in Indonesia and Malaya: A study in economic development*. London: George Allen & Unwin.

Arndt, T. W. (1957). Overseas borrowing – The new model. *Economic Record, XXXIII* (August).

Bain, J. S. (1956). *Barriers to new competition*. Cambridge, Mass: Harvard University Press.

Barlow, E. R. (1953). *Management of foreign manufacturing subsidiaries*. Cambridge, Mass: Harvard University Press.

Barlow, E. R., & Wender, I. T. (1955). *Foreign investment and taxation*. Englewood Cliffs, NJ: Prentice-Hall.

Barratt Brown, M. (1974). *The economics of imperialism*. Harmondsworth: Penguin.

Benaerts, P. (1933). *Les Origines de la Grande Industrie Allemande*. Paris: Editions F H Turot.

Blyth, C. D., & Carty, E. B. (1956). Non resident ownership of Canadian Industry. *Canadian Journal of Economics and Political Science*, 452–458.

Brecher, I., & Reisman, S. S. (1957). *Canada–United States economic relations*. Ottawa: Royal Commission on Canada's Economic Prospects.

90 *Peter J. Buckley*

Buckley, P. J. (1989). Foreign direct investment by small and medium-sized enterprises: The theoretical background. *Small Business Economics, 1*(2): 89–100 (reprinted in Peter J Buckley (1989). The multinational enterprise: theory and application, Basingstoke: Macmillan).

Buckley, P. J. (Ed.) (2003). *International business*. Aldershot: Ashgate (History of Management Thought Series).

Buckley, P. J. (2006). Stephen Hymer: Three phases, one approach? *International Business Review, 15*(2): 140–147 (Special Issue on Stephen Herbert Hymer and/or the (Theory of the) MNE and International Business).

Buckley, P. J., & Casson, M. (1976). *The future of the multinational enterprise*. London: Macmillan.

Buckley, P. J., & Ghauri, P. N. (2004). Globalisation, economic geography and the strategy of multinational enterprises. *Journal of International Business Studies, 35*(2): 81–98.

Buckley, P. J., Casson, M., & Gulamhussen, M. A. (2002). Internationalisation – Real options, knowledge management and the Uppsala approach. In Virpi Havila, M. Mats Forsgen, & H. Hakansson (Eds.), *Critical perspectives on internationalisation* (pp. 229–262). Oxford: Elsevier Science.

Buckley, P. J., & Lessard, D. R. (2005). Regaining the edge for international business research. *Journal of International Business Studies, 36*(6): 595–599.

Bukharin, N. (1918). *Imperialism and world economy*. London: Merlin Press. (1970 edition).

Burns, A. R. (1936). *The decline of competition: A study of the evolution of american industry*. New York: McGraw-Hill.

Byé, M. (1958a). *Self-financed multi territorial units and their time horizon*. International Economic Association International Economic papers No. 8, New York: the Macmillan Company (original French version 1957).

Byé, M. (Ed.). (1958). *Lo politique industrielle de L'Europe Integrée et L'Apport Des Capitaux Exteriérs*. Paris: Presses Univeritaires de France.

Cairncross, A. K. (1953). *Home and foreign investment 1870–1913*. Cambridge: Cambridge University Press.

Callis, H. G. (1942). *Foreign capital in South East Asia*. New York.

Casson, M. (1985a). Multinational monopolies and international cartels. In Peter J. Buckley & Mark Casson (Eds.), *The economic theory of the multinational enterprise*. London: Macmillan.

Casson, M. (1985b). The theory of foreign direct investment. In J. Peter, Buckley, & Mark Casson (Eds.), *The economic theory of the multinational enterprise*. London: Macmillan.

Coase, R. H. (1937). The nature of the firm. *Economica (new series), 4*: 386–405.

Contributions to Political Economy. (2002). In C. N. Pitelis, & R. Sugden (Eds.), Vol. 21, No. 1, Special Issue on Stephen Hymer and the Multinational Enterprise.

Dunning, J. H. (1958). *American investment in British manufacturing industry*. London: George Allen & Unwin.

Dunning, J. H. (1972). *International investment*. Harmondsworth: Penguin Books.

Dunning, J. H. (1977). Trade, location of economic activity and the MNEs. In B. Ohlin, P. Hesselborn, & P. Wijkman (Eds.), *The international allocation of economic activity* (pp. 395–418). London: Macmillan.

Dunning, J. H., & Lundan, S. M. (2008). *Multinational enterprises and the global economy*. Cheltenham: Edward Elgar.

The Theory of International Business Pre-Hymer 91

Dunning, J. H., & Pitelis, C. N. (2008). Stephen Hymer's contribution to international business scholarship: An assessment and extension. *Journal of International Business Studies, 39*(1): 167–176.

Fellner, W. (1949). *Competition among the few*. New York: Alfred A Knopf.

Frankel, S. H. (1938). *Capital investment in Africa: Its courses and effects*. London: Oxford University Press.

Frolich, P. (1940). *Rosa luxemburg*. London: Victor Gollancz.

Hexner, E. (1946). *International cartels*. London: Sir Isaac Pitman & Sons Ltd.

Hilferding, R. (1910). Das Finanzkapital. Translation edited by Tom Bottomore (1981) as Finance Capital: A study of the latest phase of capitalist development. London: Routledge and Keegan Paul.

Hilton Young, E. (1912). *Foreign companies and other corporations*. Cambridge: Cambridge University Press.

Hobson, J. A. (1902). *Imperialism: A study*. London: Unwin Hyman. Third Edition 1988.

Hobson, C. K. (1914). *The export of capital*. London: Constable (Reprinted 1963 with Introduction by Roy Harrod, London: Constable).

Hubbard, G. E. (1935). *Eastern industrialization and its effect on the West: With special reference to Great Britain and Japan*. London: Oxford University Press.

Hymer, S. H. (1960). *The international operations of national firms*. Cambridge, Mass: MIT Press. (published 1976).

Hymer, S. H. (1968). The impact of the multinational firm. In Maurice Byé (Ed.), *La Politique Industrielle de L'Europe Integrée et L'Apport des Capitaux Exteriéurs* (pp. 7–29). Paris: Presses Universitaires de France.

Hymer, S. H. (1970). The efficiency (contradictions) of the Multinational Corporation. *Papers and Proceedings of the American Economic Association*, May.

Hymer, S. H. (1971). The multinational corporation and the law of uneven development. In J. Bhagwati (Ed.), *Economics and world order* (pp. 113–140). New York: World Law Fund.

International Business Review. (2006). Vol. 15 No. 2 Special Issue on S. H. Hymer and the theory of the MNE and International Business edited by C. N. Pitelis.

Iversen, C. (1935). *Some aspects of the theory of international capital movements*. Copenhagen: Einer Munksgaard.

Jasay, A. E. (1960). The social choice between home and overseas investment. *Economic Journal, 70*: 105–113.

Jenks, L. H. (1927). *The migration of British capital to 1875*. New York: Knopf.

Kindleberger, C. P. (1969). *American business abroad*. New Haven: Yale University Press.

Kindleberger. C. P. (1988). The "New" multinationalization of business. *ASEAN Economic Bulletin, 5*(November), 113–124.

Knox, F. A. (1957). United States capital investments in Canada. *American Economic Review, Papers and Proceedings, 47*(2): 596–609.

Lenin, V. I. (1917). *Imperialism – The highest stage of capitalism*. London: Progress Publishers. (1970 edition).

Lewis, C. (1938). *America's stake in international investments*. Washington D.C. The Brookings Institution.

Lewis, C. (1948). *The United States and foreign investment*. Washington D.C. The Brookings Institution.

Lund, A. (1944). Kapitalbevaegelses – teorien og de direkte investeringer. *Nationalokonomisk Tidsskrift*, 28–57.

Luxemberg, R. (1913). (English edition 1951) *The accumulation of capital*. London: Routledge.

Ma, X., & Delios, A. (2007). A new tale of two cities: Japanese FDIs in Shanghai and Beijing, 1979–2003. *International Business Review, 16*(2): 207–228.

MacDougall, G. D. A. (1960). The benefits and costs of private investment from abroad: A theoretical approach. *Economic Record, 36*: 13–35.

Marshall, H., Southard, F. A., Jr., & Taylor, K. W. (1936). *Canadian-American industry: A study of international investment*. New Haven: Yale University Press.

Mason, E. S. (1946). *Controlling world trade: Cartels and commodity agreement*. New York: McGraw-Hill.

McLean, J. C., & Haigh, P. W. (1954). *The growth of integrated oil companies*. Boston: Harvard Business School Press.

Mommsen, W. J. (1980). *Theories of imperialism (Translated P. S. Falla)*. Chicago: University of Chicago Press.

Mun, T. (1664). *England's Treasure by Foreign Trade*. London: Thomas Clark. Republished in J. R. McCulloch (1954) *Early English Tracts on Commerce*, Cambridge: Cambridge University Press.

Nurkse, R. (1933). Causes and effects of capital movements. In H. John & Dunning (Eds.), *International Investment*. Middlesex: Penguin Books.

Pedersen, K., & Strandskov J. (2006). Arne Lund. 1944. *On FDI – A neglected Danish contribution*. Mimeo: University of Aarhus, Denmark.

Penrose, E. T. (1956). Foreign investment and the growth of the firm. *Economic Journal, 66*: 220–235.

Penrose, E. T. (1959). *The theory of the growth of the firm*. Oxford: Basil Blackwell.

Phelps, D. M. (1936). *Migration of industry to South America*. New York: McGraw-Hill.

Plummer, A. (1934). *International combines in modern industry*. London: Isaac Pitman. (second edition 1938, Third edition 1951).

Radice, H. (Ed.). (1975). *International firms and modern imperialism*. Harmondsworth: Penguin Books.

Remer, C. F. (1933). *Foreign investment in China*. New York: Macmillan. Second edition with new introduction (1968) New York: Howard Fertig.

Rippy, J. F. (1944, 1947). *Latin America and the industrial age*. New York: G. P. Putnam's Sons (reprinted 1971, Greenwood Press, Wesport, Conn).

Robinson, J. (1953). Imperfect competition revisited. *Economic Journal*, September.

Sammonds, R. L., & Abelson M. (1942). *American Direct Investments in foreign countries–1940*. US Department of Commerce, Economic Series No. 20.

Sanchez-Peinado, E., & Pla-Barber, J. (2006). A multidimensional concept of uncertainty and its influence on the entry mode choice: An empirical analysis in the service sector. *International Business Review, 15*(3): 215–232.

Schumpeter, J. (1934). *The theory of economic development: An inquiry into profits, capital, credit, interest and the business cycle. (Translated R. Opie)*. Cambridge, MA: Harvard University Press.

Schumpeter, J. (1942). *Capitalism, socialism and democracy*. New York: Harper & Brothers.

Schumpeter, J. (1951). In Paul M. Sweezy (Ed.), *Imperialism and social classes*. Oxford: Oxford University Press.

Smith, A. (1976). *An inquiry in the nature and causes of the wealth of nation*. Chicago: University of Chicago Press.

Southard, F. A. (1931). *American industry in Europe*. Boston: Houghton Mifflin Company.

Staley, E. (1935). *War and the private investor.* New York: Doubleday Doran & Company Inc.

Staley, E. (1939). *World economy in transition.* New York: Kennikat Press (1971 Reprint).

Teece, D. J. (2006). Reflections on the Hymer thesis and the multinational enterprise. *International Business Review, 15*(2): 124–139.

Townshend, J. (1990). *J. A. Hobson,* Manchester: Manchester University Press.

United States Department of Commerce, Bureau of Foreign and Domestic Commerce. (1931). *A new estimate of American investments abroad.* Trade Information Bulletin No. 767, Washington DC: US Department of Commerce.

Vernon, R. (1966). International investment and international trade in the product cycle. *Quarterly Journal of Economics, 80*: 190–207.

Wilkins, M. (1977). Modern European economic history and the multinationals. *Journal of European Economic History, 6*(3): 575–595.

Williams, J. H. (1929). The theory of international trade reconsidered. *Economic Journal, 39*(154): 195–209.

Williamson, A. (1894). *British industries and foreign competition.* London: Simpkin Marshal Hamilton Kent & Co.

Wilson, C. H. (1954). *The history of Unilever: a study in economic growth and social change.* London: Cassell.

Wu, Y. (1946). International capital investment and the development of poor countries. *Economic Journal, 56*(221): 86–101.

5
The Governance of the Multinational Enterprise: Insights from Internalization Theory

Co-authored with Roger Strange

Introduction

Internalization theory has long provided one of the main theoretical rationales for the existence of the multinational enterprise. It is founded on the basic idea that the exploitation of firms' knowledge-based assets across national boundaries is often most efficiently undertaken internally within the hierarchical structure of the multinational enterprise (MNE). Internalization theory has not been without its critics, notably by proponents of the evolutionary theory of the firm (Kogut and Zander, 1993). We believe that much of this criticism is misplaced, but that nevertheless the extant literature on internalization theory has focused too much on imperfections in the external markets for knowledge transfer. We argue below that not enough attention has been given to both the nature and the significance of the transactions costs associated with the internal transfer of knowledge and to some of the underlying assumptions of the theory.

In particular, we wish to suggest two promising lines of future research. The first focuses on the internal transaction costs associated with the governance and organization of the activities within the MNE, and here we highlight the costs of information acquisition and transmission, the costs of coordination, and the costs of aligning the interests of different stakeholders within the MNE. The second addresses the implications of different assumptions about the risk propensity of the MNE. Internalization theory implicitly assumes that the MNE is risk-neutral, but we argue that there are many reasons to believe that this assumption is unrealistic. Further to this point, different attitudes to risk can have an impact upon the preferred governance structure for international transactions (Chiles and McMackin, 1996).

Internalization theory

Internalization theory has its origins in the work of Coase (1937), who sought to explain the existence of the firm as an institution, and why is came to

The Governance of the Multinational Enterprise   95

supersede the market. His answer, in short, was that there were transaction costs in effecting exchanges through the market, and that the firm would emerge if the costs of organizing these exchanges within a firm were lower. Internalization theory (Buckley and Casson, 1976; Hennart, 1982; Hymer, 1968; McManus, 1972; Rugman, 1981) extends these arguments to the MNE, and emphasizes the relative costs and benefits of coordinating economic activities across national boundaries internally by the management of a firm rather than externally through the market.

Buckley and Casson (1976) point out that the production of most goods and/or services involves a range of activities, which are connected by flows of intermediate products. These intermediate products include not only semi-processed materials passed from one industry to another, but also various types of knowledge and expertise embodied in human capital, patents, and other intangible assets. The efficient coordination of these activities requires a complete set of markets in the intermediate products, involving large numbers of buyers and sellers, no information asymmetries, and no externalities. But the external markets for many intermediate products suffer from a range of imperfections (DeGennaro, 2005). These imperfections typically include: (a) the lack of futures markets for the coordination of activities involving significant time lags; (b) the impracticability of discriminatory pricing to efficiently exploit market power; (c) indeterminate bargaining situations resulting from bilateral concentrations of market power; (d) buyer uncertainty about the nature and quality of the intermediate product; and (e) government interventions such as tariffs, taxes, and restrictions on capital movements (Buckley and Casson, 1976, pp. 37–8). These imperfections are particularly significant in the markets for knowledge-based assets and capabilities (e.g. R&D), and there is thus an incentive to bypass them and bring the activities under common ownership. If these activities are located in different countries, then an MNE will result.

Internalization theory has been characterized as a static theory, though a dynamic element can be introduced by incorporating an analysis of the innovation process (Buckley and Casson, 1976, pp. 34–86). Internalization theory is primarily a theory of the MNE as a governance mechanism, rather than a theory of what underpins the growth of MNEs (Cantwell, 2001). This latter issue is the concern of resource-based theory (Barney, 1986; 1991, Peteraf, 1993; Wernerfelt, 1984) and the evolutionary theory of the MNE (Kogut and Zander, 1993): theories which emphasize the heterogeneous firm-specific advantages that enable some firms to develop sustainable competitive advantages, and thus earn above-normal rents and grow. Notwithstanding the differences in emphasis, the two approaches are essentially complementary. As Mahoney (2001, pp. 655–6) points out, resource-based theory delineates the set of market imperfections that lead to sustainable rents, while internalization theory hypothesizes that the existence of those rents is sufficient to explain the existence of the MNE.

Governance and internal transaction costs

The internalization decision has been well analysed in the analysis of the growth of the (multinational) firm. What has not been so well analysed is the precise configuration of the internal architecture of the firm; that is, its governance structure (Buckley and Carter, 1996, 2002, 2003).

An attempt to show the power of these ideas was made by Teece (1983), who investigated technological and organizational factors as determining the scope of the firm through production costs. Teece's analysis of horizontal integration envisages governance costs and production costs as both being a function of an 'index of the complexity of know-how' in the firm. Governance costs of different forms of doing business abroad (licensing versus foreign direct investment, FDI) are a function of the complexity of technology. He assumes that the FDI mode is invariant to increasing complexity of knowledge because of the ease with which tacit knowledge can be transferred by internal markets. In contrast, the governance costs of licensing increase with the complexity of knowledge because of increasing costs of firm-to-firm transfer. A similar evaluation is made of the production costs in each mode. Production costs and governance costs are then summed to give the total costs of the modes of doing business abroad so that an optimal scope of horizontal integration is given for each level of complexity of know-how. A parallel exercise is conducted for vertical integration. Market-based relations are contrasted with vertically integrated relations by making their governance costs of market relations and vertical integration functions of an index of asset specificity where vertical integration has both a set-up cost (higher than setting up market relationships) and a lower variable cost of operation. As asset specificity increases, so does the possibility of integration.

In Teece's model (which has much in common with Buckley and Casson, 1981), governance costs are a function of complexity of knowledge and asset specificity. There is also a (minor) international determinant of governance costs of integration – the risk of expropriation. The greater these risks, the more international governance costs will rise, favouring arm's length relationships (licensing, purchasing) rather than internal ones (FDI, integration). Teece's analysis is an interesting attempt to put governance costs centre-stage in the analysis of MNEs, but it does so only as an intermediate variable – the real drivers are complexity of (tacit) knowledge and asset specificity – and it has a weak international dimension. That governance costs and production costs are separable and additive also requires justification, at the least.

If we step back from Teece's exposition to Williamson's basic framework, we can first agree with Williamson's most recent work that markets and hierarchies are not dichotomous alternatives, but may be more like extreme points on a continuum. Williamson (1979, p. 103) argues that 'governance structures – the institutional matrix within which transactions are negotiated and executed – vary with the nature of the transaction'. All transactions are not equal. Some may be endowed with social characteristics which others lack. Moreover, repeated transactions may take on a different character than one-off deals. This opens the possibilities for a more rounded discussion of governance costs.

These theoretical arguments on the internal organization of the firm suggest two polar extremes. On the one hand, there is the purist view of internalization, expounded by Buckley and Casson (1976, 1985), in which the firm functions as an approximation to a perfect market. This can be contrasted, on the other hand, with the 'markets and hierarchies' approach of Williamson (1975, 1979), which considers that integration (internalization) is accompanied by suspension of the price mechanism and the allocation of internal resources by management fiat. In the first of these approaches, the firm's internal organization is designed so as to transmit shadow prices to managers between decentralized cost centres and profit centres, so that the overall profits are maximized (Buckley, 1983). Each decision-maker within the firm maximizes profits, given the internal prices; in effect, the firm includes in these prices an optimal tax, leaving members with an income which is just enough to keep them in their present employment (Hirshleifer, 1956). In contrast, the 'markets and hierarchies' approach asserts either that bounded rationality and opportunism render it impossible to find the 'correct' prices even in an internalized market, or that individuals' responses to price would result in damaging externalities for the rest of the organization. Hierarchy overcomes these problems by constraining actions through management directive rather than price signals, replacing the market by another mechanism and not merely internalizing it.

In practice, internal organization often lies between these two extremes. The activities within the firm are many and various, and are undertaken by many different individuals. There are linkages between the activities of different individuals, in that the actions of one are typically complementary to those of other individuals. The strategy followed by the firm, and ultimately the value of the firm, depends upon how these activities are coordinated (Buckley and Carter, 1996). But the actual internal division of labour gives rise to three problems of organizational design. The first is the information problem, which arises because few individuals within the firm are likely to possess all the information that they require to choose the optimal action for which they have responsibility. The division of labour within the firm suggests that the requisite information is likely to be held by different individuals, and furthermore there will typically be uncertainty over the effects of any particular course of action. The second is the coordination problem, which arises from the complementarity of actions. Perfect coordination can typically only be achieved by allocating all tasks to the same individual, but an approximation to this may be achieved through individuals working together within teams. The third is the motivation problem, which arises from the differences between the goals of the employees, the managers, and the shareholders. Each will typically favour actions which maximize their own utility, but which may or may not be consistent with the objective function of the firm. For instance, employees may shirk in their duties, whilst managers may initiate firm strategies from which they derive private benefits even if such strategies are non-optimal for the firm. Now it would be possible to formulate an optimal strategy to maximize the objective function of the firm (e.g. to maximize the value of the firm) if:

- all members of the firm had access to the best decision-relevant knowledge (perfect information);
- all complementary actions were chosen jointly (perfect coordination); and
- all members of the firm shared the firm's objective function (perfect motivation).

In practice, this is highly unlikely and there will be both *costs* and *losses* which are the result of derogation from the optimal set of actions. These internal transaction *costs* include: the costs of acquiring and transmitting information (information costs); the costs of communication about complementary actions or of providing for them to be combined (coordination costs); and the cost of incentive schemes to align the actions of the members of the firm with the objectives of the firm (motivation costs). These motivation costs would include both the costs of managerial supervision and monitoring of employees' actions and/or the costs of training and socializing designed to induce employees to adopt the firm's objectives, and the agency costs which arise from the fact that the principals (shareholders) have delegated responsibility of the day-to-day operations of the firm to agents (managers). The *losses* include: the reduction in the optimal pay-off to the firm caused by members not having the best available information (information loss); the reduction in the pay-off to the firm arising when complementary actions are not chosen jointly (coordination loss); and the reduction in the pay-off to the firm caused by members pursuing their own objectives (motivation loss). These losses are, in effect, internal 'externalities' arising from the division of managerial labour within the firm, and the associated costs measure the resources deployed in correcting the externalities. The goal of the firm's governance structure is to minimize the sum of these internal transaction costs and the losses.

The organizational externalities and costs (information, coordination, and motivation), and therefore problems of governance, will be more severe in MNEs than in purely domestic firms (Buckley and Carter, 1996). The simplest set of factors which increase the *information* costs of communication and the

The Governance of the Multinational Enterprise 99

exchange of ideas and knowledge is the spatial separation of individuals who hold complementary knowledge and who could gain from coordinating the actions. Spatially-separated individuals are also likely to have different first languages, notwithstanding the adoption of English as the world's business language. Furthermore, there may be more fundamental differences between national outlooks and routines, which fundamentally influence communication and *coordination*. Hedlund and Nonaka (1993) examine the way in which information and knowledge are constructed in different cultures. They summarize common perceptions about the differences between Japanese and Western firms in terms of differences in the extent to which the firm's knowledge is 'tacit' or 'articulated' and the degree to which knowledge is held by individuals or groups. Western firms are characterized by individually held, articulated knowledge and Japanese firms by tacit knowledge held at the level of the group. More generally, there are numerous differences in the everyday assumptions (norms) which individuals make about the actions of others in a given situation, about the standards of acceptable behaviour and the interpretation of tacit signals such as body language, which play a major part in the successful coordination of the actions of groups. These differences in routines may in themselves imply differences in performance of some kinds of task (cf. Buckley and Casson, 1992, pp. 228–31), but where related tasks are to be carried out by individuals who hold different social and cultural assumptions, the dangers of misunderstanding and misinformation may detract significantly from the joint effectiveness of the collaboration, unless considerable time (and expense) is spent in developing mutual understanding. There is considerable evidence that cross-border knowledge transfer within the MNE suffers from 'internal stickiness', and typically requires adaptation to the local context. Furthermore, the need for adaptation increases as the institutional distance between the home and host countries increases (Jensen and Szulanski, 2004).

It may be particularly difficult to *motivate* individuals in different countries diligently to pursue the interests of the organization as a whole. Jensen and Meckling (1976, pp. 328–30) suggest that the magnitude of these agency costs depend *inter alia* on the inherent complexity and geographic dispersion of the firms' activities, and are thus likely to be more substantial in MNEs. In the conventional economic arguments on moral hazard and adverse selection in organizations, the monitoring problem is exacerbated by the geographic and cultural distances involved in multinational operations. The risks of opportunism may therefore be higher, and the costs of counter-measures may be higher too. In cultures which do not conform to the individualist stereotype, individuals may identify with a group or community, within which they behave altruistically, or with the shared interest of the community in mind. Thus, it may be expected that individuals will favour the perceived interests of their national subsidiary rather than the overall interests of the firm.

Governance and attitudes to risk

An implicit assumption in internalization theory is that the MNE is risk-neutral, and thus that the optimal governance structure can be determined simply by reference to the comparative costs of effecting exchanges through the market and within the hierarchy of the MNE. But this assumption is too simplistic for several reasons.

First, firms do not exhibit stable risk preferences, but 'show unstable risk-taking behavior in the neighbourhood of death, relatively high levels of risk taking when slack resources are large, risk seeking in the neighbourhood of a target, a tendency to change risk preference over time with the same resources, and a tendency to underestimate risks as a result of favourable experience with them' (March and Shapira, 1992, p. 181). Chiles and McMackin (1996, p. 82) argue that, when a firm is more risk-seeking, the level of asset specificity at which hierarchical organization will be preferred to the market will *ceteris paribus* be greater. In other words, risk-seeking firms are less likely to be hierarchical than risk-averse firms when faced with the same configuration of transaction costs. One implication of this is that the boundary choice made by the MNE depends not only upon an evaluation of relative transactions costs, but also upon its wider context and upon its past history.

Second, firms do not make decisions about strategy: managers do. Managers may well be less risk-averse than the firm's shareholders, and thus may not actually seek out and/or implement the most efficient governance structure. Hermalin (1993) suggests that managers prefer risky strategies, since these are least informative about their abilities. Reputational risk is not the same as project risk, and the two do not even need to be highly correlated. Managers may also derive various private benefits from certain governance structures, and may favour a more hierarchical structure because their compensation is linked to firm size (Baker et al., 1988); because they derive power and prestige from being associated with a larger firm (Jensen, 1986); because their job security is enhanced (Shleifer and Vishny, 1989); or because a more diversified firm reduces the risks attached to their undiversified personal portfolios (Amihud and Lev, 1981). The shareholders may introduce monitoring and/or bonding mechanisms to curb this managerial discretion, but these add to the internal transaction costs. Such motivation costs, as noted above, are likely to be more significant in MNEs than in purely domestic firms. And, as Filatotchev and Wright note in their companion paper, different types of shareholders (family, institutions, the state) are also likely to have different attitudes towards risk (Eisenhardt, 1989).

Third, the various stakeholders' risk preferences – and hence the risk preference of the MNE – are likely to be influenced by volatility in the global economy. When markets are stable and stakeholders are able to predict comparative transaction costs with some certainty, then all stakeholders

The Governance of the Multinational Enterprise   101

will be prepared to be more risk-seeking (at least in relative terms) and the firm may rely more on market transactions. But when product, factor, and financial markets are volatile, all stakeholders are likely to become more risk-averse. The analysis of Chiles and McMackin (1996) suggests that this may increase the perceived costs of market governance and give rise to greater levels of hierarchical control over flows of intermediate products. This volatility will be all the more apparent in international markets for intermediate products, and greater hierarchical control within the MNE is to be expected.

In short, we thus suggest that the chosen governance structure will depend not only upon comparative transaction costs, but also upon the risk preferences of the key decision-makers, the extent of organizational slack, the firm's previous (favourable or unfavourable) experience of risky investments, and the health of the global economy.

A research agenda

The objectives of this paper have been to outline the contribution of internalization theory to our understanding of the governance of the MNE, and to highlight aspects of the theory that we believe have received insufficient attention and put forward some issues that merit further research. Figure 5.1 provides a diagrammatic representation of our arguments.

First, we have drawn attention to the various internal transactions costs associated with the governance and organization of activities within the MNE. It is not clear how substantial these costs might be in practice, although Tomassen and Benito (2009) report in their study of Norwegian MNEs that close to 40 per cent of the variation of subsidiary performance can be attributed to governance costs. More work quantifying the size and significance of governance costs would be welcome. Furthermore, it is not obvious how internal governance costs might be affected by the widespread adoption of information and communication technologies (ICT). Certainly, it might be expected that ICT should reduce information and coordination costs (Afuah, 2001), particularly in MNEs, but the impact upon motivation costs is unclear. On the one hand, ICT should facilitate managerial supervision and monitoring of the employees, but on the other hand, ICT might make it easier for managers to initiate non-optimal strategies from which they derive private benefits. It is also likely that ICT will reduce market transaction costs, so *a priori* the net impact upon the internalization decision will be indeterminate. A related issue is that internal transaction costs are likely to be very difficult to assess *ex ante*, particularly within the context of MNE operations in emerging markets, and may only become apparent in the post-contractual phase. This may lead to a reassessment of the optimal governance structure of overseas affiliates (Puck et al., 2009).

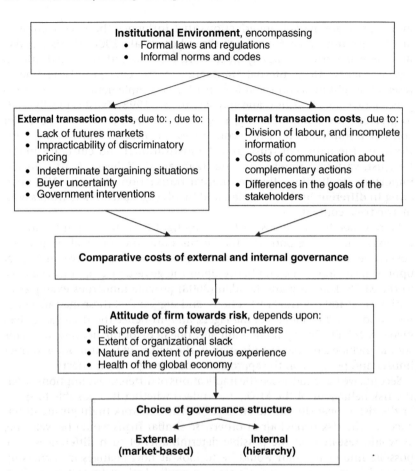

Figure 5.1 The choice of governance structure

There has been a considerable amount of published research on the interaction between the institutional environment and external transaction costs, and the implications for the governance structure of firms. For instance, Kogut and Singh (1988) considered the effects of national culture on entry mode. Oxley (1999) suggested that firms adopt more hierarchical governance structures in countries where the regimes for the protection of intellectual property are weak, whilst Brouthers (2002) found that MNEs favoured international joint ventures (IJVs) in markets characterized by stringent legal restrictions. Luo (2005) reported that the contractual structure of IJVs was contingent upon both the nature of the transactions and the institutional environment. Countries' institutional environments may also create market imperfections that influence the effectiveness of MNEs' resource-based advantages (Brouthers et al., 2008; Henisz, 2003). But there has been relatively little work on how different institutional environments affect internal transaction costs. One promising line of research might focus on the role of trust as a complement to more formal governance mechanisms (Lane and Bachmann, 1998). Trust typically leads to greater information sharing, more cooperative behaviour, and easier conflict resolution, and thus economizes on internal transaction costs. However, the nature of trust, and the institutional and cultural support for trust, vary in different countries (Zaheer and Zaheer, 2006). This has important implications for the internal transaction costs of MNEs operating in different host economies, and involving stakeholders from asymmetric trust contexts.

More generally, these observations highlight how differing institutional contexts – including both the formal rules and the informal norms that govern behaviour and structure social interaction – may have an impact upon transaction costs, and hence upon the governance options available to the MNE. Dunning and Lundan (2008) provide numerous examples of both formal and informal institutions, and suggest that these may affect the perceptions and ideologies of managers, and influence the strategic choices made by MNEs. Clearly there is ample scope here for further research. This should include a deeper examination of the nature of institutions and their impact and progress on the appropriate modelling of their effects.

Second, we have addressed the implications of different assumptions about the risk behaviour of the MNE, and indeed whether it is possible to speak of the risk propensity of the MNE *per se*. Further work highlighting differences in the risk behaviour of otherwise similar firms would be welcome, as would research on the possible determinants of such differences. One possible line of research would be to look at how changes in ownership (through, for instance, privatization or public listing) impact upon firm boundary decisions. It might be expected that firms with private owners would be more risk-averse than the same firms under public ownership, and thus that privatization should lead to a greater reliance on hierarchical governance structures. Equally, firms with widely-dispersed share ownership are likely to be more risk-seeking compared to the same firms under family ownership, as it is well established that family owners are typically risk-averse because much of their wealth is tied up in the one firm. Related to these points, what is the impact of acquisitions by shareholders from different countries? We have also drawn attention to the fact that it is the managers that make decisions about firm strategy, and that managers may well be less risk-averse than the shareholders. This highlights the need for further research on the process of (international) strategy formation by the managers of MNEs (Buckley et al., 2007), and the constraints under which such managers operate. It also points to the possibility of agency conflicts

104   *Peter J. Buckley and Roger Strange*

between the managers and the shareholders, and to the potential useful-ness of agency theory as a complement to internalization theory in under-standing the governance of the MNE.

Conclusions

Internalization theory has long provided a compelling rationale for the existence of the MNE as a governance mechanism, notwithstanding the rival claims of resource-based theory and the evolutionary theory of the firm. Despite its longevity, we would nevertheless argue that more research is required on the nature and significance of the internal transaction costs and on the actual process of strategy formulation by MNE managers. In this regard, there is scope for combining the insights of internalization theory with those of institutional analysis and agency theory, such as in the Counter–Point to this Point (Filatotchev and Wright, 2010).

References

Afuah, A. (2001). 'Dynamic boundaries of the firm: are firms better off being verti-cally integrated in the face of technological change?' *Academy of Management Journal*, **44**, 1211–28.

Amihud, Y. and Lev, B. (1981). 'Risk reduction as a managerial motive for conglom-erate mergers'. *Bell Journal of Economics*, **12**, 605–17.

Baker, G. P., Jensen, M. C. and Murphy, K. J. (1988). 'Compensation and incentives'. *Journal of Finance*, **43**, 593–616.

Barney, J. B. (1986). 'Strategic factor markets: expectations, luck and business strategy'. *Management Science*, **32**, 1231–41.

Barney, J. B. (1991). 'Firm resources and sustained competitive advantage'. *Journal of Management*, **17**, 99–120.

Brouthers, K. D. (2002). 'Institutional, cultural and transaction cost influences on entry mode choice and performance'. *Journal of International Business Studies*, **33**, 203–22.

Brouthers, K. D., Brouthers, L. D. and Werner, S. (2008). 'Resource-based advantages in an international context'. *Journal of Management*, **34**, 189–217.

Buckley, P. J. (1983). 'New theories of international business: some unresolved issues'. In Casson, M. (Ed.), *The Growth of International Business*. London: George Allen.

Buckley, P. J. and Carter, M. J. (1996). 'The economics of business process design: motivation, information and coordination within the firm'. *International Journal of the Economics of Business*, **3**, 5–24.

Buckley, P. J. and Carter, M. J. (2002). 'Process and structure in knowledge manage-ment practices of British and US multinational enterprises'. *Journal of International Management*, **8**, 29–48.

Buckley, P. J. and Carter, M. J. (2003). 'Governing knowledge sharing in multinational enterprises'. *Management International Review*, **43**, 7–25.

Buckley, P. J. and Casson, M. (1976). *The Future of the Multinational Enterprise*. Basingstoke: Macmillan.

Buckley, P. J. and Casson, M. (1981). 'The optimal timing of a foreign direct invest-ment'. *Economic Journal*, **91**, 75–87.

The Governance of the Multinational Enterprise 105

Buckley, P. J. and Casson, M. (1985). *The Economic Theory of the Multinational Enterprise.* London: Macmillan.

Buckley, P. J. and Casson, M. (1992). 'Organising for innovation: the multinational enterprise in the twenty-first century'. In Buckley, P. J. and Casson, M. (Eds), *Multinational Enterprises in the World Economy: Essays in Honour of John Dunning.* Aldershot: Edward Elgar, 212–32.

Buckley, P. J., Devinney, T. M. and Louviere, J. J. (2007). 'Do managers behave the way theory suggests? A choice-theoretic examination of foreign direct investment location decision-making'. *Journal of International Business Studies*, **38**, 1069–94.

Cantwell, J. (2001). 'A survey of theories of international production'. In Pitelis, C. N. and Sugden, R. (Eds), *The Nature of the Transnational Firm.* London: Routledge, 10–56.

Chiles, T. H. and McMackin, J. F. (1996). 'Integrating variable risk preferences, trust, and transaction cost economics'. *Academy of Management Review*, **21**, 73–99.

Coase, R. (1937). 'The nature of the firm'. *Economica*, **4**, 386–405.

DeGennaro, R. P. (2005). 'Market imperfections'. Federal Reserve Bank of Atlanta, Working Paper 2005–12.

Dunning, J. H. and Lundan, S. M. (2008). 'Institutions and the OLI paradigm of the multinational enterprise'. *Asia Pacific Journal of Management*, **25**, 573–93.

Eisenhardt, K. M. (1989). 'Agency theory: an assessment and review'. *Academy of Management Review*, **14**, 57–74.

Filatotchev, I. and Wright, M. (2010). 'Agency perspectives on corporate governance of multinational enterprises'. *Journal of Management Studies*, **48**, 471–86.

Hedlund, G. and Nonaka, I. (1993). 'Models of knowledge management in the West and Japan'. In Lorange, P., Chakravarty, B., Roos, J. and Van de Ven, A. (Eds), *Implementing Strategic Processes: Change, Learning and Cooperation.* London: Blackwell, 117–44.

Henisz, W. J. (2003). 'The power of the Buckley and Casson thesis: the abilities to manage institutional idiosyncrasies'. *Journal of International Business Studies*, **34**, 173–84.

Hennart, J.-F. (1982). *A Theory of Multinational Enterprise.* Ann Arbor, MI: University of Michigan.

Hermalin, B. S. (1993). 'Managerial preferences regarding risky projects'. *Journal of Law, Economics and Organization*, **9**, 127–35.

Hirshleifer, J. (1956). 'On the economics of transfer pricing'. *Journal of Business*, **29**, 172–84.

Hymer, S. H. (1968). 'La grande "corporation" multinationelle: analyse de certaines raisons qui poussent à l'intégration internationale des affaires'. *Revue Economique*, **14**, 949–73.

Jensen, M. (1986). 'Agency costs of free cash flow, corporate finance and takeovers'. *American Economic Review*, **76**, 323–9.

Jensen, M. and Meckling, W. (1976). 'Theory of the firm: managerial behaviour, agency costs and ownership structure'. *Journal of Financial Economics*, **3**, 305–60.

Jensen, R. and Szulanski, G. (2004). 'Stickiness and the adaptation of organizational practices in cross-border knowledge transfers'. *Journal of International Business Studies*, **35**, 508–23.

Kogut, B. and Singh, H. (1988). 'The effect of national culture on the choice of entry mode'. *Journal of International Business Studies*, **19**, 411–32.

Kogut, B. and Zander, U. (1993). 'Knowledge of the firm and the evolutionary theory of the multinational enterprise'. *Journal of International Business Studies*, **24**, 625–45.

106 *Peter J. Buckley and Roger Strange*

Lane, C. and Bachmann, R. (Eds) (1998). *Trust Within and Between Organizations.* Oxford: Oxford University Press.

Luo, Y. (2005). 'Transactional characteristics, institutional environment and joint venture contracts'. *Journal of International Business Studies*, **36**, 209–30.

Mahoney, J. (2001). 'A resource-based theory of sustainable rents'. *Journal of Management*, **27**, 651–60.

March, J. G. and Shapira, Z. (1992). 'Variable risk preference and the focus of attention'. *Psychological Review*, **99**, 172–83.

McManus, J. C. (1972). 'The theory of the international firm'. In Pacquet, G. (Ed.), *The Multinational Firm and the Nation State.* Toronto, ON: Collins and Macmillan.

Oxley, J. E. (1999). 'Institutional environment and the mechanisms of governance: the impact of intellectual property protection on the structure of inter-firm alliances'. *Journal of Economic Behavior and Organization*, **38**, 283–309.

Peteraf, M. (1993). 'The cornerstones of competitive advantage: a resource-based view'. *Strategic Management Journal*, **14**, 79–92.

Puck, J. F., Holtbrügge, D. and Mohr, A. T. (2009). 'Beyond entry mode choice: explaining the conversion of joint ventures into wholly owned subsidiaries in the People's Republic of China.' *Journal of International Business Studies*, **40**, 388–404.

Rugman, A. M. (1981). *Inside the Multinationals: The Economics of Internal Markets.* New York: Columbia University Press.

Shleifer, A. and Vishny, R. W. (1989). 'Management entrenchments: the case of manager-specific investments'. *Journal of Financial Economics*, **25**, 123–39.

Teece, D. J. (1983). 'Technological and organizational factors in the theory of the multinational enterprise'. In Casson, M. (Ed.), *The Growth of International Business.* London: George Allen, 51–62.

Tomassen, S. and Benito, G. R. G. (2009). 'The costs of governance in international companies'. *International Business Review*, **18**, 292–304.

Wernerfelt, B. (1984). 'A resource-based view of the firm'. *Strategic Management Journal*, **5**, 171–80.

Williamson, O. E. (1975). *Markets and Hierarchies: Analysis and Anti-Trust Implications.* New York: The Free Press.

Williamson, O. E. (1979). 'Transaction-cost economics: the governance of contractual relations'. *Journal of Law and Economics*, **22**, 233–61.

Zaheer, S. and Zaheer, A. (2006). 'Trust across borders'. *Journal of International Business Studies*, **37**, 21–9.

6
Formalizing Internationalization in the Eclectic Paradigm

Co-authored with Niron Hashai

Introduction

Thirty years have passed since John Dunning first articulated the eclectic paradigm (Dunning, 1977). Dunning's approach to the complex phenomenon of the multinational enterprise (MNE) has proved robust and, over time, has become one of the most influential streams of thought in the international business literature. The eclectic paradigm explains the emergence of MNEs according to three types of competitive advantage: ownership advantage, location advantage and internalization advantage (Dunning, 1977, 1981, 1988, 1993, 1998). Despite its dominant position within the field of international business, the eclectic paradigm has not yet been formalized across all of its elements (ownership, location and internalization advantages) within a general equilibrium model. While some scholars have borrowed partial insights from the eclectic paradigm in their formal modeling of MNEs (e.g., Carr, Markusen, & Maskus, 2001; Ethier, 1986; Horstman & Markusen, 1987; Markusen, 1998), many others claim that the paradigm is too rich to be formalized, and that it is more of a "broad tent" rather than a model (Cantwell & Narula, 2001; Eden, 2003).

The purpose of the current paper is to offer a simple general equilibrium model that formalizes internationalization within the eclectic paradigm. The novelty of our approach lies in the formalization of all three constructs within the eclectic paradigm, rather than relating to one or two of them. The model is essentially based on a simple reconfiguration of concepts taken from recent new classical economics literature (e.g., Yang, 1994, 2001; Yang & Ng, 1995) to analyze the impact of labor and knowledge productivity on the utility of both entrepreneurs and workers.

In the next section we briefly survey the vast literature on firm internationalization and the emergence of MNEs. In the following section, we present the features of our model. The model is then used to compare the utilities of entrepreneurs and workers in various possible operation modes. The emergence of the MNE is explained endogenously within a unifying

108 *Peter J. Buckley and Niron Hashai*

framework that compares domestic production for exports and local consumption, international licensing and foreign direct investment (FDI). We then incorporate knowledge-asset-seeking motivations for FDI into the model, and conclude by presenting the implications of the proposed model, suggesting how it could be empirically verified, and highlighting opportunities for future theoretical advances. It is evident that other areas of the paradigm could be similarly formalized, and this paper provides a generalizable means of so doing.

A brief literature review

Over the last three decades, two major schools of thought have tried to explain the phenomenon of the MNE. Both schools' point of departure was orthodox economics, or more specifically the Heckscher–Ohlin–Samuelson theory of trade, but they have diverged quite substantially from each other and, by and large, have ignored each other (Markusen, 2001). One school of thought, dominated by international trade economists, remained in the domain of orthodox economics in the sense that it introduced general-equilibrium models with strict assumptions to explain the emergence of the MNE. While this stream of research has gradually moved away from assumptions of perfect competition and constant returns to models incorporating imperfect competition, economies of scale and differentiated products, its main focal point has remained the explanation of patterns of production, consumption and trade at the country level rather than the firm level. Some major contributions are Brainard (1997), Ethier (1986), Grossman and Helpman (2002), Helpman (1984), Helpman and Krugman (1985), Markusen (1984) and Markusen and Venables (1998, 2000).

The other school of thought, consisting of international business scholars, chose to move into heterodox economics and introduce partial equilibrium models based on more relaxed underlying assumptions. This line of research is mainly interested in explaining the firm's strategic motivation to choose FDI over other entry modes when internationalizing. Dunning's eclectic paradigm (Dunning, 1977, 1981, 1988, 1993, 1998) offers a straightforward articulation of the major insights of this school of thought by referring to the combined impact of ownership advantage, location advantage and internalization advantage on foreign entry mode selection by internationalizing firms.

Ownership advantage is a firm characteristic. It is manifested by firm-specific ownership of intangible assets such as technological or marketing knowledge, as well as by superior managerial capabilities (in comparison with those of indigenous competitors) to control and coordinate international transactions. The factors constituting ownership advantage are viewed as an "intra-firm public good", transferable between different units of an MNE around the world.

Location advantage is a country-specific characteristic. Conceptually it is similar to comparative advantage, familiar from international trade theory. Location advantage is represented by the comparative cost of country-specific inputs (e.g., materials, labor, natural resources) accessible by enterprises operating within that country's borders, or by the cost of trade barriers between countries, which may include transportation costs, tariffs and non-tariff barriers. The factors that constitute location advantage are country specific and are location bound – they are internationally immobile.

Internalization advantage is a transaction attribute. It stems from the fact that the factors constituting ownership advantage become a private good once transferred outside the boundaries of the firm. Internalization advantage applies to the case where the firm prefers to exploit its ownership advantage internally, rather than by licensing or any other collaborative mode, in order to minimize the transaction costs associated with the inter-firm transfer of proprietary knowledge and capabilities.[1]

In his earlier work, Dunning assumed that a firm's ownership advantage originates in its home country, where its motivation to internationalize is market seeking, or resource seeking, or efficiency seeking, or other global strategic considerations (Dunning, 1977, 1988, 1993). However, more recently Dunning and other scholars (e.g., Almeida, 1996; Cantwell, 1995; Dunning & Narula, 1995; Kogut & Chang, 1991) have given more attention to knowledge-asset-seeking motivations of internationalization. Knowledge asset seeking essentially implies that ownership advantage does not necessarily originate in a firm's home country, but rather may be acquired and augmented abroad, and thus serves as a motivation for firm internationalization.

General properties of the model

Consider a world comprising two countries, A and B. A single good (g) can be produced in A and B, by using two intermediate goods: labor (l) and know-how (k). We assume that there are two types of "consumer-producer" individual in A and B: "entrepreneurs" and "workers". The entrepreneurs supply technological, marketing or managerial know-how, which is transformed by the workers into units of g. For simplicity we assume that there are n_A identical entrepreneurs in A and n_B identical entrepreneurs in B.

While g can be produced through either a firm or a non-firm production mode (Alchian & Demsetz, 1972), we assume that the firm production mode is more efficient than the non-firm production mode, as it enables transaction costs between individuals with different specializations to be minimized. We also assume that entrepreneurs use their know-how to become employers that offer contracts in which the workers get payment for their labor and the entrepreneur gets the residual returns from selling the workers' output (g) in the market (Milgrom & Roberts, 1988; Yang, 2001; Yang

110   *Peter J. Buckley and Niron Hashai*

& Ng, 1995). We ignore the possibility whereby a worker employs entrepreneurs to produce g, and the possibility that an entrepreneur employs another entrepreneur.

The production function of g is assumed to be of a Cobb-Douglas type, in the following structure:

$$G = aK^\alpha L^\beta \tag{1}$$

where G is the output volume of g, K is the required quantity of k to produce g,[2] L is the quantity of l required to produce g, and α and β are productivity constants. The costs of producing a given quantity of K are assumed to be sunk costs, and L is subject to a per-unit cost of w_i (i=A, B). Constants a, α and β are positive, with $a>1$, $0<\alpha<1$ and $0<\beta<1$. Know-how productivity (α) is assumed to be equal in A and in B, but labor productivity is assumed to be different: accordingly we shall refer to workers' productivity in A (β_A) and workers' productivity in B (β_B). This Ricardian view of differences in labor productivities represents another important component of location advantage, and its logic dates back to Solow (1957).[3]

Entrepreneurs are free to move between A and B, and their k can be sold across borders. Entrepreneurs may also supply know-how (k) to other entrepreneurs in the market. Since in each country entrepreneurs are assumed identical, the sale of k is relevant only between A and B. Thus k is an intangible tradable intermediate good, where entrepreneurs with higher K are said to have an ownership advantage. The quantity of k offered to the market in A (B) is denoted by K_i^s (i=A, B). The quantity of k purchased by an entrepreneur in the market in A (B) is denoted by K_i^d (i=A, B), which, allowing for transaction costs, is given by

$$K_i^d = te_{kij} K_i^s, 0 < te_k < 1, i, j = A, B, i \neq j \tag{2}$$

where te_k is the transaction efficiency of the sale of know-how to the market. Thus, in the case where k is traded in the market, it is subject to a transaction cost coefficient of $1-te_k$. Intra-firm transaction costs are assumed to be zero (i.e., te_k=1), and hence reflect the internalization advantage.[4]

In addition, we assume that workers cannot move between A and B: thus l is a country-specific intermediate good representing an important component of location advantage. The overall quantities of labor available in A and B are denoted by L_A and L_B, respectively.

An additional major factor in the model is the efficiency of operating in a foreign country, denoted as $te_{f,AB}$. Thus $1-te_{f,AB}$ may be regarded as a fixed learning cost that stems from the "liability of foreignness" (Hymer, 1976; Zaheer, 1995). Entrepreneurs from A are foreigners in B (and vice versa), and thus have to pay a certain "cost premium" over indigenous entrepreneurs who are more familiar with the local business, legal and political

Formalizing Internationalization 111

environments. These costs may derive from the need to communicate in two or more languages, overcome cultural differences, and accommodate different legal and regulatory systems (Hofstede, 1980; Hymer, 1976; Kogut & Singh, 1988; Martin & Salomon, 2003; Zaheer, 1995).

The good (g) can be self-consumed, supplied to the workers in return for their l, or supplied to other entrepreneurs in return for their k. The self-consumed quantity of g in A (B) is denoted by G_i^c (i=A, B). The quantity of g supplied by entrepreneurs in A (B) to workers or other entrepreneurs, be they located domestically or internationally, is denoted by G_i^s (i=A, B, where i determines the location of the entrepreneur who supplies g). The quantity of g received by entrepreneurs and workers in A (B) from other entrepreneurs, be they located domestically or internationally, is denoted by G_i^d (i=A, B, where i determines the location of the workers or entrepreneurs receiving g).

The utility function (U_e) of an entrepreneur in A (B) is represented by the quantity of self-consumed g (G_i^c) and the quantity of g received from other entrepreneurs (G_i^d), as follows:

$$U_{ei} = G_i^c + G_i^d, \ i = A, B \tag{3}$$

This utility function captures the value of "self-produced and self-consumed" goods in A or in B as well as of goods that are purchased from other entrepreneurs locally or internationally.

The utility function (U_w) of a worker in A (B) is represented by the wages compensation he or she receives for their work, as follows:

$$U_{wi} = w_i L_i', \ i = A, B \tag{4}$$

where w_i represents the price of l in terms of g, and L_i' is the quantity of labor conducted by the worker (e.g., number of hours or a fraction of his or her overall working time).

Finally, each entrepreneur's supply of k and g to the market should equal his or her demand for k and g. Hence each entrepreneur in A (B) faces a budget constraint:

$$P_k K_i^d + G_i^d = P_k K_i^s + G_i^s, \ i = A, B \tag{5}$$

where P_k represents the price of k in terms of g, and G_i^s is the quantity of supplied g.

Utility from different operation modes

Each entrepreneur decides how much to produce and how much to consume of the product g in order to maximize his OR her utility. A combination of transactions between individuals (entrepreneurs and/or workers) where l and

112 Peter J. Buckley and Niron Hashai

k are exchanged for g is defined as an "operation mode". A feasible operation mode is composed of a set of transactions conducted by individuals so that the market-clearing conditions are met. Each operation mode has an equilibrium solution in which the market is cleared and the entrepreneurs and subsequently their workers maximize their utility (Yang & Ng, 1995). This equilibrium reflects the maximal quantity of g that is producible under the constraints of a given operation mode.

The entrepreneurs from A and B face five alternative operation modes: domestic production for exports and local consumption; international licensing from A to B; international licensing from B to A; FDI in A; and FDI in B. Since the focus of this paper is ON the emergence of the MNE, we ignore the domestic licensing alternative. This alternative has more to do with the question of the firm's boundaries (i.e., integration vs outsourcing) than with firms' internationalization and thus will be analyzed here only in the international context.

By applying marginal analysis to these alternatives we can obtain the entrepreneurs' utility (or real income) from each operation mode. The basic features of the five operation modes that we examine are as follows:

(1) *Domestic production for exports and local consumption.* Each entrepreneur in i (i=A, B) hires workers from i to transform k into g. An entrepreneur pays his or her workers' labor and collects the whole net revenues (total revenues minus workers' wages). Hence this operation mode involves the exchange of l for g, which is denoted as: L_i/G_i^s in both A and B.

(2) *International licensing from A to B.* In addition to engaging in domestic production in A as described above, each entrepreneur in A provides k to licensees, being entrepreneurs in B who produce g using the purchased k and workers from B. The produced amount of g is then exchanged by the entrepreneurs from B as wages compensation and in exchange for the supplied k. Two transactions are implied by international licensing from A to B: entrepreneurs from A trade k for g (denoted as K_A^s/G_B^s) and, on the basis of this know-how, entrepreneurs from B hire workers to produce g, thus exchanging l for g (denoted as: L_B/G_B^s).

(3) *International licensing from B to A.* Each entrepreneur in A obtains k from a licensor, being an entrepreneur from B, and then produces g using the purchased k and workers from A. The produced amount of g is then exchanged locally (as wages compensation) and internationally (in exchange for the supplied k). Two transactions are implied by international licensing from B to A: entrepreneurs from A trade k for g (denoted as K_B^s/G_A^s) and, on the basis of this know-how, hire workers to produce g, thus exchanging l for g (denoted as L_A/G_A^s). In addition, each entrepreneur in B engages in domestic production as described above.

(4) *FDI in B.* In addition to engaging in domestic production in A, each entrepreneur in A sets up a firm (subsidiary) in B. Then g is produced

using local workers in B and know-how brought in from A. FDI in B implies the exchange of l for g, which is denoted by L_B/G_B^s. B's entrepreneurs remain unemployed in this operation mode.

(5) *FDI in A.* In addition to engaging in domestic production in B, each entrepreneur in B sets up a firm (subsidiary) in A. Thus g is produced using local workers in A and know-how brought in from B. FDI in A implies the exchange of l for g, which is denoted by L_A/G_A^s. A's entrepreneurs remain unemployed in this operation mode.

The possible five operation modes discussed above are summarized in Table 6.1.

It is noteworthy that our model ignores the costs of transferring goods between A and B. We refer only to alternative operation modes in which the aim is to maximize the overall quantity of produced g. The efficiency of transferring goods between A and B (denoted by $te_{g,ij}$, $0 < te_g < 1$, $i, j = A, B$, $i \neq j$) actually represents an inter-country "tax" that reduces the total utility obtained by any given operation mode. The quantity of g that is shipped between A and B is therefore reduced by an inter-country "transfer" cost. Since, in all five operation modes, production takes place in both A and B, the decision of entrepreneurs to ship some of the produced goods to

Table 6.1 Production characteristics in different operation modes

Operation mode	Production characteristics in A	Production characteristics in B	Comments
Domestic production for exports and local consumption	A's entrepreneurs use their k to produce g with L_A	B's entrepreneurs use their k to produce g with L_B	
International licensing from A to B	A's entrepreneurs use their k to produce g with L_A	B's entrepreneurs use k from A's entrepreneurs to produce g with L_B	
International licensing from A to B	A's entrepreneurs use k from B's entrepreneurs to produce g with L_A	B's entrepreneurs use their k to produce g with L_B	
FDI in B	A's entrepreneurs use their k to produce g with L_A	A's entrepreneurs use their k to produce g with L_B	B's entrepreneurs remain unemployed
FDI in A	B's entrepreneurs use their k to produce g with L_A	B's entrepreneurs use their k to produce g with L_B	A's entrepreneurs remain unemployed
Knowledge-asset-seeking FDI in B	A's entrepreneurs use their k to produce g with L_A	A's entrepreneurs employ B's entrepreneurs and use their k to produce g with L_B	

114   *Peter J. Buckley and Niron Hashai*

another country (in exchange for a different good g') is essentially derived from comparative advantage of A (B) in producing g and g' and "transfer" costs considerations, as well as (to some extent) the relative sizes of A and B (Ohlin, 1933; Heckscher, 1949). Nevertheless, the decision on where to produce these products (in A and/or B) and under which operation mode would still be the outcome of the relative maximal utilities of the operation modes discussed.

Next, we calculate the utility of A's and B's entrepreneurs from each of the above operation modes.

Utility from domestic production for exports and local consumption

In this operation mode each entrepreneur from i (i = A, B) uses a certain amount of g to pay workers (G_i^s), and consumes the remaining quantity of g (G_i^c). The decision problem of each entrepreneur is

$$\text{Max} \, U_{ei} = G_i^C (i = \text{A}, \text{B})$$

subject to

$$G = G_i^C + G_i^s = a\left(K_i'\right)^\alpha \left(\frac{L_i}{n_i}\right)^{\beta_i} \quad \text{(production function)}$$

$$G_i^s = w_i \left(\frac{L_i}{n_i}\right) \quad \text{(workers' wages constraint)}$$

where K_i' represents the quantity of k held by each entrepreneur in i; L_i/n_i is the quantity of labor required by each entrepreneur in i (where n_i represents the number of entrepreneurs in country i; i=A, B), assuming a uniform distribution of labor between all identical entrepreneurs; and w_i is the appropriate wage rate in terms of g, as noted earlier. G_i^s is the quantity of g paid to workers by the entrepreneur, G_i^c is the entrepreneur's residual return, and β_i is an indicator of the workers' productivity in i.

The entrepreneurs from i are always expected to utilize their maximal level of k in order to maximize utility: hence by differentiating U_{ei} with respect to L_i/n_i and setting the result equal to zero we can derive the maximal utility of each entrepreneur from domestic production for exports and local consumption in i:[5]

$$U_{ei,\text{domestic}-i} = a\left(1-\beta_i\right)\left(K_i'\right)^\alpha \left(\frac{L_i}{n_i}\right)^{\beta_i}, \quad i = \text{A}, \text{B} \tag{6a}$$

Since it is now straightforward to calculate the workers' utility from domestic production for exports and local consumption, we can also derive the total utility of this operation mode. The *total* utility of domestic production for exports and local consumption is represented by the utility of *all* entrepreneurs and workers in A and in B, and is given by

$$U_{\text{domestic}} = n_A a \left(K_A'\right)^\alpha \left(\frac{L_A}{n_A}\right)^{\beta_A} + n_B a \left(K_B'\right)^\alpha \left(\frac{L_B}{n_B}\right)^{\beta_B} \tag{6b}$$

Utility from international licensing from A to B

In the case of international licensing of know-how from A to B, the individual decision problem of each entrepreneur in A in the exchange of K_A^s/G_B^s is

$$\text{Max}U_{eA} = P_k K_A^s$$

The utility of each entrepreneur in A represents the amount of g that he or she receives in exchange for his or her k. Thus in this case the utility of each entrepreneur from A depends on the quantity of k that entrepreneurs from B are willing to purchase, and on the price these entrepreneurs are willing to pay. Since B's entrepreneurs also maximize their utility, the quantity and price of k will be determined so that the utility of the entrepreneurs from B is maximized. Thus the utility of each entrepreneur in A from being an international licensor is determined according to the maximization of the utility of the entrepreneurs from B who purchase k. We would therefore calculate maximal U_{eB} and then compute U_{eA} in order to derive the maximal utility of an A's entrepreneur from being an international licensor. The individual decision problem of B's entrepreneurs is

$$\text{Max}U_{eB} = G_B^c$$

subject to

$$G_B^c + G_B^s = a \left(te_{k,AB}K_A^s\right)^\alpha \left(\frac{L_B}{n_B}\right)^{\beta_B}$$

$$G_B^s = w_B \left(\frac{L_B}{n_B}\right) + P_k K_A^s$$

where L_B/n_B is the quantity of labor required for each entrepreneur in B, and w_B is the wage rate in terms of g. The transaction efficiency coefficient for know-how transfer from A to B is denoted by $te_{k,AB}$: hence $1-te_{k,AB}$ represents the transaction costs for know-how transfer, that is, the dissipation of an A's entrepreneur's proprietary know-how when it is transferred to an independent foreign entrepreneur (Martin & Salomon, 2003; Rugman,

1981). The quantity of g sold by each entrepreneur in B in order to pay for K_A^s and L_B is G_B^s, and G_B^c is the residual return of each entrepreneur in B.

Differentiating U_{eB} with respect to L_B/n_B, differentiating U_{eB} with respect to K_A^s, and setting the differentiated terms equal to zero enables us to derive the maximal utility of a B's entrepreneur from being international licensee as per the two intermediate products he or she uses. Results show that this utility is maximized in the case where $K_A^s = K_A'$: that is, when an A's entrepreneur supplies all the knowledge he or she retains. Based on the computed U_{eB} we can derive U_{eA}, as follows:

$$U_{eA,\text{license}-\text{A to B}} = a\alpha \left(te_{k,AB}\right)^\alpha \left(K_A'\right)^\alpha \left(L_B/n_B\right)^{\beta_B} \tag{7a}$$

The total utility of this operation mode is represented by the utility of B's entrepreneurs, the utility of n_B A's entrepreneurs who sold their k to B's entrepreneurs,[6] the utility of A's entrepreneurs from domestic production, and the utility of the workers in A and B, as follows:

$$U_{\text{license}-\text{A to B}} = a\left(K_A'\right)^\alpha \times \left[\left(te_{k,AB}\right)^\alpha \left(L_B/n_B\right)^{\beta_B} n_B + n_A \left(L_A/n_A\right)^{\beta_A}\right] \tag{7b}$$

Utility from international licensing from B to A

The case of international licensing of know-how from B to A is symmetric to the previous operation mode, where the maximal utility of an entrepreneur from A being an international licensee is

$$U_{eA,\text{license}-\text{B to A}} = a\left(te_{k,BA}\right)^\alpha \left(K_B'\right)^\alpha \left(\frac{L_A}{n_A}\right)^{\beta_A} \times (1-\beta_A-\alpha) \tag{8a}$$

The total utility from this operation mode is

$$U_{\text{license}-\text{B to A}} = a\left(K_B'\right)^\alpha \times \left[\left(te_{k,BA}\right)^\alpha \left(\frac{L_A}{n_A}\right)^{\beta_A} n_A + n_B \left(\frac{L_B}{n_B}\right)^{\beta_B}\right] \tag{8b}$$

Utility from FDI in B

In the case of FDI in B, the decision problem of each entrepreneur in A is

$$\text{Max} U_{eA} = G_B^C$$

subject to

$$G_B^C + G_B^s = a\left(te_{f,AB}K_A'\right)^\alpha \left(\frac{L_B}{n_A}\right)^{\beta_B}$$

$$G_B^s = w_B L_B$$

Formalizing Internationalization 117

where $te_{f,AB}$ represents the efficiency of operating in a foreign country.

Differentiation of U_{eA} with respect to L_B/n_B and setting the result equal to zero yields the maximal utility of an A's entrepreneur from FDI in B:

$$U_{eA,FDI-B} = a(1-\beta_B)(te_{f,AB})^\alpha (K_A')^\alpha \left(\frac{L_B}{n_A}\right)^{\beta_B} \qquad (9a)$$

In this operation mode B's entrepreneurs remain unemployed, and total utility is reflected by the utility of A's entrepreneurs from producing in A and B as well as the utility of the workers they employ, as follows:

$$U_{FDI-B} = n_A a(K_A')^\alpha \left[\left(\frac{L_A}{n_A}\right)^{\beta_A} + (te_{f,AB})^\alpha \left(\frac{L_B}{n_A}\right)^{\beta_B}\right] \qquad (9b)$$

Utility from FDI in A

The case of FDI in A is symmetric to the previous operation mode where A's entrepreneurs remain unemployed and a B's entrepreneur utility is given by

$$U_{eB,FDI-A} = a(1-\beta_A)(te_{f,BA})^\alpha (K_B')^\alpha \left(\frac{L_A}{n_B}\right)^{\beta_A} \qquad (10a)$$

and the total utility of this operation mode is

$$U_{FDI-A} = n_B a(K_B')^\alpha \left[\left(\frac{L_B}{n_B}\right)^{\beta_B} + (te_{f,BA})^\alpha \left(\frac{L_A}{n_B}\right)^{\beta_A}\right] \qquad (10b)$$

The emergence of the MNE

By comparing the maximal total utility obtained from the different operation modes we can define the set of necessary and sufficient conditions for the emergence of the MNE. Entrepreneurs are expected to prefer the operation mode where they obtain the highest utility. Workers, on the other hand, are expected to prefer the operation mode that yields the highest wages for their level of productivity, and thus would prefer to work for the entrepreneur with the highest utility level.[7] Hence the operation mode that yields the highest total utility would be selected in equilibrium.

Let us consider, for instance, the conditions under which FDI in B emerges as the selected operation mode.[8] This will be the case if: $U_{FDI-B} > U_{domestic}$, $U_{FDI-B} > U_{license-A\ to\ B}$, $U_{FDI-B} > U_{license-B\ to\ A}$, and $U_{FDI-B} > U_{FDI-A}$. The set of necessary and sufficient conditions for FDI in B is specified by inequalities (11a)–(11d), which represent, respectively, the conditions under which the utility from FDI in B is greater than the utility in each of the above operation modes.

$$\frac{(K_A')^\alpha \left[n_A^{1-\beta_A} (L_A)^{\beta_A} + n_A^{1-\beta_B} (te_{f,AB})^\alpha (L_B)^{\beta_B}\right]}{n_A^{1-\beta_A} (K_A')^\alpha (L_A)^{\beta_A} + n_B^{1-\beta_B} (K_B')^\alpha (L_B)^{\beta_B}} > 1 \qquad (11a)$$

$$\frac{n_{\mathrm{A}}^{1-\beta_{\mathrm{A}}}\left(L_{\mathrm{A}}\right)^{\beta_{\mathrm{A}}}+n_{\mathrm{A}}^{1-\beta_{\mathrm{B}}}\left(te_{\mathrm{f,AB}}\right)^{\alpha}\left(L_{\mathrm{B}}\right)^{\beta_{\mathrm{B}}}}{n_{\mathrm{B}}^{1-\beta_{\mathrm{B}}}\left(te_{k,\mathrm{AB}}\right)^{\alpha}\left(L_{\mathrm{B}}\right)^{\beta_{\mathrm{B}}}+n_{\mathrm{A}}^{1-\beta_{\mathrm{A}}}\left(L_{\mathrm{A}}\right)^{\beta_{\mathrm{A}}}}>1 \tag{11b}$$

$$\frac{\left(K_{\mathrm{A}}'\right)^{\alpha}}{\left(K_{\mathrm{B}}'\right)^{\alpha}}\cdot\frac{n_{\mathrm{A}}^{1-\beta_{\mathrm{A}}}\left(L_{\mathrm{A}}\right)^{\beta_{\mathrm{A}}}+n_{\mathrm{A}}^{1-\beta_{\mathrm{B}}}\left(te_{\mathrm{f,AB}}\right)^{\alpha}\left(L_{\mathrm{B}}\right)^{\beta_{\mathrm{B}}}}{n_{\mathrm{A}}^{1-\beta_{\mathrm{A}}}\left(te_{k,\mathrm{BA}}\right)^{\alpha}\left(L_{\mathrm{A}}\right)^{\beta_{\mathrm{A}}}+n_{\mathrm{B}}^{1-\beta_{\mathrm{B}}}\left(L_{\mathrm{B}}\right)^{\beta_{\mathrm{B}}}}>1 \tag{11c}$$

$$\frac{\left(K_{\mathrm{A}}'\right)^{\alpha}}{\left(K_{\mathrm{B}}'\right)^{\alpha}}\cdot\frac{n_{\mathrm{A}}^{1-\beta_{\mathrm{A}}}\left(L_{\mathrm{A}}\right)^{\beta_{\mathrm{A}}}+n_{\mathrm{A}}^{1-\beta_{\mathrm{B}}}\left(te_{\mathrm{f,AB}}\right)^{\alpha}\left(L_{\mathrm{B}}\right)^{\beta_{\mathrm{B}}}}{n_{\mathrm{B}}^{1-\beta_{\mathrm{B}}}\left(L_{\mathrm{B}}\right)^{\beta_{\mathrm{B}}}+n_{\mathrm{B}}^{1-\beta_{\mathrm{A}}}te_{\mathrm{f,BA}}\left(L_{\mathrm{A}}\right)^{\beta_{\mathrm{A}}}}>1 \tag{11d}$$

It is straightforward to see how inequalities (11a)–(11d) represent the various parameters of the eclectic paradigm. Internalization advantage is represented by $te_{k,\mathrm{AB}}$ and $te_{k,\mathrm{BA}}$: the higher $te_{k,ij}$ ($i,\ j$=A, B), the lower the internalization advantage. The lower the transaction efficiency of the international markets for know-how, the greater the likelihood that an MNE will emerge. This view is consistent with mainstream literature on the emergence of MNEs, of both international trade economists and international business scholars.

Ownership advantage is represented by $K_{\mathrm{A}}'/K_{\mathrm{B}}'$. The higher the $K_{\mathrm{A}}'/K_{\mathrm{B}}'$ ratio, the greater the likelihood that A's entrepreneurs will engage in FDI in B. Nevertheless, ownership advantage is also affected by the efficiency of operating in a foreign country, denoted by $te_{\mathrm{f,AB}}$ and $te_{\mathrm{f,BA}}$. The higher $te_{\mathrm{f,AB}}$ is (for instance as a result of previous experience of A's entrepreneur in B's market), the higher the likelihood that A will maintain the ownership advantage that stems from a high $K_{\mathrm{A}}'/K_{\mathrm{B}}'$ ratio, and thus the higher the likelihood that FDI in B will occur.

The role of location advantage is somewhat more complicated. While location advantage essentially refers to the $\left(L_{\mathrm{B}}\right)^{\beta_{\mathrm{B}}}/\left(L_{\mathrm{A}}\right)^{\beta_{\mathrm{A}}}$ ratio, the impact of this ratio on the likelihood of FDI in B is strongly affected by the terms $te_{\mathrm{f,AB}}$, $te_{\mathrm{f,BA}}$, $te_{k,\mathrm{AB}}$ and $te_{k,\mathrm{BA}}$. The higher $te_{\mathrm{f,AB}}$ and the lower $te_{k,\mathrm{AB}}$ ($te_{k,\mathrm{BA}}$) are, the higher the probability is for FDI in B to occur, rather than international licensing (inequalities (11b) and (11c)). The higher $te_{\mathrm{f,AB}}$ and the lower $te_{\mathrm{f,BA}}$ are, the higher the probability is for FDI in B to occur, rather than FDI in A (inequality (11d)). Moreover, according to inequality (11d) it is not comparative labor quantities or labor productivities that determine whether FDI in A or FDI in B will occur; rather it is the impact of the comparative liability of foreignness that determines which of the two operation modes will yield a higher total utility.

Deeper investigation of inequalities (11a)–(11d) clarifies the main factors affecting the attractiveness of FDI in B, compared with alternative operation modes. Inequality (11a) implies that the likelihood of FDI in B compared with domestic production for exports and local consumption in both A and B increases when $K_{\mathrm{A}}' \times te_{\mathrm{f,AB}} > K_{\mathrm{B}}'$: that is, when A's k discounted by the liability of foreignness exceeds B's k. Inequality (11b) implies that the likelihood of FDI in

Formalizing Internationalization 119

B compared with international licensing of k from A to B increases when $te_{k,AB} < te_{f,AB}$: that is, when the inefficiency of the market for know-how has a stronger impact over k dissipation than the liability of foreignness. Inequality (11c) implies that the likelihood of FDI in B compared with international licensing of k from B to A increases when $te_{k,BA} < te_{f,AB}$: that is, when the efficiency of transferring k from B to A is lower than the liability of foreignness faced by A's entrepreneurs operating in B. While the feasibility of FDI in B in this case is by and large conditioned by the K'_A/K'_B ratio, the impact of the market for k and of the liability of foreignness may clearly revert this ratio, implying that, albeit having a lower k, FDI in B is still feasible for A's entrepreneurs in this case. Inequality (11d) implies that the likelihood of FDI in B compared with FDI in A increases when $te_{f,BA} < te_{f,AB}$: that is, when the foreignness faced by A's entrepreneurs operating in B is lower than that faced by B's entrepreneurs operating in A. It is noteworthy again that while the feasibility of FDI in B in this case is by and large conditioned by the K'_A/K'_B ratio, the impact of relative liabilities of foreignness may revert this ratio, implying once again that, albeit having a lower k, FDI in B is still feasible for A's entrepreneurs. As noted by Shenkar (2001), some of the major factors affecting the liability of foreignness, such as cultural distance, are not necessarily symmetric, implying that differences in bidirectional liabilities of foreignness are not unlikely.

Finally, it follows from inequalities (11a)–(11d) that the larger the number of entrepreneurs in A is relative to entrepreneurs in B, the higher the probability is for FDI in B to occur, rather than the respective alternative operation modes. This implies that, other things being equal, we should expect countries with a larger number of entrepreneurs to have a higher propensity for outgoing FDI.

Overall, inequalities (11a)–(11d) demonstrate how ownership advantage, location advantage and internalization advantage interact in determining the set of necessary and sufficient conditions for the emergence of MNEs (in this case FDI in B). As mentioned before, much of the strength of the eclectic paradigm lies in the perception that the interaction between ownership advantage, location advantage and internalization advantage determines the feasibility of the emergence of an MNE. Our formalization of the eclectic paradigm can further contribute to this strength of the original paradigm, since inequalities (11a)–(11d) enable us to specifically observe the relationships between the various elements of the eclectic paradigm. According to these inequalities, each of these elements (ownership, location and internalization advantages) may strengthen or counteract the impact of the others, depending on its relative magnitude. For instance, our discussion regarding the factors affecting location advantage implies that location advantage by itself is of little importance (note that in each of the inequalities (11a)–(11d) we get L_B and L_A in both the numerator and the denominator), and that the magnitude of the $\left(L_B\right)^{\beta_B}/\left(L_A\right)^{\beta_A}$ ratio is actually shaped by the efficiency of the market for know-how (i.e., the existence of an internalization advantage) and the extent of the liability of foreignness in A and B, which is related to firms' ability to exploit

120 *Peter J. Buckley and Niron Hashai*

their ownership advantage. Likewise the emergence of FDI in B compared with international licensing of k, either from A to B or vice versa, is determined by the interaction between ownership advantage (represented by the K'_A/K'_B ratio discounted by the liability of foreignness) and internalization advantage (represented by the efficiency of the market for k).

Hence, while the eclectic paradigm does not specify the relations between its elements, our model explicitly addresses this issue. According to our model, the emergence of FDI in B should not be regarded as the product of binary values that represent the existence or non-existence of ownership, location and internalization advantages (for example, 1 = a specific advantage exists; 0 = a specific advantage does not hold). This line of thinking would lead to the faulty conclusion that the nonexistence of one of these advantages is sufficient to prevent FDI from taking place. Our model captures ownership, location and internalization advantages as the product of continuous (non-zero) variables, with the magnitude of each variable affecting the probability of the emergence of an MNE. Thus, even in cases where one advantage is low, other advantages that are exceptionally high can counterbalance this disadvantage, and FDI may still occur.

Finally, under the current model the functional relationship between ownership and advantages can be explicitly specified. Following Buckley and Casson (1976), Kogut and Zander (1993) and Martin and Salomon (2003), the greater ownership advantage is, the greater is internalization advantage, since complex firm-specific knowledge can be more efficiently transferred within firms than between firms. Following our specifications of ownership and internalization advantages, Eq. (12) is a possible formulation of this relationship:

$$1 - te_{kij} = \mu \frac{K'_A}{K'_B} te_{fij}, \quad 0 < te_k < 1, 0 < te_f < 1; \quad \mu > 0, i,j = A, B, \quad i \neq j \qquad (12)$$

Insertion of Eq. (12) into Eqs (11b) and (11c) enables us to compare the attractiveness of FDI in B with licensing. A simple mathematical manipulation indicates that in both cases the impact of $te_{f,ij}$ on the chosen operation mode diminishes, and that the probability of FDI occurring in B is higher, the higher the knowledge wedge is between A and B entrepreneurs (i.e., the higher K'_A/K'_B is).

Knowledge-asset-seeking FDI

Relaxing our underlying assumptions to allow entrepreneurs to employ foreign entrepreneurs and use these entrepreneurs' know-how to produce g either in A or in B may enable us to relate to the phenomenon of knowledge asset seeking FDI (Almeida, 1996; Cantwell, 1995; Dunning & Narula, 1995; Kogut & Chang, 1991). Knowledge asset seeking essentially implies that ownership advantage (associated with having a superior k) should not

Formalizing Internationalization 121

necessarily originate in a firm's home country, but rather may be obtained by accessing more superior k abroad.

In the context of the current model knowledge asset seeking implies that, if K_B'/K_A', an entrepreneur from A may employ an entrepreneur from B and pay for the latter's k with g units (as done with his or her workers), rather than purchasing the k of a B's entrepreneur in the market for knowhow.[9] In this case the k of B entrepreneurs becomes an additional part of B's location advantage, which in turn becomes A's entrepreneurs' ownership advantage (Cantwell & Narula, 2001).

The utility of an entrepreneur from A represents the amount of g that he or she receives for K_B', and his or her individual decision problem is

$$\text{Max} U_{eA} = g_A^c$$

subject to

$$G = G_i^c + G_A^s = a \left(te_{f,A,B} K_B' \right)^\alpha \left(\frac{L_A}{n_A} \right)^{\beta^A} \text{ (production function)}$$

$$G_A^s = w_A \left(\frac{L_A}{n_A} \right) + w_B' K_B' \text{ (wages constraint)}$$

Knowledge-asset-seeking FDI by A's entrepreneurs differs from FDI in B in the fact that K_B' is used to produce g rather than K_A'; however, it is noteworthy that using B entrepreneur's K_B' does not eliminate the liability of foreignness associated with operating in a foreign country, as discussed earlier.[10] Differentiation of U_{eA} with respect to L_A/n_A and K_B', setting the results equal to zero and then computing U_{eA} enables us to derive the maximal utility of A's entrepreneur from knowledge assets seeking FDI. This utility equals

$$U_{eA,k-\text{seeking}} = a\alpha \left(te_{f,AB} K_B' \right)^\alpha \left(\frac{L_A}{n_A} \right)^{\beta_A} \left(1 - \beta_A - \alpha \right) \tag{13a}$$

Hence the total utility of this operation mode is represented by the utility of the employing entrepreneurs, the utility of the n_A employed entrepreneurs from B,[11] and the utility of the workers in A and B employed by A's entrepreneurs (see Table 6.1), as follows:

$$U_{k\text{seeking}} = a \left(te_{f,AB} K_B' \right)^\alpha \left[n_A^{-\beta_B} \beta_B L_B^{\beta_B} + n_A^{1-\beta_A} L_A^{\beta_A} \right] \tag{13b}$$

Since we have argued earlier that the operation mode yielding the highest total utility is the one likely to emerge, it follows that knowledge asset seeking will be preferred over, for instance, international licensing (arguably its natural alternative) from B to A when

122 Peter J. Buckley and Niron Hashai

$$\frac{a\left[\left(te_{f,AB}\right)^\alpha n_A^{-\beta_B} \beta_B L_B^{\beta_B} + n_A^{1-\beta_A} L_A^{\beta_A}\right]}{n_A^{1-\beta_A}\left(te_{k,BA}\right)^\alpha L_A^{\beta_A} + n_B^{1-\beta_B} L_B^{\beta_B}} > 1 \tag{14a}$$

which indicates that low efficiency of the market for know-how from B to A and high productivity of B's workers lead to knowledge-asset-seeking FDI rather than licensing k from B to A.

Likewise, knowledge asset seeking will be preferred over FDI in B when

$$\left(\frac{K_B'}{K_A'}\right)^\alpha \frac{a\left[\left(te_{f,AB}\right)^\alpha n_A^{-\beta_B} \beta_B L_B^{\beta_B} + n_A^{1-\beta_A} L_A^{\beta_A}\right]}{n_A^{1-\beta_A} L_A^{\beta_A} + n_A^{1-\beta_B}\left(te_{f,AB}\right)^\alpha L_B^{\beta_B}} > 1 \tag{14b}$$

which implies that the higher the wedge is between K_B' and K_A', the higher is the liability of foreignness for A's entrepreneurs operating in B, and the higher the productivity of B's workers is, the higher is the likelihood of knowledge-asset-seeking FDI in B.

Finally, we compare the utility of knowledge asset seeking in B by A's entrepreneurs with the alternative of B's entrepreneurs engaging in FDI in A. Here knowledge asset seeking is preferred when

$$\frac{\left(te_{f,AB}\right)^\alpha n_A^{-\beta_B} \beta_B L_B^{\beta_B} + n_A^{1-\beta_A} L_A^{\beta_A}}{n_B^{1-\beta_A}\left(te_{f,BA}\right)^\alpha L_A^{\beta_A} + n_B^{1-\beta_B} L_B^{\beta_B}} > 1 \tag{14c}$$

which implies that the relative liabilities of foreignness of A and B entrepreneurs as well as the relative number of entrepreneurs from each country are the major determinants of the type of FDI that will emerge in equilibrium.

Overall, inequalities (14a)–(14c) exemplify once again how ownership, location and internalization advantages interact to yield the emergence of an optimal operation mode.

Discussion and conclusion

This paper has constructed a simple general equilibrium model that formalizes the predictions of the eclectic paradigm regarding the emergence of MNEs. To the best of our knowledge it is the first attempt to formalize internationalization within the eclectic paradigm. Our model constitutes an intermediate route between the view of MNEs taken by international trade economists and that taken by international business scholars. It presents a formal decision-making model that simplifies reality while retaining relaxed underlying assumptions to explain simultaneously the location and control dilemmas of internationalizing firms. We incorporate the concepts of ownership, location and internalization advantages, familiar from international business literature, into a general equilibrium model, usually preferred by international economists. Our model endogenously explains FDI as the operation mode that maximizes the total utility of entrepreneurs and workers while clearing the markets for know-how and labor.

By examining comparative labor productivities, comparative firm-specific know-how levels, the transaction efficiency of the international market for know-how, and entrepreneurs' efficiency of operating in a host country, we are able to introduce a set of necessary and sufficient conditions for the emergence of the MNE, so that the total utility derived from FDI in a host country exceeds the utility from domestic production for exports and local consumption, international licensing and incoming FDI. Moreover, we are able to model the emergence of knowledge-asset-seeking FDI with the same modeling tools as used to model more conventional operation modes (e.g., international licensing and FDI).

Our model is able to explain the simultaneous existence of domestic production for exports and local production and FDI and the simultaneous existence of such domestic production and international licensing. It is explicit in its formulation of the structure of the firm's production function, and in the residual rights allocation between entrepreneurs and workers. As such, while remaining simple, it encompasses multiple combinations of alternative operation modes. More specifically, several insights may be gained from our formalization of the eclectic paradigm. The first insight is the observation that the impact of comparative labor quantities and labor productivities on the likelihood that an MNE will emerge is moderated by comparative liability of foreignness and the efficiency of the markets for know-how. As the market for know-how transfer (from B to A) becomes more efficient, and as the liability of foreignness decreases, labor cost and labor productivity considerations become less substantial in explaining the emergence of the MNE.[12] The second insight is the perception of ownership, location and internalization advantages as continuous, rather than dichotomous, variables, which may counteract or support each other. Here, we assert that even when one of these advantages is very low the other advantages may still compensate for it and justify the emergence of an MNE. The interaction between the different types of advantage can be further manifested by referring to specific functional relationships between them. We have demonstrated the impact of a positive linear relationship between ownership and internalization advantages. Other functional relationships between ownership and internalization advantages or between other elements of the paradigm can obviously be further analyzed using our model. Finally, the impact of the relative number of entrepreneurs in A and B on the emergence of the MNE, as identified in our model, supports the notion that countries that are comparatively abundant with entrepreneurs are expected to have a positive FDI balance with less abundant countries.

A major benefit of our formalization of the eclectic paradigm is that it paves the way for testing the paradigm empirically, a need identified by many scholars (e.g., Casson, 2000). The variables specified in our model are either measurable or are variables for which reasonable proxies can be proposed. Data on domestic production volumes are obviously available, and data on production volumes of foreign affiliates within a host country have been used before (e.g., Carr et al., 2001; Markusen, 2001). Data on labor productivity in different countries are often published by international organizations such as the International Labor Organization, UNCTAD and the WTO. It is more difficult to measure firm-specific know-how; however, measures such as the ratio of a specific firm's R&D expenses to its overall costs of production, or the number of patents a firm holds (e.g., Cantwell, 1995), may be used as proxies for firm-specific know-how. Such data may be used at both the country and the sector levels to enable an analysis of both inter-country and inter-sector differences in the levels of FDI. Similarly, data on patents registered in various countries (sectors) and the enforceability of intellectual property rights in these countries could serve as a proxy for the efficiency of the market for know-how transfer. As for the excess costs of operating in a different country, measures of cultural distance between countries (Kogut & Singh, 1988; Ronen & Shenkar, 1985) or data on the differences between countries' income per capita (Linder, 1961) may be used as rough measures for the difficulty of doing business abroad. Other parameters that can be used in this respect are the indexes of the difficulty of investing in a host country published by the World Economic Forum (Carr et al., 2001; Markusen, 2001), or the costs attributed to institutional differences between countries (Henisz, 2005). Therefore we believe that future research should aim to quantify or proxy the variables suggested in this paper and subsequently test our model against the FDI patterns of different countries and sectors (as reported for instance in UNCTAD, 2005). This is essential in order to verify the robustness of the proposed model.

Our proposed model can be expanded in several directions. For instance, one may refer to nonidentical entrepreneurs originating in A and B respectively. For such entrepreneurs one may, for instance, assume that $K'_A > K'_B$ for a specific subgroup of entrepreneurs in A, but that this relationship reverses for a different subgroup. This modification may enable us to relate to additional issues such as the labor allocation between different entrepreneurs according to their specific quantity of know-how, the coexistence of FDI in A and FDI in B, and so on. Other modifications may be to allow multiple stages of production and hence relate to vertically integrated MNEs (Brainard, 1997; Teece, 1981) rather than relating only to horizontally integrated ones, or to refer to the impact of increasing returns to scale (rather than the constant returns assumed in our model). Another route in which our model can be expanded is adding an additional product g' so that classic comparative advantage considerations are also taken into account. This should also enable us to specifically incorporate the efficiency of transferring goods between A and B (te_g) in the model. Finally, a further expansion route might be to specifically model the competition on talented employees between entrepreneurs from different countries (Lewin & Peeters, 2006).

This requires specific modeling of the allocation of incentives offered by entrepreneurs to workers (in terms of the good g) in order to attract the most productive ones under conditions of worker scarcity. Such modifications complicate the mathematical formulation of the model considerably, and are beyond the scope of the current paper.

Dunning's original intention may have been to step out from orthodox economics modeling and present a heterodox paradigm that is richer and more realistic. At the time this was probably the best way to offer progress in our understanding of the complex phenomenon of the MNE. However, 30 years later it may be the time to offer models that formalize the basic notions of the eclectic paradigm. Such models should still preserve the richness of the original paradigm, but should also enable us to build refutable hypotheses. While such lines of modeling may confine the paradigm to specific contexts (such as internationalization in the current case), it is essential to do so in order to make the paradigm more robust and to gain further insights from it. Our model provides a straightforward example that this task is feasible.

Acknowledgements

We thank Editor-in-Chief Arie Y Lewin and two anonymous *JIBS* reviewers for their guidance. Niron Hashai thanks the Asper Center for Entrepreneurship at the Hebrew University for its financial support.

Notes

1. A similar view is also taken by Buckley and Casson (1976, 1998), Hirsch (1976), Hennart (1982, 1993) and Rugman (1981, 1986).
2. K can be thought of as the quantity of tacit and codified technological know-how, patents and designs obtained by entrepreneurs.
3. Physical capital costs are assumed to converge around the globe, and hence are ignored in this model (Casson, 1985). Differences in production output are expected to be mainly a function of know-how level, labor volume and labor productivity.
4. Strictly speaking we should refer to intra-firm and inter-firm transaction costs where the latter are expected to exceed the former (Buckley & Casson, 1976; Williamson, 1975, 1985). Ignoring intra-firm transaction costs is done for simplicity and does not change the results of our model.
5. For simplicity we assume that the parameters a and α are identical for entrepreneurs in A and in B.
6. Or alternatively the utility of n_B transactions in which K_A' was transferred by any number of A's entrepreneurs smaller than n_B.
7. This is so because such entrepreneurs will always be able to offer them marginally higher wages in terms of g (i.e., $w_i + \varepsilon$, where ε = incremental wage difference).
8. The case where FDI in A is selected is perfectly symmetric.
9. Since all entrepreneurs in B are identical, enrolling a single entrepreneur will suffice.
10. We are in debt to an anonymous reviewer for this comment.

126   *Peter J. Buckley and Niron Hashai*

11. Or alternatively the utility of n_A transactions in which K'_B was transferred by any number of B's entrepreneurs smaller than n_A.
12. As they appear in both the numerators and the denominators of Eqs (11a)–(11d).

References

Alchian, A. A., & Demsetz, H. 1972. Production, information costs and economic organization. *American Economic Review*, 62(5): 775–795.

Almeida, P. 1996. Knowledge sourcing by foreign multinationals: Patent citation analysis in the US semiconductor industry. *Strategic Management Journal*, 17(Winter Special Issue): 155–165.

Brainard, S. L. 1997. An empirical assessment of the proximity-concentration tradeoff between multinational sales and trade. *American Economic Review*, 87(4): 520–544.

Buckley, P. J., & Casson, M. C. 1976. *The future of the multinational enterprise*. London: Macmillan.

Buckley, P. J., & Casson, M. C. 1998. Analyzing foreign market entry strategies: Extending the internalization approach. *Journal of International Business Studies*, 29(3): 539–562.

Cantwell, J. 1995. The globalisation of technology: What remains of the product cycle model? *Cambridge Journal of Economics*, 19(1): 155–174.

Cantwell, J., & Narula, R. 2001. The eclectic paradigm in the global economy. *International Journal of the Economics of Business*, 8(2): 155–172.

Carr, D., Markusen, J. R., & Maskus, K. E. 2001. Estimating the knowledge-capital model of the multinational enterprise. *American Economic Review*, 91(3): 693–708.

Casson, M. 1985. Multinationals and intermediate product trade. In P. J. Buckley & M. Casson (Eds), *The economic theory of the multinational enterprise*: 144–171. London: Macmillan.

Casson, M. 2000. *The economics of international business: A new research agenda*. Cheltenham: Edward Elgar.

Dunning, J. H. 1977. Trade, location of economic activity and the MNE: A search for an eclectic approach. In B. Ohlin, P.-O. Hesselborn, & P. M. Wijkman (Eds), *The international allocation of economic activity*: 395–418. London: Macmillan.

Dunning, J. H. 1981. *FDI and the multinational enterprise*. London: Allen & Unwin.

Dunning, J. H. 1988. The eclectic paradigm of FDI: A restatement and some possible extensions. *Journal of International Business Studies*, 19(1): 1–31.

Dunning, J. H. 1993. *Multinational enterprises and the global economy*. Reading, MA: Addison-Wesley.

Dunning, J. H. 1998. Location and the multinational enterprise: A neglected factor? *Journal of International Business Studies*, 29(1): 45–66.

Dunning, J. H., & Narula, R. 1995. The R&D activities of foreign firms in the United States. *International Studies of Management and Organization*, 25(1–2): 39–73.

Eden, L. 2003. A critical reflection and some conclusions on OLI. In J. Cantwell & R. Narula (Eds), *International business and the eclectic paradigm*: 277–297. London: Routledge.

Ethier, W. J. 1986. The multinational firm. *Quarterly Journal of Economics*, 101(4): 805–833.

Grossman, G. M., & Helpman, E. 2002. Integration vs outsourcing in industry equilibrium. *Quarterly Journal of Economics*, 117(1): 85–120.

Heckscher, E. 1949. The effect of foreign trade on the distribution of income. In H. S. Ellis & L. A. Metzler (Eds), *Readings in international trade*: 43–69. Philadelphia: The Blakiston Co.

Helpman, E. 1984. A simple theory of international trade with multinational corporations. *Journal of Political Economy*, 92(3): 451–471.

Helpman, E., & Krugman, P. R. 1985. *Market structure and foreign trade: Increasing returns, imperfect competition and the international economy*. Cambridge, MA: MIT Press.

Henisz, W. J. 2005. The institutional environment for international business. In P. J. Buckley (Ed.), *What is international business?*: 85–109. Basingstoke: Palgrave Macmillan.

Hennart, J.-F. 1982. *A theory of multinational enterprise*. Ann Arbor, MI: University of Michigan Press.

Hennart, J.-F. 1993. Explaining the swollen middle: Why most transactions are a mix of "market" and "hierarchy". *Organization Science*, 4(4): 529–547.

Hirsch, S. 1976. An international trade and investment theory of the firm. *Oxford Economic Papers*, 28(2): 258–270.

Hofstede, G. 1980. *Culture's consequences: International differences in work-related values*. Beverly Hills, CA: Sage Publications.

Horstman, I. J., & Markusen, J. R. 1987. Strategic investments and the development of multinationals. *International Economic Review*, 28(1): 109–121.

Hymer, S. H. 1976. *The international operations of national firms: A study of direct foreign investment*. Unpublished 1960 Ph.D. thesis, Massachusetts Institute of Technology, Cambridge, MA.

Kogut, B., & Chang, S.-J. 1991. Technological capabilities and Japanese foreign direct investment in the United States. *Review of Economics and Statistics*, 73(3): 401–413.

Kogut, B., & Singh, H. 1988. The effect of national culture on the choice of entry mode. *Journal of International Business Studies*, 19(3): 411–423.

Kogut, B., & Zander, U. 1993. Knowledge of the firm and the evolutionary theory of the multinational corporation. *Journal of International Business Studies*, 24(4): 625–645.

Lewin, A. Y., & Peeters, C. 2006. Offshoring work: Business hype or the onset of fundamental transformation? *Long Range Planning*, 39(3): 221–239.

Linder, S. B. 1961. *An essay on trade and transformation*. New York: John Wiley & Sons.

Markusen, J. R. 1984. Multinationals, multi-plant economies, and the gains from trade. *Journal of International Economics*, 16(3–4): 205–226.

Markusen, J. R. 1998. Multinational firms, location and trade. *The World Economy*, 21(6): 733–755.

Markusen, J. R. 2001. International trade theory and international business. In A. M. Rugman & T. L. Brewer (Eds), *The Oxford handbook of international business*: 69–87. New York: Oxford University Press.

Markusen, J. R., & Venables, A. J. 1998. Multinational firms and the new trade theory. *Journal of International Economics*, 46(2): 183–203.

Markusen, J. R., & Venables, A. J. 2000. The theory of endowment, intra-industry and multinational trade. *Journal of International Economics*, 52(2): 209–234.

Martin, X., & Salomon, R. 2003. Knowledge transfer capacity and its implications for the theory of the multinational corporation. *Journal of International Business Studies*, 34(4): 356–373.

Milgrom, P., & Roberts, J. 1988. Economic theories of the firm: Past, present, and future. *Canadian Journal of Economics*, 21(3): 444–458.

Ohlin, B. 1933. *Interregional and international trade*. Boston: Harvard University Press.

128 *Peter J. Buckley and Niron Hashai*

Ronen, S., & Shenkar, O. 1985. Clustering countries on attitudinal dimensions: A review and synthesis. *Academy of Management Review*, 10(3): 435–454.

Rugman, A. M. 1981. *Inside the multinationals: The economics of internal markets*. New York: Columbia University Press.

Rugman, A. M. 1986. New theories of the multinational enterprise: An assessment of internalization theory. *Bulletin of Economic Research*, 38(2): 101–119.

Shenkar, O. 2001. Cultural distance revisited: Towards a more rigorous conceptualization and measurement of cultural differences. *Journal of International Business Studies*, 32(3): 519–536.

Solow, R. 1957. Technical progress and the aggregate production function. *Review of Economics and Statistics*, 39(3): 312–320.

Teece, D. 1981. The multinational enterprise: Market failure and market power consideration. *Sloan Management Review*, 22(3): 3–17.

UNCTAD. 2005. *World investment report*. Geneva: United Nations.

Williamson, O. E. 1975. *Markets and hierarchies: Analysis and anti-trust applications*. New York: Free Press.

Williamson, O. E. 1985. *The economic institutions of capitalism*. New York: Free Press.

Yang, X. 1994. Endogenous vs exogenous comparative advantages and economies of specialization vs economies of scale. *Journal of Economics*, 60(1): 29–54.

Yang, X. 2001. *Economics: New classical versus neoclassical analysis*. Oxford: Blackwell.

Yang, X., & Ng, Y. K. 1995. Theory of the firm and structure of residual rights. *Journal of Economic Behavior and Organization*, 26(1): 107–128.

Zaheer, S. 1995. Overcoming the liability of foreignness. *Academy of Management Journal*, 38(2): 341–363.

7
The Impact of the Global Factory on Economic Development

This paper advances four propositions.

1. A complex of causal factors under the umbrella term of globalisation have caused an international configuration of economic activities labelled 'the global factory' that dominates large areas of the world economy.
2. The existence of global factory system constrains the development options of a large number of developing countries.
3. Difficulties of mobilising entrepreneurial abilities in many countries react with these constraints to produce a difficult environment for economic development.
4. The paths to economic development under this system are:
   (a)   Incrementally upgrading activities within existing global factories.
   or
   (b)   Develop global factories under local control.

All of these development options are immensely difficult to implement. This paper suggests that although there has been a radical shift in the *location* of activities within the global economy, the *control* or orchestration of these activities remains very firmly within the metropolitan (advanced) countries.

Proposition 1. *Globalisation pressures have reconfigured the world economy and created "global factories."*

"Globalisation is essentially a process driven by economic forces. Its immediate causes are: the spatial reorganisation of production, international trade and the integration of financial markets." It is not therefore uniform across economic space – "the segmentation of the manufacturing process into multiple partial operations which combined with the development of cheap transportation and communication networks, has brought the increasing division of production into separate stages carried out in different locations." (Sideri, 1997, p. 38). The strategies of

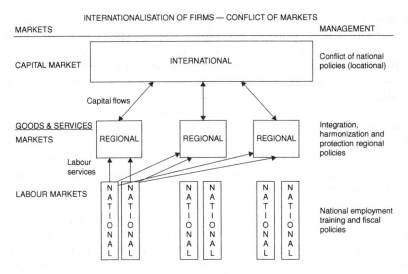

Figure 7.1 Internationalisation of firms – conflict of markets

multinational firms are therefore crucial to the causes and consequences of globalisation.

We can examine globalisation as a conflict between markets and management (government policies). Figure 7.1 identifies three levels of markets – financial markets, markets in goods and services and labour markets. Each of these is moving at a different speed towards global integration. Financial markets are already very closely integrated internationally. No individual 'national capital markets' can have a sustainable independent existence. However, attempts at national regulation do persist (Laulajainen, 2000) and the role of localities in the financial markets still provides differentiation (Berg & Guisinger, 2001; Tickell, 2000). Despite this, it is legitimate for analytical purposes to hypothesise a single integrated global capital market. Regional economic integration is becoming increasingly effective in integrating goods and services markets at the regional level. The relationship between company strategy and policy making within regional blocs, such as the European Union (EU), is a fascinating area for the development of new research streams (Chapman, 1999; Raines & Wishlade, 1999, see also Wood, 2003 on the Industrial Midwest of America). Labour markets, however, are functionally separate at the national level and here integration is largely resisted by national governments (Buckley et al., 2001).

The largest multinational enterprises are already perfectly placed to exploit these differences in the international integration of markets (Buckley, 1996). However, regional economic integration offers both large and small firms the opportunity to enjoy the advantages of a large 'home' market, whether it is their native home or their adoptive home. The operation of international capital markets (which allow firms to drive their capital costs down to a minimum) has largely transcended policy on regional integration, although each region would hope to retain its own regional financial centre. It is primarily in the arena of the creation and fostering of regional goods and services markets that enable firms to exploit economies of scale across several countries. Regional economic integration offers the most substantial size-of-country benefits. However, regional integration that encompasses countries with differential labour markets is becoming increasingly beneficial. This regional integration enables costs to be reduced by locating the labour intensive stages of production in the cheaper labour economies within the integrated area. Firms that serve just one regional market, as well as those that serve several of the regional goods and services markets of the world through horizontally integrated foreign direct investment (FDI), are able to complement this with vertically integrated FDI in quality-differentiated labour markets. Vertical integration also reflects the spatial distribution of supplies of key inputs and raw materials. The multinational enterprise achieves advantages through both vertical and horizontal integration. Each strategy is promoted by the 'size-of-country benefits' of regional economic integration in goods and services markets, which reduce or eliminate artificial barriers to trade between the members. This maximises the ability of firms to exploit intra-regional differences in factor abundance, including differentiated human capital.

On an industry level, globalisation can be shown to have an increasing impact. Gersbach (2002, p. 209) defines globalisation at the micro level as "the exposure of a productivity follower industry in one country to the productivity leader in another country". The transmission mechanisms of change across country borders are trade and FDI. Gersbach found a strong relationship between globalisation and productivity differences with the most efficient producers. He concludes that globalisation matters and that its influence spreads beyond a single region (e.g., Europe, North America).

More attention has been paid to vertical relationships (the supply chain or value chain). The differentiation of labour markets is most acute between advanced and less developed countries which are typically not part of the same regional bloc. The managers of multinational enterprises (MNEs) are increasingly able to segment their activities and to seek the optimal location for increasingly specialized slivers of activity. This ability to separate and relocate stages of production has led to a boom in manufacturing in China and service activities in India. MNEs are also increasingly able to co-ordinate these activities by means of a wide variety of mechanisms from wholly owned FDI through licensing and subcontracting to market relationships. The more precise use of location and ownership strategies by MNEs is the very essence of increasing globalisation. This is the emergence of the 'global factory' (Buckley, 2004).

132   *Peter J. Buckley*

In parallel with the growth of the globalisation of production, globalisation of consumption has accelerated and it is perhaps this which has excited most opposition. The alleged globalisation of tastes provokes nationalistic protectionist sentiments and is here analysed in terms of the balance of strategies within MNEs between "local" and "global" pressures on the firm.

1. Location factors

The process of globalisation is thus not only beginning to reorganise power at world level but also at national and sub-national levels (Alden, 1999; Dunning & Wallace, 1999; Graham, 2003; Mirza, 1998; Peck & Durnin, 1999; Pike, 1999; Yeung, 2003). As domestic firms move part of their production to other countries, technology, knowledge and capital become more important than land, the traditional source of state power. This redefines the function of the state (Rosecrance, 1996; Sideri, 1997). The loss of sovereignty to supra-national regional institutions is more acceptable than to international institutions which are more remote. The EU is an example of such regional integration and governance (Bressand, 1990). Social programmes within the EU are enforcing major redistributions of revenue between the individual nations—a process currently (2006) being challenged. The nation state as the possessor of the sense of identity is being replaced by sub-nations and internal regions as government is devolved.

A recent study by Subramanian and Lawrence (1999) found that national locations remained distinctive. Policy barriers at the borders, differences in local cultures in their widest sense and nature and geography, contribute to distinctiveness. This, together with the ability of incumbents to keep outsiders at a disadvantage (Buckley et al., 2001) and the first entrant benefits of local firms, reinforce the differentiation of national economies. International competition remains imperfect and international price differences persist because arbitrage is costly. Domestic market conditions largely determine prices and wages. Multinational firm affiliates remain firmly embedded in their local economy and such local firms identify closely with the national government. Subramanian and Lawrence (1999) conclude that national borders still matter. Borders continue to engender and to coincide with important discontinuities stemming from government policies, geography and societal differences. The authors stress information discontinuities which coincide with national boundaries and so create search and deliberation problems for trading and manufacturing firms. These issues also account for the alleged 'home bias' of multinational firms. Foreign direct investment is the key tool by which multinationals bridge cross-border discontinuities.

The two contrasting paradigms of a world made up of self-contained national economies and a 'borderless world' are incomplete and capture only part of a complex and subtle story. Lenway and Murtha (1994) examine the

The Impact of the Global Factory   133

role of the state as strategist along four dimensions: authority versus markets, communitarianism versus individualism, political versus economic objectives and equity versus efficiency. They state that international business scholarship "places a benchmark value on efficient international markets and tends to regard states as causes of deviation from this ideal" (p. 530).

2. Driving factors in globalisation and the global factory

On the demand side, producers can make substitute or competing products increasingly easily. In addition, consumers are willing to switch between products, particularly when prices fall for some classes of product. This produces increasing volatility and creates pressures on producers to lock consumers in by branding (and by extending brands across a wider product range).

On the supply side, rapid innovation occurs and this leads to mass production of standardized offerings which creates opportunities for economies of scale. (The "product cycle" process has become foreshortened (Vernon, 1966, 1979).) Crucially, access to cheap labour has become much easier. The combined effect of the need for flexibility to meet consumer demand and downward pressure on prices through competition induces increased demands for outsourcing and offshoring. The costs of adopting flexible manufacturing are now much lower than before. Companies are thus faced with protecting their ownership advantages even when externalising differentiated activities.

Technological changes, including the rise of e-commerce, have made global operations cheaper and more manageable. Managers in companies with global operations have learned to "fine slice" their activities and to locate each "stage" of activity in its optimal location and to control the whole supply chain, even when not owning all of it. These technological and managerial drivers have been augmented by political changes towards far more openness in previously closed economies. Even local factors can be seen to support global development. For instance, biases in the local capital market in China discriminate against whole swathes of local activity in the domestic private sector and make foreign ownership more likely than the growth of smaller indigenous firms (Huang, 2003). The nature of the global factory varies over time and space. Differences in industrial systems across countries have been frequently noted (Whitley, 1999). Particular differences can be noted in the degree of vertical integration (or internalisation of the value chain) as between Japanese and U.S. industry, Taiwan and South Korea, the rest of Italy versus the Emilia-Romagna region, and the British and U.S. textile industries in the first half of the nineteenth century. In all these examples, the first half of the pairing is much less vertically integrated (McLaren, 2000). From a country's point of view, is it good to attempt to host the location of the whole of the value chain? A more reasonable question is:

134   *Peter J. Buckley*

how far is it possible to secure the governance (or primary governance) or a global factory?

The true enemy of single nation global factories (even single region ones) is comparative advantage. Global factories are global because of differences in location give rise to national comparative advantages. The creation of *ersatz* global factories in single countries is often doomed to failure because no single country can replicate the cost and dynamic advantages of global competitors. The location of different stages of the global factory is determined by the advantages of different host countries. These can be augmented "artificially" by education, agglomeration advantages (giving rise to clustering) and investment in research, development and entrepreneurship. Host country policies designed to produce improvements in their dynamic comparative advantage can act as a magnet for economic activity. The attempt to design policies to attract all the stages of the global factory is futile. The issue of control of the governance of global factories is a more subtle issue. There are barriers to entry to markets, to locations, to new functions (R&D, marketing) and to *new* products (innovation, product improvement). These barriers often are of different natures, for instance the barriers to diversification (of products) differ from the barriers to internationalisation.

3. Elements of the global factory

The notion of the global factory was introduced in Buckley (2004) and developed in Buckley and Ghauri (2004). The key idea is that MNEs are becoming much more like differentiated networks. They choose location and ownership policies so as to maximise profits but this does not necessarily involve internalising their activities. Indeed, they have set a trend by outsourcing or offshoring their activities. Outsourcing involves utilising "buy" rather than "make" in the Coasean "externalise or internalise" decision (Coase, 1937). Offshoring involves both the externalisation option together with the 'make abroad' location decision (Buckley & Casson, 1976). MNEs have developed the ability to 'fine slice' their activities on an even more precise calculus and are increasingly able to alter location and internalisation decisions for activities which were previously locationally bound by being tied to other activities and which could only be controlled by internal management fiat.

The opening up of the global factory has provided new opportunities for new locations to enter international business. Emerging countries such as India and China are subcontracting production and service activities from the brand-owning MNEs. The use of the market by MNEs enables new firms to compete for business against the internalised activities of the MNE. This not only subjects every internalised activity to "the market test", it also results in a differentiated network (as presented in Figure 7.2) which we term "the global factory."

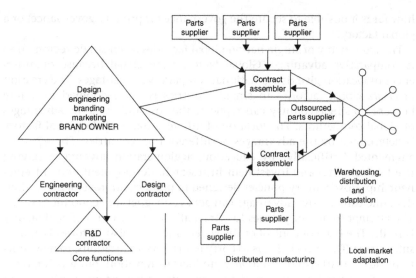

Figure 7.2 The global factory – globally distributed operations

The global supply chain is divided into three parts. The original equipment manufacturers (OEMs) control the brand and undertake design, engineering and R&D for the product (although there may be outsourced (see Figure 7.2)). They are customers for contract manufacturers (CMs) who perform manufacturing (and perhaps logistics) services for OEMs. In this so called modular production network, CMs need to possess capabilities such as mix, product and new product flexibilities while at the same time carrying out manufacturing activities at low costs with mass production processes. Flexibility is necessary to fulfil consumers' product differentiation needs (local requirements) and low cost for global efficiency imperatives (see Wilson & Guzman, 2005). The third part of the chain is warehousing, distribution and adaptation carried out on a 'hub and spoke' principle in order to achieve local market adaptation through a mix of ownership and location policies. As Figure 7.3 shows, ownership strategies are used to involve local firms with marketing skills and local market intelligence in international joint ventures (IJVs) whilst location strategies are used to differentiate the wholly owned 'hub' (centrally located) from the jointly owned 'spokes.'

4. The information structure of the global factory

Casson (1997a) highlights the importance of information costs in the structure of business organisation. He sees the brand owner as essentially a specialist in the search and specification functions (for customers and

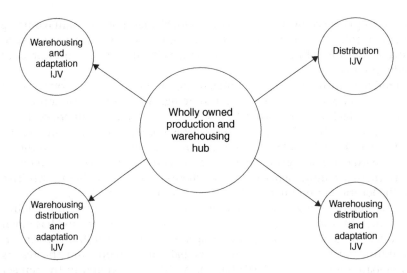

Figure 7.3 'Hub and spoke' strategies: an example

products respectively). "The brand owner, by intermediating between the producer and the retailer, co-ordinates the entire distribution channel linking the worker to the final customer" (Casson, 1997b, p. 159). This intermediation by the brand owner/market maker is intermediation of information, not production. The information structure of the global factory is shown schematically in Figure 7.4. This shows that the brand owner is the information hub of the global factory. The brand owner organises the market process itself. The organisation of production is conventionally within firms but the organisation of the whole production and trade sequence is intermediated by the market-making global factory. In many industries, particularly service industries, such as banking and insurance, the essence of competitiveness is the processing of information.

Fragmentation of the production chain can be accompanied by spatial disaggregation if:

(a) there are technological discontinuities between different stages,
(b) the stages are characterised by different factor intensities, and
(c) the costs of coordination and transport are sufficiently low to make the process economic (Deardorff, 2001).

Each of these elements has a technical, a managerial and a political dimension. Strategies of "fine-slicing" the production chain have combined with technological change, notably the development of the internet and other communications technologies to allow control at a distance (and without ownership) to become more feasible even for elements of the chain requiring fine control. The opening up of China (and now India) creates access to cheap, well disciplined labour and the development of logistics practice reduces costs.

Products with standard manufacturing interfaces and services with standard processes are ideal for outsourcing. A lack of interaction of the offshored facility with other functions enables a clean interface to be created and a "fine-slicing" cut to be made. Products which should not be outsourced include those where protection of intellectual property is crucial, those with extreme logistics requirements, with high technology content or performance requirements and those where consumers are highly sensitive to the location of production (Boston Consulting Group, 2004).

The literature on global commodity chains, latterly global value chains, has much in common with the analysis of the global factory and has much to offer in furthering the research agenda. This is true both in understanding the relationships between global value chains and the results of globalisation (Gereffi, 2001; Kaplinsky, 2001, 2004) and in the impact that value chains have on (the problems) of emerging economies, principally by investigating the prospects of upgrading the parts of the value chain that benefit poorer economies (Barnes, Kaplinsky, & Morris, 2004; Gereffi, 1999; Gereffi & Memedovic, 2003; Kaplinsky, Memedovic, Morris, & Readman, 2003). Issues of governance within global value chains have also been investigated (Gereffi, Humphrey, & Sturgeon, 2005) in ways that parallel the discussion of the global factory. Sadly, transaction and economics is treated solely as if it explained only internalisation (not externalisation too). "Conversely, the transaction costs approach offers various reasons why firms will bring certain activities in house" (Gereffi et al., 2005, p. 80). Research on governance of value chains – "a theory of value chain governance" (Gereffi et al., p. 85) relies on "complexity of information and knowledge transfer...the extent to which this...can be codified and...capabilities" as key drivers in the theory. This collapses into classification of five governance types and thus research agenda needs to be carried beyond typology.

Much of the work on first "commodity chains" then "value chains" is strongly empirically based and provides a well thought out research programme, as exemplified by "A Handbook for Value Chain Research" (Kaplinsky & Morris, 2001). This research programme has gone beyond the original distinction between "producer driven" and "buyer driven" chains (Gereffi, 2001) and Bair (2005) notes that there remains much to do in relating descriptions of varieties of "chains" to development outcomes. A key contribution of the commodity-chain literature is to move away from arid analyses of industries, sectors or even strategic groups to focus on links between firms and other entities that compete in networks against each

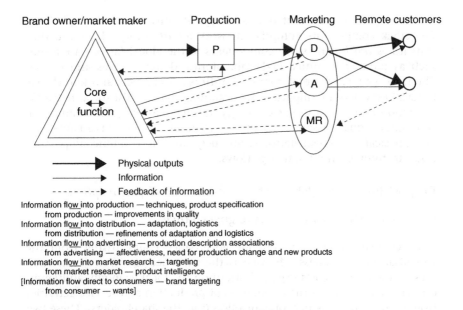

Figure 7.4 The information structure of the global factory

other. This feature of global capitalism is central to understanding the difficulties of upgrading facing emerging countries in having to deal with global factories.

5. The assets of the global factory

Strategies used in the global factory require a rethink of our notion of the stock of investment. Focal firms have decreased their ownership of productive capacity and increased their stocks of intangible assets. Thus production is outsourced to firms who specialise in maintaining and expanding production capacity. Focal firms invest in intangible assets such as: (1) brand equity; (2) management skills; (3) innovative capacity (R&D labs, design facilities); (4) distribution networks.

These assets are embedded within the firm. They are difficult to disentangle and disengage from the firm as a whole and they have an element of non-substitutability. It is difficult for other firms to copy or to replicate these intangible assets. Particular types of intangible assets that have achieved salience and value in the global factory are brand image, embedded supply chain management, design and new product development facilities, distribution networks with local adaptation capabilities and the ability of the management team to achieve customer lock-in.

Casson (2006) notes that networks typically involve stocks and flows. The stock components comprise network *infrastructure*, whilst the flow constitutes *traffic*. The stock components of the global factory are assets, such as production units, R&D laboratories, design centres and offices. The flows generated are of goods, semi-finished products and knowledge. Physical networks are important in sustaining trade whilst social networks are important in sustaining technology transfer, marketing and managerial communications (Casson, 2006, pp. 6–7). The global factory is an amalgam of a physical and social network, uniquely fitted to combine support for trade, technology and knowledge flows.

Proposition 2. *The global factory constrains development options*

6. Globalisation and corporate governance

Two key issues interact to provide governance issues arising from the globalisation of business. The first is the existence of unpriced externalities. These impose costs (e.g., pollution) on the local economy and environment. The second is the remoteness of production and service activities from their ultimate owners or controllers (e.g., the shareholders). These two factors interact because the mechanism for correcting negative externalities becomes difficult to implement due to remoteness and lack of immediate responsibility.

Perceived difficulties of global governance in multinational firms are exacerbated by the current crises in governance of firms in the West. The shareholder return driven environment which prevails today is very much the creature of the merger wave of the 1980s (Buckley & Ghauri, 2002). The feeling that corporations are outside social controls and that current forms of governance benefit only executives (and owners) rather than other stakeholders contribute to the concerns of critics. MNE–host country relations in middle-income countries have fully emerged onto the world stage, leaving behind a group of largely inert less developed countries which have so far been bypassed by globalisation. Large, emerging countries, which contain significant middle class markets, cheaper and well educated labour and stabilising political regimes (India, China, Brazil) are no longer seen just as new markets for old products (Prahalad & Lieberthal, 1998) but as significant locations requiring reconfigurations of the economic geography of MNE's operations. Not only do MNEs adapt products to local markets – local markets also provide ideas for new global products (Murtha, Lenway, & Hart, 2001). Increasing location 'tournaments', to attract FDI may have reduced the benefits to the host countries as have the increasing skill of the *managers* of MNEs in making their investments more 'footloose'. Corresponding skills on the part of host countries to make FDI 'sticky' are not developing at the same rate. Differences within developing countries may lead to divergence

140   *Peter J. Buckley*

between those which can develop the velocity to catch up and those which will fall behind as the world economy becomes more interdependent.

7. The power of the global factory

What then gives the global factory its power? Why should the global factory be able to hire the contract manufactures, sales outlets, design houses, logistics companies, advertising consultants and research laboratories rather than the other way round? How can global factories exercise this power without ownership? The answers, as always, are a combination of factors. These factors are entrepreneurship, control and selection of information, finance and innovation. They are combined within the enabling institutions of the parent country which nurture and foster the exercise of entrepreneurship and encourage risk taking and experimentation. They are able to orchestrate supply chains (Hinterhuber, 2002) without necessarily owning all the elements in the chain.

8. Constraints on development

Not only do global factories provide strong global competition for local firms, based on internationally recognised brand names and control of global marketing and distribution networks, they also have financial strength that among other things, enable global factories to purchase potentially competitive firms in host countries. This is allied to control of internalised technology and research skills that provide state-of-the-art products and a pipeline of future products. In globalised markets, access to high-income markets is largely shut off from less developed country firms (indeed all firms not part of the global factory networks) through control of distribution. This makes export of all but commodities difficult from less developed countries. Often the choice for such firms is to subcontract for the global factory or to struggle to establish outlets in high-income countries, which incurs high up-front sunk costs. The latter strategy is often impossible for financial reasons.

The purchasing power, often verging on monopsony, of the global factory can be utilised to reduce prices of inputs from the host country. This applies to physical and service inputs and to the price of labour. Multinational firms in less developed countries pay higher wages than local firms in general but it is possible to envisage an alternative position where local firms emerge to raise the wage rate above the going rate – set by agricultural wages. The factor that prevents this alternative position from emerging is the lack of entrepreneurial ability available to host country firms. At least part of this deficiency is because local entrepreneurs are bid away from local firms (by the higher wages alluded to above) to become managers and entrepreneurs in the global factory.

Is it therefore better for less developed countries to host portions of the global factory? The short run answer is probably yes because wages, taxes, spillover benefits and training benefits accrue to the local economy. This will generally be a benefit greater than the cost of relying on purely traditional employment (in agriculture largely – rural poverty). However, the answer in the long run depends on the potential of the host economy to develop in the absence of global factories and inward investment. The more practical policy question is how far global factories should be encouraged in particular host countries.

Proposition 3. *Difficulties of mobilising and concentrating entrepreneurship in poorer countries further inhibit development*

Economic theory tends to underestimate the obstacles that lie in the path of realising the potential for exploitation of resources in any locality. Concentration on traditional concepts of resource endowment (land, labour, capital) has had only a limited success in exploring national differences in material economic performance (as conventionally measured by per capita GNP). Even adding differences in education and training does not go far enough as these are embedded in general culture. Thus two main obstacles to the efficient use of natural resources can be identified. The first is geographical: the inability to effect a division of labour due to obstacles of transportation, including transaction costs. The second is the absence of an entrepreneurial culture which provides the economy with flexibility – in particular, the structural flexibility to cope with changes in the division of labour. These issues can also be developed in the context of the firm.

9. Dynamics: transaction costs and entrepreneurship

Why do entrepreneurs hire assets rather than asset owners hire entrepreneurs? The answer lies in non-contractibility. The key function of the entrepreneur is to exercise judgement in the face of uncertainty (Casson, 1982; Knight, 1921). Incomplete contracts have a positive effect on the exercise of entrepreneurship – they allow sequential adaptation to changing circumstances in an uncertain world. The firm is thus the agency by which the entrepreneur (whose services is the most difficult to measure or evaluate) combines his assets (judgement) with physical assets. The firm enables previously segmented areas of judgement and skills to be blended together and thus individual entrepreneurship becomes collective organisation. Individuals with entrepreneurial judgement can thus coalesce within the organisation and combine their skills. Because of the non-contractibility (or rather the extremely high costs of contracting) of these skills, this coalition becomes embedded in the firm, thus giving a transactions cost rationale

142 *Peter J. Buckley*

for 'competencies' residing for a finite period of time in certain companies. "Sticky capabilities" thus emerge.

Baumol (2007) distinguishes "replicative" entrepreneurship from innovative entrepreneurship. The former is simply the organiser (or undertaker) of a firm. This may be a way out of individual poverty – operating as a peddler and hiring no one for example and such tiny enterprises may well grow in huge numbers in poor economies. Indeed they may well appear *because* the economy is relatively stagnant. Innovative entrepreneurs are characterised by the supply of new products, new production methods, market-making and the creation of new forms of organisation. They are the organisers of innovation – taking an entire process from the generation of a novel idea (invention) through to marketability and entry of the product or service to the (global) market place. Such activities (as defined by Say, 1819 and Schumpeter, 1911) include the risk bearing function and thus involve the mobilisation of capital, but also the exercise of judgement (Casson, 1982). It is the combination of these attributes that is crucial and the existence of an environment that nurtures and rewards them that leads to success. Retention of entrepreneurs, against the centrifugal tendencies of metropoles in the global economy, is also a factor in long term success and in the creation of global factories.

Proposition 4. *Constrained paths to development result in changes in the location but not the control of economic activity.*

10. The least developed countries – starting development

A necessary condition for development in any locality is that there are resources with a potential for exploitation. Economic theory tends to underestimate the obstacles that lie in the path of realising this potential, however. Working with traditional concepts of resource endowment – land, labour and capital – cross-section regressions using the total factor productivity approach have only limited success in explaining international differences in material economic performance (as measured by per capita GNP) (Pack & Westphal, 1987). Some countries clearly under-perform by failing to realise their potential, and the question is why this should be so (Leibenstein, 1968).

Differences in education and training are commonly cited as a possible explanation, and the analysis presented here is generally consistent with this view. It goes beyond it, however, in recognising that education takes place largely outside formal institutions. Early education, in particular, is effected through family influence, peer group pressure within the local community and so on. To benefit fully from formal education it may be necessary for people to 'unlearn' beliefs from their informal education. But if the conflict between the two sets of beliefs is acute then psychological

The Impact of the Global Factory 143

obstacles to unlearning may arise. Measures of educational input based on gross expenditure fail to capture these important factors. The analysis in this paper helps to identify those aspects of the formal curriculum which are crucial in supporting economic development. It also identifies those elements of general culture which prepare people to benefit from such education.

Two main obstacles to the efficient use of national resources have been identified. The first is geographical: the inability to effect a division of labour due to obstacles to transportation. In this context, the presence of a potential entrepôt centre is crucial in facilitating the development of a region. The second is the absence of an entrepreneurial culture. An entrepreneurial culture provides an economy with flexibility – in particular, the structural flexibility to cope with changes in the division of labour. These changes may be progressive changes stemming from essentially autonomous technological innovations, or defensive changes made in response to resource depletion or various environmental disturbances. These are not new ideas. Kreutz (1991) notes "There is a marked emphasis on trade and its virtues in the writings of tenth-century Muslim geographers such as Ibn Hawqal. Speaking disparagingly of contemporary Sicily, which he found dirty and impoverished, lbn Hawqal blamed its sorry condition on heavy taxation and execrable treatment of merchants. Elsewhere, he admired, above all, busy harbors and the steady flow of goods" (p. 84).

11. Emerging countries

Three possible strategies suggest themselves to create a global factory under a single country (or region) governance. First is to expand from the subordinate contractual manufacturing provider by adding activities. The second is to internationalise from an 'almost complete' local factory lacking perhaps, branding or R&D. The third is to build a full range of activities in the host country or regions and then internationalise the whole range from a domestic base. We will analyse the first strategy in detail. The second strategy, feasible only where global networks are patchy or intrinsically difficult to create, is on first sight more hopeful. However, 'gaps' in global factories are difficult to fill because they represent deficiencies in local conditions. They are most usually in branding, distribution or R&D and are, as we shall see, the most difficult and complex part of the network of the global factory to enter. Alliances are a potential means of filling gaps but are open to potential power inequalities and to the threat of takeover. Finally, building a local network and then internationalising the whole of it is a formidable task. Such a strategy only arises when the local economy is large (China, India, Brazil, Russia) or is protected by artificial barriers (such as tariffs) or cultural barriers. Korean Chaebols might be an example and their extremely patchy success rate is an example of the difficulties of internationalising even from

Figure 7.5 Original equipment manufacturer

a strong, artificially protected and culturally distorted base. It could also be argued that Korean firms lacked the basic R&D strength to anchor a true global factory, being dependent on second generation Japanese technology.

In emerging countries (*par excellence* China) the first step is produce components or complete products to the specifications of foreign firms who market the final product. Such "original equipment manufacturers" (Figure 7.5) are a subservient part of the global factory's network and are often in a weak bargaining position vis-à-vis the principal. There are many OEMs to play off against one another and OEMs are often forced to be price takers.

A crucial and neglected (Casson, 1999) aspect of breaking in to the global factory is the ability of indigenous firms to assume the role of market-making intermediaries. A market-making intermediary establishes trading links that would not otherwise exist. In so doing, such a firm creates a network of buyers and sellers that could not easily trade with each other. This requires negotiating skills, a reputation for honesty and, crucially, the firm must recognise systematic changes in demand and supply conditions that create opportunities to profit from the creation of new markets. Therefore, information costs are vital. The entrepreneur's task is to collect the relevant information and to identify opportunities to satisfy latent demand. The creation of a new market involves set up costs. These are non-recoverable sunk costs analogous to those involved in innovation. In order to recover these costs, a degree of monopoly is essential. The first mover advantages which confer such a monopoly can be protected by secrecy or some form of legal entry prevention – a patent or licence. An effective form of protection is to reach customers quickly and defend a reputation for quality by branding.

The status of OEM allows benefits to the emerging country firm (Shenkar, 2005). The firm can achieve incremental upgrading of quality and manufacture to customer requirements. It is plugged into the network of the global factory (albeit in a subservient position) and gains access, indirectly, to the global market. The OEM also receives technological support derived from the detailed specification of the customer. More enlightened principals also supply financial and managerial help and may impose health and safety and environmental standards as well as upgrading the labour force.

Step 2 involves performing design and some development work and becoming an original design manufacturer (ODM) (Figure 7.6). This strategic decision requires a significant upgrading of technological capability

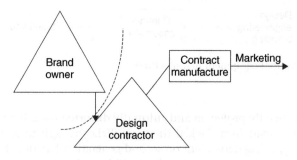

Figure 7.6 Original design manufacturer

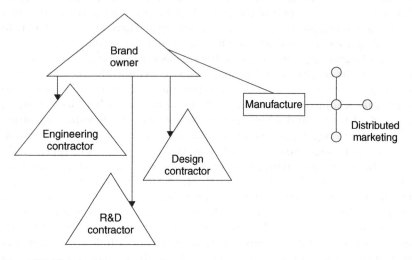

Figure 7.7 Original brand manufacture

and the recruitment of engineers and designers capable of meeting world standards. It is significant that these categories of skills are priorities of the Chinese leadership (Shenkar, 2005, p. 89). A successful ODM can bypass middlemen and go direct to the buyer (usually the brand owner will control this process). The move from OEM to ODM is a profound one requiring high levels of managerial and technological skill and political nous. An UNCTAD (2005) study identifies need for host countries for textile MNEs to develop the ability to upgrade from simple assembly to "full package production" (in textiles). It provides the following list of key policy areas to enable this to happen: identify specialist niches; skills and technological upgrading; investment in information technology; improvement of infrastructure and utilising tariff preferences. This is a formidable list for low and even

146 *Peter J. Buckley*

middle-income countries and firms to achieve, especially in view of their competitors also attempting to achieve the same goal.

The final step is to design, manufacture and sell the product under the firm's own name. This move to original brand manufacturer (OBM) involves control not only of production engineering and design, but also of branding and marketing as shown in Figure 7.7. It requires marketing and research skills. Given the global market it will also require exporting and FDI and the establishment of the brand in foreign markets. Some Chinese firms (Haier, Huawi Technologies) have achieved modest success in creating their own global factories. Some outward FDI from China is designed to support such activities. Other outward FDI from emerging countries is intended to secure brands to be exploited worldwide. The main reasons why Shanghai Automotive Industry Corporation (SAIC), China's biggest car maker was interested in buying Rover in 2005 were (1) to obtain the Rover brand (2) to obtain the ability to design and manufacture cars (Financial Times, 2005a, "What Shanghai sought from Longbridge", p. 15).

12. Entry by buying brands

Brands, just like any other asset, can be acquired. It might seem to be a relatively easy way for outsiders to enter the global factory by purchasing brands. This will usually mean the acquisition of the whole company because brands are embedded and are often unavailable except as part of the takeover of the brand owner. However, it is often ailing companies that are most likely to be takeover targets and such companies may be owners of tired, dated or obsolescent brands. Moreover, because of the potential value as assets, brands are expensive to acquire and this may put good healthy brands with potential longevity beyond the purchasing power of emerging country firms.

In his analysis of the takeovers of IBM's personal computing business by Lenovo the Chinese computer maker and Siemens of Germany paying BenQ, the Taiwanese company to take over its ailing mobile telephone business, Kroeber (2005, p. 19) shows that the Chinese company did so on for less favourable conditions than the Taiwanese company. Moreover, when the Chinese television maker TCL took control of the television business of Thomson SA of France, they acquired these assets for virtually no cash payment but Thomson retained a one-third stake in the TV business with an option to convert it into TCL shares. Lenovo paid IBM $1.75 billion in combined cash and debt assumption and this also gave IBM a 19% stake in Lenovo (Biediger et al., 2005). These Western companies disengaged from unprofitable businesses at no cost and gained a low cost option on the future profits if the Chinese companies turned the business around. The desperation of the Chinese companies compares unfavourably with the good deal that BenQ obtained. BenQ gained rights to all the patents held by

The Impact of the Global Factory 147

the Siemen's mobile handset unit whereas when TCL acquired Thomson's TV business the highest value activity (tube production) was left out.

Kroeber (2005, p. 19) suggests an explanation of this phenomenon that accords perfectly with the underlying rationale of the global factory. Taiwanese companies have great strengths in supply chain management whereas the big Chinese manufacturing companies are trading groups that have exploited temporary arbitrage opportunities. Taiwanese equipment manufacturers rely on dense networks of highly specialized component suppliers. These suppliers and the ultimate assemblers (such as BenQ) operate with high flexibility and fast turnaround times. Thus, Taiwanese companies can bring new designs to market rapidly and can move into new product lines as new electronic gadgets are invented. Since, the mid-1990s, Taiwanese companies have gained cost advantages by moving most low-end production to China. In contrast, Chinese companies, such as Lenovo and TCL, have taken advantage of low purchasing power and inefficiencies in the Chinese market. They offer cheap versions of electronic products in a market where Chinese consumers cannot afford the higher quality but more expensive foreign products. These advantages diminish as Chinese income and purchasing power grows. Low profit margins mean that Chinese companies (such as TCL and Lenovo) cannot afford the R&D expenditure necessary to create new products and brands. In addition they have underdeveloped manufacturing and supply chain management skills. Entrepreneurial and market-making skills are weak in China and so acquiring weaker brands at high prices seems the best way forward to establish independent global factories.

Bids from China National Offshore Oil Corporation (CNOOC) for the U.S. oil group Unocal and by a group led by Haier (the leading Chinese domestic appliance company) for Maytag, the owner of Hoover vacuum cleaners have led to Chinese companies being termed 'aberrant buyers' (Financial Times, 24.06.05, p. 17). The desire of Chinese companies to buy not only global brands but also natural resources combined with the notoriously imperfect domestic capital market (Huang, 2004) means that these companies often outbid more traditional purchasers. As all outward investment by Chinese companies requires approval from the state Council, flexibility in negotiations is not an asset they possess.

The purchase of Ingersall Production systems by Dalian Machine Tool (China's largest machine tool manufacturer) in 2002 was driven by the desire to acquire American management techniques and the takeover depended on retaining the local Chief Executive. A long term learning perspective is essential in building the global factory and brand. The value of a brand depends upon what the (prospective) owner can do to enhance it. This value enhancement depends crucially upon sales, marketing and distribution abilities. Smaller and inexperienced firms typically do not have this range of skills. Purchasing of brands alone will not secure long run global competitiveness. Brands, like all other assets, require constant reinvestment

148   *Peter J. Buckley*

(and reinvigoration). They also require a wide range of supporting skills. Without these, brand value will atrophy.

13. The dynamics of upgrading

The move from contract OEM to ODM, to OBM and finally to full global factory, involving contracting out of activities is a set of enormous leaps. The degree of skill and managerial resources can only be accumulated, financed and protected by an immense effort of will and concentration of resources. There is a requirement for entrepreneurial ability of a high order and, moreover, the type of entrepreneurial skill required varies over time. Initially, the entrepreneur has to secure and to fulfil demanding and competitive contracts in order to secure a position as OEM in the global factory. Reliability and quality of output must be achieved. Upgrading to ODM requires real vision, a global outlook, long term planning and the ability to build a high level multi-disciplinary team. Designers and engineers have to be integrated into the firm and they require a different style of management from production workers. A shift from accepting design and engineering specifications to the creation of them is a profound step change. The final stage – the move to OBM – is even more difficult to achieve. The creation of an original brand is a huge undertaking. Quality, reliability, a good design and the maintenance of world class standards are not easily achieved. This has to go together with the creation of global distribution and marketing. Thus a primarily national, dependant organisation needs to become international and independent, central to a new global factory.

14. Consolidation

It is clear that OEMs have little bargaining power and this constrains their ability to amass the resources necessary to break out of their subservient role in the global factory. There is evidence that this is happening and situations approaching bilateral monopoly (or at least oligopoly) are occurring in several sections where one or more powerful principals confront multi skilled "factories for hire" which are approaching a scale, competence and self confidence to break out of the role of mere contractors.

A clear example of this process occurs in the textile and clothing sector (UNCTAD, 2005). A small number of large retailing companies transmit demands from Western consumers and largely shape trade and production patterns. However, with the removal of tariff protection from manufacturing in selected lower cost production locations, there is increasing pressure on producers to consolidate production into larger factories to gain economies of scale and reduce costs. This consolidation produces MNEs – mainly from East Asia (Hong Kong, Taiwan, Korea) with multiple production locations to supply the retailers.

The Impact of the Global Factory   149

15. The role of the state

The relationship between the global factory and state intervention to bolster developments is a complex one. The global factory results from managerial decisions on insourcing versus outsourcing (the make-or-buy decision) and location decisions which are unconstrained geographically. The developmental state as it has so far been conceived and implemented restricts both decision sets. Historically, developmental states (Japan and South Korea) fostered national champions. These have been conglomerate firms centred on a bank or a family – Kiertsu and Chaebols. Internal capital markets within these conglomerates have reinvested 'soft' money (raised cheaply from the bank or the state) and this has resulted in over-diversification. Parallel global factories would have utilised market relationships and avoided excessive internalisation. Similarly, the conglomerates, because of state direction or bias in investment decision, invested heavily at home rather than undertaking foreign investment. It is arguable that old-style conglomerate state championed firms like the Keiretsu and Chaebol were overwhelmed by the inability to compete with rival global factories even with state backing and 'economic patriotism'. This does not necessarily mean that no form of developmental state could be successful. Such a state would have to be far more intelligent in design and flexible in operation. Future developmental states would have to combine judicious investment in locationally fixed endowments to attract and retain economic activity, to foster domestic entrepreneurship and to abandon opposition to market imperatives, including the necessity for home based firms to invest abroad in order to attain or retain international competitiveness. Focus rather than diversification would be the hallmark of future national champions. More open strategies would be required – for instance, family centred firms would have to recruit talent from outside the family to key managerial positions and less ethnocentric attitudes would be necessary for success. Investment in particular types of locationally fixed infrastructure to support key activities might be a feature of future strategies together with active policies to acquire and retain key individuals (scientists, designers) and groups (top managers, financiers). The strategies might resemble a more refined version of Singaporean strategies over the last 30 years.

There is a key requirement to balance state direction with innovative and entrepreneurial attitudes and behaviour which require freedom and individual risk taking. Subsidies and handouts require funding and funding requires a solid tax base. In addition, developmental states have been riddled with corruption. Moves away from market-based rewards provide opportunities for opportunism. Developmental states need to be open, transparent and to implement predictable policies and administration.

Future successful developmental states will have to perform a balancing act between direction and noninterference that requires sensitive, flexible and honest policies on a long term consistent basis. It is not clear that many

150 *Peter J. Buckley*

(if any) states will be able to achieve these requirements and their decision makers must avoid the temptations of appropriating the rents that could accrue to the state.

16. Sovereign wealth funds

Government intervention in the global economy has recently been via sovereign wealth funds through which Governments buy foreign assets. Originally such funds were invested conservatively, buying largely US Treasury Bonds and other foreign paper assets. These assets can be used to support the country's exchange rate as they are highly liquid. Now China and other countries have more reserves than they need for this purpose and can move into vehicles for long term saving and to more risky assets – such as acquiring equities. Singapore has two such funds (G1C and Temasek) and oil and commodity – rich countries model their funds on Norway's Government Pension Fund (Economist, 2007, p. 77). These funds acquire large equity stakes in foreign companies, including banks. Many sovereign wealth funds lack expertise in appraising foreign companies for equity acquisition purposes. China has therefore purchased equity (9.9%) in Blackstone's, a private equity company with outstanding expertise in valuing and acquiring large companies. This acquisition by China's sovereign wealth fund is a first step to taking control of global factories, using global financial companies as captive advisors.

In a global economy dominated by global factories, sovereign wealth funds represent a rational response by emerging countries. Not only do these funds represent a long term source of funds (albeit more risky than short term paper assets) they also provide management expertise on how to acquire global factories (via private equity stakes) and a direct purchase of management control (or at least a share in the management) of global factories. It is the ultimate management of the factories themselves that poses the largest question mark against the success of these ventures. Political interference is a threat to success as is the ability of the emerging country to retain the loyalty and expertise of key managers down the chain of control.

17. Conclusion: the global factory and its impact on development

The analysis of the global factory within a Coasean framework puts the issues of development in a new light. Developing countries are constrained by the existence and power of global factories. They are frequently constrained to be suppliers of labour intensive manufacturing goods into the global factory system. Breaking into the global factory by emerging country firms is formidably difficult. It requires a combination of strong finance, effective promotion, the training and recruitment of skilled personnel (which requires an excellent educational system) and a dedicated long term strategy. Developing countries can attempt to upgrade from this position gradually by the set of steps outlined above or they can attempt to set up new global factories in competition with existing ones. This latter strategy requires a concentration of resources available through large Sovereign Wealth Funds but beyond the scope of most emerging countries. Acquisition elements of this strategy in particular, such as buying established brands, require particular managerial skills. Development issues can be analysed within the framework above which pay particular attention to dynamics and to the context of the individual developing country which is crucial in determining outcomes.

18. Research agenda

This paper suggests an extensive research agenda. The shifts in the location of economic activity, to India and China for example, are well documented. What is less clear is the mechanisms of control over these activities. The power of "orchestration" of the global factory requires a refined conceptual framework and a good deal of micro-economic analysis – much of it is in a qualitative framework. The crucial elements of control in the system may not be easily replicable. The power of brand names, innovation and financing combined with an efficient distribution network provide formidable entry barriers to new entrants.

References

Alden, J. (1999). The impact of foreign direct investment on job creation: The experience of Wales. In N. A. Phelps & J. Alden (Eds.), *Foreign direct investment and the global economy* (pp. 204–220). London: The Stationery Office.

Bair, J. (2005). From Commodity Chains to Value Chains and Back Again? *MIMEO*, Yale University Department of Sociology, p. 125.

Barnes, J., Kaplinsky, R., & Morris, M. (2004). Industrial policy in developing economies: Developing dynamic comparative advantage in the South African Automobile sector. *Competition and Change, 8*(2): 153–172.

Baumol, W. J. (2007). Entrepreneurship and innovation: The (Micro) theory of price and profit. Working Paper, Yale University.

Berg, D. M., & Guisinger, S. E. (2001). Capital flows, capital controls and international business risk. In A. M. Rugman & T. L. Brewer (Eds.), *The Oxford handbook of international business* (pp. 259–281). Oxford: Oxford University Press.

Biediger, J., DeCicco, T., Green, T., Hoffman, G., Lei, D., Mahadevan, K. (2005). Strategic action at Lenovo. *Organizational Dynamics, 34*(1): 89–102.

Boston Consulting Group. (2004). *Capturing global advantage.* Boston, MA: Boston Consulting Group.

Bressand, A. (1990). Beyond interdependence: 1992 as a global challenge. *International Affairs, 66*(1): 47–65.

Buckley, P. J. (1996). Government policy responses to strategic rent-seeking transnational firms. *Transnational Corporations, 5*(2): 1–17.

152 *Peter J. Buckley*

Buckley, P. J. (2004). Government policy responses to strategic rent-seeking transnational firms. *Transnational Corporations, 5*(2): 1–17 1996.

Buckley, P. J., & Casson, M. C. (1976). *The future of the multinational enterprise.* London: Macmillan.

Buckley, P. J., & Ghauri, P. N. (Eds.) (2002). *International mergers and acquisitions: A reader.* London: International Thomson Press.

Buckley, P. J., & Ghauri, P. N. (2004). Globalisation, economic geography and the strategy of multinational enterprises. *Journal of International Business Studies, 35*(2): 81–98.

Buckley, P. J., Clegg, L. J., Forsans, N., & Reilly, K. T. (2001). Increasing the size of the 'country', regional economic integration and foreign direct investment in a globalized world economy. *Management International Review, 41*(3): 251–274.

Casson, M. (1982). *The entrepreneur.* Oxford: Martin Robertson.

Casson, M. (1997a). Entrepreneurial networks in international business. *Business and Economic History, 26*(2): 3–17.

Casson, M. (1997b). Institutional economics and business history: A way forward? *Business History, 39*(4): 151–171.

Casson, M. (1999). The organisation and evolution of the multinational enterprise. *Management International Review, 39*(Special Issue 1): 77–121.

Casson, M. (2006, April). *Networks: A new paradigm in international business history?* UK Academy of International Business Conference, Manchester.

Chapman, K. (1999). Merger/acquisition activity and regional cohesion in the EU. In N. A. Phelps & J. Alden (Eds.), *Foreign direct investment and the global economy* (pp. 121–138). London: The Stationery Office.

Coase, R. H. (1937). The nature of the firm. *Economica, 4*: 386–405.

Deardorff, A. (2001). Fragmentation across cones. In S. Ardnt & H. Kierzkowski (Eds.), *Fragmentation: new production patterns in the world economy.* Oxford: Oxford University Press.

Dunning, J. H., & Wallace, L. (1999). New Jersey in a globalising economy. In N. A. Phelps & J. Alden (Eds.), *Foreign direct investment and the global economy* (pp. 253–269). London: The Stationery Office.

Sovereign Wealth Funds: Keep your T-bonds, we ' ll take the bank. (2007, July 28). *Economist,* p. 77.

What Shanghai sought from Longbridge. (2005, June 1). *Financial Times,* p. 15.

A new Asian invasion: China' s champions bid high for American brands and resources. (2005, June 24) *Financial Times,* p. 17.

Gereffi, G. (1999). International trade and upgrading in the apparel commodity chain. *Journal of International Economics, 48*: 37–70.

Gereffi, G. (2001). Beyond the producer driven/buyer driven dichotomy. *IDS Bulletin, 32*(2): 30–40.

Gereffi, G., Humphrey, J., & Sturgeon, T. (2005). The governance of global value chains. *Review of International Political Economy, 12*(1): 78–104.

Gereffi, G., & Memedovic, O. (2003). *The global apparel value chain: What prospects for upgrading by developing countries?* Vienna: UNIDO.

Gersbach, H. (2002). Does and how does globalisation matter at industry level? *World Economy, 25*(2): 209–229.

Graham, E. M. (2003). Attracting foreign direct investment to the United States: The joust between the federal government and the states. In N. A. Phelps & P. Rains (Eds.), *The new competition for inward investment* (pp. 61–78). Cheltenham: Edward Elgar.

The Impact of the Global Factory 153

Hinterhuber, A. (2002). Value chain orchestration in action and the case of the global agrochemical industry. *Long Range Planning, 35*(6): 615–635.

Huang, Y. (2003). *Selling China – Foreign Direct Investment during the Reform Era.* Cambridge: Cambridge University Press.

Kaplinsky, R. (2001). Is globalization all it is cracked up to be? *Review of International Political Economy, 8*(1): 45–65.

Kaplinsky, R. (2004). Spreading the gains from globalization? What can be learned from value-chain analysis? *Problems of Economic Transition, 47*(2): 74–115.

Kaplinsky, R., Memedovic, O., Morris, M., & Readman, J. (2003). *The global wood furniture value chain: What prospects for upgrading by developing countries?* The Case of South Africa Vienna: UNIDO.

Kaplinsky, R., & Morris, M. (2001). *A handbook for value chain research.* Brighton: University of Sussex Institute for Development Studies.

Knight, F. (1921) . In G. J. Stigler (Ed.), *Risk, uncertainty and profit.* Chicago: University of Chicago Press (1971).

Kreutz, B. M. (1991). *Before the Normans: Southern Italy in the ninth and tenth centuries.* Philadelphia: University of Pennsylvania Press.

Kroeber, A. (2005, June 23). China's century is still a long march away. *Financial Times,* p. 19.

Laulajainen, R. I. (2000). The regulation of international finance. In G. L. Clark, M. P. Feldman, & M. S. Gertler (Eds.), *The Oxford handbook of economic geography* (pp. 215–229). Oxford: Oxford University Press.

Leibenstein, H. (1968). Entrepreneurship and Development. *American Economic Review (papers and proceedings), 58:* 72–83.

Lenway, S. A., & Murtha, T. P. (1994). The state as strategist in international business research. *Journal of International Business Studies, 25:* 513–535.

McLaren, J. (2000). Globalization and vertical structure. *The American Economic Review, 90*(5): 239–1254.

Mirza, H. (1998). *Global competitive strategies in the new world economy: Multilateralism, regionalization and the transnational firm.* Northampton, MA: Edward Elgar.

Murtha, T. P., Lenway, S. A., & Hart, J. A. (2001). *Managing new industry creation.* Stanford University Press.

Pack, H., & Westphal, L. E. (1987). Industrial strategy and technological change: Theory versus reality. *Journal of Development Economics, 22*(1): 86–128.

Peck, F., & Durnin, J. (1999). Institutional marginalisation and inward investment strategies in the North of England: The case of Cumbria. In N. A. Phelps & J. Alden (Eds.), *Foreign direct investment and the global economy* (pp. 237–252). London: The Stationery Office.

Pike, A. (1999). In situ restructuring in branch plants and their local economic development implications. In N. A. Phelps & J. Alden (Eds.), *Foreign direct investment and the global economy* (pp. 221–236). London: The Stationery Office.

Prahalad, C. K., & Lieberthal, K. (1998, July–August). The end of corporate imperialism. *Harvard Business Review,* 69–79.

Raines, P., & Wishlade, F. (1999). E.C. policy-making and the challenges of foreign investment. In N. A. Phelps & J. Alden (Eds.). *Foreign direct investment and the global economy* (pp. 71–86). London: The Stationery Office.

Rosecrance, R. (1996, July–August). The rise of virtual state. *Foreign Affairs, 47*(1): 45–61.

Say, J-B. (1819). *Traite d'economic politique* (4th edition, C. Prinsep, Trans.). Boston: Wells and Lilley (1821).

154　*Peter J. Buckley*

Schumpeter, J. (1911). *The theory of economic development* (R. Opie, Trans.). Cambridge, Mass: Harvard University Press (1934).

Shenkar, O. (2005). *The Chinese century: The rising Chinese economy and its impact on the global economy, the balance of power and your job.* Upper Saddle River, N.J. Wharton School.

Sideri, S. (1997). Globalisation and regional integration. *European Journal of Development Research, 9*(1): 38–81.

Subramanian, R., & Lawrence, R. Z. (1999). *A prism on globalization: Corporate responses to the dollar.* Washington, DC: Brookings Institution Press. p. 198.

Tickell, A. (2000). Finance and localities. In G. L. Clark, M. P. Feldman, & M. S. Gertler (Eds.), *The Oxford handbook of economic geography* (pp. 230–252). Oxford: Oxford University Press.

UNCTAD. (2005). *TNCs and the removal of textiles and clothing quotas.* Geneva: UNCTAD.

Vernon, R. (1966). International trade and international investment in the product cycle. *Quarterly Journal of Economics, 80*: 190–207.

Vernon, R. (1979). The product cycle hypothesis in a new international environment. *Oxford Bulletin of Economics and Statistics, 41*: 255–267.

Whitley, R. (1999). *Divergent capitalisms: the social structuring change of business systems.* Oxford University Press.

Wilson, J., & Guzman, G. A. C. (2005, July). *Organisational knowledge transfer in modular production networks: The case of Brazil.* Paper presented to AIB World conference, Quebec.

Wood, A. (2003). The politics of orchestrating inward investment: Institutions, policy and practice in the industrial Midwest. In N. A. Phelps & P. Rains (Eds.), *The new competition for inward investment* (pp. 79–98). Cheltenham: Edward Elgar.

Yeung, G. (2003). Scramble for FDI: The experience of Guangdong province in Southern China. In N. A. Phelps & P. Rains (Eds.), *The new competition for inward investment* (pp. 193–212). Cheltenham: Edward Elgar.

Part II
Knowledge, Innovation and Management

8
Under What Conditions Do Firms Benefit from the Research Efforts of Other Organizations?

Co-authored with Mario I. Kafouros

1. Introduction

It has been recognized that industrial Research and Development (R&D) may affect not only the productivity performance of the organization that undertakes such activities (Griliches, 1986; Hall and Mairesse, 1995), but also the performance of other firms. Empirical research confirms the existence of R&D spillovers, indicating that the productivity achieved by a firm depends on the pool of scientific knowledge accessible to it (Adams and Jaffe, 1996; Geroski, 1995; Griliches, 1992; Scherer, 1982). However, past empirical results are conflicting: even though many studies find the impact of R&D spillovers to be both positive and high (Bernstein, 1988; Brandstetter, 1996; Raut, 1995), for reasons that are often unclear, other studies find that spillovers have negligible or even negative consequences for firm performance (Antonelli, 1994; Geroski, 1991; Wakelin, 2001). Although it is known that in order to unlock their economic potential, companies must actively search for and exploit external ideas and technologies (Chesbrough, 2003, 2007), there is a question that remains unanswered. When do firms utilize successfully external knowledge to create additional value, and when do they fail to do so?

This study extends previous research by addressing the above question and indicating that the reason for previously conflicting results may be an incomplete understanding of the factors influencing the spillovers performance relationship. Put differently, drawing on theories of innovation and knowledge externalities, it examines the conditions under which a firm benefits from the technological achievements and research discoveries of other firms. Specifically, the study focuses on three factors that may influence the assets, resources and market positions of companies and in turn, the impact that spillovers have on their productivity performance. Initially, we analyze the role of technological opportunities and firm size. Although

158   *Mario I. Kafouros and Peter J. Buckley*

past studies have evaluated how these two factors impact on a firm's own innovation, there has been little research concerning their impact on the ability of organizations to benefit from external R&D. The third factor that the study investigates is that of competitive conditions. Theory suggests that higher competitive pressure is associated with imperfect appropriability and in turn, with stronger spillovers. We test this theoretical prediction and examine whether variations in the effects of R&D spillovers may be attributable to the level of competition. This is particularly important as existing research often ignores that the R&D undertaken by other firms increases not only the pool of scientific knowledge, but also the level of competitive pressure (Aghion et al., 2001).

In addition to the examination of the role of technological opportunities, firm size and competition, this paper differs from previous studies in a number of other ways. First, it distinguishes between the R&D undertaken by intra-industry competitors and that undertaken by external (inter-industry) innovators. Employing a variety of different weighting methods, it investigates whether firms successfully utilize knowledge gained from their rivals (whose products are often substitutes for their own products), or whether they gain more from firms in more distantly related industries (whose products either complement their own or are not directly related to them). Second, the study utilizes firm-level data (for the UK manufacturing sector). The use of micro-level data allows the separation of productivity advances that are result of a firm's specific capabilities, from those improvements that are general to the industry (Wakelin, 2001). Third, in contrast to studies that use the GDP price index to deflate R&D expenditures, this paper uses recently constructed R&D price indices, thereby capturing R&D-cost idiosyncrasies that vary across sectors. Indeed, the data indicate that R&D costs tend to rise more rapidly for low-tech sectors, implying that these firms have to pay more for industrial research.

The paper is organized as follows. Sections 2 and 3 present the theoretical context of the study, and describe the methodology and the data. Section 4 presents the findings concerning intra- and inter-industry spillovers. We then explore the role of technological opportunities and firm size in Section 5, while Section 6 investigates the role of competition. Conclusions are drawn in Section 7.

2. Positive and negative R&D spillovers

The rationale behind R&D spillovers is that the technology and scientific knowledge developed by one firm is often useful to others as well (Griliches, 1992; Scherer, 1982). Hence, R&D may improve not only a firm's own productivity but also that of other firms of the same industry or even of other industries. R&D spillovers may occur through trade, i.e. when the new products that a firm develops are used as inputs by other firms (Mohnen,

1999). A good example is that of the IT industry, the products of which have advanced the productivity of many other sectors (Brynjolfsson and Hitt, 2003). R&D spillovers also occur when a firm exploits the knowledge and ideas that other firms have developed. As knowledge can be easily transferred through publications, reverse engineering, exchange of scientists and collaborations, firms can often build on external knowledge without having to pay for it (Geroski, 1995; Los and Verspagen, 2000).

What has not attracted much interest, however, is the negative effect of spillovers. Jaffe (1986) was one of the first to report that positive spillovers are confounded with negative effects such as lower profits and a higher depreciation rate of knowledge. In line with Jaffe (1986), a recent study of Bitzer and Geishecker (2006) finds that negative intra-industry spillovers often dominate their corresponding positive effects. Indeed, the R&D that a firm's rivals undertake, improves not only society's pool of knowledge but also their own products, processes and productivity. Although one might expect that the increased productivity levels of rivals would not negatively affect the productivity of a firm, frequently this appears to be the case.

Aitken and Harrison (1999) refer to a market-stealing effect that may force an organization to reduce output in response to competition from technologically superior rivals. In turn, this may shift its cost curve higher, resulting in lower productivity. De Bondt (1996) emphasizes that whilst R&D improves the competitiveness of one firm, it may reduce its rivals' profits. McGahan and Silverman (2006) argue that external innovations may negatively influence organizational performance either through direct market-stealing or indirect appropriation through licensing. Furthermore, as sales and productivity are correlated, what academic studies estimate is a comparative (or relative) measure of productivity.[1] When a firm loses market share because of the technological advances and the better competitive position of its rivals, a reduction in its measured 'comparative' productivity may be observed, despite the fact that its production capacity remains the same. Negative spillovers also imply some form of labour hoarding; otherwise, the drop in firms' output should be accompanied by a proportionate decrease in labour force.[2] Overall, these arguments suggest that R&D investments may impose negative externalities on rivals, even though positive knowledge transmission occurs (De Bondt, 1996).

Consider for example the computer processor industry, which is dominated by Intel and AMD. If Intel, by developing a new powerful processor, succeeds in significantly increasing its market share, the sales and consequently the measured productivity of AMD will be lower (even though Intel has created knowledge on which AMD can build). Thus, as Griliches (1979) emphasized, measured output goes up in terms of the revenues received, and productivity depends on the amount of returns that an innovator succeeds in appropriating for himself. However, the conditions for positive and negative spillovers vary between firms, and theory does not so far indicate

160 *Mario I. Kafouros and Peter J. Buckley*

which effect is likely to dominate. As noted earlier, this study analyzes three factors (technological opportunities, firm size and competition) that may influence the direction of the 'net' spillover effect, i.e. when the positive effect outweighs the negative (market-stealing) effect.

3. Research methods and data overview

3.1. Measuring spillover effects

Following past literature (Griliches, 1979; Scherer, 1982), our analysis is based on a production function. Besides the ordinary inputs of capital (K) and labour (L), it also includes the R&D capital (R) of a firm, as well as a measure of the aggregate R&D (s_{int}) undertaken by intraindustry competitors. This model however, becomes more complicated because 'we do not deal with a closed industry but with a whole array of firms and industries which borrow different amounts of knowledge from different sources according to their economic and technological distance from them' (Griliches, 1992, p. 35). To represent the R&D undertaken by the firms in external industries (inter-industry spillovers), we have added one more variable (s_{ext}):

$$Q = f\left(K, L, R, s_{int}, s_{ext}\right) \tag{1}$$

This production function after accounting for time (t) and firm (i) differences and after transforming it into logarithmic form is

$$q_{it} = a + \alpha k_{it} + \beta l_{it} + \gamma r_{it} + \delta s_{int,it} + \zeta s_{ext,it} + \varepsilon_{it} \tag{2}$$

The lower case letters (q, k, l, r, s_{int} and s_{ext}) denote the logarithms of the variables whereas α, β, γ, δ and ζ are the elasticities of capital, labour, R&D capital, intra- and inter-industry spillovers, respectively. The term a is the residual of the production function and ε_{it} is the disturbance term. To serve the objectives of the study and examine the impact of R&D spillovers on firms' productivity performance, Eq. (2) is re-written below in terms of labour productivity (output/labour):

$$q_{it} - l_{it} = a + \alpha\left(k_{it} - l_{it}\right) + \gamma\left(r_{it} - l_{it}\right) + (\mu - 1)l_{it} \\ + \delta\left(s_{int,it} - l_{it}\right) + \zeta\left(s_{ext,it} - l_{it}\right) + \varepsilon_{it} \tag{3}$$

We have not imposed the assumption of constant returns to scale (CRS), when $(\mu - 1) \neq 0$ the CRS assumption is rejected. To avoid biased estimates, the model also includes dummy variables to control for time and industry effects (not shown in Eq. (3)). The model will be estimated using the ordinary least squares (OLS) method.[3] The construction of the R&D and spillover variables is described below.

3.1.1. R&D capital (R)

Following Griliches (1979), the R&D capital (or stock of scientific knowledge) is taken to be a measure of past and current R&D expenditures (RD):

$$R_{\text{it}} = \text{RD}_{\text{it}} + \text{RD}_{i(t-1)} + \text{RD}_{i(t-2)} + \dots \tag{4}$$

However, in order to innovate continuously, firms have to abandon past knowledge. Therefore, past research – as any other type of capital – depreciates and becomes less valuable over time. Additionally, part of a firm's research findings will be diffused, used and thus neutralized by other firms. In order to account for the declining usefulness of R&D, a depreciation factor (δ) is introduced to convert the gross research to net (the term k represents the lagged year)[4]:

$$R_{\text{it}} = \text{RD}_{\text{it}} + \sum_{1}^{k} (1-\delta)^k \text{RD}_{i(t-k)} \tag{5}$$

3.1.2. R&D undertaken by intra-industry competitors (s_{int})

A measure of the aggregate R&D undertaken by intra-industry rivals was constructed in order to investigate whether their spillover effect has a positive or negative impact on productivity. In contrast to other studies that only take into account the R&D undertaken by the firms of their samples, following Harhoff (2000) this paper allows all private R&D in the population of the UK R&D-performing firms to enter the spillover pool. Using Eq. (5), we have constructed an intra-industry spillover capital for each firm separately.[5] This measure was also corrected for double counting.[6]

3.1.3. Inter-industry spillovers (s_{int})

To examine whether firms borrow knowledge from inventors of external industries, we have calculated an inter-industry spillover capital. Initially, we constructed a proximity matrix (W) that identified the technological distance between firms, i.e. the extent to which the technologies developed in different industries were useful for each firm of the sample. Earlier studies used either a patent-based or an input–output weighting. As patent data were not available in this study, we used input–output data on the use of intermediate goods to construct a technological-proximity matrix.[7] The data included a 122 × 122 dimensions table with information on the intermediate goods used to produce 122 different product categories. We grouped those products relevant to the study into 15 two- or three-digit industries. For example, products such as inorganic, organic and 'other' chemical goods were incorporated into the chemical industry. Hence, we constructed a table of 15 × 15 dimensions. Each firm's inter-industry

162　*Mario I. Kafouros and Peter J. Buckley*

spillover capital was thus the weighted sum of 14 different R&D capital stocks:

$$s_i = \sum_{j=1}^{14} w_{ij} R_j \qquad (6)$$

R_j represents the R&D capital of industry j, whilst w_{ij} is the weighting factor of the technological distance between firm i and industry j (taken from the input–output table).

3.2. Data overview

To investigate the extent to which a firm (rather than an industry) benefits from external R&D, as well as to examine the differences across firms within an industry and to avoid inferences biased by idiosyncrasies associated with a specific period, we collected firm-level panel data. Using datastream, a wide range of data including firms' sales, capital, labour and R&D expenditure were collected for an 8-year period (1995–2002). The sample includes 138 UK manufacturing firms that reported their R&D expenditure. Data were also collected for the total R&D undertaken by each two- or three-digit UK industry.[8]

Although the UK accounting rules suggest that firms should report their R&D expenditure, there is no law to enforce this (Stoneman and Toivanen, 2001). As a result, 9 of the 138 firms reported zero R&D expenditure and thus were eliminated. Twelve more were eliminated either because of more than three missing R&D observations or because of their small size. The final balanced sample comprised 117 firms that accounted for approximately 80% of the total private R&D investment (thereby reducing the possibility of having a serious sample selectivity bias). Table 8.1 presents the sector analysis of the sample. To achieve the objectives of the paper, the model will be re-estimated for a number of sub-samples separately. For that reason, we divided the sample into smaller- and larger-firms sub-samples.[9] Additionally, following past studies (Griliches and Mairesse, 1984; Harhoff, 1998), we included industries such as metal manufacturing, minerals and mechanical machinery in the low-tech sample whereas industries such as pharmaceutical, electronics and aerospace were included in the high-tech sample.[10]

Using the raw data, several variables were constructed. As Jorgenson (1963) suggested, capital input should be a measure of the services flowing from it (rather than capital stock). Following Griliches (1980), the study approximated capital services using the depreciation of fixed capital stock (which is in fact the actual cost that a firm pays for using its capital assets). To minimize the danger of biased results, we also estimated the model using a measure of the net fixed capital stock. Labour input is defined as the number of employees. Both capital and labour input were corrected for double counting.[11] As a proxy for output, the sales of each firm were used. Although this is in line

Under What Conditions Do Firms Benefit 163

Table 8.1 Sectoral analysis of the sample (117 UK firms, 1995–2002)

	SIC 80 code	No. of firms
Low-technology industries		
Metal products	22 and 31	3
Minerals	23 and 24	4
Machinery and mechanical engineering	32	28
Motor vehicle parts	35	6
Textiles	43	1
Paper and printing	47	2
Rubber and plastics	48	3
Other manufacturing	49	1
Total		48
High-technology industries		
Chemicals	25	15
Pharmaceuticals	257	6
Computing and office equipment	33	3
Electrical and electronics	34	21
Telecommunication	344	10
Aerospace	364	6
Instrument engineering	37	8
Total		69

with the practice of many previous papers (Griliches and Mairesse, 1984; Goto and Suzuki, 1989; Hall, 1993; Harhoff, 2000; Wakelin, 2001), it may not be optimal. As Cuneo and Mairesse (1984) found, using sales instead of valueadded may bias the elasticity of R&D downwards. Nevertheless, the results of Mairesse and Hall (1996) (who used both sales and value-added) showed that sales as dependent variable performs relative well.

Using the procedures described earlier, we constructed measures of R&D capital, intra-industry and inter-industry spillovers. Due to the lack of official R&D price indices, published studies usually utilize the GDP price index to convert R&D expenditures to constant prices. However, as the cost of R&D does not follow the path of prices within the economy as a whole (Mansfield, 1987), this approach does not measure accurately the level of R&D activity. In contrast to past research, the analysis undertaken in this study includes the fact that (depending on the industry involved) the cost of R&D may rise at different rates. To do so, it employs industry-specific R&D price indices (rather than the GDP index).[12]

Table 8.2 presents the descriptive statistics for the sample. Although the R&D-intensity (R&D/sales) of the high-tech and smaller firms is 6.9 and 6.7%, respectively, it is much lower at 1.6 and 2.7% for the low-tech

164 *Mario I. Kafouros and Peter J. Buckley*

and larger firms. Interestingly, whilst the productivity for the technologically advanced and larger firms does not differ by much, the corresponding productivity for the low-tech and smaller firms is much lower. As was expected, the average intra- and inter-industry spillover capital per employee is very high for both high-tech firms and for smaller firms, implying that their employees may draw knowledge from a large spillover pool.

4. Main findings: intra- and inter-industry spillovers

It is frequently argued that corporate performance may be affected differently by the R&D undertaken by intra- or inter-industry firms. Mohnen (1996) explains that if the new product from outside R&D could replace the firm's own product, then R&D spillovers may decrease the price that a producer can charge for it. Similarly, McGahan and Silverman (2006) argue that the strength of such an effect depends on whether innovation has come from potential rivals or not. To examine the validity of these predictions, this section analyzes separately the impacts of the R&D undertaken by intraindustry competitors and that undertaken by external inventors.

Table 8.2 Descriptive statistics (mean values)[a]

	Whole sample	High-tech firms (69)	Low-tech firms (48)	Larger firms (63)	Smaller firms (54)
Sales/employee[b]	97	105	89	101	90
Capital/employee[b]	27	28	26	29	24
Number of employees	5998	5523	6452	11,049	487
R&D capital/ employee[b]	17	25	7	12	19
Intra-industry spillover capital[c]	2851	3166	2609	2,772	2,881
Intra-industry spillover capital/ employee[b]	6593	9228	2550	783	13,807
Inter-industry spillover capital[c]	1009	1153	787	846	1,127
Inter-industry spillover capital/ employee[b]	2441	3447	791	242	5,209
R&D intensity (%)	4.30	6.90	1.60	2.70	6.70

[a] The mean values have been estimated using 8 years of observation (1995–2002). Extreme values have been eliminated. The statistics for the spillover capitals indicate their approximate values as they may change depending on the weighting method utilized.
[b] These monetary values are in £1,000.
[c] These monetary values are in £1,000,000.

4.1. The impact of the R&D undertaken by intra-industry competitors

Table 8.3 presents the findings concerning intra-industry spillovers.[13] These are based on Eq. (3).[14] The first model includes an unweighted spillover variable. The elasticity of R&D capital is high at 0.13, showing that a firm's own R&D investments increase significantly its productivity performance. To examine the impact of R&D price indices on the results, we re-estimated the model using the GDP deflator (rather than our R&D price indices). As a result of this, the elasticity of R&D decreased from 0.13 to 0.11. This suggests that as R&D-cost idiosyncrasies vary across industries, the lack of R&D price indices may bias the coefficient of R&D downwards, and underestimate the contribution of R&D.

The coefficient of intra-industry spillovers is zero and statistically insignificant, implying that intense R&D competition neutralizes positive spillovers.[15] This finding is consistent with Wakelin's (2001) work for the UK which found the effects of spillovers to be statistically insignificant between 1988 and 1992. However, it contradicts other studies that found positive spillover effects (Adams and Jaffe, 1996; Brandstetter, 1996; Los and Verspagen, 2000). To incorporate in the analysis the possibility that the maximization of these effects may take some time, we employed 1- and 2-year lagged variables (not shown in Table 8.3). Despite the fact that the elasticity of R&D increased to 0.16, the effects of spillovers remained insignificant.[16]

Model 2 goes one step further. According to the absorptive-capacity hypothesis, the capability of capturing external know-how relates to a firm's prior R&D (Cohen and Levinthal, 1990). Levin et al. (1987) found that firms' own research was an effective way of investigating rival technologies.

Table 8.3 Intra-industry spillovers[a]

	Model 1	Model 2	Model 3
Log (K/L)	0.18*** (0.02)	0.18*** (0.02)	0.18*** (0.02)
Log L	0.03 ns (0.02)	0.01 ns (0.01)	0.035** (0.01)
R&D elasticity	0.13*** (0.01)	0.17*** (0.03)	0.13*** (0.01)
Intra-industry spillovers	0.00 ns (0.02)	–	–
Intra-industry spillovers (weighted by absorptive capacity)	–	–0.02 (0.009)	–
Intra-industry spillovers (weighted by I/O flows)	–	–	0.00 ns (0.01)
Control for industry	Yes	Yes	Yes
Control for time	Yes	Yes	Yes
R^2	0.32	0.33	0.35

ns = not significant, (*) 5% level of significance, (**) 1% level of significance, (***) 0.1% level of significance; the absence of a star indicates a level of significance of 10%.

[a] The dependent variable is labour productivity.

166 Mario I. Kafouros and Peter J. Buckley

Similarly, studies of technological diffusion found that R&D-intensive companies adopted new technologies faster than less R&D-intensive firms (Baldwin and Scott, 1987). To test whether the data supported these arguments, we included an interaction variable (following the work of Harhoff, 2000). This variable is a measure of intra-industry spillovers weighted by each firm's own R&D (i.e. $\log s \times \log R$). The coefficient of the new intra-industry spillover variable is slightly negative at –0.02 (but still not statistically significant). Additionally, because each firm's own R&D capital is incorporated in the new variable, multi-collinearity problems ensue, the effects of which are severe increasing the coefficient of R&D from 0.13 to 0.17. For that reason, we used a third approach.

The first two models include an unweighted measure of spillovers. As such, they implicitly assume that all rivals' R&D activities are relevant and useful to the firm. The usefulness of rivals' knowledge, however, may differ across industries. Calculations based on UK input–output data showed that approximately 40% of the inputs of firms such as electrical and electronics come from their own industry. By contrast, the corresponding figure for minerals and instruments manufacturers is less than 9%. For that reason, we weighted the spillover variable according to the extent to which a firm uses the technologies of its own industry. Model 3 presents the results. Once again the spillovers coefficient is zero, indicating that on average the spillover effects of intra-industry competitors are insignificant (rather than simply being an artifact of a particular variable construction process).

4.2. Inter-industry spillovers and the role of technological distance

Table 8.4 presents the findings concerning the relationship between inter-industry spillovers and productivity performance. Model 1 indicates that this relationship is positive at 0.02, suggesting that the R&D undertaken by organizations in external industries has a positive – but relatively low – impact on productivity. To investigate whether the absorptive-capacity hypothesis is valid for inter-industry spillovers, Model 2 presents the results when the spillover variable is weighted by each firm's own R&D. The statistical significance of spillovers is now greater (at the 0.1% level) and the coefficient is slightly higher at 0.03. Although the findings favor the relevant hypothesis, the new coefficient is not significantly higher. The reason for this result may be the ease with which products may be imitated in a digital age without the need to possess basic scientific understanding (Liu and Buck, 2007).

Our previous models do not take into account the arguments of Griliches (1992) that the stock of knowledge available in an industry is not in itself indicative of how much of this knowledge spills over to other firms, nor who the potential recipients of the knowledge will be. Indeed, spillover effects may be weak when external technologies are so different from a firm's own know-how that they cannot be absorbed (De Bondt, 1996). Large

Table 8.4 Inter-industry spillovers[a]

	Model 1	Model 2	Model 3	Model 4
Log (K/L)	0.17*** (0.02)	0.17*** (0.02)	0.17*** (0.02)	0.17*** (0.02)
Log L	0.04*** (0.01)	0.04*** (0.01)	0.06*** (0.01)	0.05*** (0.009)
R&D elasticity	0.13*** (0.01)	0.07*** (0.02)	0.13*** (0.01)	0.13*** (0.01)
Inter-industry spillovers	0.02** (0.007)	–	–	–
Inter-industry spillovers (weighted by absorptive capacity)	–	0.03*** (0.005)	–	–
Inter-industry spillovers $\hat{0}.33$	–	–	0.05*** (0.01)	–
Inter-industry spillovers 2	–	–	–	0.015** (0.006)
Control for industry	Yes	Yes	Yes	Yes
Control for time	Yes	Yes	Yes	Yes
R^2	0.32	0.3	0.31	0.31

ns = not significant, (*) 5% level of significance, (**) 1% level of significance, (***) 0.1% level of significance; the absence of a star indicates a level of significance of 10%.
[a] The dependent variable is labour productivity.

and diversified firms may draw knowledge from a much wider knowledge pool than that constructed. Conversely, as smaller firms usually specialize in a specific niche (Griliches, 1992), they may draw knowledge from a much narrower product field. If this argument is valid, then our technological-proximity matrix may not represent accurately the real technological relationship between firms. As Cincera (1998, p. 178) argues 'it may be the case that firms characterized by an intermediary technological distance, i.e. P_{ij} =. 5, actually benefit much more or much less from R&D spillovers than firms at the extreme, i.e. firms very close or very distant from other firms'.

To test the above arguments, we re-estimated the model using other definitions of technological proximity. Following Cincera (1998) and Harhoff (2000), we used weighting metrics that are nested within an exponential transformation. We transformed the weighting matrix w_{ij} as $w'_{ij} = w^a_{ij}$ (with $a > 0$). The rationale behind this transformation is that the distance between a firm's own R&D and external R&D might be a non-linear function of the matrix w_{ij}. Hence, whilst the initial linearly weighted spillover variable was based on $a = 1$, two new spillover variables were constructed for values of a equal to 0.33 and 2 (named SPILLS033 and SPILLS2, respectively). Figure 8.1 depicts the effects of these transformations. When a takes values smaller than 1, it allows distant R&D to be weighted more strongly in the

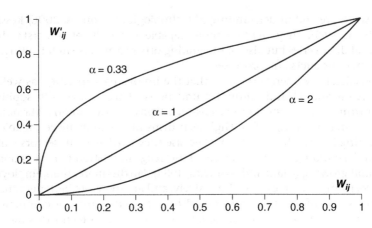

Figure 8.1 Transformation of the weighting matrix

constructed spillover variable. Conversely, when $a > 1$ then distant R&D is weighted less strongly (Harhoff, 2000).

The last two models of Table 8.4 report the findings when the SPILLS033 or SPILLS2 variable took the place of the initial variable. The elasticity of SPILLS033 (giving emphasis to distant R&D) increased at 0.05, and became highly significant at the 0.1% level. In contrast, the coefficient of SPILLS2 (based on the notion that the R&D of neighbor firms is more important) slightly decreased at 0.015. These findings favor a broader definition of the spillover pool. It seems that when firms capture knowledge from firms outside their own industry, they draw knowledge successfully even from more technologically distant industries. This finding, however, contradicts Harhoff (2000) who found that the impacts of R&D spillovers for German firms remained relatively stable when alternative values of a were used. Another noteworthy observation not shown in Table 8.4, is that although the use of lagged variables did not change the intra-industry results presented in the previous section, they increased significantly the coefficient of inter-industry spillovers (from 0.02 to 0.05), implying that knowledge from outside industries takes some time to be absorbed.

5. Technological opportunities and firm size

The previous section assumed that R&D spillovers impact on the performance of heterogeneous firms in a similar way. This section examines two factors (technological opportunities and firm size) that may influence a firm's ability to benefit from external R&D, and in turn the magnitude and direction of such externalities. A number of theoretical arguments guide the selection of these two factors. For instance, high-tech firms have a better infrastructure and understanding of technologies (Kafouros, 2006; Kessler, 2003). As such, they may be more capable not only of understanding external discoveries but also of integrating other firms' research findings in their own products and processes.

Considerable evidence suggests that the innovative capacities, as well as the organizational and cultural foundations of technologically sophisticated firms differ from those of low-tech firms (Matheson and Matheson, 1998; Wang and Tsai, 2003). High-tech firms may also be more capable of benefiting from spillovers, simply because they participate in sectors where the understanding and the scientific knowledge in relation to innovation is rich and growing (Clark and Griliches, 1984). Furthermore, their employees use electronic resources more intensively, and are therefore better equipped to access the information transmitted from associate firms or competitors (Kafouros, 2005). Accordingly, spillover effects for high-tech firms may be more positive than for lowtech firms.

By contrast, the role of firm size is more ambiguous. On the one hand, theory suggests that larger firms are better equipped to benefit from knowledge externalities because they possess the technological expertise, know-how, and managerial qualities that could improve the understanding of inventions developed externally (Mansfield, 1968). They may also be able to use the research findings of other firms more efficiently as they can afford to have specialized scientists working on the systematic collection, analysis

Table 8.5 The role of firm size and technological opportunities[a]

	Whole sample (117 firms)	High-tech firms (69 firms)	Low-tech firms (48 firms)	Larger firms (63 firms)	Smaller firms (54 firms)
Log (K/L)	0.18***	0.19***	0.16***	0.15***	0.13***
	(0.02)	(0.03)	(0.02)	(0.03)	(0.04)
Log L	0.03 ns	0.10***	−0.02 ns	−0.10***	0.12***
	(0.02)	(0.03)	(0.03)	(0.03)	(0.04)
R&D elasticity	0.13***	0.18***	0.09***	0.18***	0.11***
	(0.01)	(0.02)	(0.01)	(0.02)	(0.02)
Intra-industry spillovers	0.00 ns	0.07**	−0.06*	−0.11***	0.12***
	(0.02)	(0.02)	(0.02)	(0.03)	(0.04)
Inter-industry spillovers	0.02**	0.03**	−0.10**	−0.01 ns	0.05***
	(0.007)	(0.009)	(0.03)	(0.01)	(0.01)
Control for industry	Yes	Yes	Yes	Yes	Yes
Control for time	Yes	Yes	Yes	Yes	Yes
R^2	0.32	0.33	0.34	0.51	0.2

ns = not significant, (*) 5% level of significance, (**) 1% level of significance, (***) 0.1% level of significance; the absence of a star indicates a level of significance of 10%.
[a] The dependent variable is labour productivity.

and circulation of information regarding newly developed technologies and recently registered patents (Kafouros, 2008).

Nevertheless, there is also a case for suggesting the converse – that smaller firms are actually better able to profit from external technological information. First, it may prove more difficult for the R&D teams of larger firms to trace the relevant knowledge for their numerous products, processes and technologies. Tsai (2001) demonstrated that their limited degree of autonomy may hinder the monitoring of, and rapid response to the latest technological trends. Second, the net effect of spillovers depends on the extent to which external knowledge is crucial to a firm. The higher a firm's reliance on external technologies, the greater the likelihood that the positive spillover effects outweigh the negative effects (McGahan and Silverman, 2006). Similarly, Geroski (1995) argued that if technologies stand alone as isolated discoveries, R&D spillovers will substitute for a firm's own R&D. Conversely, in situations where external technologies are crucial and can be used as a base for future inventions, spillovers will be complementary to a firm's research. Previous research suggests that smaller firms develop incremental (rather than radical) innovations that are frequently characterized by a strong reliance on external technologies (Bound et al., 1984; Kleinknecht, 1989; Pavitt et al., 1987; Piergiovanni et al., 1997). As such, it is likely that the positive effect will dominate. As theory does not identify a clear relationship between firm size and spillovers, the following section examines this issue empirically.

5.1. Findings and discussion

To examine the role of technological opportunities and firm size, after splitting the sample into different sub-samples, we re-estimated the model. Consistent with previous studies, the results of Table 8.5 shows that whilst high-tech firms enjoy good returns to their own R&D, the corresponding payoff for low-tech firms is lower. Concerning the impact of the R&D undertaken by intraindustry rivals, the results for technologically advanced companies show that the positive effect dominates. This confirms the theoretical predictions discussed earlier that high-tech firms achieve success utilizing the ideas and technologies of competitors. But these results could be interpreted differently by an R&D director who might simply see the research efforts of his own company improving the productivity of his rivals. The relationship is totally reversed in the case of low-tech firms. It appears that because of their limited ability to draw on external scientific knowledge, negative spillovers dominate, decreasing their performance.

The last two columns report the findings on firm size. The contribution of their own R&D to productivity is high for larger firms but much lower for smaller firms. In contrast, the opposite is true regarding the contribution of the information transmitted by intra-industry competitors. Its impact on smaller firms' productivity is not only positive, but also higher than that arising from their own R&D. Conversely, the R&D undertaken by intra-industry rivals has a strong negative impact on the productivity of larger firms, suggesting strongly that the negative effects of competition outweigh the positive ones.

Table 8.5 also presents the results for inter-industry spillovers. These spillovers are particularly important because as the data show, in industries such as motor vehicles, paper and printing, only 17% of intermediate inputs are taken from the other 14 industries of the sample. On the other hand, for industries such as metals this figure may be as high as 70%. The results indicate that inter-industry spillovers are positive for high-tech firms, showing that these companies profit from the R&D of firms in different external industries. Interestingly however, for firms in less technology-oriented sectors, spillovers are once again negative.

The findings of inter-industry spillovers for larger versus smaller firms are similar to those found for intra-industry spillovers. They suggest that firm size is negatively associated with the contribution of external R&D. These support the prediction that as smaller firms develop incremental technologies (Pavitt et al., 1987; Piergiovanni et al., 1997), there is a strong reliance on external knowledge, and therefore the positive effects outweigh the negative ones. Another explanation for this result relates to previous findings showing that small firms which are R&D-intensive have a better absorptive capacity (Cohen and Levinthal, 1990), and tend to adopt and respond to new technologies faster (Baldwin and Scott, 1987).[17]

Generally, the results show that when the positive spillover effect dominates, its magnitude is higher for the R&D undertaken by intra-industry rivals and lower for that undertaken by other inventors. This confirms the argument of Griliches (1992) that the usefulness of external R&D tends to be highest if it is undertaken by intra-industry firms. Indeed, firms in the same industry may benefit not only from the ideas of other companies, but also through the hiring of other firms' scientists and R&D engineers (Hall, 1996). Consistent with our results, Bernstein (1988) showed that intra-industry spillovers are more significant than inter-industry spillovers. Similarly, Adams and Jaffe (1996) concluded that R&D outside the product field is less effective than R&D within the product field.

6. The role of competition

Another factor that plays an important role in the appropriation (or not) of innovation is that of competition. Although the relationship between competition and innovation has been examined for more than six decades, it is still a subject for debate (Tang, 2006). Schumpeter (1942) suggested and many others argued similarly (e.g. Grossman and Helpman, 1991), that because oligopolistic and monopolistic environments provide profitable innovative opportunities, they are likely to promote R&D. In contrast, Arrow (1962) argued that markets with the characteristics of perfect competition provide more incentives to innovate. The rationale behind this claim is that intellectual-property law may allow an inventor to license his innovations to many firms, and thus maximize the returns to his research efforts.

It has also been recognized that R&D investments may allow a firm to gain a more advantageous competitive position in relation to its rivals (Aghion et al., 2001). Nevertheless, although firms innovate in order to escape competition, it may also be argued that when they invest in similar practices that involve new knowledge, many benefits are forwarded to other firms (Chen and Miller, 1994; Porter, 1980). In cases where a firm's R&D investments are neutralized by rivals' investments, R&D is no longer a decisive strategic weapon and there may even be an adverse effect on corporate performance. Indeed, a firm that participates in an R&D-intensive environment may capture the full value of its innovations only for a short period of time, as the inventions of rivals reduce the life cycle of technologies and lead to quick obsolescence of products.

Many studies have investigated the relationship between competition and a firm's own innovation. That objective, however, differs from the aim of this section, which is to examine whether competition influences the impact of external R&D on corporate performance. Theory suggests that the appropriability of the benefits of R&D may vary depending on competitive conditions. McGahan and Silverman (2006) argue that even an important innovation may not have a significant effect if competition is high and does not allow a firm to capture its full value (which spills over to other firms). This implies that the presence of a high level of competition may lead to low returns to a firm's own R&D but may permit other firms to exploit successfully external R&D. In such cases of imperfect appropriability, we should expect the effects from R&D spillovers to be more positive. In contrast, lower competitive pressure may allow firms to better appropriate the full value of R&D, resulting in either less positive or negative spillovers.

Nevertheless, although one might expect that the magnitude and direction of spillovers may depend on the appropriability regime in an industry, this may not always be the case. The above arguments do not take into account the non-rival and non-excludable properties of knowledge: in contrast to a tangible good, knowledge can be used by many firms and it is difficult for the producer of knowledge to stop others from using it (Geroski, 1995). These suggest that it is possible for R&D to benefit simultaneously both the firm that undertakes such activities and other firms as well. Utilizing industry- and firm-level measures of competition, the following section tests these arguments and examines empirically the relationship between competition and spillovers.

6.1. Findings and discussion

To examine the role of competition, we need to measure the competitive pressure that a firm faces, and generally the competitive conditions in each industry. To do so, previous research utilized a wide range of proxies such as profitability, barriers to entry, market concentration and market share (Greenhalgh and Rogers, 2006). One of the measures adopted here is that of concentration ratio. This industry-level proxy refers to the extent to which the largest firms contribute to the activity in an industry. It is defined as the 'sum of sales for the largest firms over total sales for an industry' and has been calculated for the top 15 firms of each industry of our sample.[18] This ratio varies widely between 10 and 80%, depending on the industry involved.[19]

After splitting the sample into lower- and higher-concentration subgroups, we re-estimated the model.[20] The first sub-sample contains industries that tend to have characteristics of perfect competition, whilst the second one includes industries that tend to have oligopolistic characteristics (i.e. a few firms dominate the market). Table 8.6 (Model 1) reports the results. These clearly support the Schumpeterian hypothesis and stand in direct contrast with the claims of Arrow (1962). They indicate that when a market tends to have perfect-competition conditions (first column), the returns to a firm's own R&D are significantly lower (at 0.09) than the corresponding returns (of 0.19) enjoyed by firms in oligopolistic markets.

The results confirm previous studies which showed that firms in oligopolistic or monopolistic environments face less market uncertainty, and can more easily appropriate the benefits of R&D (Kamien and Schwartz, 1982; Tang, 2006). In line with the previous theoretical discussion, however, this relationship is reversed in the case of spillovers. We find that when the coefficient of R&D is low (i.e. when firms appropriate only a small portion of the fruits of their own innovation), the spillover effects are more positive, confirming that many of the relevant benefits are forwarded to other firms. This finding is consistent not only with theory but also with the fact that as less concentrated markets contain many firms, the likelihood that newly developed knowledge will be exploited by external agents is higher. This result is also in line with the argument of McGahan and Silverman (2006) that in the presence of weak appropriabilty regime, a firm should benefit more readily from external innovations. In contrast, the results of the second column indicate that in oligopolistic markets where the economic payoff for R&D is high (i.e. when firms capture the benefits of their own research efforts), the elasticity of intra-industry spillovers is negative.

Model 1 utilized an industry-level proxy of competition. As such, it is based on the assumption that all firms within an industry face similar competitive pressure. To confirm our previous findings and to investigate

174   *Mario I. Kafouros and Peter J. Buckley*

if there existed intra-industry differences under competitive conditions, we also employed a firm-level proxy of competition: the market share of each firm.[21] This approach has been used widely, and it has been theoretically accepted that the larger the market share a firm has, the lower is the competition that it faces. After splitting the sample into lower- and higher-market share subgroups, we re-estimated the model.[22] Model 2 of Table 8.6 reports the results (third and fourth column). These confirm the findings of Model 1. They indicate that market share has a positive association with the returns to innovation, i.e. the lower the competition that a firm faces, the better it can appropriate the benefits of its own R&D.

The results support Tang (2006) who argued that firms with significant market power can better finance their R&D activities because of the supranormal profits arising from such power. They are also in line with the results of Greenhalgh and Rogers (2006) who found that a higher market share increases the market valuation of patent activity. The findings concerning spillover effects are also consistent with both the theoretical predictions discussed earlier and our industry-level results. On average, they tend to be more positive when competition is intense, and less positive where there are lower levels of competition. The implication of this finding is important suggesting that even when firms do not capture the full value of their R&D, they may still increase their performance by exploiting successfully external discoveries.

Table 8.6   The role of competition[a]

| | Model 1 (industry-level data) | | Model 2 (firm-level data) | |
| | | | High-competition | Low-competition |
	Competition	Oligopoly		
Log (K/L)	0.19*** (0.03)	0.11*** (0.03)	0.16*** (0.03)	0.24*** (0.03)
Log L	0.05* (0.03)	−0.05** (0.02)	0.28*** (0.05)	0.14*** (0.03)
R&D elasticity	0.09*** (0.01)	0.19*** (0.02)	0.11*** (0.02)	0.16*** (0.02)
Intra-industry spillovers	0.02 ns (0.02)	−0.05*** (0.02)	0.10*** (0.02)	0.09*** (0.03)
Inter-industry spillovers	0.06*** (0.01)	0.00 ns (0.01)	0.19*** (0.06)	0.02* (0.01)
Control for industry	Yes	Yes	Yes	Yes
Control for time	Yes	Yes	Yes	Yes
R^2	0.26	0.50	0.40	0.45

ns = not significant, (*) 5% level of significance, (**) 1% level of significance, (***) 0.1% level of significance; the absence of a star indicates a level of significance of 10%.
[a] The dependent variable is labour productivity.

7. Summary and conclusions

Although prior studies recognize the importance of monitoring external technological advances, they frequently (but incorrectly) assume that the impacts of R&D spillovers on productivity performance are similar across diverse firms. However, depending on their resources, assets, size and market positions, firms look at external inventions differently (Chesbrough, 2007). This study contributes to the innovation literature by examining under what conditions firms may benefit from the research efforts of other innovators. The analysis delivered a number of findings that may update the academic and managerial understanding of the spillovers-performance relationship. In order to survive the battle for technological leadership, firms must create additional value by exploiting external sources of innovation (Chesbrough, 2007), but our findings suggest that not all firms are able to do this. Rather, we found that depending on technological opportunities, firm size and competition, the net impact of R&D spillovers can be either positive or negative. An implication for theory is that future predictions about the net effect of spillovers should be linked to the above market- and firm-specific characteristics. Equally, in order to avoid inaccurate results, social scientists who empirically examine the mechanisms underlying R&D should incorporate these factors in their analyses.

The current study demonstrated that spillovers are positively associated with the technological opportunities that a firm faces. This finding is consistent with the behavior of high-tech firms to invest heavily in R&D, showing that they reap rewards not only from their own R&D but also from that undertaken by other companies. Conversely, negative market-stealing effects dominate in the case of low-tech firms, decreasing their productivity. As it is likely that a firm will experience more positive spillovers when its innovations place emphasis on technical information gathered from outside sources, it is advisable for low-tech firms to build more on external inventions. Improving the understanding of discoveries developed externally should be a central part of their strategy.

The analysis of the role of firm size demonstrated that it enhances a firm's capacity to improve performance through its own R&D. Contrary to theoretical expectations however, the impact of spillovers is negatively associated with firm size: external R&D has a strong but negative impact on the performance of larger firms. Because large firms have the financial resources to develop technologies internally, it seems that they are too self-reliant, ignoring the potential benefits of external R&D. However, the increasing complexity of products implies that firms – even the largest – can no longer rely only on their internal knowledge reservoir. To keep their innovation leadership, large corporations should refine their strategic plans in a way that effectively incorporates external inventions in their R&D processes (Chesbrough, 2007). Many innovation strategists have already started doing so by giving rewards and recognition to people who adopt ideas from elsewhere (De Bondt, 1996). Interestingly, the contribution of spillovers to smaller firms' productivity is higher than that of their own R&D. This finding reflects their strong reliance on external technologies and explains why despite the low returns to their R&D, smaller firms continue to be R&D-intensive. Even though their own research was not particularly important for performance, it may have enabled them to catch up with outside leading-edge technologies and increase productivity using the knowledge transmitted by other innovators.

The current research has also demonstrated that another key factor that explains variations across firms is that of competition. Irrespective of the data analyzed (industry- or firm-level), the results showed that the economic payoff for firms' own R&D was lower when they participated in environments of perfect-competition and generally when they face intense competition. In such cases however (where appropriability is low), spillover effects were more positive allowing firms to increase performance by using the discoveries of others. The implication of this finding is that innovation generates value regardless of the degree of competition: some firms gain more from their own research (but not from external R&D), whilst other organizations gain less from their own R&D but benefit significantly from R&D spillovers. The study also distinguished between the R&D undertaken by intra-industry competitors and that of other inventors. Although one might expect that firms would focus on the know-how of technologically close firms, the findings indicate the opposite. They support the notion that firms utilize research results from apparently technologically unrelated industries. This has implications for academic research, suggesting that our understanding of the concept of technological distance may be incomplete.

The analysis has a number of limitations that offer opportunities for future research. Firstly, the study has not identified the types of R&D that are spilled over more (or less) easily. More detailed data may allow us to shed light on the spillover mechanisms for basic, applied and outsourced R&D or for process and product R&D. Secondly, we used an imperfect measure of output (sales) that may bias the results. Another potential bias may come from the fact that our model does not incorporate the knowledge created by government laboratories, universities and international inventors outside the UK. Thirdly, proxies such as 'concentration ratio' and 'market share' do not measure accurately the level of competition, despite their wide use by prior studies. Future research should explore other factors that influence competitive conditions, such as the time needed by rivals to imitate a firm's products or to introduce a competing innovation (Levin et al., 1987). It is also interesting to note that although the existing empirical framework relies only on the level of firms' R&D, theoretically the effects of innovation and competition depend not only on how much R&D a firm undertakes, but also on how much is undertaken by its rivals. A better framework should allow for not only a firm's level of R&D, but also the difference of this level from the average level of competitors' R&D (Kafouros, 2008). Put simply, it should take into account that whilst R&D for some firms may work as a competitive weapon, in very competitive environments where firms are 'running to stand still', R&D may simply be a defense mechanism.

Acknowledgements

The financial support of the UK Economic and Social Research Council (ESRC) is gratefully acknowledged (PTA-026–27–0800). We would like to thank John Sharp and John Mingers for their comments. We are also grateful to the editor, Nick Von Tunzelmann, and three anonymous referees for their useful suggestions.

Notes

1. Sales and productivity are correlated simply because output, which is the numerator of any productivity measure, is usually defined as sales or value added (sales minus the materials that were used in production). Hence, both measures of output (and thus productivity) depend on sales.
2. We would like to thank an anonymous referee for this comment.
3. The model could also be estimated using the generalized method of moment (GMM), random effects or by using other instrumental variable methods such as the two stage least square (2SLS) or the indirect least squares (ILS) (also known as reduced form). As each method has its own advantages and faults, it is difficult to claim that one method is superior or that it yields less biased estimates. Many researchers have discussed the issue of the appropriate method. Griliches (1986) argues that such methods do not solve the important problem of simultaneity but merely shift it to the validity and exogeneity of external instruments. Gujarati (1995) points out that although some instrumental variable methods may decrease simultaneity, if there is no simultaneity then the estimates become less efficient, having larger variance. Taking into account the problems above, along with the fact that in practice, the findings of studies using methods such as the 2SLS and ILS (Cuneo and Mairesse, 1984; Griliches, 1980; Sassenou, 1988) are similar or only marginally better than those obtained from the ordinary least squares method (Mairesse and Sassenou, 1991), we prefer to use OLS that the majority of similar studies have employed.
4. Based on the findings of Pakes and Schankerman (1984) and Goto and Suzuki (1989), Eq. (5) is calculated using a depreciation rate of 20%. Additional measures of R&D capital are also calculated using rates of 15 and 25%. In line with the findings of other studies however (e.g. Harhoff, 1998), we found that the rate of depreciation did not have a significant impact on the findings.
5. Following the work of Pakes and Schankerman (1984) and Goto and Suzuki (1989), the depreciation rate of this stock was set at 20% per year.
6. Each firm's own R&D capital was deducted from the total intraindustry spillover capital.
7. The input-output table was obtained from the UK Office for National Statistics.

8. These data were acquired from the UK Office for National Statistics.
9. Following Griliches (1980), the large firm sub-sample comprises firms with over 1000 employees whereas the second sub-sample includes all firms which have fewer than 1000 employees. Smaller firms account for 46% of the whole sample; the remaining 54 percent are larger firms. Nevertheless, although firms which have less than 1000 employees are only a small fraction of other firms which may have a six digit number of employees, they still cannot be considered as small firms.
10. The low-technology sample comprises 48 firms whereas the remaining 69 firms belong to high-technology industries.
11. We deducted from ordinary fixed capital, plant and equipment devoted solely to the R&D department. Similarly, we deducted from ordinary employees, those who belong to R&D department.
12. These price indices were constructed recently. For a full description of their construction process, see Kafouros (2008). The findings indicate that the difference between the GDP deflator and the industryspecific price indices is considerable in many sectors. The costs of R&D tend to rise more rapidly for low-tech firms, showing that they have to pay more for undertaking R&D.
13. Although the results are presented separately, both the intra- and inter-industry variables are included in the model (in order to avoid the bias due to inter-correlation of the two variables).
14. These findings (as well as subsequent findings) are heteroscedasticity-robust. To investigate this problem, we initially conducted a 'white' heteroscedasticity test. This indicated that the null hypothesis of homoscedasticity cannot be rejected (at the 5% level). We also used the so-called Goldfeld-Quandt test to examine the null hypothesis that the variance of error terms is homoscedastic. The findings indicated that the null hypothesis cannot be rejected (at the 1% level), confirming that there is no evidence of heteroscedasticity.
15. When we re-estimated the model by using the unbalanced sample of 129 firms, we found similar results.
16. The econometric framework described earlier assumes that the disturbance term ε_{it} is composed of two other types of disturbances: a permanent disturbance (v_i) specific to the firm, and a transitory disturbance (w_{it}) (see Cuneo and Mairesse, 1984). The breakdown of the disturbance term leads to two types of estimates. The estimates of Table 8.3 have the advantage of being unaffected by biases coming from the correlation between explanatory variables and the disturbance w_{it}. These estimates, however, do not take into account the efficiency characteristics of the firm (e.g. managerial capability). To avoid this bias and ensure that the estimates are unaffected by v_i disturbances, we re-estimated the model using differences (the equivalent of doing 'within firm' analysis; see Odagiri and Iwata, 1986). Other advantages of this method are that firstly it includes not only the characteristics of a specific industry but also the characteristics of each individual firm (Mairesse and Sassenou, 1991), and secondly, as Griliches (1986) suggested, it is a simple but effective way to remedy the problem of simultaneity that besets productivity studies. The new findings yielded by this method are consistent with the findings of Table 8.3, confirming that intra-industry spillovers are insignificant (the elasticity of R&D increased only slightly from 0.13 to 0.14).
17. The descriptive statistics of Table 8.2 confirm this, showing that the R&D intensity of the smaller firms of the sample is very high at 6.7%.

18. The data were collected from the database of the UK Office for National Statistics.
19. In some industries the sales of the top 15 firms accounted for about 10% of the total industry sales. By contrast, in other industries (with high concentration) the corresponding figure was 80%. We should also note that the rank order remained similar when we used value added (rather than sales) and when we calculated the ratio for the top 5 (rather than top 15) firms of each industry.
20. The sample was split by using the median of the concentration ratio, which was 50%.
21. The market share of each firm is defined as the ratio of its sales over the total sales of the industry to which this firm belongs.
22. To do so, we used the median of the market share, which was approximately 1%.

References

Adams, J.D., Jaffe, A.B., 1996. Bounding the effects of R&D: an investigation using matched establishment-firm data. The RAND Journal of Economics 27, 700–721.

Aghion, P., Harris, C., Howitt, P., Vickers, J., 2001. Competition, imitation and growth with step-by-step innovation. Review of Economic Studies 68, 467–492.

Aitken, B., Harrison, A., 1999. Do domestic firms benefit from foreign direct investment? Evidence from panel data. American Economic Review 89, 605–618.

Antonelli, C., 1994. Technological districts localized spillovers and productivity growth. The Italian evidence on technological externalities in the core regions. International Review of Applied Economics 8, 18–30.

Arrow, K., 1962. Economic welfare and the allocation of resources for invention. In: Nelson, R. (Ed.), The Rate and Direction of Inventive Activity. Princeton University Press, Princeton.

Baldwin, W., Scott, J., 1987. Market Structure and Technological Change. Harwood Academic Publishers, London.

Bernstein, J., 1988. Costs of production, intra- and inter-industry R&D spillovers: Canadian evidence. Canadian Journal of Economics 21, 324–347.

Bitzer, J., Geishecker, I., 2006. What drives trade-related R&D spillovers? Decomposing knowledge-diffusing trade flows. Economics Letters 93, 52–57.

Bound, J., Cummins, C., Griliches, Z., Hall, B., Jaffe, A., 1984. Who does R&D and who patents? In: Griliches, Z. (Ed.), R&D, Patents, and Productivity. University of Chicago Press, Chicago, pp. 21–54.

Brandstetter, L., 1996. Are knowledge spillovers international of intranational in scope? Microeconometric evidence from the US and Japanese R&D intensive sectors. National Bureau of Economic Research Working Paper 5800.

Brynjolfsson, E., Hitt, L., 2003. Computing productivity: firm-level evidence. Review of Economics and Statistics 85, 793–808.

Chen, M.J., Miller, D., 1994. Competitive attack, retaliation and performance: an expectancy-valence framework. Strategic Management Journal 15, 85–102.

Chesbrough, H.W., 2003. Open Innovation: The New Imperative for Creating and Profiting from Technology. Harvard Business School Press, Boston.

Chesbrough, H.W., 2007. Why companies should have open business models. MIT Sloan Management Review 48, 22–28.

Cincera, M., 1998. Economic and Technological Performance of International Firms. Ph.D. Thesis, Universite Libre of De Bruxelles.

Clark, B., Griliches, Z., 1984. Productivity and R&D at the firm level in French manufacturing. In: Griliches, Z. (Ed.), R&D, Patents, and Productivity. University of Chicago Press, Chicago, pp. 393–416.

Cohen, W.M., Levinthal, D.A., 1990. Absorptive capacity: a new perspective on learning and innovation. Administrative Science Quarterly 35, 128–152.

Cuneo, P., Mairesse, J., 1984. Productivity and R&D at the firm level in French manufacturing. In: Griliches, Z. (Ed.), R&D, Patents, and Productivity. University of Chicago Press, Chicago, pp. 375–392.

De Bondt, R., 1996. Spillovers and innovative activities. International Journal of Industrial Organisation 15, 1–28.

Geroski, P.A., 1991. Innovation and the sectoral sources of UK productivity growth. The Economic Journal 101, 1438–1451.

Geroski, P., 1995. Markets for technology: knowledge, innovation, and appropriability. In: Stoneman, P. (Ed.), Handbook of the Economics of Innovation and Technological Change. Blackwell, Oxford, pp. 90–131.

Goto, A., Suzuki, K., 1989. R&D capital, rate of return on R&D investment and spillover of R&D on Japanese manufacturing industries. The Review of Economics and Statistics 71, 555–564.

Greenhalgh, C., Rogers, M., 2006. The value of innovation: the interaction of competition, R&D and IP. Research Policy 35, 562–580.

Griliches, Z., 1979. Issues in assessing the contribution of research and development to productivity growth. Bell Journal of Economics 10, 92–116.

Griliches, Z., 1980. Returns to research and development expenditures in the private sector. In: Kendrick, J., Vaccara, B. (Eds.), New Developments in Productivity Measurement and Analysis. University of Chicago Press, Chicago, pp. 419–461.

Griliches, Z., 1986. Productivity, R&D, and basic research at the firm level in the 1970s. American Economic Review 76, 141–154.

Griliches, Z., 1992. The search for R&D spillovers. Scandinavian Journal of Economics 94, 29–47.

Griliches, Z., Mairesse, J., 1984. Productivity and R&D at the firm level. In: Griliches, Z. (Ed.), R&D, Patents, and Productivity. University of Chicago Press, Chicago, pp. 339–374.

Grossman, G., Helpman, E., 1991. Innovation and Growth, Technological Competition in the Global Economy. MIT Press, Cambridge.

Gujarati, D.N., 1995. Basic Econometrics. New York, McGraw-Hill.

Hall, B., 1993. Industrial R&D during the 1980s: Did the rate of return fall? Brookings Papers on Economic Activity (Microeconomics) 2, 289–343.

Hall, B., 1996. The private and social returns to research and development. In: Smith, B., Barfield, C. (Eds.), Technology, R&D and the Economy. The Brookings Institution.

Hall, B., Mairesse, J., 1995. Exploring the relationship between R&D and productivity in French manufacturing firms. Journal of Econometrics 65, 263–293.

Harhoff, D., 1998. R&D and productivity in German manufacturing firms. Economics of Innovation and New Technology 6, 28–49.

Harhoff, D., 2000. R&D spillovers, technological proximity, and productivity growth – evidence from German panel data. Schmalenbach Business Review 52, 238–260.

Jaffe, A., 1986. Technological opportunity and spillovers of R&D'. American Economic Review 76, 984–1001.

Jorgenson, D.W., 1963. Capital theory and investment behavior. The American Economic Review, Papers and Proceedings of the Seventy Fifth Annual Meeting of the American Economic Association 53, 247–259.

Kafouros, M.I., 2005. R&D and productivity growth: evidence from the UK. Economics of Innovation and New Technology 14, 479–497.

Kafouros, M.I., 2006. The impact of the Internet on R&D-efficiency: theory and evidence. Technovation 26, 827–835.

Kafouros, M.I., 2008. Industrial Innovation and Firm Performance: The Impact of Scientific Knowledge on Multinational Corporations. Edward Elgar.

Kamien, M., Schwartz, N., 1982. Market Structure and Innovation. Cambridge University Press, Cambridge.

Kessler, E.H., 2003. Leveraging e-R&D processes: a knowledge-based view. Technovation 23, 905–915.

Kleinknecht, A., 1989. Firm size and innovation: observations in Dutch manufacturing industry. Small Business Economics 1, 215–222.

Levin, R.C., Klevorick, A.K., Nelson, R.R., Winter, S.G., 1987. Appropriating the returns from industrial research and development. Brookings Papers on Economic Activity 3, 783–820.

Liu, X., Buck, T., 2007. Innovation performance and channels for international technology spillovers: evidence from Chinese high-tech industries. Research Policy 36, 355–366.

Los, B., Verspagen, B., 2000. R&D spillovers and productivity: evidence from U.S. manufacturing microdata. Empirical Economics 25, 127–148.

Mairesse, J., Hall, B., 1996. Estimating the productivity of research and development: an exploration of GMM methods using data on French and United States manufacturing firms. National Bureau of Economic Research Working Paper 5501.

Mairesse, J., Sassenou, M., 1991. R&D and productivity: a survey of econometric studies at the firm level. The Science Technology and Industry Review 8, 317–348.

Mansfield, E., 1968. The Economics of Technological Change. Norton, New York.

Mansfield, E., 1987. Price indexes for R&D inputs 1969–83. Management Science 33, 124–129.

Matheson, D., Matheson, J., 1998 . The Smart Organization: Creating Value Through Strategic R&D. Harvard Business School Press, Boston.

McGahan, A.M., Silverman, B.S., 2006. Profiting from technological innovation by others: the effect of competitor patenting on firm value. Research Policy 35, 1222–1242.

Mohnen, P., 1996. R&D externalities and productivity growth. STI Review 18, 39–66.

Mohnen, P., 1999. International R&D spillovers and economic growth. Université du Québec à Montréal and CIRANO.

Odagiri, H., Iwata, H., 1986. The impact of R&D on productivity increase in Japanese manufacturing companies. Research Policy 15, 13–19.

Pakes, A., Schankerman, M., 1984. The rate of obsolescence of patents, research gestation lags, and the private rate of return to research resources. In: Griliches, Z. (Ed.), R&D, Patents and Productivity. University of Chicago Press, Chicago, pp. 98–112.

Pavitt, K., Robson, M., Townsend, J., 1987. The size distribution of innovating firms in the UK: 1945–1983. The Journal of Industrial Economics 55, 291–316.

Piergiovanni, R., Santarelli, E., Vivarelli, M., 1997. From which source do small firms derive their innovative inputs? Some evidence from Italian industry. Review of Industrial Organization 12, 243–258.

182   *Mario I. Kafouros and Peter J. Buckley*

Porter, E.M., 1980. Competitive Strategy: Techniques for Analyzing Industries and Competitors. The Free Press, New York.

Raut, L., 1995. R&D spillovers and productivity growth: evidence from Indian private firms. Journal of Development Economics 48, 1–23.

Sassenou, M., 1988. Recherche-developpment et productivity dans les enterprizes Japonaises: Une etude econometrique sur donnees de panel. Doctoral Dissertation, Ecole des Hautes Etudes en Sciences Sociales, Paris.

Scherer, F.M., 1982. Inter-industry technology flows and productivity growth. The Review of Economics and Statistics 64, 627–634.

Schumpeter, J.A., 1942. Capitalism, Socialism and Democracy. Harper and Row, New York.

Stoneman, P., Toivanen, O., 2001. The impact of revised recommended accounting practices on R&D reporting by UK firms. The International Journal of the Economics of Business 8, 123–136.

Tang, J., 2006. Competition and innovation behavior. Research Policy 35, 68–82.

Tsai, K.H., 2001. The factors speeding up the pace of new product development: the case of taiwan's ic design industry. Dissertation of the Department of Business Administration, National Taipei University, Taipei.

Wakelin, K., 2001. Productivity growth and R&D expenditure in UK manufacturing firms. Research Policy 30, 1079–1090.

Wang, J., Tsai, K., 2003. Productivity growth and R&D expenditure in Taiwan's manufacturing firms. National Bureau of Economic Research Working Paper 9724.

9
The Role of Internationalization in Explaining Innovation Performance

Co-authored with Mario I. Kafouros,
John A. Sharp, and Chengqi Wang

1. Introduction

Economic-growth theorists and management scholars have proposed that innovation has a positive impact on corporate performance. That is, increasing investments in innovation allows firms to develop and license new technologies, adopt more efficient production techniques, introduce new products and processes, and consequently become more competitive and increase their economic performance. However, past empirical results are mixed, not always confirming this theoretical proposition. Many studies find the private returns to innovation to be both positive and high (Hall and Mairesse, 1995; Adams and Jaffe, 1996). By contrast, several other studies indicate that although a firm's innovative efforts advance significantly society's pool of scientific knowledge, they make a limited or even negative contribution to the firm's own economic performance (Link, 1981; Sassenou, 1988). Hence, even though a number of studies have evaluated the relationship between innovation and performance, it is often unclear why some firms benefit from their innovative efforts, yet others fail to do so.

Extending past research on innovation, this study develops and tests empirically a framework that links together these apparently conflicting results. Drawing on theoretical knowledge from the disciplines of innovation and international business, it is argued that not all firms are able to benefit from innovation. Rather, it is proposed that the innovation–performance relationship is moderated by a firm's degree of internationalization (DOI), i.e. the extent to which it operates beyond its national borders (Kotabe et al., 2002). In other words, it is suggested that firms need some threshold of internationalization and to be able to access a broad range of markets in order to benefit sufficiently from their new products and processes. Initially, the study offers a theoretical framework that explains why the observed variations in the returns to innovation may be attributed to a firm's DOI. It then empirically tests this proposition and provides econometric evidence

184   *Mario I. Kafouros et al.*

showing that internationalization affects the economic payoff from industrial innovation.

2. Innovation and firm performance

The literature on innovation points out that Research and Development (R&D) leads to the creation of a stock of scientific knowledge (Griliches, 1979; Mansfield, 1984). A firm can use this knowledge in different ways to develop innovations and competencies, and improve its performance. By developing more efficient processes, for example, it can reduce the costs associated with the production of its goods. By introducing new products or by improving the quality of its existing products, it can increase its market share and sales (Mansfield, 1968). A firm can also increase its revenues through the royalty fees it receives from patent licenses. However, R&D also has indirect impacts. Cohen and Levinthal (1990) suggested that innovation increases a firm's ability to capture, assimilate and utilize external knowledge. It has also been argued that innovative firms are qualitatively different from non-innovative firms (Wakelin, 2001), and that R&D drives significant organizational adaptations that favor performance (Kafouros, 2008).

However, although one might expect that the contribution of innovation to a firm's performance would always be positive, frequently this does not occur. Due to intense competition and rivals' imitations, firms do not always appropriate the fruits of innovation, which frequently spill over to society (Arrow, 1962). Furthermore, strategic-management research demonstrates that the innovations of a firm's competitors may neutralize some (or even all) of the gains arising from its own investments in innovation (Porter, 1980; Chen and Miller, 1994). As noted earlier, past empirical studies have confirmed this, with results ranging from a strongly positive relationship between innovation and economic performance (Hall and Mairesse, 1995; Adams and Jaffe, 1996; Kafouros, 2005) to an insignificant-or even negative-effect (Link, 1981; Sassenou, 1988).

Trying to explain the variation in the returns to innovation, many writers have argued that because technologically sophisticated firms participate in sectors where the understanding and the scientific knowledge related to innovation is rich and growing, their innovative efforts significantly influence their performance (Clark and Griliches, 1984). Technology-management researchers have also argued that the good infrastructure and understanding of technologies (Kessler, 2003), makes high-tech firms more capable of integrating external research findings in their products and processes (Kafouros, 2006). Empirical findings have supported these propositions, indicating that the returns to innovation tend to be very positive for high-tech firms (Griliches and Mairesse, 1984; Wang and Tsai, 2003). Other scholars have suggested that various factors such as economies of scale and scope, technical expertise and managerial qualities allow large firms to enjoy high returns to innovation (Mansfield, 1968). However, the empirical findings concerning the role of firm size are inconclusive. Some studies indicate that the effects of innovation depend on firm size (Lichtenberg and Siegel, 1991; Cohen and Klepper, 1996), yet others found no evidence of such an association (Griliches, 1980; Wang and Tsai, 2003).

Although past research has investigated the effects of factors such as firm size and technological opportunities, it has not examined other firm-specific characteristics that may be needed to capture successfully the value of innovation. As noted earlier, this study focuses on one of these characteristics and suggests that a firm's degree of internationalization affects its ability to benefit from innovation. Before testing this proposition and showing that internationalization moderates the innovation–performance relationship, the next section draws on a variety of theoretical grounds and explains how and why internationalization is likely to influence the returns to innovation.

3. How does internationalization affect the returns to innovation?

Internationalization can be broadly defined as 'expanding across country borders into geographic locations that are new to the firm' (Hitt et al., 1994, p. 298). We have deliberately adopted this definition because depending on factors such as firm size and industry, firms may adopt a different internationalization approach. Whilst some firms may prefer to internationalize their production more, others may place emphasis on the internationalization of their business. A more recent phenomenon is the internationalization of R&D network. Even though these measures of internationalization are usually correlated, past empirical evidence indicates that the internationalization of R&D is lower than that of sales (von Zedtwitz and Gassmann, 2002).

One way of understanding how internationalization influences the returns to innovation is to focus on how it affects the factors that determine the economic payoff from innovation. Simplifying the conceptual framework, these factors may be grouped into two categories. The first relates to the factors that influence a firm's ability to produce technological innovations (innovative capacity). R&D departments with high innovative capacity can develop better products and processes, faster and at lower cost and therefore contribute more to a firm's performance. The second category includes the wide range of factors that allow a firm firstly, to better exploit its technological developments and secondly, to protect and appropriate the fruits of innovation. The following subsections explain how internationalization may affect innovative capacity as well as the exploitation and the appropriability of innovation, and thereby the innovation–performance relationship. The framework is also outlined in Figure 9.1.

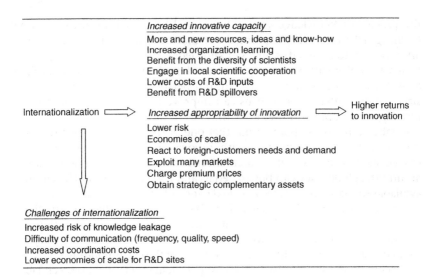

Figure 9.1   The main implications of internationalization

3.1. The connection between internationalization and innovative capacity

Increased R&D competition, along with continually shorter product life cycles, have made the achievement of technological breakthroughs difficult. As a result, the development of innovations requires substantial and diverse resources. Kobrin (1991) demonstrated that internationalization helped to generate these R&D resources. It has also been suggested that internationally diversified firms can improve their innovative capacity by being better able to utilize the wider range of resources available globally (Kotabe, 1990), and which are often unavailable to domestic firms. Furthermore, they can promote innovation by using the specific advantages of different countries (Hitt et al., 1997), and by making contacts and establishing alliances with local suppliers, universities, research centers and competitors (Santos et al., 2004).

In a similar vein, the knowledge-based view of the firm suggests that innovation is an information- and knowledge-intensive process (Nonaka and Takeuchi, 1995). In order to be creative and efficient, R&D teams need to access and retrieve information from as many sources as possible. As highly international firms tend to have geographically dispersed R&D departments (von Zedtwitz and Gassmann, 2002; Kurokawa et al., 2007), they can increase their innovative capacity by utilizing knowledge and ideas from several countries and from a broader group of scientists (Kafouros, 2006). Hitt et al. (1997) demonstrated that the greater knowledge of national idiosyncrasies, available to culturally diverse teams, facilitates coordination. Internationalization can also advance innovative capacity by improving

The process of knowledge accumulation and by increasing organizational learning. Hitt et al. (1997) pointed out that internationalization not only allows a firm to enrich its sources of knowledge, but also provides the opportunity to capture ideas from a greater number of new and different markets, as well as from a wide range of cultural perspectives. Thus, they emphasized, highly international firms can improve their ability to innovate by having greater opportunities to learn.

Kotabe et al. (2002) pointed out that one of the main aims of firms is to minimize the costs associated with innovation. Internationalization can reduce such costs. As highly international firms can access many markets around the globe, they can buy materials and R&D inputs from the cheapest available sources, and locate their R&D and other departments in the most productive regions. Many researchers have suggested that multinational companies can establish their facilities in regions where land, capital and scientific talent are cheap. Granstrand et al. (1993) observe that the salary of a well-educated researcher in India is one-tenth of the corresponding salary of a researcher in Sweden. Similarly, the cost per square meter for a biotech lab in the US is approximately ten times that of the corresponding cost in India.

Internationalization can also improve the ability to innovate by allowing firms to hire better technologists and access skilled technical expertise (Cheng and Bolon, 1993). A higher DOI may improve the quality of new products through network mechanisms that enable a continuous flow of information about the changing needs and requirements of customers (Kafouros, 2006). It may also allow a company to adapt its technologies to the local market needs, thereby improving its responsiveness (Cheng and Bolon, 1993), providing technical support and engaging in local scientific cooperation (von Zedtwitz and Gassmann, 2002).

Nevertheless, researchers often make a distinction between an 'international' and a 'global' innovation network, arguing that the latter requires coordination and integration of dispersed departments (Shenkar and Luo, 2004). Kuemmerle (1997) suggested that only a few companies are able to create a 'cohesive research community'. Similarly, Doz et al. (2001) and Santos et al. (2004) use the term 'metanationalization' to suggest that only those firms that are truly global innovators, can exploit 'localized pockets of technology, market intelligence and capabilities'. For these companies, they argue, technology has become a decisive competitive weapon as they are able to develop more, higher-value innovation at a lower cost.

Another theoretical explanation relates to R&D spillovers. According to the relevant literature, both innovative capacity and firm performance depend on the size of the 'pool' of scientific knowledge that a firm can access (Griliches, 1979; Jaffe, 1986; Scherer, 1982). As international diversification allows firms to access a larger pool of scientific knowledge created in different markets, it makes them more capable of borrowing and exploiting new ideas, of imitating other firms' developments, of integrating

188   *Mario I. Kafouros et al.*

new research findings in their products and processes, and consequently of further increasing their innovative capacity. Generally, it has been recognized that in order to unlock their economic potential, organizations must search for and exploit external ideas and sources of innovation (Chesbrough, 2003). Similarly, Kuemmerle (1997) argues that in order to innovate with the speed required to remain competitive, firms must absorb new research results from foreign universities, competitors and clusters of scientific excellence. Santos et al. (2004) emphasize that if companies utilize similar knowledge reservoirs, uninspired products are likely to be developed.

On the other hand though, a high degree of internationalization increases the risk of knowledge leakage. It is frequently argued that one of the disadvantages of decentralization is the unwitting dissemination of knowledge from poorly-controlled departments (Fisch, 2003), increasing the likelihood of know-how spillovers to competitors (Sanna-Randaccio and Veugelers, 2007). Indeed, when the knowledge pool within the local economy is poor, the costs from outgoing spillovers may even outweigh the benefits from incoming spillovers (SannaRandaccio and Veugelers, 2007). For that reason, many innovation strategists argue that a centralized network is required in order to protect corporate technology.

Another negative consequence of internationalization relates to the substantial cost that the coordination and control of a global network requires. Granstrand et al. (1993) explain that in order to promote learning and avoid duplication, information exchange between individuals, teams and divisions is required. This cost can be substantial as the exchange of tacit knowledge and the creation of trust necessitates personal face-to-face meetings (von Zedtwitz and Gassmann, 2002). As such, both managers and scientists need to travel to different locations in order to visit affiliated suppliers, collaborators and universities. Other writers emphasize that geographical distance between departments also influences communication in terms of frequency, quality and speed (von Zedtwitz and Gassmann, 2002); and that the efficiency of communication between teams decreases exponentially with geographic distance, raising the risk of misunderstandings (Fisch, 2003). Other arguments favoring centralization relate to the economies of scale and 'critical mass' that an R&D site must have in order to operate efficiently (Granstrand et al., 1993). These arguments refer to the expensive instruments and equipment as well as to the scientists and technologists needed to ensure that the benefits of a new R&D lab will outweigh the vast costs associated with the investment in it.

3.2. The connection between internationalization, and the exploitation and appropriability of innovation

At this point, it is important to distinguish between technological achievement and economic payoff. In the previous section, it was argued that the returns to innovation depend on the ability of a firm to develop

The Role of Internationalization 189

technological innovations. However, they also depend on the ability to exploit and appropriate the returns from technological developments (Griliches, 1979), as well as the ability to implement strategies that allow a firm to benefit economically through innovation. As noted earlier, inventors cannot always appropriate the benefits of their research efforts; thus, these may easily spillover to other firms and consumers. In other words, high technological performance does not necessarily go hand in hand with high economic performance. We argue that internationalization is one of those firm-specific characteristics that allow a firm to better exploit and appropriate the benefits of innovation.

Caves (1982) was one of the first to argue that firms that expanded to other markets enjoyed higher returns to innovation. Recently, the work of some other researchers also supported this proposition. Santos et al. (2004) discuss the importance of combining technical know-how and market expertise. Hitt et al. (1997) suggested that firms that operate in a limited number of markets might not be able to cover the costs associated with innovation. Indeed, the substantial costs of such investments, along with the short product life cycles and the fact that the depreciation rate of investments in innovation is usually high (Pakes and Schankerman, 1984; Goto and Suzuki, 1989), might not allow firms with a limited DOI to benefit from such investments. By contrast, highly international firms could charge premium prices for their products (Kotabe et al., 2002), and offer them to a large number of potential buyers, thereby spreading the costs. Fisch (2003) argues that internationalization allows firms to recognize and react to foreign customer demands, support local production units, and implement incentives or regulations of host governments. Sanna-Randaccio and Veugelers (2007) analyze the importance of similar market-driven motives in relation to higher responsiveness to local differences, understanding of the local context, and proximity to lead users. Moreover, internationalization might lower the risk of R&D by avoiding fluctuations and business cycles specific to a single market or region. Hence, as Lu and Beamish (2004) emphasized, only firms that deployed their intangible assets in many markets could exploit them to their full value.

Another researcher who suggested that the boundaries of a firm might affect the appropriability of innovation was Teece (1986). He argued that the ownership of complementary assets, which needed to be employed to convert a technological success into a commercial one, determined who benefits and who loses from innovation. Hence, he concluded, as internationalization raised the possibility of obtaining such complementary assets (e.g. through international alliances), it was an important strategic variable that provided the opportunity for innovating firms to outperform their competitors. The link between the effects of innovative activity and internationalization is also provided by the framework of the 'internalization' of markets across international frontiers (Buckley and Casson, 1976). The researchers argue

190 *Mario I. Kafouros et al.*

that there are distinct advantages in internalizing markets in innovation-intensive intermediate products. These include the ability to forward plan by integrating the outputs of R&D with the marketing and production functions, the ability to use discriminatory pricing, the avoidance of buyer uncertainty in the (international) market for licenses, as well as the ability to use internal transfer prices internationally to increase appropriation.

Multinational firms can also benefit from economies of scale. Rugman (1981) argued that international diversification could yield a competitive advantage by allowing a firm to perform more activities internally. Nelson (1959) suggested that diversified firms might have more opportunities to exploit any unpredictable outcomes of R&D. Furthermore, innovative firms that operate in many regions can lower production costs and increase their performance by transferring and applying their process innovations to many production plants (Kotabe et al., 2002). Overall then, it may be concluded that internationalization moderates the innovation–performance relationship, influencing the economic payoff a firm receives from innovation.

4. Method and data

4.1. Model

Having explained how and why internationalization may influence the returns to innovation, the next step is to test this proposition empirically. The ideal empirical approach would be to estimate the impacts of internationalization on innovative capacity and appropriability of innovation separately. However, given that it is impossible to find accurate proxies for 'innovative capacity' and 'appropriability', the study estimates the total impact that internationalization has on the economic payoff from innovation. The model adopted here is based on the work of Griliches (1979) who presented a Cobb–Douglas production function that correlated firm output not only with the conventional inputs of capital and labor, but also with the stock of 'R&D capital'. However, this model has the drawback that because the depreciation rate of innovation is unknown it is difficult to estimate the stock of R&D capital precisely.

For that reason, we have utilized a transformation of this model that has been used widely in the econometric literature, to assess the returns to innovation (Goto and Suzuki, 1989; Hall and Mairesse, 1995; Wakelin, 2001). This transformation (see Eq. (1) below) associates innovative activity with differences in firm performance (ΔP). The fact that it allows us to assess what advances in performance can be attributed to investments in innovation, makes this model ideal for serving the objective of this research. This specification (also known as 'rate of return') is characterized by a number of attractive properties. Firstly, it uses current R&D expenditure so it is not necessary to estimate the stock R&D capital. Secondly, it calculates directly the rate of return to innovation, i.e. it estimates the marginal product of

The Role of Internationalization 191

innovation (rather than its elasticity). Furthermore, it has the advantage of avoiding the possible bias due to simultaneous decisions in relation to firm inputs and outputs (Odagiri and Iwata, 1986). For more technical details concerning how this model is derived, see Goto and Suzuki (1989), Hall and Mairesse (1995) and Wakelin (2001).

$$\Delta P_{it} = \lambda + \alpha \Delta K_{it} + \beta \Delta L_{it} + \rho I_{it} + \sum \gamma D_i + \varepsilon_{it}, \tag{1}$$

where $\Delta X_{it} = X_{it} - X_{it-1}$, P_{it} is the economic performance of firm i in year t, K_{it} is a measure of tangible assets of firm i in year t, L_{it} is the labor input of firm i in year t, I_{it} is the innovative activity of firm i in year t, $\sum D_i$ is a number of dummy/control variables, ε_{it} is the error term of firm i in year t, λ is a constant, ρ is the rate of return to innovation, and α, β, γ are other parameters to be estimated.

Assuming that the theoretical framework is valid then (1) the contribution of innovation to the performance of firms with a higher DOI should differ considerably from the corresponding contribution to the performance of firms with a lower DOI, and (2) the extent to which a firm is international should moderate the innovation–performance relationship. To examine empirically our propositions, we initially split the sample into firms with a higher and lower degree of internationalization. We then estimate Eq. (1) for each subgroup separately. We finally compare the average returns to innovation for the two subgroups, and determine the extent to which the impact of innovation on performance differs across firms.

Furthermore, the model of Eq. (1) was extended by using moderated regression analysis. According to the relevant literature, in order to test whether a variable is indeed a moderator, one should examine whether the regression coefficient between the dependent and independent variables is a function of that moderator (Le et al., 2006), i.e. in statistical terms, that the corresponding interaction variables are significant. Testing the proposition that internationalization influences the payoff from innovation, we estimate Eq. (2). This includes a variable of innovative activity, weighted by the DOI of firm i in year t. If the theoretical framework is valid, then the rate of return to innovation (ρ) estimated from Eq. (2) should differ considerably from that estimated from Eq. (1).

$$\Delta P_{it} = \lambda + \alpha \Delta K_{it} + \beta \Delta L_{it} + \rho I_{it} DOI_{it} + \sum \gamma D_i + \varepsilon_{it}. \tag{2}$$

4.2. Variables

4.2.1. Dependent variable

Measures of performance usually focus on indices that relate to either firm profitability or revenues. Because firms' profitability is highly volatile and sometimes negative, and because the time lag between innovation and

192   *Mario I. Kafouros et al.*

profitability is likely to be much longer than that between innovation and revenues, this study utilizes the second one. The dependent variable of economic performance is a deflated measure of each firm's sales revenue per employee (this is also a measure of labor productivity). As emphasized by many previous studies, although financial measures (such as profitability) have problems associated with the handling of royalties, management fees, and accounting standards (Buckley, 1996, p. 162), labor productivity is less subject to manipulation (Wagner, 2004). One practical problem is that the data include R&D employees twice, once in the conventional input of labor and a second time in the input of R&D. To correct this problem and estimate the returns to innovation more accurately, the R&D employees were subtracted from the total number of employees.

4.2.2. Independent variables

Tangible assets: This variable is a deflated measure of the available capital services for each firm's employee. This followed the work of Jorgenson (1963) who suggested that the input of tangible assets must be a measure, not of capital stock, but of the services flowing from it. According to this framework, the cumulative stock of capital produces a flow of services that are the conceptual capital input. The ideal method of measuring capital services is to use the so-called rental price, i.e. the cost that a firm pays, either to other firms or to itself, for having and using a number of assets. Following Griliches (1980), the rental price of capital services was approximated using the depreciation of fixed capital stock, as this is in effect, the actual cost that a firm pays for having and using its capital assets.

Labor input: This variable was measured by using each firm's number of employees. It is important to explain that because the model is a transformation of the Cobb-Douglas production function and because labor is also included in the variables of firm performance and tangible assets, the coefficient of labor does not represents its contribution to firm performance. Researchers usually include it in the model to test whether the assumption of constant returns to scale (CRS) is valid. One can reject the CRS assumption when regression coefficient of labor is significantly different from zero.

Innovation: Researchers have used different approaches to operationalize innovation. Some previous studies quantified innovation by measuring the number of each firm's patents or actual innovations (Griliches et al., 1987). These approaches have raised many concerns because the outcomes of industrial research and development are not always successful. In any case, even when the outcomes are successful, they are not always patentable. Similarly, the approach of asking R&D directors about their firm's actual innovations has its own problems because firstly, directors do not always provide objective responses about the technological developments of their own firms and secondly, it is difficult to weight and assess the importance of each innovation appropriately. To avoid such criticisms and following previous similar studies (e.g. Hall and Mairesse, 1995; Wakelin, 2001), innovation in this study is a measure of R&D intensity, i.e. the ratio of the R&D expenditure that each firm spends over its sales.

Innovation × internationalization: To examine whether internationalization moderates the innovation–performance relationship, we estimated a measure of innovation that is weighted by the degree of internationalization. A firm can increase its degree of internationalization in many ways. For instance, it can find representatives in other countries, develop collaborations and export its products. Alternatively, internationalization can be increased by establishing its own subsidiaries in foreign markets. To proxy this variable, researchers have used a wide range of measures including the ratio of foreign sales to total sales, foreign sales to total assets or the number of countries in which a firm operates (Kotabe et al., 2002). Because internationalization does not only relate to the number of markets or regions that a firm has accessed, but also to the size of these markets or regions, we do not use the last proxy. Instead, following the majority of previous studies (e.g. Grant, 1987; Kotabe et al., 2002), and the suggestions of Sullivan (1994) who examined the suitability of these indices, this study quantifies internationalization by using the ratio of foreign sales to total sales.

4.2.3. Control variables

As discussed earlier, the innovation–performance relationship depends on a number of factors. Considerable evidence suggests that the innovative capacities, as well as the organizational and cultural foundations of technologically sophisticated firms, such as pharmaceuticals and electronics, differ from those of low-tech firms such as metals and textiles manufacturers (Harhoff, 1998; Matheson and Matheson, 1998; Wang and Tsai, 2003). Other studies have supported the idea that the returns to innovation depend on firm size (Lichtenberg and Siegel, 1991; Cohen and Klepper, 1996). Additionally, firm performances and characteristics may vary not only over time but also across industries. In order to capture these variations and avoid biased estimates, a number of dummy variables have been included for high- and low-tech firms, firm size, year and the industry to which each firm belongs.

4.3. Sample

To empirically test whether internationalization affects the returns to innovation, it is essential to use firm-level data. The use of such data is particularly important for this study, as it allows the separation of advances in performance that are result of a firm's specific capabilities from those improvements that are general to the sector as a whole (Wakelin, 2001). For two main reasons, we also decided to use panel data. Firstly, a sample that includes several years is essential in order to capture the international expansion of firms across time, and how this affected the innovation–performance relationship. Secondly, as Kotabe et al. (2002) pointed out, inferences drawn

194   *Mario I. Kafouros et al.*

by pure cross-section data are biased by idiosyncrasies associated with that specific period. Thus, only a sample that includes many years can safeguard against any business-cycle biases and any market fluctuations caused by economic recessions or revivals (Kafouros, 2005).

To estimate the model, we used data for the UK manufacturing sector. These were obtained from Data-stream, the UK R&D Scoreboard Survey and firms' financial reports. In order to choose the sample, we performed a search based on two criteria: For each firm (1) data should be available for performance, tangible assets, number of employees, innovation and internationalization, and (2) the data should be available for at least 14 years. The search returned a sample of 84 large manufacturing firms for the period between 1989 and 2002 (i.e. 1176 observations). In 2002, the total private R&D investment of the whole UK manufacturing sector was £10.14 billion (ONS, 2002). In that same year, the R&D expenditures of the 84 firms of the sample accounted for £4.9 billions. So even though the sample does not include many firms, the R&D undertaken by those firms accounted for approximately 50% of the total UK R&D investment. Although we had the opportunity to use a larger sample (but for a shorter period), a long time horizon is required in order to capture the international expansion of firms over time.

Table 9.1 provides details on the industries included in the sample. To estimate the model we used the two-year differences of each variable, because one-year differences tend to be affected by extreme short-term variations of the variables (Mairesse and Sassenou, 1991). Indeed, it was observed that estimates based on 1-year differences were unstable. We also took into account the possibility that innovation might take some time to improve

Table 9.1   Sectoral analysis (84 UK manufacturing firms, 1989–2002)

	SIC 80 code	No. of firms
Metal products	22 & 31	2
Minerals	23 & 24	3
Machinery and mechanical engineering	32	23
Motor vehicle parts	35	6
Paper and printing	47	2
Rubber and plastics	48	2
Other manufacturing	49	2
Chemicals and pharmaceuticals	25	16
Electrical and electronics	34	15
Telecommunication	344	4
Aerospace	364	5
Instrument engineering	37	4
Total		84

performance. Based on the findings of Pakes and Schankerman (1984), we lagged the innovation variable by two years. Table 9.2 presents means and standard deviations for a number of variables, as well as correlation coefficients for the final variables included in the model. It is important to emphasize that the sample firms are very large, averaging 9347 employees. The fact that the correlation between the *innovation × internationalization* and *innovation* variables is high does not engender any econometric problems, as the model does not include them simultaneously.

5. Evidence

5.1. Empirical results

Table 9.3 reports the regression findings. These resulted from the model described earlier and the method of ordinary least squares (OLS). Both Models 1 and 2 are based on Eq. (1). Although the first one does not include any control variables, Model 2 includes dummies for size, technological opportunities, years and industries. As the results show, the goodness of fit (R^2) for Model 2 is significantly higher than that for Model 1, confirming that control variables are important in order to avoid biases associated with time- and industry-specific idiosyncrasies. Although R^2 is relatively low at 0.29, it is higher than that of many previous studies (Odagiri and Iwata, 1986; Griliches and Mairesse, 1990).

Model 2 is similar to those that previous studies have estimated. As the results indicate, the rate of return to innovation is 0.26 (statistically significant at the 5% level). This suggests that investments in innovation had a significant and positive effect on the performance of UK manufacturing MNEs. The results are consistent with earlier findings. For instance, using a sample of UK firms for the 1988–1992 period, Wakelin (2001) found the

Table 9.2 Descriptive statistics and correlations[a]

	Mean	S.D.	2	3	4	5
1. ΔPerformance[b]	0.025	0.111	0.39	−0.41	0.03	0.05
2. ΔTangible assets[b]	0.048	0.151		−0.55	−0.03	−0.03
3. ΔEmployees[b]	−0.002	0.152			0.14	0.14
4. Innovation	0.026	0.025				0.89
5. Innovation × internationalization	0.015	0.017				
Performance	95 910	95 130				
Tangible assets	24 440	18 440				
Number of employees	9347	16 526				
Internationalization	0.65	0.22				

Note: [a] Correlations greater than 0.15 are significant at the 0.01 level.
[b] Two-year differences of the variables.

196   *Mario I. Kafouros et al.*

Table 9.3 Regression results for firm performance (84 UK manufacturing MNEs, 1989–2002)

	Model 1		Model 2		Model 3	
	Coefficient	SE	Coefficient	SE	Coefficient	SE
Tangible assets	0.16**	0.023	0.21**	0.026	0.21**	0.026
Labor	−0.21**	0.024	−0.21**	0.024	−0.21**	0.024
Innovation	0.23*	0.121	0.26*	0.116		
Innovation × internationalization					0.56**	0.185
Firm size	−0.006	0.007	−0.002	0.007	−0.002	0.007
High/low tech dummy	0.021**	0.007	−0.012	0.007	−0.015	0.017
Time dummies			Yes		Yes	
Industry dummies			Yes		Yes	
R^2	0.22%		0.29%		0.31%	
R^2-adjusted	0.22%		0.28%		0.29%	

Note: A number of time and industry dummies are included in the models. However, because these dummies are many, their coefficients are not shown in the table.
*$p<0.05$.
**$p<0.01$.

returns to innovation to be 0.29. The results are also similar to those of some other studies that found that the payoff from innovation for the US, France and Japan was around 0.30 (Griliches and Mairesse, 1983; Griliches and Mairesse, 1990). The coefficient for the control variable of firm size is statistically insignificant. As the sample comprises only large firms, however, this is not surprising. It also seems that the industry dummies absorbed firms' heterogeneity, thereby leading to a statistically insignificant effect for the high/low-tech control variable.

In order to test whether internationalization affects the capability of firms to benefit economically through innovation, Eq. (2) was estimated. As noted earlier, if our research proposition is valid, then the rate of return to innovation estimated from Eq. (2) should differ considerably from that estimated from Eq. (1). Indeed, the results of Model 3 confirm this. The estimated returns to innovation increased remarkably from 0.26 to 0.56, and the goodness of fit of the model has been further improved. The good fit of the new interaction variable is also reflected in the statistical significance level, which improved from 5% to 1%. The positive and much higher coefficient suggests that, on average, the returns to innovation become higher as the firm becomes more international. That is, the benefits a firm receives from its innovative activity depend on the extent to which it operates in markets beyond its national boundaries.

To examine the robustness of the findings, we examined their sensitivity to changes in the definitions of tangible assets, as well as to changes in the price indices utilized to deflate the variables. Despite different specifications, the findings remained approximately the same. The findings were approximately the same even when the random-effect estimator was employed. Additionally, a Durbin–Watson test indicated that there was no evidence of positive or negative auto-correlation (d statistic = 2.07). We also investigated the possibility of 'reverse causality'. This problem arises when the independent variables are not exogenously determined (as they should be), but there is a degree of feedback from output to inputs. In other words, although performance may depend on corporate innovation and internationalization, there is also a possibility that those organizations with high performance invest more in innovation and internationalization. In order to examine this, we reversed the model, i.e. we used the variable of 'innovative activity' as dependent variable, and a 1-year lagged measure of performance as independent variable. The results indicated that the impact of performance on innovation was statistically insignificant, thereby rejecting the possibility of reverse causality. This result remained the same when a 2-year lagged measure of performance was utilized, as well as when 'internationalization' was used as dependent variable.

To confirm the findings of Table 9.3, we also examined whether the impact of innovation on performance is greater for firms that are more international. To do so, the sample was divided into firms with higher and lower DOI, and Eq. (1) was estimated for each subgroup separately. The value of the 'internationalization' variable of the firms in the sample ranges widely from 0.20 to 0.95. In other words, whilst the foreign sales of some firms comprised only the 20% of their total sales, as much as 95% of other firms' sales were made in international markets.

To divide the sample in two subgroups of lower and higher DOI, following previous studies we used the above and below levels of the median (which was 0.69%). Hence, 42 firms that had a DOI higher than 69% were included in the higher-internationalization group. The remaining firms of the sample, the foreign sales of which ranged from 20% to 69%, were included in the lower-internationalization group. The descriptive statistics for the two subgroups indicated that their R&D-intensity was exactly the same (at 2.6%). Hence, although more international firms may have the incentives to increase their R&D investment as a proportion of sales, the descriptive statistics do not support this. Contrary to our expectations, the descriptive statistics also revealed that the performance of firms with lower DOI was slightly higher than the corresponding performance of higher-internationalization firms.

Table 9.4 compares the average returns to innovation for the two subgroups. The findings are consistent with those of Table 9.3. They confirm that internationalization is a firm-specific characteristic that affects the payoff from innovation. Specifically, the rate of return to innovation for the firms with lower DOI is only 0.12 and statistically insignificant, thereby implying that

198 *Mario I. Kafouros et al.*

Table 9.4 Regression results for firms with lower and higher degree of internationalization (DOI)

	Firms with lower DOI		Firms with higher DOI	
	Coefficient	SE	Coefficient	SE
Tangible assets	0.16**	0.038	0.11**	0.024
Labor	−0.17**	0.034	−0.10**	0.026
Innovation	0.12	0.156	0.34**	0.105
Firm size	−0.006	0.011	0.003	0.005
High/low tech dummy	−0.02	0.021	0.002	0.016
Time dummies	Yes		Yes	
Industry dummies	Yes		Yes	
R^2	0.23%		0.30%	
R^2-adjusted	0.20%		0.26%	

Note: A number of time and industry dummies are included in the models. However, because these dummies are many, their coefficients are not shown in the table.
*$p<0.05$.
**$p<0.01$.

innovation may not contribute to their performance. It appears that because their technological discoveries are not marketed in many countries, the significant costs associated with innovation dominate the benefits. In line with the previous theoretical discussion however, the relationship is totally reversed in the case of higher-internationalization organizations. The corresponding rate of return for these firms is 0.34 (statistically significant at the 1% level), indicating that internationalization is indeed a factor that allows these firms to profit from innovation.

5.2. Discussion

The empirical results given above support our proposition, showing that internationalization moderates the innovation–performance relationship. The analysis demonstrates that highly international firms enjoy high returns to their innovative efforts. This finding is consistent with many theoretical predictions. Although the costs of developing new ideas are similar whether offered to one market or to many (Zachary, 1995), being more international allows a firm to achieve greater returns from innovation by utilizing many markets (Hitt et al., 1997). The results also confirm that firms with high DOI outperform their less internationalized competitors, as they can increase their innovative capacity by engaging in local scientific cooperation, lowering the costs of R&D, and benefiting from new resources, ideas and technologists. Additionally, because investments in innovation depreciate rapidly (Goto and Suzuki, 1989), a firm that markets its inventions in a small number of countries may capture the full value of its innovations only for a short period of time. For this reason, it is particularly important for R&D-intensive firms to be able to exploit the value of their developments by reaching a large number of potential buyers through the operation of internal markets in the MNE (Buckley and Casson, 1976).

Another noteworthy result is that the weighting of innovative activity by the DOI doubled the coefficient of the returns to innovation. An implication for academic research is that the actual returns to such investments may be higher than previous studies have indicated. Hence, those firms that reduce R&D spending because of their low expectations of adequate payoff (Ravenscraft and Scherer, 1982) may be encouraged to increase their investments in R&D again. The study may also assist in resolving the inconsistency of some of the previous findings. As discussed earlier, it is often unclear why whilst some studies find the effects of innovation to be positive and high, other studies find these impacts to be insignificant. Our findings imply that the reason for such conflicting results may be the fact that even though prior research controlled for the effects of technological opportunities and firm size, it did not control for the effects of internationalization.

Interestingly, the findings also show that the impact of innovation on performance is statistically insignificant for firms with lower degree of internationalization. This implies that there is a threshold for these moderating effects, under which the costs of innovation may exceed its potential benefits. Although this threshold may be lower for some industries and higher for others, the fact that the value of DOI for the first subgroup ranges between 20% and 69% implies that this threshold is probably quite high. Nevertheless, one should be very careful when interpreting the findings about the lower-internationalization subgroup. The insignificant returns to innovation do not imply that these firms should reduce their investments in innovation. Although they may not receive any direct economic payoff for their investments, innovation is necessary for firms to remain competitive (Teece, 1986).

The results may also help to explain why the previous findings concerning the effects of firm size are contradictory. The subgroup analysis supports the notion that even when firms are large, they cannot benefit from innovation unless they are sufficiently international. As firm size and internationalization are inevitably correlated, it is likely that the small-firm subgroups of previous studies included firms that operated in a single market. Hence, as these firms had not only small size but also a lower degree of internationalization, researchers cannot be sure whether variations in the returns to innovation may be attributable merely to firm size, rather than to the degree of internationalization. Nevertheless, one could make the same criticism for this study, i.e. argue that some of the variation of the estimates may be a result of the varying firm size. To show that this is not the case, we used the below and above median of firm sales and divided the data into smaller- and larger-firms. We then estimated the model for each subgroup separately. The

200   *Mario I. Kafouros et al.*

findings showed that the payoff from innovation was approximately the same for both subgroups; thereby suggesting that as the sample comprises relatively large firms, the variation of the results of Table 9.4 is caused by internationalization (rather than by firm size).

6. Conclusions, implications and future research

Although prior studies recognize the importance of innovation in allowing a firm to develop competitive advantages (Artz et al., 2003) and in surviving the battle for technological leadership (Chesbrough, 2007), they often focus on the role of firm size and technological opportunities. This study contributes to the innovation literature by suggesting that another significant firm-specific factor that allows companies to improve performance through innovation is that of 'internationalization'. Initially, the study offered a conceptual framework that explained how and why internationalization, by influencing innovative capacity and appropriability, is likely to affect the returns to innovation. Then, utilizing a sample of firms with different degree of internationalization and a 14-year time horizon that captured their international expansion, it provided evidence that confirmed the critical role of DOI in reaping rewards from innovation.

The findings suggest that not all firms are able to create additional value by exploiting their research discoveries. Rather, we found that depending on DOI, the impact of innovation on corporate performance can be either positive or insignificant. An implication for theory is that future predictions about the impacts of industrial research should be linked to a firm's degree of internationalization. Similarly, an implication for empirical research is that models that do not control for the effects of internationalization may yield biased results that underestimate the consequences of innovation for firms' economic performance. A third implication of our findings relates to the role of firm size. As discussed earlier, social scientists need to be cautious in attributing variations in the innovation–performance relationship to firm size. Although the size of an organization plays an important role in explaining innovation performance, we found that large firms with low degree of internationalization do not outperform their competitors. This result provides support to the arguments emphasizing that organizations – even the largest – can no longer rely only on their own technologies and knowledge reservoir (Chesbrough, 2007; Santos et al., 2004).

As firms invest vast amounts of money in innovation, the results may update not only scholarly knowledge but also managerial understanding and practice. Even though firms' innovation efforts lead to significant technological and scientific breakthroughs, the analysis demonstrated that only firms with high DOI were able to enjoy the fruits of innovation. This result confirms the argument of Frohman (1982) that large investments in innovation alone do not ensure the successful exploitation of technology as a decisive strategic weapon. It also suggests that although the potential benefits of such investments are many, to be successful in capturing these benefits organizations need to coordinate innovation strategy with international-business strategy (Kotabe et al., 2002). Therefore, one recommendation to firm strategists is to focus not only on the development of new products and processes but also on the expansion to new markets. That is, before making large investments in innovation, firms should plan a strategy that will ensure that they can successfully exploit their new developments in a wide range of markets.

However, the study has a number of limitations. Firstly, the innovation expenditures reported by firms are the sum of different R&D activities. Researchers could replicate the findings using specific types of innovation, such as process and product innovations or outsourced innovation. Similarly, different measures of performance such as profitability can be used. Secondly, the current study utilized UK data. To generalize the results more reliably, future research should re-estimate the model using data from other countries. Thirdly, the study operationalized 'internationalization' by using the ratio of foreign sales to total sales. This proxy however, does not measure accurately the level of internationalization, despite its wide use by prior studies. Because of limited data availability, it was impossible to reproduce the results using alternative definitions. Future studies could re-estimate the model using more accurate measures for each firm's internationalization of sales, production and R&D network.

Another interesting avenue for future work relates to firms' international-expansion strategy. Out dataset did not indicate what proportion of each firm's foreign sales were exports and what proportion of such sales were generated by subsidiaries. More precise data could allow researchers to examine whether one of these two international expansion strategies is preferable for enhancing the value found in innovation. Utilizing such data, researchers could also create separate ratios for the US, Europe and Asia, and examine whether the returns to innovation for firms that increased their international expansion in one region outperformed the returns obtained by those firms that increased their international expansion in another region.

Acknowledgements

This paper is part of a larger research project funded by the UK Economic and Social Research Council (ESRC) (PTA-026–27–0800).

References

Adams, J.D., Jaffe, A.B., 1996. Bounding the effects of R&D: an investigation using matched establishment-firm data. RAND Journal of Economics 27 (4), 700–721.

Arrow, K., 1962. The economic implications of learning by doing. Review of Economic Studies 29, 155–173.

Artz, K.W., Norman, P.M., Hatfield, D.E., 2003. Firm performance: a longitudinal study of R&D, patents, and product innovation. Academy of Management, Best Conference Paper.

Buckley, A., 1996. International Capital Budgeting. Prentice-Hall, NJ.

Buckley, P.J., Casson, M., 1976. The Future of the Multinational Enterprise. Macmillan, London.

Caves, R.E., 1982. Multinational Enterprise and Economic Analysis. Cambridge University Press, Cambridge.

Chen, M.J., Miller, D., 1994. Competitive attack, retaliation and performance: an expectancy-valence framework. Strategic Management Journal 15, 85–102.

Cheng, J.L.C., Bolon, D.S., 1993. The management of multinational R&D: a neglected topic in international business research. Journal of International Business Studies 24, 1–18.

Chesbrough, H.W., 2003. Open Innovation: The New Imperative for Creating and Profiting from Technology. Harvard Business School Publishing Corporation, Cambridge, Mass.

Chesbrough, H.W., 2007. Why companies should have open business models. MIT Sloan Management Review 48 (2), 22–28.

Clark, B., Griliches, Z., 1984. Productivity and R&D at the firm level in French manufacturing. In: Griliches, Z. (Ed.), R&D, Patents, and Productivity. University of Chicago Press, Chicago, 393–416.

Cohen, W.M., Klepper, S., 1996. Firm size and the nature of innovation within industries: the case of product and process R&D. Review of Economics and Statistics 78 (2), 232–243.

Cohen, W.M., Levinthal, D.A., 1990. Absorptive capacity: a new perspective on learning and innovation. Administrative Science Quarterly 35 (1), 128–152.

Doz, Y., Santos, J., Williamson, P., 2001. From Global to Metanational: How Companies Win in the Knowledge Economy. Harvard Business School Publishing Corporation, Cambridge, Mass.

Fisch, J.H., 2003. Optimal dispersion of R&D activities in multinational corporations with a genetic algorithm. Research Policy 32, 1381–1396.

Frohman, A.L., 1982. Technology as a competitive weapon. Harvard Business Review 60 (1), 97–104.

Goto, A., Suzuki, K., 1989. R&D capital, rate of return on R&D investment and spillover of R&D on Japanese manufacturing industries. Review of Economics and Statistics 71 (4), 555–564.

Granstrand, O., Hikanson, L., Sjiilander, S., 1993. Internationalization of R&D-a survey of some recent research. Research Policy 22, 413–430.

Grant, R.M., 1987. Multinationality and performance among British manufacturing companies. Journal of International Business Studies 22, 249–263.

Griliches, Z., 1979. Issues in assessing the contribution of research and development to productivity growth. Bell Journal of Economics 10, 92–116.

Griliches, Z., 1980. Returns to research and development expenditures in the private sector. In: Kendrick, J., Vaccara, B. (Eds.), New Developments in Productivity Measurement and Analysis. University of Chicago Press, Chicago, Ill., 339–374.

Griliches, Z., Mairesse, J., 1983. Comparing productivity growth: an exploration of French and US industrial and firm data. European Economic Review 21, 89–119.

Griliches, Z., Mairesse, J., 1984. Productivity and R&D at the firm level. In: Griliches, Z. (Ed.), R&D, Patents, and Productivity. University of Chicago Press, Chicago, 339–374.

Griliches, Z., Mairesse, J., 1990. R&D and productivity growth: comparing Japanese and US manufacturing firms. In: Hulten, C. (Ed.), Productivity Growth in Japan and the United States. University of Chicago Press, Chicago, Ill., 317–348.

Griliches, Z., Pakes, A., Hall, B., 1987. The value of patents as indicators of inventive activity. In: Dasgupta, P., Stoneman, P. (Eds.), Economic Policy and Technological Performance. Cambridge University Press, Cambridge, 97–124.

Hall, B., Mairesse, J., 1995. Exploring the relationship between R&D and productivity in French manufacturing firms. Journal of Econometrics 65, 263–293.

Harhoff, D., 1998. R&D and productivity in German manufacturing firms. Economics of Innovation and New Technology 6, 28–49.

Hitt, M.A., Hoskisson, R.E., Ireland, R.D., 1994. A mid-range theory of the interactive effects of international and product diversification on innovation and performance. Journal of Management 20, 297–326.

Hitt, M., Hoskisson, R., Kim, H., 1997. International diversification: effects on innovation and firm performance in product-diversified firms. Academy of Management Journal 40 (4), 767–798.

Jaffe, A., 1986. Technological opportunity and spillovers of R&D. American Economic Review 76 (5), 984–1001.

Jorgenson, D.W., 1963. Capital theory and investment behavior. The American Economic Review, Papers and Proceedings of the Seventy Fifth Annual Meeting of the American Economic Association 53 (2), 247–259.

Kafouros, M.I., 2005. R&D and productivity growth: evidence from the UK. Economics of Innovation and New Technology 14 (6), 479–497.

Kafouros, M.I., 2006. The impact of the Internet on R&D-efficiency: theory and evidence. Technovation 26 (7), 827–835.

Kafouros, M.I., 2008. Industrial innovation and firm performance: the impact of scientific knowledge on multinational corporations. Edward Elgar.

Kessler, E.H., 2003. Leveraging e-R&D processes: a knowledge-based view. Technovation 23, 905–915.

Kobrin, S., 1991. An empirical analysis of the determinants of global integration. Strategic Management Journal 12, 17–31.

Kotabe, M., 1990. The relationship between offshore sourcing and innovativeness of US multinational firms: an empirical investigation. Journal of International Business Studies 21 (4), 623–638.

Kotabe, M., Srinivasan, S.S., Aulakh, P.S., 2002. Multinationality and firm performance: the moderating role of R&D and marketing capabilities. Journal of International Business Studies 33 (1), 79–97.

Kuemmerle, W., 1997. Building effective R&D capabilities abroad. Harvard Business Review 75 (2), 61–70.

Kurokawa, S., Iwata, S., Roberts, E.B., 2007. Global R&D activities of Japanese MNCs in the US: a triangulation approach. Research Policy 36, 3–36.

Lc, S.A., Walters, B., Kroll, M., 2006. The moderating effects of external monitors on the relationship between R&D spending and firm performance. Journal of Business Research 59 (2), 278–287.

Lichtenberg, F., Siegel, D., 1991. The impact of R&D investment on productivity-new evidence using linked R&D-LRD data. Economic Inquiry 29 (2), 203.

Link, A., 1981. Research and Development Activity in US Manufacturing. Praeger, New York.

Lu, J.W., Beamish, P.W., 2004. International diversification and firm performance: the S-curve hypothesis. Academy of Management Journal 47 (4), 598–609.

Mairesse, J., Sassenou, M., 1991. R&D and productivity: a survey of econometric studies at the firm level. Science Technology and Industry Review 8, 317–348.

Mansfield, E., 1968. The Economics of Technological Change. Norton, New York.

Mansfield, E., 1984. R&D and innovation: some empirical findings. In: Griliches, Z. (Ed.), R&D, Patents, and Productivity. University of Chicago Press, Chicago, 127–148.

Matheson, D., Matheson, J., 1998. The Smart Organization: Creating Value Through Strategic R&D. Harvard Business School Press, Boston.

Nelson, R.R., 1959. The simple economics of basic scientific research. Journal of Political Economy 67, 297–306.

Nonaka, I., Takeuchi, H., 1995. The Knowledge-Creating Company. Oxford University Press, Oxford.

Odagiri, H., Iwata, H., 1986. The impact of R&D on productivity increase in Japanese manufacturing companies. Research Policy 15, 13–19.

ONS, 2002. Research and Development in UK Businesses: Business Monitor MA14. UK Office for National Statistics.

Pakes, A., Schankerman, M., 1984. The rate of obsolescence of patents, research gestation lags, and the private rate of return to research resources. In: Griliches, Z. (Ed.), R&D, Patents and Productivity. University of Chicago Press, Chicago, 98–112.

Porter, E.M., 1980: Competitive Strategy: Techniques for Analyzing Industries and Competitors. The Free Press.

Ravenscraft, D., Scherer, F.M., 1982. The lag structure of economic returns to research and development. Applied Economics 14, 603–620.

Rugman, A.M., 1981. Inside the Multinationals: The Economics of International Markets. Croom Helm, London.

Sanna-Randaccio, F., Veugelers, R., 2007. Multinational knowledge spillovers with decentralised R&D: a game-theoretic approach. Journal of International Business Studies 38, 47–63.

Santos, J., Doz, Y., Williamson, P., 2004. Is your innovation process global? Sloan Management Review 45 (4), 31–37.

Sassenou, M., 1988. Recherche-developpment et productivity dans les enterprizes Japonaises: Une etude econometrique sur donnees de panel', Doctoral Dissertation, Ecole des Hautes Etudes en Sciences Sociales, Paris.

Scherer, F.M., 1982. Inter-industry technology flows and productivity growth. Review of Economics and Statistics 64 (4), 627–634.

Shenkar, O., Luo, Y., 2004. International Business. Wiley, New York.

Sullivan, D., 1994. Measuring the degree of internationalization of a firm. Journal of International Business Studies 25 (2), 325–342.

Teece, D.J., 1986. Profiting from technological innovation. Research Policy 15, 285–306.

von Zedtwitz, M., Gassmann, O., 2002. Market versus technology drive in R&D internationalization: four different patterns of managing research and development. Research Policy 31, 569–588.

Wagner, H., 2004. Internationalization speed and cost efficiency: evidence from Germany. International Business Review 13 (4), 447–463.

Wakelin, K., 2001. Productivity growth and R&D expenditure in UK manufacturing firms. Research Policy 30, 1079–1090.

Wang, J., Tsai, K., 2003. Productivity growth and R&D expenditure in Taiwan's manufacturing firms. NBER Working Paper 9724, National Bureau of Economic Research.

Zachary, G.P., 1995. Behind stocks surge is an economy in which big firms survive. Wall Street Journal 22, A1.

10
Knowledge Accession and Knowledge Acquisition in Strategic Alliances: The Impact of Supplementary and Complementary Dimensions

Co-authored with Keith W. Glaister, Elko Klijn, and Hui Tan

The authors would like to thank managing editor Sebastian Stegmann, associate editor Véronique Ambrosini and two anonymous reviewers for their valuable comments on this paper.

Introduction

Knowledge transfer has been a major area of academic focus in recent years (Gupta and Govindarajan, 2000; Luo, 2002; Simonin, 1999; Teece, 1977; Tsai, 2001; Wang, Tong and Koh, 2004). Many scholars claim that knowledge transfer is a key route for organizations to share and create knowledge (Conner and Prahalad, 1996; Grant, 1996; Pak and Park, 2004). This can result in enhanced competitive advantages (Desouza and Evaristo, 2003; Hansen, Nohria and Tierney, 1999; Nonaka, 1991; Penrose, 1959). Researchers have traditionally linked knowledge transfer to organizational learning (Doz and Prahalad, 1991; Hamel, 1991; Inkpen, 1995, 1998; Kim and Inkpen, 2005; Kogut and Zander, 1993; Lyles and Baird, 1994; Lyles and Schwenk, 1992). In contrast to this literature, Grant and Baden-Fuller (2004) argue that firms can pursue knowledge transfer without the ambition to learn. This is an important but rarely explored area. Grant and Baden-Fuller (2004) make a distinction between knowledge accession and knowledge acquisition within the setting of strategic alliances. They propose that organizations do not in all cases pursue knowledge transfer with the ambition to learn, i.e. to acquire knowledge. On the contrary, alliance formation is often pursued for knowledge accession.

The purpose of this paper is to extend Grant and Baden-Fuller's theory by incorporating two further dimensions in knowledge transfer, namely the supplementary and complementary aspects of knowledge transfer. We will explore how knowledge flows in the context of knowledge accession and knowledge acquisition and examine how various knowledge transfer activities are differentiated due to their complementary and supplementary dimensions. While trust and cost have frequently been identified as two of the important factors in knowledge transfer (e.g. Adler, 2001; Bresman, Birkinshaw and Nobel, 1999; Das and Teng, 1998; Inkpen and Tsang, 2005; Simonin, 1999; Zander and Kogut, 1995), they have rarely been explored with respect to different modes of knowledge transfer. Thus, the aim of our paper is to provide insights in the discussions on the different dimensions of knowledge transfer modes, as well as their impact on cost and trust in the knowledge transfer process.

The rest of the paper is set out as follows. In the next section, we review the modes of knowledge transfer. We then introduce the concepts of complementary knowledge and supplementary knowledge and examine these dimensions of knowledge transfer in the context of knowledge accession and knowledge acquisition. Next, we identify how the configuration of knowledge transfer modes and the dimensions of knowledge transfer affect the cost level of knowledge transfer. We further examine the implications for trust in strategic alliances in the context of this configuration. In examining costs and trust we develop a number of propositions which offer new insights into the knowledge transfer process. Conclusions follow in the last section.

Modes of knowledge transfer

Inter-firm knowledge transfer takes place when specific knowledge is passed on from one firm to the other, normally in strategic alliances (Argote and Ingram, 2000; Koza and Lewin, 1998; Song, Almeida and Wu, 2003). The formation of alliances with other organizations thus creates learning opportunities (Cohen and Levinthal, 1990; Grant, 1996; Lane, Salk and Lyles, 2001; Stuart, 1998). A first attempt to distinguish the various modes of knowledge transfer was made by Grant and Baden-Fuller (2004). They differentiate knowledge accession and knowledge acquisition in strategic alliances. Knowledge accession is the combination of knowledge resources of different firms in the partnership to develop new products or services (Buckley and Carter, 2004; Inkpen and Beamish, 1997). '[...] Each member firm *accesses* its partner's stock of knowledge in order to exploit complementarities, but with the intention of maintaining its distinctive base of specialized knowledge' (Grant and Baden-Fuller, 2004, p. 64, italics added). In contrast, the purpose of knowledge acquisition is to obtain knowledge which has the potential to change the scope of an acquiring firm's specialized knowledge.

Grant and Baden-Fuller (2004) argue that, in most cases, knowledge accession occurs within the strategic alliance, because firms tend not to depart often from their core competence and the respective knowledge that is associated with it. Thus, a partner does not have the urge to acquire knowledge from the alliance which is unlikely to augment its specialized knowledge stock. For instance, when partners come from different industries, there is a less strong incentive to conduct knowledge acquisition as they will wish to maintain their current specialized knowledge in respective sectors (Barney, 1991; Grant, 1996). Consequently, it is knowledge accession and not knowledge acquisition which features most prominently in strategic alliance relationships (Grant and Baden-Fuller, 2004).

Knowledge accession

Knowledge accession describes organizational action between firms to access each other's knowledge stock. It is concerned with the amalgamation of existing specialized knowledge of the partner(s) to create synergetic effects. The focus of knowledge accession does not rest on learning. As shown in Figure 10.1, partner firms contribute knowledge to the focal unit (assumed to be the strategic alliance). The new stock of combined specialized knowledge can help firms A and B to achieve a shared goal that is not attainable by them individually. The nature of the combination process is not based on knowledge exchange, but rather a process of inputting knowledge into the focal unit. We eschew the term 'exchange' because this implies an economic relationship where a 'seller' expects a return from the 'buyer' for the provision of its knowledge. Instead, each firm selects knowledge out of

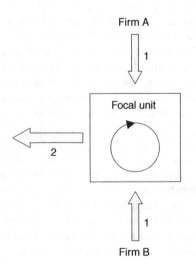

1 Knowledge Inflow
2 Knowledge outflow (i.e. in the form of products/services)

Figure 10.1 Knowledge accession

their own stock and shares this in association with the other firm in order to accomplish a common goal.

A key feature of knowledge accession is that there is no reverse knowledge transfer that flows from the focal unit to the contributing firms. Knowledge accession is normally associated with either process innovation (production/marketing), or product innovation (new product/services), or a combination of the two. Thus, the combined specialized knowledge may be embedded in a new product or service, or attached to the process of delivering the product/service to the target market. The synergetic effects arising from knowledge accession should enhance the competitiveness of the alliance, resulting in higher obtainable economic rents for each of the partners.

The transfer of knowledge between firms can be examined in terms of complementary or supplementary combinations, adding a new dimension to knowledge transfer.

Complementary knowledge accession

In this case, the new stock of knowledge in the focal unit encompasses similar specialized knowledge of the partners. Here, 'complementary' is used to reflect the similarity of knowledge between the firms. However, this does not indicate an extensive overlap. Rather, it can be knowledge which is different but related to the same product or service. For example, the mobile phone software developer Symbian is owned by hardware manufacturers Ericsson (15.6%), Nokia (47.9%), Panasonic (10.5%), Samsung (4.5%), Siemens (8.4%) and Sony Ericsson (13.1%). The aim of the joint venture was to produce the most intelligent software for mobile phones, enabling users to access telephony, email, web, electric diary and entertainment in one device. It achieved this objective within a few years of its establishment and became the dominant mobile operational system in the market. While any one of the above hardware manufacturers would find it difficult to develop a new mobile phone operating system, this successful joint venture has benefited from the knowledge contributed by each of the above shareholders, namely technologies relating to different aspects of integrated mobile or wireless communication solutions where these firms have an existing advantage over other competitors (Ancarani and Shankar, 2003). Thus, being complementary gives firms the opportunity to build on their existing knowledge stock and deepens the knowledge specialization of the partnership, rather than broadening its knowledge scope. Complementary knowledge accession can enhance the efficiency and economies of scale of the partnership and reduce uncertainty, as it provides a critical mass of knowledge (Buckley and Carter, 2002, 2003).

Supplementary knowledge accession

Supplementary knowledge accession reflects the difference in specialized knowledge between firms. The purpose of supplementary knowledge

210   *Peter J. Buckley et al.*

transfer is to widen the knowledge scope of the alliance. In order to create synergetic effects, the firms involved must possess distinctive competences. An example of supplementary knowledge accession is the British grocery retailer Tesco's entry into the Polish retailing market. British managers worked with Polish managers to set up local suppliers in different areas of the country to cater for different tastes and styles of Tesco's food offerings (*Financial Times*, 2004). Here, British managers and their Polish partners each contributed a different set of knowledge to the new Tesco subsidiary: the British brought managerial expertise and applied Tesco's rules and procedures in the new market, while Polish partners provided knowledge of local products and the local market which were not known to the British. Another example is the Sony Ericsson alliance in producing mobile phone handsets: Sony brought in the design of mobile handsets and Ericsson contributed software development and branding (Ariño and Reuer, 2004).

Thus, supplementary knowledge accession can be used to improve an existing product or service, or as a springboard to help launch a new product or service. The combination of dissimilar knowledge from the contributing firms can enable the partnership to extend its knowledge range and firm resources. This can strengthen the competitiveness and performance of the partnership in the market.

Knowledge acquisition

Knowledge *acquisition* is the transfer of knowledge resources between firms with the aim of acquiring knowledge in order to learn. Figure 10.2 shows two streams of knowledge flows for each firm. One stream, knowledge inflow, is from the partner firms A and B to the focal unit. The other stream, knowledge outflow, is from the focal unit to each of firms A and B. Knowledge acquisition occurs when at least one firm receives knowledge that comes from the focal unit. This indicates that knowledge acquisition results in reverse knowledge transfer (where new knowledge is transferred back to a contributing partner) (Buckley, Clegg and Tan, 2003; Håkanson and Nobel, 2001) and leads to learning (Dhanaraj *et al.*, 2004).

Complementary knowledge acquisition

When the partners acquire complementary knowledge from the focal unit, they can increase their knowledge concentration and deepen their field of specialization, because the knowledge that the firm acquires complements the knowledge about their current core competences. This can lead to higher efficiency (Grant, 1996). However, greater specialization can reduce the adaptability of the firm concerned (Porter, 1980). In complementary knowledge acquisition, the acquired knowledge is likely to be transferred relatively easily, because the partner firms possess similar specialized knowledge

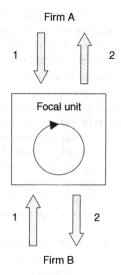

1 Knowledge inflow
2 Reverse knowledge transfer

Figure 10.2 Knowledge acquisition

which facilitates the process of assimilation by the learning organization. This reduces the costs involved in knowledge transfer. One special case of complementary knowledge acquisition is the licensing agreement. As licensing agreements are primarily concerned with the transfer of specific technical and manufacturing knowledge from the licensor to the licensee, the licensee needs to absorb the transferred technology in its own production process/product based on learning and assimilation. In most cases the licensee already has knowledge related to this field of specialization and it is therefore relatively easy for this firm to acquire additional knowledge that is specific for the service that it will carry out for the licensor.

The recent rise of the Chinese automotive industry has been underpinned by inter-firm complementary knowledge acquisition from foreign partners, such as the partnership between Chery Automobile of China and Italian design houses Bertone and Pininfarina (*Financial Times*, 2005). While Chery is revving fast to become a low cost manufacturer of cars based on mature production technologies, it lacks expertise in modern car design and development. The Italian partner's contribution in this area can help Chery in exploring the international market while strengthening its position in the domestic market. Whether Chery has sufficient concentration of similar specialized knowledge and ability to absorb the newly acquired knowledge from Bertone and Pininfarina, instead of taking the design only, remains to be tested.

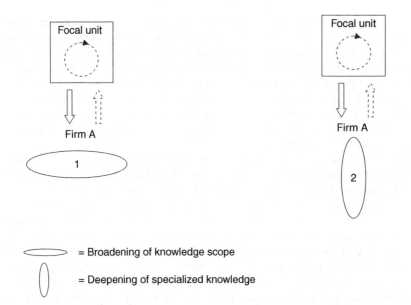

Figure 10.3 Supplementary versus complementary knowledge acquisition

Supplementary knowledge acquisition

When partner firms each possess distinctive knowledge and have the ambition to learn, the knowledge transfer is supplementary knowledge acquisition in nature. The firms can extend their scope of specialization by acquiring supplementary knowledge from the focal unit thereby broadening their range of specialization. Supplementary knowledge acquisition can help firms to be more adaptable to market changes. Caution should be exercised, however, because supplementary knowledge acquisition can present the risk of diluting the firm's specialization and losing core competence. The fact that the firms do not possess similar specialized knowledge means that the recipient will find it difficult to assimilate the transferred knowledge due to barriers to knowledge transfer. Thus, supplementary knowledge acquisition is likely to be a slower process and more costly than complementary knowledge acquisition. Constraints on knowledge transfer exist not only in the form of limits to absorptive capacity on the part of the recipient firm, but also in the capability of the transferor to express the knowledge, i.e. there are also limits to eloquent capacity (Buckley *et al.*, 2005). Figure 10.3 is a schematic overview of complementary and supplementary knowledge acquisition.

One example of inter-firm supplementary knowledge acquisition is the joint venture, NUMMI, set up by GM and Toyota. One of the reasons for establishing this partnership by both sides was to learn from each other, i.e. GM learned 'the Toyota way' of production and quality control and Toyota acquired GM's skills in product design and marketing in the American market (Liker, 2004). Reverse knowledge transfer from NUMMI helped both partners to improve their product offering and production technologies. Another example is Huawei Technologies, one of China's telecommunications equipment manufacturers. This company is working with Siemens on third-generation mobile phone technology and with Infineon to make chipsets for mobile handsets that use the W-CDMA 3G standard. Huawei Technologies also has a stake in an R&D joint venture between NEC and Matsushita to develop W-CDMA phones, and it has shared laboratories with Microsoft and Sun Microsystems of the USA (*Financial Times*, 2003). Through these collaborations, Huawei Technologies has gained access to its partner companies' advanced technology, research and development resources and their brand recognition and sales channels in developed markets. In return, Huawei Technologies can offer its foreign partners techniques of volume manufacturing of high-tech products with assured quality and channels of access to the fast-expanding Chinese domestic market.

To summarize, Figure 10.4 shows the two-by-two configuration of knowledge transfer modes and the dimensions of knowledge transfer.

	Inter-Firm Knowledge Transfer Mode	
	Knowledge accession	Knowledge acquisition
Complementary	*Cell 1* Complementary knowledge accession	*Cell 3* Complementary knowledge acquisition
Supplementary	*Cell 2* Supplementary knowledge accession	*Cell 4* Supplementary knowledge acquisition

Dimensions of Knowledge Transfer

Figure 10.4 Supplementary and complementary knowledge transfer modes

214 *Peter J. Buckley et al.*

Implications on costs and trust of the different transfer modes

In this section we build on this configuration and examine how costs and trust of knowledge transfer are affected by the different combinations of knowledge transfer modes and knowledge transfer dimensions. We also consider the role of trust in the context of this configuration.

Cost and knowledge transfer

Knowledge transfer is never costless: language barriers, spatial distances and cultural differences can result in misinformation and misunderstanding and therefore impose real costs on the partner firms (Buckley and Carter, 2004). Knowledge stickiness can impede the effective knowledge transfer process (Szulanski, 1996; Von Hippel, 1998). Stickiness is related to the tacit knowledge that restricts the ease of knowledge transfer between partners (Szulanski, 1996). The higher the extent of tacit knowledge involved, the more difficult it is to transfer the knowledge and the more costs incurred in the execution of the transfer. Hence, the costs associated with knowledge transfer are a function of the transferor firm's ability to articulate the knowledge to be transferred to the recipient firm and the absorptive capacity of the receiving firm (Cohen and Levinthal, 1990). While we focus our discussion on knowledge transfer cost, we are aware that cost is an input factor in the knowledge transfer process. Performance enhancement as a result of knowledge transfer, whether it be knowledge accession or knowledge acquisition, is the standard against which to evaluate its cost of transfer. As long as there is a marked improvement in firm performance (i.e. high benefit) after conducting knowledge transfer, high cost is acceptable. In contrast, even low cost transfers are not effective if the benefit is negligible.[1]

Complementary and supplementary knowledge characteristics are variables that influence the cost of the knowledge transfer. Knowledge acquisition involves extensive organizational learning and is constrained by the capability of the transferor (in expressing the knowledge) and the transferee (in absorbing and understanding the knowledge). Misinterpretation by either side is possible and can result in high costs. Furthermore, in the case of knowledge acquisition, transfer costs are higher, because an alliance partner faces both the costs of transferring know-how into the alliance and the costs of learning from the alliance (Hansen, Mors and Løvås, 2005). Knowledge accession, in contrast, does not require organizational learning. It is a process of knowledge combination rather than of learning. It involves pooling knowledge resources from the collaborating partners to the focal unit; therefore it incurs less cost in the treatment of the transferred knowledge. This leads us to the following proposition.

> *P1:* Knowledge acquisition incurs higher costs than knowledge accession.

We argue that there is no cost difference between complementary knowledge accession and supplementary knowledge accession. This is because knowledge accession is a process of inputting knowledge into the partnership to achieve a shared goal that is not attainable by the partners individually. Each firm of the partnership presents its knowledge to the focal unit under the contract to enrich the knowledge collection, regardless of its supplementary or complementary nature. No reverse knowledge transfer takes place in this case, and therefore no learning is engaged. This leads to the second proposition.

> *P2:* There is no cost difference between supplementary knowledge accession and complementary knowledge accession.

Supplementary knowledge acquisition indicates that the partner firm learns distinctive knowledge that is dissimilar but supplements their current specialized knowledge, thereby extending the knowledge scope. However, 'distinctive' implies that the process of knowledge transfer and learning is time consuming, because the recipient has to assimilate the acquired knowledge that is relatively different from their current field of specialization. The knowledge is relatively new to them because they are not familiar with it. This means that the recipient needs to nurture and enhance its absorptive capacity (Cohen and Levinthal, 1990).

On the other hand, complementary knowledge acquisition takes place when partners learn similar knowledge from each other to create a critical mass of knowledge in the relevant area, leading to efficiency and economies of scale. As a result, the recipient should have some familiarity with this newly acquired knowledge and be able to assimilate the acquired knowledge relatively easily. The firm's original knowledge base, prior to the knowledge transfer, should be sufficient to support the undertaking of assimilation of the newly acquired knowledge. There are fewer uncertainties and risks in the assimilation of similar or complementary knowledge than with distinctive knowledge as in supplementary knowledge acquisition. Consequently, we argue that supplementary knowledge acquisition is more costly than complementary knowledge acquisition. Hence, we develop the following proposition.

> *P3:* Supplementary knowledge acquisition incurs higher costs than complementary knowledge acquisition.

Trust and knowledge transfer

The formation of strategic alliances creates a set of reciprocal dependences between partner firms. This together with the potential for competition between partners can establish a dynamic that enhances the risk and instability of the venture. Although partners have a wide array of formal

216   *Peter J. Buckley et al.*

governance mechanisms that can potentially reduce the downsides of alliance formation (e.g. threat of opportunistic behaviour), trust is necessary to reduce such hazards and to contribute to the success of the inter-organizational relationship (Glaister, Husan and Buckley, 2003). There is a widely held view that mutual trust is important for strategic alliances to be successful (Buckley and Casson, 1988; Inkpen and Beamish, 1997; Madhok, 1995; Yan and Gray, 1994) and that it is indeed part of alliance governance mechanisms contributing to success (Dhanaraj *et al.*, 2004; Dyer and Singh, 1998; Kale, Singh and Perlmutter, 2000; Parkhe, 1998; Williamson, 1991). Trust stabilizes the relationship between partners, reduces the need to specify and monitor contracts, permits open exchange of information and reduces uncertainty and transaction costs (Berger, Noorderhaven and Nooteboom, 1995; Bradach and Eccles, 1989; Casson, 1995; Chiles and McMackin, 1996; Gulati, 1995; Hill, 1990; Nooteboom, 1996; Nooteboom, Berger and Noorderhaven, 1997; Powell, 1990). The strength of social ties between the parent and the alliance stimulates trust (Cohen and Prusak, 2001; Kale, Singh and Perlmutter, 2000; Uzzi, 1997; Uzzi and Lancaster, 2003). Dhanaraj *et al.* (2004) identify those high levels of interactions that lead to a level of comfort between partners in a partnership. As Uzzi (1997) defines it, trust can lead to the accession by one partner to certain resources of the other partner. Although the establishment of trust is primarily associated with the duration of the alliance, it can further depend on the knowledge transfer mode. The different knowledge transfer modes examined in this paper add a new dimension to the discussion of trust.

Knowledge accession does not involve learning from the strategic alliance by a partner. When one partner understands that no learning by the other partner takes place, it will be less protective about the knowledge it possesses – whether it be complementary knowledge or supplementary knowledge – and will be more willing to use it in the strategic alliance. Hence, the different dimensions of knowledge accession between partners do not make a significant impact on the trust involved. In contrast to knowledge accession, inter-firm knowledge acquisition is characterized by the ambition of the recipient to replicate transferred knowledge. This prospect can mean that the transferor has to be vigilant about its knowledge contributions so that its core competence will not be imitated. The inter-firm partnership under this knowledge transfer mode is more 'structured and formal', and is often governed by contracts (Wang and Nicholas, 2005). Consequently, with knowledge accession, a trusting relationship will be easier to create and to maintain than with knowledge acquisition which involves reverse knowledge transfer and organizational learning. This leads to the following propositions.

P4: Trust between knowledge transferor and recipient is easier to establish in knowledge accession than in knowledge acquisition.

Knowledge Accession and Knowledge Acquisition 217

P5: Complementary knowledge accession and supplementary knowledge accession do not have different implications for trust between the partners.

While it costs more to acquire supplementary knowledge than complementary knowledge (Proposition 3), complementary knowledge acquisition demands a higher trust relationship than supplementary knowledge acquisition to take place effectively. This arises because of the readiness of the partners in learning similar knowledge from each other based on embedded absorptive capacity. Partners share the same specialized knowledge backgrounds and in some cases they can even be potential competitors. Leaking of knowledge is more possible when the partners possess similar types of knowledge, but more difficult when they possess different types of knowledge that require a different set of skills and the absorptive capacity to facilitate the transfer process and overcome knowledge stickiness (Jensen and Szulanski, 2004; Szulanski, 1996). Thus, partners are more vigilant and protective in complementary knowledge acquisition than in supplementary knowledge acquisition. For this reason trust between the partners is more difficult to maintain in complementary knowledge acquisition than in supplementary knowledge acquisition. This leads to the following proposition.

P6: Trust between knowledge transferor and recipient is more difficult to maintain in complementary knowledge acquisition than in supplementary knowledge acquisition.

It should be noted that there is a significant caveat associated with Propositions 4, 5 and 6. This is because the situation may be more ambiguous than is implied here. Knowledge acquisition requires a very close working relationship between partners in order to learn, e.g. intensive social interaction is

Table 10.1 Relative cost and trust implications of inter-firm knowledge transfer

Inter-firm knowledge transfer	Cost implications for each transfer mode	Trust implications for each transfer mode
1. Complementary knowledge accession	Low	Low
2. Supplementary knowledge accession	Low	Low
3. Complementary knowledge acquisition	Medium	High
4. Supplementary knowledge acquisition	High	Medium

Note: 1–4 correspond to cells in Figure 4.

218   *Peter J. Buckley et al.*

required for acquiring tacit knowledge (Polanyi, 1966). Such a close working relationship might thus foster greater levels of trust in knowledge acquisition than a less close working relationship as in knowledge accession. One way of resolving this ambiguity would be to undertake an empirical investigation to compare the development and levels of trust between partners involved in knowledge accession alliances and those involved in knowledge acquisition alliances (see Table 10.1).

To help manage the dynamic internal processes at inter-firm level, partners sometimes seek direct controls in the partnership (Makhija and Ganesh, 1997), probably based on equity ownership (Mowery, Oxley and Silverman, 1996; Pak and Park, 2004). This can pre-empt any negative consequences of mistrust or failed trust in the partnership on knowledge acquisition. Hence, we have the following proposition.

P7: Trust in inter-firm knowledge acquisition between the transferor and the recipient can be reinforced (institutionalized) by direct equity control.

Conclusions

The aim of this paper is to make a contribution through extending our understanding of the inter-firm knowledge transfer modes of knowledge accession and knowledge acquisition in strategic alliances as first highlighted by Grant and Baden-Fuller (2004). In doing so, we introduce and examine the dimensions of knowledge transfer in terms of complementary knowledge and supplementary knowledge. The differentiations between complementary knowledge accession and supplementary knowledge accession, and between complementary knowledge acquisition and supplementary knowledge acquisition, aid our understanding of the nature of knowledge transfer between partners in an international strategic alliance.

Knowledge accession involves the contribution of knowledge between partners to the alliance. This may involve two types of knowledge accession partnerships: one in pursuit of efficiency and productivity based on complementary knowledge transfer and the other in pursuit of business scope and product adaptability based on supplementary knowledge transfer. In contrast, knowledge acquisition is underpinned by reverse knowledge flows from the alliance to the partner firms. It also involves two types of knowledge transfer between partner firms through the alliance: complementary knowledge acquisition to strengthen individual partners' core knowledge base and supplementary knowledge acquisition to widen their knowledge range.

This highlights the critical difference in partner firm strategies between those involved in knowledge accession and those involved in knowledge acquisition. Strategic alliances are used to achieve a common goal by firms undertaking knowledge accession. The firms work together to make the alliance a stronger entity, which we term partnership enhancing knowledge transfer. Complementary knowledge accession can help the alliance to strengthen its specialization and core competence, while supplementary knowledge accession leads to a wider knowledge base and business adaptation. In contrast, a strategic alliance can also be a vehicle for strengthening the partner firms' own competitiveness where firms undertake knowledge acquisition. The partners collaborate to make each firm a stronger entity, which we term self-enhancing knowledge transfer. In this case, complementary knowledge acquisition is used to pursue efficiency and to improve the partner firms' existing competitiveness, whereas supplementary knowledge acquisition is a shortcut to business expansion and firm growth.

We also examined the implications of the knowledge transfer modes and dimensions configuration on the costs and trust of knowledge transfer. We argue that there is no cost difference between knowledge transfer modes characterized by either supplementary knowledge accession or complementary knowledge accession. We further posit that knowledge acquisition incurs a higher cost than knowledge accession and that supplementary knowledge acquisition is more costly than complementary knowledge acquisition. We expect that, in strategic alliances formed for knowledge acquisition purposes, it is more difficult to establish trust than in alliances formed for knowledge accession purposes.

In alliances where knowledge accession is a dominant transfer mode, whatever the scale of dissimilarities between the knowledge stocks of the partner firms, the mode of knowledge transfer will not affect trust significantly, because no reverse knowledge transfer is intended. On the other hand, partner firms pursuing expansion or growth strategies need to prepare better for knowledge acquisition in order to try and overcome the various barriers in the process of knowledge assimilation. The costs of knowledge transfer can escalate if the transferred knowledge is deemed to be part of the core competence of one partner. The difficulty in establishing trust in this situation will directly contribute to cost escalation. We argue that institutional arrangements based on equity ownership can mitigate the cost and trust implications associated with the knowledge acquisition mode of knowledge transfer. This, however, is not sufficient to prevent the emergence of the uncertainties and risks in alliances, such as knowledge leakage and threat from partner competition. Clearly, future research should undertake an empirical examination in order to test our propositions and to establish their validity in different country markets. In addition, more research is needed to explore whether international alliances stay with the knowledge transfer mode (e.g. knowledge accession) through their lives, and the barriers that prevent an alliance from moving from one knowledge transfer mode to another.

Note

1. We would like to thank one of the anonymous reviewers for this suggestion.

References

Adler, P. S. (2001). 'Market, hierarchy, and trust: the knowledge economy and the future of capitalism', *Organization Science*, **12**, pp. 215–234.

Ancarani, F. and V. Shankar (2003). 'Symbian: customer interaction through collaboration and competition in a convergent industry', *Journal of Interactive Marketing*, **17**, pp. 56–76.

Argote, L. and P. Ingram (2000). 'Knowledge transfer: a basis for competitive advantage in firms', *Organizational Behavior and Human Decision Processes*, **82**, pp. 150–169.

Ariño, A. and J. Reuer (2004). 'Designing and renegotiating strategic alliance contracts', *Academy of Management Executive*, **18**, pp. 37–48.

Barney, J. B. (1991). 'Firm resources and sustained competitive advantage', *Journal of Management*, **17**, pp. 99–120.

Berger, J., N. G. Noorderhaven and B. Nooteboom (1995). 'The determinants of supplier dependence: an empirical study'. In J. Groenewegen, C. Pitelis and S. E. Sjostrand (eds), *On Economic Institutions: Theory and Applications*, pp. 195–212. Aldershot: Edward Elgar.

Bradach, J. and R. Eccles (1989). 'Price, authority and trust: from ideal types to plural forms', *Annual Review of Sociology*, **15**, pp. 97–118.

Bresman, H., J. Birkinshaw and R. Nobel (1999). 'Knowledge transfer in international acquisitions', *Journal of International Business Studies*, **30**, pp. 439–462.

Buckley, P. J. and M. J. Carter (2002). 'Process and structure in knowledge management practices of British and US multinational enterprises', *Journal of International Management*, **8**, pp. 29–48.

Buckley, P. J. and M. J. Carter (2003). 'Governing knowledge sharing in multinational enterprises', *Management International Review*, **43**, pp. 7–25.

Buckley, P. J. and M. J. Carter (2004). 'A formal analysis of knowledge combination in multinational enterprises', *Journal of International Business Studies*, **35**, pp. 371–384.

Buckley, P. J. and M. Casson (1988). 'A theory of co-operation in international business'. In F. J. Contractor and P. Lorange (eds), *Co-operative Strategies in International Business*. Lexington, MA: Lexington Books.

Buckley, P. J., J. Clegg and H. Tan (2003). 'The art of knowledge transfer: secondary and reverse transfer in China's telecommunications manufacturing industry', *Management International Review*, **43**, pp. 67–93.

Buckley, P. J., K. W. Glaister, E. Klijn and H. Tan (2005). 'Eloquent capacity and absorptive capacity in the knowledge transfer process. Working paper, Centre for International Business, University of Leeds.

Casson, M. (1995). *The Organization of International Business: Studies in the Economics of Trust*. Aldershot: Edward Elgar.

Chiles, T. H. and J. F. McMackin (1996). 'Integrating variable risk preferences, trust, and transaction cost economics', *Academy of Management Review*, **21**, pp. 73–99.

Cohen, W. M. and D. A. Levinthal (1990). 'Absorptive capacity: a new perspective on learning and innovation', *Administrative Science Quarterly*, **35**, pp. 128–152.

Cohen, W. M. and L. Prusak (2001). *In Good Company: How Social Capital Makes Organizations Work*. Boston, MA: Harvard Business School Press.

Conner, K. and C. K. Prahalad (1996). 'A resource-based theory of the firm: knowledge versus opportunism', *Organization Science*, 7, pp. 477–501.

Das, T. K. and B. S. Teng (1998). 'Between trust and control: developing confidence in partner cooperation in alliances', *Academy of Management Review*, 23, pp. 491–512.

Desouza, K. and R. Evaristo (2003). 'Global knowledge management strategies', *European Management Journal*, 21, pp. 62–67.

Dhanaraj, C., M. A. Lyles, H. K. Steensma and L. Tihanyi (2004). 'Managing tacit and explicit knowledge transfer in IJVs: the role of relational embeddedness and the impact on performance', *Journal of International Business Studies*, 34, pp. 428–442.

Doz, Y. and C. K. Prahalad (1991). 'Managing DMNCs: a search for a new paradigm', *Strategic Management Journal*, 12, pp. 145–164.

Dyer, J. H. and H. Singh (1998). 'The relational view: cooperative strategy and sources of inter-organizational competitive advantage', *Academy of Management Review*, 42, pp. 37–43.

Financial Times (2003). 'Big names help close Chinese credibility gap'. 13 November, p. 33.

Financial Times (2004). 'Tesco conquers in its march on central Europe'. 20 January, p. 14.

Financial Times (2005). 'China looms in rear view mirror. FT Motor Industry supplement, 1 March, p. 1.

Glaister, K. W., R. Husan and P. J. Buckley (2003). 'Learning to manage international joint ventures', *International Business Review*, 12, pp. 83–108.

Grant, R. M. (1996). 'Towards a knowledge-based theory of the firm', *Strategic Management Journal*, 17, pp. 109–122.

Grant, R. M. and C. Baden-Fuller (2004). 'A knowledge accessing theory of strategic alliances', *Journal of Management Studies*, 41, pp. 61–84.

Gulati, R. (1995). 'Does familiarity breed trust?: the implications of repeated ties for contractual choice in alliances', *Academy of Management Journal*, 38, pp. 85–112.

Gupta, A. K. and V. Govindarajan (2000). 'Knowledge flows within multinational corporations', *Strategic Management Journal*, 21, pp. 473–496.

Håkanson, L. and R. Nobel (2001). 'Organizational characteristics and reverse technology transfer', *Management International Review*, 41, pp. 395–420.

Hamel, G. (1991). 'Competition for competence and inter-partner learning within international strategic alliances', *Strategic Management Journal*, 12, pp. 83–103.

Hansen, M. T., M. L. Mors and B. Løvås (2005). 'Knowledge sharing in organizations: multiple networks, multiple phases', *Academy of Management Journal*, 48, pp. 776–793.

Hansen, M. T., N. Nohria and T. Tierney (1999). 'What's your strategy for managing knowledge?', *Harvard Business Review*, 77, pp. 106–116.

Hill, C. W. L. (1990). 'Cooperation, opportunism and the invisible hand: implications for transaction cost theory', *Academy of Management Review*, 15, pp. 500–513.

Inkpen, A. C. (1995). 'Organizational learning and international joint ventures', *Journal of International Management*, 1, pp. 165–198.

Inkpen, A. C. (1998). 'Learning, knowledge acquisition, and strategic alliances', *European Management Journal*, 16, pp. 223–229.

Inkpen, A. C. and P. W. Beamish (1997). 'Knowledge, bargaining power, and the instability of international joint ventures', *Academy of Management Journal*, 22, pp. 177–202.

Inkpen, A. C. and E. Tsang (2005). 'Social capital, networks, and knowledge transfer', *Academy of Management Review*, 30, pp. 146–165.

222 *Peter J. Buckley et al.*

Jensen, R. and G. Szulanski (2004). 'Stickiness and the adaptation of organizational practices in cross-border knowledge transfers', *Journal of International Business Studies*, 35, pp. 508–523.

Kale, P., H. Singh and H. Perlmutter (2000). 'Learning and protection of proprietary assets in strategic alliances: building relational capital', *Strategic Management Journal*, 21, pp. 217–237.

Kim, C. and A. C. Inkpen (2005). 'Cross-border R&D alliances, absorptive capacity and technology learning', *Journal of International Management*, 11, pp. 313–329.

Kogut, B. and U. Zander (1993). 'Knowledge of the firm and the evolutionary theory of the multinational corporation', *Journal of International Business Studies*, 24, pp. 625–645.

Koza, M. P. and A. Y. Lewin (1998). 'The co-evolution of strategic alliances', *Organization Science*, 9, pp. 255–264.

Lane, P., J. E. Salk and M. A. Lyles (2001). 'Absorptive capacity, learning, and performance in international joint ventures', *Strategic Management Journal*, 22, pp. 1139–1162.

Liker, J. K. (2004). *The Toyota Way*. New York: McGraw-Hill.

Luo, Y. (2002). 'Stimulating exchange in international joint ventures: an attachment-based view', *Journal of International Business Studies*, 33, pp. 169–181.

Lyles, M. A. and I. S. Baird (1994). 'Performance of international joint ventures in two Eastern European countries: a case of Hungary and Poland', *Management International Review*, 34, pp. 313–329.

Lyles, M. and C. Schwenk (1992). 'Top management, strategy and organizational knowledge structures', *Journal of Management Studies*, 29, pp. 155–173.

Madhok, A. (1995). 'Revisiting multinational firms tolerance for joint ventures: a trust-based approach', *Journal of International Business Studies*, 26, pp. 117–137.

Makhija, M. and U. Ganesh (1997). 'Control and partner learning in learning-related joint ventures', *Organization Science*, 8, pp. 508–527.

Mowery, D. C., J. E. Oxley and B. S. Silverman (1996). 'Strategic alliance and interfirm knowledge transfer', *Strategic Management Journal*, 17, pp. 77–91.

Nonaka, I. (1991). 'The knowledge-creating company', *Harvard Business Review*, 69, pp. 96–104.

Nooteboom, B. (1996). 'Trust, opportunism and governance: a process and control model', *Organization Studies*, 17, pp. 985–1010.

Nooteboom, B., H. Berger and N. G. Noorderhaven (1997). 'Effects of trust and governance on relational risk', *Academy of Management Journal*, 40, pp. 308–338.

Pak, Y. S. and Y. R. Park (2004). 'A framework of knowledge transfer in cross-border joint ventures: an empirical test of the Korean context', *Management International Review*, 44, pp. 417–434.

Parkhe, A. (1998). 'Understanding trust in international alliances', *Journal of World Business*, 33, pp. 219–240.

Penrose, E. T. (1959). *The Theory of the Growth of the Firm*. Oxford: Basil Blackwell.

Polanyi, M. (1966). *Personal Knowledge: Towards a Post-critical Philosophy*, 3rd edn. London: Routledge and Kegan Paul.

Porter, M. (1980). *Competitive Strategy*. New York: Free Press.

Powell, W. W. (1990). 'Neither market nor hierarchy: network forms of organisation'. In B. M. Staw and L. L. Cummings (eds), *Research in Organizational Behavior*, Vol. 12, pp. 295–336. Greenwich, CT: JAI Press.

Simonin, B. L. (1999). 'Ambiguity and the process of knowledge transfer in strategic alliances', *Strategic Management Journal*, 20, pp. 595–623.

Song, J., P. Almeida and G. Wu (2003). 'Learning by hiring: when is mobility more likely to facilitate interfirm knowledge transfer?', *Management Science*, **49**, pp. 351–365.

Stuart, T. E. (1998). 'Network positions and propensities to collaborate: an investigation of strategic alliance formation in a high-technology industry', *Administrative Science Quarterly*, **43**, pp. 668–698.

Szulanski, G. (1996). 'Exploring internal stickiness: impediments to the transfer of best practice within the firm', *Strategic Management Journal*, **17**, pp. 27–43.

Teece, D. J. (1977). 'Technology transfer by multinational firms: the resource costs of transferring technological knowhow', *Economic Journal*, **87**, pp. 242–261.

Tsai, W. (2001). 'Knowledge transfer in intraorganizational networks: effects of network position and absorptive capacity on business unit innovation and performance', *Academy of Management Journal*, **44**, pp. 996–1004.

Uzzi, B. (1997). 'Social structure and competition in interfirm networks: the paradox of embeddedness', *Administrative Science Quarterly*, **42**, pp. 35–67.

Uzzi, B. and R. Lancaster (2003). 'Relational embeddedness and learning: the case of bank loan managers and their clients', *Management Science*, **49**, pp. 383–399.

Von Hippel, E. (1998). 'Sticky information and the locus of problem solving: implications for innovation'. In A. D. Chandler Jr, P. Hagström and Ö. Sölvell (eds), *The Dynamic Firm: The Role of Technology Strategy, Organization and Regions*, pp. 60–77. Oxford: Oxford University Press.

Wang, P. and S. Nicholas (2005). 'Knowledge transfer, knowledge replication, and learning in non-equity alliances: operating contractual joint ventures in China', *Management International Review*, **45**, pp. 99–119.

Wang, P., T. W. Tong and C. P. Koh (2004). 'An integrated model of knowledge transfer from MNC parent to China subsidiary', *Journal of World Business*, **39**, pp. 168–182.

Williamson, O. E. (1991). 'Comparative economic organization: the analysis of discrete structural alternatives', *Administrative Science Quarterly*, **36**, pp. 269–296.

Yan, A. and B. Gray (1994). 'Bargaining power, management control, and performance in United States–China joint ventures: a comparative case study', *Academy of Management Journal*, **37**, pp. 1478–1517.

Zander, U. and B. Kogut (1995). 'Knowledge and the speed of the transfer and imitation of organizational capabilities: an empirical test', *Organization Science*, **6**, pp. 76–92.

11
Do Managers Behave the Way Theory Suggests? A Choice-Theoretic Examination of Foreign Direct Investment Location Decision-Making

Co-authored with Timothy M. Devinney and Jordan J. Louviere

Foreign direct investment choice: theory and empirical limitations

The location and control decisions of multinational enterprises are at the core of managerial decision-making and academic theorising in international business. For each activity the firm undertakes, it has two critical decisions: (1) Where should the activity be located? (2) How should it be controlled? (Buckley, 2004). The control decision is whether to own and operate the function in house, or subcontract or outsource it to an independent company. Joint ventures are an intermediate stage between ownership and contract. Strictly speaking, foreign direct investment (FDI) implies control of the operation involving the investment, but there are many ways to control a facility beyond ownership. For example, foreign investors with minority ownership may well have power over an entity through the control of technology, management or key organisational systems.

Research in this area is derived from two intertwined theoretical traditions. The first derives from trade theory and the economics of industrial organisation, following Hymer (1960). Within the international business literature the two most dominant paradigms are those related to Dunning (1981) and Buckley and Casson (1976). According to this tradition, the choice of location for foreign investment is a deliberate, if rationally bounded, decision made with the primary goal of profitability and rent extraction, which may be combined with secondary goals of asset seeking or protection of profitability and rent. A second approach is the more loosely structured internationalisation process model associated with the 'Uppsala tradition' (e.g., Johanson and Vahlne, 1977, 1990). According to this approach, managers make iterative decisions that are dominated by limited information and risk aversion. Such behaviour leads to a staged approach to entry that has specific characteristics and patterns. This approach emphasises that the subsidiary goal of 'learning to internationalise' is as important to explaining internationalisation patterns as a purely rational calculative approach.

Location decisions for FDI have received relatively little attention in the literature. Mudambi and Navarra (2003) consider location choice shortlisting to be a lacuna in the literature. It is also known that FDI is not a point-of-time 'go/no-go' decision but a process (this has been known right from the inception of studies of managerial decision-making in FDI – see the title of Aharoni's (1966) book, *The Foreign Investment Decision Process*). An examination of this process yields important changes over its duration, as we shall see.

Empirically, there has been far more work utilising and attempting to validate the economics tradition (e.g., Mucchielli and Mayer, 2004; Wei *et al.*, 2005), with the more behavioural- and managerial-based internationalisation process model being relegated to case studies of small numbers of individual companies (e.g., Fina and Rugman, 1996; Sarkar *et al.*, 1999; Chetty and Blankenburg Holm, 2000) or cross-sectional surveys (e.g., Sullivan and Bauerschmidt, 1990; Eriksson *et al.*, 1997; Luo and Peng, 1999). However, both of these approaches have natural limitations and strong biases. The limitations of the internationalisation process model have been well documented, and are related mainly to the lack of a link between the empirical studies and a formal structural model (e.g., Melin, 1992; Andersen, 1993) and concerns about the domain of the firms studied (e.g., Sullivan and Bauerschmidt, 1990). But what is more worrying from our perspective are the unrecognised limitations of tests of the economics-based approach. Because most empirical FDI studies rely on panel or survey data they fail to address several issues highlighted by Devinney *et al.* (2003):

(1) The samples are based on final location choice only. Hence we do not know:
   (a) which options were considered by the firms and discarded (because they are not in the database); and
   (b) how these discarded options differed in terms of their perceived value to the managers making them.
(2) The samples are based on intra-firm choice. Hence we do not know to what extent:
   (a) the choices are idiosyncratic to the firms or managers making them (the assumption is that all managers are the same, and firm differences can be captured by covariates); and
   (b) the consideration sets of the firms differed (an implicit but binding assumption is that the choices the firms/managers are making were possible choices of the firms not making them).

226　*Peter J. Buckley et al.*

In the present study we explore the above issues by relying on choice-theoretic empirical methods (e.g., Hensher *et al.*, 2000; Train, 2003) to capture the preference structures of managers either actively or potentially actively involved in FDI location choices. The benefit of this approach is that it allows for the examination of combinations of investment and environmental features and the relative value of each in determining the choice of managerially preferred outcomes in a more controlled setting. In addition, it allows for the direct testing of the degree of managerial variation from a purely rational model, and in this way serves as a more direct comparison between the rational calculative model and the internationalisation process model.

The next section provides a review of recent literature and then a brief summary of the economics-based calculative model and behavioural-based internationalisation process model on FDI location choice. We then move on to the heart of the paper to describe the methods and results. As this paper is aiming to present a methodology as well as some exploratory findings relating to a comparison of theories, more of the paper is devoted to a description of the methods and results than to the theories being examined. The conclusions will show that the nature of FDI investment choice is, at one and the same time, both clearer and more complex than normally discussed. We will also speculate on some of the implications of the application of experimental approaches in international business research.

Recent literature on FDI location decisions

Appendix A lists a selection of recent studies of FDI location decisions. It covers surveys of executives and managers (10 papers), secondary data including compilations of data sets at firm level (10 papers), and one survey-based Delphi study. The publication dates range from 1980 to 2006. It is natural that secondary data studies tend to emphasise 'objective' or instrumental determinants whereas surveys focus on experiential, cultural and knowledge (or information) related variables. However, the divide is not absolute. Many of the studies are of single-country outward investors (often the USA) and/or of single host countries.

The studies based on 'objective' firm-level data tend to adopt, consciously or unwittingly, a calculative approach to location decisions. Woodward and Rolfe (1993) find conventional results from factors such as market size, wage rates and transport costs. Barkema *et al.* (1996) find that cultural distance is a prominent factor in entry, particularly where another firm is involved, in a joint venture for example. Henisz (2000) finds that host country institutions are important, and that joint ventures are preferred when hazards in the host country are greatest. Chung (2001) finds technology factors to be important: both transfer and accession of technology show up as determinants in different contexts. Feinberg and Keane (2001) show interestingly mixed results on the impact of tariff reductions, even within narrowly defined manufacturing industries. Chung and Alcacer (2002) examine location within a single country – the USA – and find that, in addition to traditional location factors, knowledge-seeking motivations may operate through laboratories and manufacturing facilities. Mitra and Golder (2002) find that cultural distance from the home market is *not* a significant factor, but knowledge about nearby markets may have a significant effect. Zhou *et al.* (2002) find government policy initiatives to be a significant determinant of location among provinces in China for incoming FDI. Henisz and Macher (2004) find differences within semiconductor firms by level of technology, and find that firms also trade off their own experience against other firms' experience as sources of critical knowledge on foreign investment environments. Nachum and Zaheer (2005) show that industries with different levels of information intensity are driven by different investment motivations. There are thus rich varieties of suggested determinants in this body of literature, but equally there are sources of differences that cannot easily be reconciled.

Survey-based results are similarly heterogeneous. Davidson's (1980) pioneering study showed that corporate experience affected location decisions in two ways. First, firms preferred nations in which they were already active to those in which they were not. Second, firms with extensive international experience exhibited less preference for near, similar and familiar markets. Markets that others might perceive as less attractive because of high levels of uncertainties are given increased priority as the firm's experience rises. Crucially, for our purposes, he found that, as firms gain experience, the location of foreign activity increasingly represents an efficient response to global economic opportunities and conditions. In a single-country study, Mudambi (1998) found that firms with a longer tenure of operations are significantly more likely to invest in the host country (UK) in any given period. Brush *et al.* (1999) in a survey of plant managers in US MNEs and finds that, for this group, manufacturing strategy dominates international strategy. This is an intriguing pointer to the fact that managers may perceive location decisions differently according to where they are in the organisation. Pedersen and Petersen (2004) find that the 'shock effect' of foreign market entry develops over time (reaching its lowest level of market familiarity 8 years after entry) and supports the 'psychic distance paradox' that adjacent countries provide high levels of shock. Time periods are important in perceptions of location. Mission also reflects location, as Ambos (2005) shows for the establishment of laboratories, a complement to Kuemmerle's (1999) argument that FDI can both augment and exploit R&D. The single Delphi study (MacCarthy and Atthirawong, 2003) found conventional results for the motivations of firms in manufacturing foreign investment location.

These results suggest that process issues in internationalisation have also been found to be significant. Learning, acculturation and cultural

228   *Peter J. Buckley et al.*

assimilation are variously found to be significant in different contexts, for different managers in the FDI location decision. We can thus oppose the two traditions – the calculative and the process – in our hypothesis construction.

The calculative *vs* the internationalisation process approach to FDI location choice

The calculative and internationalisation process approaches to FDI location choice thus have a long overlapping tradition, and comparisons between them have been attempted. However, to a greater or lesser extent, such attempts have failed to come to any definitive conclusions, mainly because they rely on different levels of analysis, different sample domains, and different empirical traditions.

The economistic approach grew from a broadening of traditional trade-theoretic approaches to account for differences in FDI and internationalisation patterns (see the 'research forum' articles by Dunning, Devinney, Tallman, Mitchell and de la Torre in Cheng and Hitt (2004), for an overview of the some of this history). Its fundamental predictions are that firms are quasi-rational in their choices, and once the costs and benefits of specific investment opportunities are considered in light of the economic and competitive constraints operating in a market, there is little room for managerial discretion. The best managers making the most financially viable location choices ultimately out-survive those making less commercially efficacious choices. Proof of the validity of the rational calculative viewpoint is typically revealed through econometric panel data-based studies that show that firms do indeed make decisions that are rational, based on components of the fit between their firm-specific advantages and the structures and needs of the markets that they enter.

The internationalisation process model has a humbler beginning, growing out of a single-industry study of expansion by Swedish logging companies. Approaching the decision to internationalise at a more micro level, this tradition concentrates more on the issues of how firms learn as they internationalise. It proposes that specific biases exist in the nature of the decisions that they make based on their experience. One of the hallmarks of internationalisation theory is a belief that less experienced managers behave in ways that overweight specific investment characteristics (such as cultural closeness to the home country), and behave in a more risk-averse manner. Proof of the validity of the internationalisation approach is typically revealed through case studies showing how a single firm or groups of firms in the same industry follow a systematic process as they become more internationally mature.

The tradition deriving from economics makes little allowance for managerial self-interest and rent-seeking behaviour, factors given considerable latitude in the internationalisation process approach. Our experimental approach allows us both to incorporate insights from the process tradition and to highlight potential managerial biases including self-interest. As it focuses on the managers who are responsible for making the decisions it removes problems of 'the level of analysis' that bedevil comparisons of different conceptual approaches. Further, our hypotheses are framed so that we can test the degree to which final decisions over time converge on what is optimal for the firm, by gradually eliminating bias and self-interest as FDI decisions are repeated by the same manager. The effect of experience may make managerial decision-making more 'rational' from the point of view of the firm's best interest.

It would be apt to say that the debate between these two traditions is something of a dance where the partners never touch. This has been due to the inability to find a level of analysis or approach that allows for a more direct test of the tenets of the theories. However, one possibility – indeed, the approach used here – is to examine managerial decisions directly (albeit experimentally) in an attempt to address some of the areas of overlap between these two theoretical traditions. A direct test of the internationalisation process approach is to examine whether or not managers with less internationalisation experience utilise models that are distinctly different from those of more experienced managers, when facing precisely the same investment opportunities. A second test is to examine whether or not the risk profile of less experienced managers is different from the risk profile of the more experienced managers. We can state these as hypotheses:

> **Hypothesis 1:** Managers with more internationalisation experience will use more calculative approaches than managers with less internationalisation experience.

> **Hypothesis 2:** Managers with more internationalisation experience will show less risk aversion than managers with less internationalisation experience.

As we have shown above, both these hypotheses have support in the prior literature.

Experimental methods

We applied two experimental methods in this study. The first is a variant of standard discrete choice methods (DCM) with an experimental manipulation. The second is a best–worst (BW) experiment aimed at validating the preferences extracted from the discrete choice experiment.

The sample

The subjects were active managers in the top management team of a selection of firms headquartered mainly in Australia, Denmark and the USA, where the sample was representative of three groups:

(1) local firms with international operations (managers answering here were located in the HQ);
(2) subsidiaries of multinational enterprises (managers answering here were located in the subsidiary); and
(3) managers in local firms with no international operations.

An attempt was made to match up a sufficient sample of firms in group (1) with those in group (2): for example, we sampled both the subsidiary of Danish firms in Australia and their Danish HQ. Firms in group (3) were sampled so as to approximate the size of the subsidiaries represented in group (2). Managers were approached via fax, and an interview was arranged with those willing to be involved in the study.

Although an attempt was made to have a balanced and moderately representative sample, the respondents were not drawn from a large sample. The task we asked managers to complete is difficult and long (a typical interview was 1.5–2h), implying that many managers were unwilling to take the time to be involved. Because we are approaching the top management team at these firms, normal random sampling was abandoned for a more targeted approach. That allowed us to get managers with both some and no international experience. Approximately 200 firms were approached, with a net sample of 70 respondents. The characteristics of these individuals are shown in Table 11.1. They are senior in their organisations – 35% were CEOs, MDs or CFOs – and the organisations are representative of the Fortune Global 500 plus a sample of smaller firms in many of the same industries – the median turnover was between US$500 million and US$1000 million. Given that the purpose of this paper is to highlight a method, the sample is sufficient for preliminary analysis and evaluation of the techniques. In addition to conducting the experimental exercise with these managers, each was interviewed both at the time of the experiment and in a debriefing in which their results were explained and discussed with them.

The choice experiment

The extant theories of FDI location choice were used to determine the features of investment alternatives that would be relevant to making a location choice decision. Based on pre-testing, we reduced an initial list down to 12 investment features and one size of investment condition (with three levels) and one political stability condition (with two levels). The features and the levels

Do Managers Behave the Way Theory Suggests? 231

Table 11.1 Sample and respondent characteristics

Headquarters location	
Australia	29.0%
Denmark	31.9%
Germany, Netherlands, Switzerland	8.6%
Japan, Malaysia, Singapore	4.2%
Singapore	2.0%
UK	2.9%
USA	23.2%
Employees (median number)	32,000
Employees (mean number)	21,147
Turnover (median range)	$500 million–$1,000 million
Median levels between respondent and CEO	1
CEOs, managing directors, CFOs	34.7%
Senior VP, directors, regional heads	33.3%
Manager personally engaged in	
Import/export	52.2%
Equity JV negotiation	50.7%
Non-equity JV negotiation	44.9%
JV or alliance	53.6%
M&A	47.8%
Traded companies	37.7%
FDI location choice (LC)	56.5%
FDI establishment (E)	59.4%
FDI operations (O)	47.8%
FDI experience (aggregation of LC or E or O)	64.1%
Number of countries in which subsidiaries operate (median)	10–25

are shown in Table 11.2. They were aimed at capturing not just investment return but also potential opportunities, exploitation and exploration of/for assets, structural barriers, market inefficiencies and cultural proximity.

Theoretically, the calculative and internationalisation viewpoints would imply that specific investment attributes would be weighed more heavily or differentially. In particular, those investment attributes most readily identified with the return characteristics of the choice – the cost of operations, return on investment, potential market size, growth and access to new resources, assets and technologies – would, according to the calculative orientation, be more important. Indeed, once accounted for, the other attributes should matter little if the returns are assured. The internationalisation orientation, with its emphasis on the cognitive, learning and resource aspects of the location choice decision, would imply that managers would put differential weight on those characteristics that would reduce risk and complexity: the existence of established relations, trade and other structural barriers, the potential for exploitation of existing resources, assets

232   *Peter J. Buckley et al.*

Table 11.2 Investment features and levels used in the choice experiment

Features of investment	Levels
The cost of operations – Choosing a specific location can lead to higher or lower costs of operation across the value chain	Decrease 10%, Decrease 5%, Increase 5%, Increase 10%
Return on investment (ROI) – Describes the rate of return expected from the investment	Less than home market and fails to meet hurdle rate, Less than home market but meets hurdle rate, Same as home market, Greater than home market
Access to new resources, assets and technologies – Choosing a specific location can lead to greater competences being developed in the firm, through access to physical resources, organisational assets, or new technologies	No New Access, Access
Pre-emption of competition – Choosing a specific location can allow a firm to pre-empt competition into a location, thereby securing a first-mover advantage	Pre-emption Important, Pre-emption Not Important
Potential market size	Large relative to home market, Same as home market, Small relative to home market
Growth – The rate of increase in sales in the market	Decline, No Growth, Low Growth, Strong Growth
The existence of established relations – Different markets will have different sets of established relationships	No established relations, Yes established relations exist
Trade and other structural barriers – Markets will have different levels of trade protection	High Barriers, No Barriers
Potential for exploitation of existing resources, assets and technologies – Companies enter markets sometimes with the intent of exploiting an existing competence in a new market	No Potential, Potential Exists
Culture/language of the new market – Indicates the natural native language used in the country	English, Arabic, Chinese, French, Portuguese, Russian, Spanish, Other
Line of business – Denotes whether the new investment is in a existing, related or new line of business	Same line of business, Related line of business, Completely new line of business
Asset protection – Denotes whether legal structures exist for the protection of assets, both physical and intellectual	No Protection, Adequate/Strong protection

and technologies, the culture/language of the market, asset protection, and whether or not the expansion was in an existing line of business. In addition, according to internationalisation theory, the size of the investment and the degree of political stability would matter more to less experienced managers. However, it should be emphasised that the important consideration laid out in the hypotheses is not the attributes that managers take into consideration alone, but that managers with different levels of experience will make quite different decisions.

Individuals made decisions about 32 investment pairs with varying levels across the 12 investment features. Each subject was put into one of six investment-political conditions – in essence nesting the choice experiment within this investment–stability condition experiment. The investment levels varied between 10, 30 and 50% of total investment funds available, and were meant to capture the importance of the magnitude of the investment being made. The political stability levels varied between politically stable and politically unstable. Details of these conditions are presented in Table 11.3. An example of a singular choice from the experiment is presented in Figure 11.1. In all, each individual would be placed in 1 of 96 possible choice experiments × investment level × political stability conditions. Our design allowed us to test all main effects and all interaction effects; however, the size of the sample restricted us to an examination of main effects only.

In addition to the choice experiment, subjects were also asked to evaluate their organisation's most recent example of FDI (e.g., establishing a call centre in New Zealand or opening a factory in China) on the 12 features presented in Table 11.2. Additional information was collected about the typicality of the most recent investment, the nature of the mode of entry, and the level of investment involved. As well as this information, standard firmographic data and information on the individual manager was collected. Information on the firm's last investment is presented in Table 11.4. It shows that 84% of the firms have engaged in FDI across a wide range of countries. In addition, it hints at what might be relevant characteristics of investment choice. The last investments show a tendency towards:

(1) markets with production cost reduction (48%);
(2) markets with larger ROI (55%);
(3) markets with larger markets (58%);
(4) markets with strong growth (66%);
(5) markets with prior investment and established relations (75%);
(6) markets where existing assets and current lines of business can be exploited (81%); and
(7) markets where they are concerned about preempting competitors (63%).

234   *Peter J. Buckley et al.*

Table 11.3   Environment and investment level conditions

Individuals were given the following information before the choice experiment:
*The investments are being made in a country that is viewed as ⟨Insert Political Condition⟩.
Your organisation is considering directly investing in operations in this country and the
investment being made represents Insert ⟨Investment Level Condition⟩ of the total cash
available for investment for the next three years.*

Political condition	Investment-level condition
Quite politically stable in the sense that there is little likelihood of either social disturbance or political transitions other than through organised or legitimate means.	A relatively small investment totalling 10%. A relatively moderate investment totalling 30%.
Somewhat politically unstable in the sense that there is a not insignificant probability that social disturbances will arise or that unpredictable political transitions might occur	A relatively significant investment totalling 50%.

Features of the Investment #3	Option A	Option B
Cost of operations	Increase 10%	Decrease 10%
Return on investment (ROI)	Greater than home market	Less than home market; fails hurdle rate
Access to new resources, assets and technologies	Access	No new access
Preemption of competition	Important	Not important
Potential market size	Smaller than home market	Larger than home market
Growth	Decline	Strong growth
Existence of established relations	Yes	No
Trade and other structural barriers	No barriers	High barriers
Potential for exploitation of existing resources, assets & technologies	Potential exists	No potential
Culture/Language of the new market	Other	English
Line of business	Same	New
Asset protection	Strong	No protection
. If the investment options described above were available to your organization, which option would you recommend giving further consideration (Tick ONE box only)?	■ A	■ B
	■ Neither	
. If the investment option described above were available to your organization, which would you undertake instead of or in addition to other currently available investments (Tick ONE box only)?	■ A	■ B
	■ Neither	

Figure 11.1   Example of an investment choice option

These items line up nicely with theory, and the question we need to ask is
whether they are simply a bias associated with the nature of recent opportunities, or whether they are truly representative of the preferences of the

Table 11.4 Characteristics of last investment made

Percent with FDI	84.1%		
Cost of operations[a]		*Asset protection*[a]	
Decrease 10%	32.7%	No protection	20.8%
Decrease 5%	15.4%	Weak protection	37.8%
Increase 5%	13.5%	Strong protection	32.1%
Increase 10%	17.3%	Not considered relevant to decision	9.3%
Not considered relevant to decision	21.1%		
Return on investment[a]		*Prior investment in this market*[a]	
Less than home market; fails hurdle rate	12.7%	Dominant nature of that investment	60.9%
Less than home market; meets hurdle rate	12.7%	Wholly owned subsidiary	42.9%
		M&A	7.1%
Same as home market	12.7%	Equity JV	28.6%
Greater than home market	54.6%	Non-equity alliance	7.1%
Not considered relevant to decision	7.3%	Import/export	14.3%
Potential market size[a]		*Compared with other investments*[a]	
Smaller than home market	17.5%	This was relatively routine	68.4%
Same as home market	10.5%	This was out of the ordinary	31.6%
Greater than home market	57.9%		
Not considered relevant to decision	14.1%		
Potential market growth[a]		*Compared with other investment*[a]	
Decline or no growth	1.8%		
Low growth	21.4%	This amount was relatively insignificant	14.0%
Strong growth	66.1%	This amount was normal	35.1%
Not considered relevant to decision	10.7%	This amount was significant	50.9%
Established relationships existed in the market[a]	74.6%	Competitive pre-emption important[a]	62.7%
Not considered relevant to decision	8.5%	Not considered relevant to decision	13.6%
High trade barriers existed in the market[a]	28.3%	*Same line of business entered*[a]	66.7%
Not considered relevant to decision	11.3%		
Exploitation of existing assets important[a]	81.3%		
Not considered relevant to decision	10.1%		
Last market entered[a]			
China	16.3%		
Other developing Asia (Vietnam, Indonesia, India, etc.)	8.4%		
Developed Asia (Korea, Taiwan, etc.)	7.1%		
Developed Western (EU-15, USA, etc.)	22.9%		
Developing Western (E. Europe, etc.)	4.3%		

[a]These questions answered only by those whose last investment involved FDI.

236 *Peter J. Buckley et al.*

managers. In other words, these are clearly factors that managers desire in the best of circumstances, but how do they make decisions when there are conflicts between these factors across investment options?

The BW experiment

To validate and further extend the models developed based on the choice-modelling experiment, we also conducted a BW experiment using the 12 features given in Table 11.2 plus four additional factors – political stability, currency value, investment assistance, and the existence of a democratic government in the host country. The use of BW scales is aimed at addressing two issues. The first is to examine any bias in the way individuals respond to the choice experiment. In theory, the DCM experiment and the BW experiments are tapping the same underlying preferences and therefore should provide confirmatory results. Second, BW experiments are relatively simple to conduct. If the results of the DCM experiment and the BW experiment are indeed equivalent, a much larger sample can be examined using the simpler method without any loss of generality of the results.

One of the biggest challenges in determining the relative importance of a set of factors in an international environment is the existence of scalar inequivalence (Cohen, 2003). Scalar inequivalence arises primarily because of differences in response styles, which are defined as 'tendencies to respond systematically to questionnaire items on some basis other than what the items were specifically designed to measure' (Paulhus, 1991: 17). There is ample empirical evidence to show that individuals in different countries differ significantly in their response styles (Chen *et al.*, 1995; Steenkamp and Baumgartner, 1998; Steenkamp and Ter Hofstede, 2002), and that these differences can lead to seriously biased conclusions (Baumgartner and Steenkamp, 2001). For example, Cohen (2003) argued that differences in international market segmentation studies may be due more to differences in scale use than to true differences in consumer needs and preferences. Although most of this work is related to consumer research, there is every likelihood that similar issues arise with respect to managerial decisions as assessed by surveys.

BW scaling is a multiple-choice extension of the paired comparison approach that is scale-free and forces respondents to make a discriminating choice among the issues under consideration. As Finn and Louviere demonstrated (1992: 13), 'BW scaling models the cognitive process by which respondents repeatedly choose the two objects in varying sets of three or more objects that they feel exhibit the largest perceptual difference on an underlying continuum of interest'. Appendix B provides a detailed discussion of the logic and algebra of BW scaling. Readers are referred to Marley and Louviere (2005) for a more detailed description of the scale properties of BW experiments. BW experiments permit intra- and inter-feature comparison of levels through the use of a common interval scale (McIntosh and Louviere, 2003; Cohen and Neira, 2003). Figure 11.2 provides an example from the BW experiment.

Empirical estimation

Choice model results

Examination of the choice-modelling responses is done through a series of binary logit models. Respondents were asked to evaluate pairs of investments by indicating which of the options: (1) they would 'recommend giving further consideration'; and (2) 'would undertake instead of or in addition to other currently available investments'. These two decisions are akin to asking the manager a 'consideration set' question and a go/no-go, or investment, question. In this sense, they can be seen to represent nested decisions. The choices from question (2) force individuals to make a definitive decision from the set generated from decision (1).

However, before proceeding to the logit analysis, it is useful to examine the tendency of respondents to indicate whether they would consider or undertake an investment based on the characteristics of those investments. Table 11.5 indicates simply whether or not an investment was chosen (in other words, the 'neither' option was not chosen) cross-tabulated against different conditions. Overall, respondents would 'consider' 26% of the investments and 'undertake' 14%. In situations where the market was politically unstable these percentages drop to 25 and 9%, respectively. The level of the investment does not seem to reveal a consistent pattern of choices. Overall, individuals are less likely to make any choice when asked the 'would invest' question.

Question No.	Which issue matters LEAST to you? (tick ONLY ONE box for each question)	Sets of social and ethical issues for you to consider	Which issue matters MOST to you? (tick ONLY ONE box for each question)
1	☐ ☐ ☐ ☐	Cost of operations Potential market size Growth Existence of established relations	☐ ☐ ☐ ☐
2	☐ ☐ ☐ ☐	Access to new resources Potential market size Trade and structural barriers Potential for exploitation of existing resources	☐ ☐ ☐ ☐
3	☐ ☐ ☐ ☐	Potential market size Culture/Language of market Line of business Strong asset protection	☐ ☐ ☐ ☐

Figure 11.2 Example of the best–worst experiment.

238   Peter J. Buckley et al.

Table 11.5   Propensity to choose any investment (percentage of all investments presented)

	Would consider an investment	Would invest
Overall (*N*=4414 choices each)	26.0	14.0
When environment is		
Unstable (*N*=2430)	25.4	8.8
Stable (*N*=1984)	26.5	14.9
When investment is		
Small (*N*=1408)	35.3	16.2
Medium (*N*=1454)	42.4	12.6
Large (*N*=1552)	37.2	13.0
Cost of production		
Declines 10%	31.8	15.2
Declines 5%	25.4	13.1
Increases 5%	20.2	8.8
Increases 10%	24.2	14.5
Return on investment		
Less than home market; fails hurdle rate	14.4	13.9
Less than home market; meets hurdle rate	21.8	10.9
Same as home market	25.7	11.2
Greater than home market	40.0	15.7
No access to new resources	23.4	13.9
Access to new resources	28.6	12.9
Pre-emption important	29.4	14.9
Pre-emption unimportant	22.7	11.9
Market size		
Smaller than home market	24.5	14.7
Same as home market	21.8	10.6
Larger than home market	32.8	15.4
Market growth		
Declining	14.9	12.9
None	18.6	10.7
Low	23.6	11.6
Strong	43.3	16.7
Established relations unimportant	21.4	11.4
Established relations important	30.7	15.4
Barriers to trade exist	21.4	12.4
Barriers to trade do not exist	30.8	14.4
No exploitation of existing assets	23.9	12.1
Exploitation of existing assets	28.1	14.7
Language		
English	24.6	12.5
Arabic	16.6	7.1
Chinese	25.4	12.3
French	23.9	9.9
Portuguese	22.0	12.8
Russian	20.1	13.1

Continued

Table 11.5 Continued

	Would consider an investment	Would invest
Spanish	24.8	10.2
Other	37.4	20.7
Diversification		
Same line of business	34.9	18.3
Related line of business	24.6	10.6
New line of business	19.0	11.8
No/weak asset protection	19.9	12.1
Strong asset protection	32.4	14.8

In addition, there are some logical patterns that arise. First, cost-of-production increases are related to a smaller likelihood of considering an investment (although not making the investment); however, the effect is not monotonic. Second, a higher ROI is positively and monotonically related to the consideration of an investment, but slightly less so in the case of the go/no-go decision. Third, access to new resources, exploitation of existing assets, pre-emption of competition, the existence of established relations in the market and avoidance of barriers to trade are all related to making or considering an investment. Fourth, market growth and market size are important to considering an investment but less so in making an investment. In both cases, large markets with strong growth are the clear choice winners. Fifth, being in the same line of business is important to considering and making an investment. Sixth, asset protection is a strong consideration factor, but less so in making the final investment. These simple results provide face validity as to the seriousness with which the managers involved considered the task.

This information provides some understanding of the nature of managerial preferences for different FDI location choices, but we need a more statistically valid approach to determine the marginal value of specific investment options. Table 11.6 presents the logit analysis for the 'consider' and 'invest' choices in the aggregate. What we see in these results is that the likelihood of considering an FDI option is more clear-cut than the likelihood of choosing the final investment, given what was considered. Ignoring the stability of the market and the level of the investment, it appears that production cost matters, as do ROI, access to resources, market size (when large), market growth, established relationships, barriers to trade, exploitation of existing assets, remaining in the same line of business, and strong asset protection. Being in an English-speaking country and not in an Arabic- or Russian-speaking country also appears as part of the criteria. When we adjust for the stability of the market and the level

240 *Peter J. Buckley et al.*

Table 11.6 Aggregate consider and invest models

	Would consider the investment option		Would invest in the option	
Cost of production				
Declines 10%	0.328***	0.330***	0.025	0.025
Declines 5%	0.217***	0.223***	0.051	0.054
Increase 5%	0.023	0.025	−0.168**	−0.166**
Return on investment				
Less than home market; fails hurdle rate	−0.573***	−0.576***	−0.073	−0.073
Less than home market; meets hurdle rate	−0.148**	−0.149**	−0.091	−0.092
Greater than home market	0.278***	0.277***	−0.071	−0.074
No access to new resources	−0.152***	−0.154***	0.046	0.054
Pre-emption important	0.053	0.054	0.017	0.021
Market size				
Smaller than home market	−0.047	−0.047	0.080	0.081
Larger than home market	0.230***	0.233***	0.109*	0.110*
Market growth				
Declining	−0.210***	−0.208***	−0.007	−0.010
Low	0.177***	0.183***	0.044	0.040
Strong	0.674***	0.680***	0.149**	0.149**
No established relations	−0.119***	−0.121***	−0.068	−0.069
Barriers to trade exist	−0.131***	−0.131***	0.048	0.048
No exploitation of existing assets	−0.141***	−0.143***	−0.109	−0.112**
Language				
English	0.084	0.098	−0.197**	−0.184**
Arabic	−0.364***	−0.354***	−0.474***	−0.458***
Chinese	−0.013	−0.003	−0.153*	−0.139
French	−0.099	−0.102	−0.286***	−0.283***
Portuguese	−0.182**	−0.173**	−0.143	−0.132
Russian	−0.233***	−0.226***	−0.118	−0.103
Spanish	−0.063	−0.068	−0.265***	−0.269***
Diversification				
Related line of business	−0.104**	−0.111**	−0.182***	−0.186***

Continued

Do Managers Behave the Way Theory Suggests? 241

Table 11.6 Continued

	Would consider the investment option		Would invest in the option	
New line of business	−0.322***	−0.329***	−0.156**	−0.162**
No asset protection	−0.259***	−0.261***	0.007	0.005
Unstable political environment		−0.037		−0.127***
Level of investment				
Small investment (10%)		0.171***		0.017***
Large investment (50%)		0.076		0.009***
Manager's FDI experience		−0.084		−0.262**
−2LL	4133.00	4117.93	3349.14	3335.36
ρ^2	0.275	0.279	0.049	0.055
Percentage classified correctly	77.7	77.5	86.6	86.6

*$P < 0.10$, **$P < 0.05$, ***$P < 0.01$.

of the investment we find that political instability is not relevant, but small and large investment amounts are related to considering more of the investments presented. Finally, accounting for the FDI experience of the manager (FDI experience) does not matter significantly. FDI experience is defined as the manager having had experience in FDI location choice, FDI establishment or FDI operations. Sixty-four per cent of managers had FDI experience. Overall, those with no FDI experience would consider an investment 28% of the time and those with FDI experience 26% of the time.

When we move to the 'invest' model, the results are less clear-cut. Indeed, one would have to say that there is greater heterogeneity in the choices made, with political stability and the FDI experience of the managers now assuming importance. Managers with less FDI experience are more likely to make any investment choice (16% of the time *vs* 13% of the time for those with experience), and all managers are less likely to make an investment when the market is politically unstable. In addition, markets with cost increases are more likely to be avoided. All of this indicates that managers are taking a slightly more risk-adverse stance when making the actual decision to invest, *vs* just considering an option, and that managers with less FDI experience appear even more risk-averse.

Tables 11.7 and 11.8 provide two more illustrative breakdowns in this analysis. Table 11.7 separates the analysis based on whether or not the manager

242 *Peter J. Buckley et al.*

in question had any prior FDI experience. The prior analysis allows us to see whether or not FDI experience matters to the tendency to accept any given investment, whereas this analysis asks whether or not the models of managers with or without experience are any different. As can be seen, the models for the experienced and inexperienced managers are similar, but do reveal a few differences. First, FDI-experienced managers are more likely to react positively to production cost reductions and market size, and negatively to moving out of their existing line of business. They also prefer smaller investments. However, they are less concerned than inexperienced managers with the existence of established relations. When it comes to the case of the investment model we see that less experienced managers are more affected by market stability and trade barriers, whereas experienced managers prefer large markets with big growth where they can exploit existing resources and lines of business.

Table 11.8 presents an analysis based on the stability of the market experimental manipulation. What we see is that the models are quite close, particularly in the case of the 'consideration' of investments. In the investment model we see that managers are more likely to engage in avoidance behaviour, putting emphasis on avoiding low-return markets and seeking markets with high growth.

Considering the limited sample size, the choice models indicate a few things of relevance. First, which options a manager is willing to consider is quite consistent with economic-based theoretical thinking about FDI location choice, and seems unaffected by the environment in which the choice is being made. Second, the actual willingness to take on an investment is less likely to match up with the economic models, and appears much more eclectic. Part of this may be due to the stylised form of our experiments. However, it is more likely that the factors that, in the end, swing the decision toward one investment *vs* another are less obvious than we are able to discern using the investment attributes we are investigating. Even more interesting is the bias that this may introduce into the decision-making process. If managers are making a 'consideration' cut that takes into account the dominant criteria of the decision (e.g., ROI) and then choosing their 'investments' conditional on this, it is hardly surprising that the marginal determinants will be the factors that were unimportant in the first stage (as these have the most variance). This is indeed confirmed by Mudambi and Navarra (2003), who show the comparability of many of the shortlists of investments investigated by firms. Third, FDI experience may be less relevant to the 'what to consider' decision and more relevant to the actual final decision being made. The implication here is that the conclusions of the internationalisation process model are less relevant for the complete investment choice decision, as even managers without much experience can make fairly rational evaluations of available alternatives.

Do Managers Behave the Way Theory Suggests? 243

Table 11.7 Consider and invest models split by manager's FDI experience

	Would consider option when FDI experience		Would invest in option when FDI experience	
	No	Yes	No	Yes
Cost of production				
Declines 10%	0.158	0.380***	−0.050	0.043
Declines 5%	0.154	0.249***	−0.074	0.075
Increase 5%	0.000	0.046	−0.187	−0.155*
Return on investment				
Less than home market; fails hurdle rate	−0.529***	−0.604***	0.141	−0.042
Less than home market; meets hurdle rate	−0.300**	−0.124*	0.046	−0.024
Greater than home market	0.318**	0.260***	0.004	0.081
No access to new resources	−0.175*	−0.152***	−0.103	0.082
Pre-emption important	0.150	0.028	−0.077	0.036
Market size				
Smaller than home market	−0.159	−0.010	0.178	0.068
Larger than home market	0.021	0.288***	−0.041	0.145**
Market growth				
Declining	−0.036	−0.258***	0.062	−0.006
Low	0.254*	0.170**	0.133	0.025
Strong	0.556***	0.711***	0.125	0.168**
No established relations	−0.238**	−0.094*	−0.059	−0.062
Barriers to trade exist	−0.052	−0.146***	−0.276**	0.002
No exploitation of existing assets	−0.072	−0.163***	0.061	−0.146**
Language				
English	−0.057	0.114	−0.357*	−0.161*
Arabic	−0.213	−0.388***	−0.256	−0.533***
Chinese	−0.023	−0.003	−0.351	−0.106
French	−0.108	−0.127	−0.340	−0.285**
Portuguese	−0.177	−0.180*	−0.413*	−0.076
Russian	−0.501***	−0.171*	−0.492**	−0.027
Spanish	−0.109	−0.080	−0.389*	−0.255**
Diversification				
Related line of business	0.074	−0.157***	−0.034	−0.227***

Continued

244   *Peter J. Buckley et al.*

Table 11.7 Continued

	Would consider option when FDI experience		Would invest in option when FDI experience	
	No	Yes	No	Yes
New line of business	−0.144	−0.372***	−0.038	−0.199**
No asset protection	−0.333**	−0.251***	0.016	−0.006
Unstable political environment	−0.069	−0.022	−0.456***	−0.129**
Level of investment				
Small investment (10%)	0.067	0.177***	−0.818***	0.139**
Large investment (50%)	−0.022	0.091*	0.025	0.103*
−2LL	751.14	3330.22	552.94	2688.64
ρ^2	0.262	0.294	0.099	0.074
Percent classified correctly	77.5	78.4	83.0	81.6

*$P < 0.10$, **$P < 0.05$, ***$P < 0.01$.

Indeed, these conclusions appear to be the same ones that the managers involved in the experiments come to themselves. In debriefing interviews managers were shown the models that were based on their own choices (as well as the aggregate models). Invariably they reacted in two ways. One was to indicate that there are many more factors going into their decisions than our experiments capture. However, when queried about this, it turned out that the attributes we used covered almost everything they brought up. What seemed to matter to them was that the number of levels in many of the attributes was broader than we used. The second was that they felt their fiduciary responsibility to their firms was to generate broad sets of options that their board of directors could discuss in line with their overall strategy. Hence their final decision was much more one of fit with their overall strategy. This would imply that the heterogeneity seen in the 'investment' choice may be reflective of the heterogeneity of the strategies of the firms involved in the study.

BW results

The BW experiment allows for a simpler means of capturing preferences, although in a situation that is less robust than the DCM experiments presented earlier. A key methodological question we need to address is whether or not the BW experiments generate conclusions in line with the DCMs. If this is the case, then we have a means of gathering much

Do Managers Behave the Way Theory Suggests? 245

Table 11.8 Consider and invest models split by market stability

	Would consider option when market is		Would invest in option when market is	
	Stable	Unstable	Stable	Unstable
Cost of production				
Declines 5%	0.323***	0.345***	0.041	−0.027
Increases 5%	0.196**	0.253***	0.047	0.073
Increases 10%	−0.054	0.118	−0.234**	−0.101
Return on investment				
Less than home market; fails hurdle rate	−0.390***	−0.919***	0.112	−0.207*
Less than home market; meets hurdle rate	−0.192**	−0.121	0.032	−0.119
Greater than home market	0.217***	0.366***	0.078	0.058
No access to new resources	−0.156***	−0.196***	0.035	0.059
Pre-emption important	0.022	0.078	0.005	0.033
Market size				
Smaller than home market	−0.041	−0.055	0.073	0.111
Larger than home market	0.165**	0.341***	0.110	0.121
Market growth				
Declining	−0.190**	−0.255***	0.114	−0.237**
Low	0.148*	0.229**	0.085	−0.035
Strong	0.599***	0.852***	0.087	0.265**
No established relations	−0.199**	−0.047	−0.108	−0.007
Barriers to trade exist	−0.122**	−0.167**	0.034	0.091
No exploitation of existing assets	−0.181***	−0.102	−0.103*	−0.116
Language				
English	0.042	0.156	−0.213*	−0.251
Arabic	−0.224**	−0.509***	−0.372**	−0.593**
Chinese	0.091	−0.129	−0.226*	−0.072
French	−0.049	−0.170	−0.306**	−0.257*
Portuguese	−0.174	−0.181	−0.018	−0.354**
Russian	−0.148	−0.359***	−0.026	−0.246
Spanish	−0.160	0.047	−0.266**	−0.352**
Diversification				
Related line of business	−0.081	−0.162**	−0.259***	−0.111
New line of business	−0.328***	−0.317***	−0.213**	−0.092
No asset protection	−0.304***	−0.229***	0.042	−0.039
FDI experience	−0.009	−0.204	−0.139	−0.681***
Level of investment				
Small investment (10%)	0.445***	−0.067	0.462***	−0.441***
Large investment (50%)	0.378***	−0.285***	0.475***	−0.639***
−2LL	2326.97	1676.03	1945.62	1262.62
ρ^2	0.261	0.367	0.092	0.118
Percent classified correctly	76.2	79.7	85.0	88.1

*$P < 0.10$, **$P < 0.05$, ***$P < 0.01$.

246 *Peter J. Buckley et al.*

more information from managers more quickly and for less expense than is normally the case with preference elicitation methods. Theoretically, we want to know what information these experiments reveal about the nature of managerial preferences with respect to FDI options that adds to what we have gathered from the DCMs. The BW experiment used here incorporated the 12 factors in the DCM experiment along with four additional FDI determinants:

(1) investment assistance (loans, grants, rebates, etc.);
(2) the fact that the government of the country is elected in democratic fair and free elections;
(3) political stability – essentially adding in the political stability condition of the DCM experiment – and;
(4) the existence of currency depreciation.

Figure 11.3 presents the aggregate scores for the BW experiment with the 16 factors arranged from 'most important' to 'least important'. The most important items factors are (from best to worst):

(1) ROI;
(2) market growth;
(3) market size;
(4) remaining in the same line of business;
(5) market stability;
(6) exploitation of assets;
(7) asset protection; and
(8) the cost of production.

The least important factors (from worst to best) are:

(16) culture;
(15) having a democratic government;
(14) investment incentives;
(13) currency depreciation;
(12) access to new resources;
(11) pre-emption of competition;
(10) barriers to trade; and
(9) having established relations in the market.

These factors fit nicely into the picture presented in the consideration models presented earlier.

Table 11.9 provides a simple mean comparison between managers with FDI experience and those without such experience. As in the case of the DCM analysis, we see that both groups have similar preference orderings,

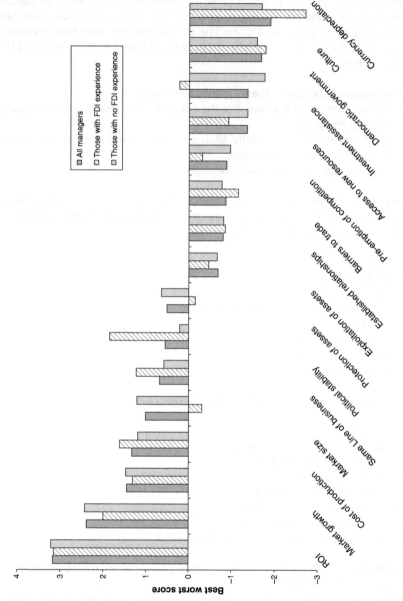

Figure 11.3 Aggregate best–worst experiment results

248   *Peter J. Buckley et al.*

Table 11.9   Differences in individual BW scores split by manager's FDI experience

| | Manager's FDI experience | | | | | | |
| | No | | Yes | | Total | | |
	BW score	Rank	BW score	Rank	BW score	Rank	F
ROI	3.15	1	3.21	1	3.17	1	0.008
Market growth	2.00	2	2.43	2	2.39	2	0.652
Cost of production	1.31	5	1.47	3	1.45	3	0.173
Market size	1.62	4	1.19	5	1.33	4	0.376
Same line of business	−0.31	10	1.21	4	1.01	5	5.528**
Political stability	1.23	6	0.58	7	0.68	6	0.807
Protection of assets	1.85	3	0.21	8	0.55	7	5.529**
Exploitation of assets	−0.15	9	0.64	6	0.51	8	2.053
Established relationships	−0.46	11	−0.66	9	−0.68	9	0.082
Barriers to trade	−0.85	12	−0.81	11	−0.80	10	0.004
Pre-emption of competition	−1.15	14	−0.77	10	−0.86	11	0.330
Access to new resources	−0.31	10	−0.96	12	−0.88	12	1.470
Investment assistance	−0.92	13	−1.36	13	−1.35	13	0.707
Democratic government	0.23	8	−1.75	16	−1.36	14	6.821**
Culture	−1.77	15	−1.57	14	−1.67	15	0.171
Currency depreciation	−2.69	16	−1.68	15	−1.88	16	2.039

*$P < 0.10$, **$P < 0.05$, ***$P < 0.01$.

with a slight preference on the part of those with FDI experience to stick to the same line of business and to be slightly less concerned about asset protection, whereas those with less FDI experience favour countries with democratic governments.

Table 11.10 is perhaps the most interesting analysis as it compares the results from the BW experiment with individual-level model estimates from the DCM experiment. For each individual, the 32 'option A' and 32 'option B' responses for the 'would consider the investment' question were aggregated to form 64 pooled observations (a similar analysis could have been conducted for the 'would invest' decision but is excluded). Multivariate ordinary least squares (OLS) regressions were estimated for each individual (estimating what is called a 'linear probability model': see Aldrich and Nelson, 1984), with the investment features used as predictors. These estimates were

Do Managers Behave the Way Theory Suggests? 249

Table 11.10 Comparison between BW and individual level DCM estimates of preference ordering (absolute correlations)

Individual estimate variable	Correlation with BW variable	
	Pearson	Rank order
Cost of production		
Declines 10%	0.329***	0.268**
Declines 5%	0.096	0.082
Increase 5%	0.042	0.054
Return on investment		
Less than home market; fails hurdle rate	−0.057	−0.088
Less than home market; meets hurdle rate	−0.161*	−0.226**
Greater than home market	0.401***	0.406***
No access to new resources	−0.454***	−0.458***
Pre-emption important	0.046	0.051
Market size		
Smaller than home market	0.063	0.101
Larger than home market	0.158	0.207*
Market growth		
Declining	−0.201*	−0.129
Low	0.067	0.085
Strong	0.177*	0.244**
No established relations	−0.217**	−0.138
Barriers to trade exist	−0.176*	−0.120
No exploitation of existing assets	−0.142*	−0.145*
Language		
English	−0.177*	−0.158
Arabic	−0.280**	−0.296**
Chinese	−0.242**	−0.293**
French	−0.094	−0.142
Portuguese	−0.298***	−0.279**
Russian	−0.249**	−0.281**
Spanish	0.128	−0.153
Diversification		
Related line of business	−0.145	−0.198*
New line of business	−0.313**	−0.392***
No asset protection	−0.347***	−0.305**

*$P < 0.10$, **$P < 0.05$, ***$P < 0.01$.

then correlated with the BW score from the appropriate measure. What we see is that the two sets of estimates are indeed quite well related, although in a complex way. In the case where we can make direct one-on-one comparisons (e.g., barriers to trade and existence of established relations) all the variables are correlated, with the exception of the pre-emption of competition measure

250   *Peter J. Buckley et al.*

(which was not significant in any of the choice models). For measures with multiple levels we see that there is always some component that is correlated with the BW measure, but normally it is the most extreme measure (e.g., production cost decreasing 10%, size greater than home market or operating in a new line of business). In the case of the culture measure it is related to the more extreme DCM variables, Arabic, Portuguese and Russian language countries.

Discussion

Most observational research on FDI uses actual stocks and flows and is unable to examine actual managerial decision-making because latent data (locations not chosen) are unobserved. This paper is an exception, because it explicitly considers hypothetical investments where we control the options being evaluated. Although this is highly stylised, it provides a unique and different window on the characteristics of managerial decision-making with respect to FDI. It also reveals the veracity of using experimental methods where previously only econometric panel data and case-theoretic methods were thought appropriate.

Our results are able to distinguish firm-focused rationality (rational from the point of view of the firm's interest as a whole) from individual-manager-focused rationality, and show an interesting interplay between these two 'rationalities'. Although it is possible that the hypothetical decision-making exercise we employed is less likely to show managerial self-interest than in actual choice situations, it does reveal a complexity that could not arise simply from managers gaming the exercise. For example, the effect of experience itself may make managerial choices more rational, and we see glimpses of this in the fact that more experience managers do indeed make different decisions. The strength of our approach is that the managers were presented with a quite complex combination of investment attributes presented in an orthogonal design. If they simply based their decisions on an overtly simple rule (choose the one with highest ROI) this would be immediately obvious in the results. Similarly, if they did not take the experiment seriously we would have found that few if any of the variables of interest were significant. Instead, we see clear, consistent patterns, both at the individual level and in the aggregate, which are confirmed by two different experimental approaches.

Our results support recent literature that has moved beyond the contrast between 'rational' and 'process' approaches to decision-making. This literature emphasises the complexity of the choices being made with respect to FDI, and we show one mechanism that may help in furthering our understanding of what managers do when faced by that complex environment. In addition, we suggest that 'when?' is as important as 'what?' in determining the outcomes of managerial decisions and their choice set. Even so, there are clearly regularities in the decision-making systems, as we suggest in the next section.

Conclusions and research implications

Our research method enables us to examine different stages of the process associated with the decision to engage in FDI (Aharoni, 1966). The first stage is the establishment of a set of potential investment destinations from a profile of attributes of alternative foreign locations that can be compared with each other across these pre-prescribed criteria. The second stage is the actual choice of an investment, either as a new investment or as an alternative to existing investments. A key conclusion from our preliminary analysis is that managers follow fairly rational rules from the point of view of the firm's interests in creating sets of investments to 'consider'. However, the choice of 'investments' in which to engage is less easy to reconcile with existing theory. One interesting conclusion that arises is that the manner in which IB researchers have analysed FDI may have introduced artefacts into their results. For example, as noted before, if managers are following a staged approach, where they narrow down investments into a smaller set and then make their final choice within that set, then it is important to understand the point in this process that is being examined. By just looking at the consideration set formation, it is likely that an investigator will walk away thinking that the rationalist theory of the firm approach is confirmed (hence rejecting Hypothesis 1 and Hypothesis 2). If one looks only at the choices within the investment model one is likely to think that the internationalisation process model is confirmed (hence accepting Hypothesis 1 and Hypothesis 2). In reality, neither is fully confirmed, because the nature of the decision-making process itself implies that factors considered in stage 1 are not going to be as relevant in stage 2.

Our results show that basic fundamental operational factors serve as the screening mechanism to determine a consideration set of investments. More country-specific factors enter the decision with higher priority when we move from 'consider' to 'invest' (a good example is host country language). Experience with FDI also figures more importantly in the 'invest' than the 'consider' decision, and perhaps this is an indication of the confidence that comes from repeating the FDI process (see also Buckley et al., 1988). In addition, one can show that the models for managers with more FDI experience are more stable and have less variance around the estimates than those for less experienced managers. Variables related to host country culture play a much greater role in the 'invest' than the 'consider' decision. These are considerations that rise to prominence in the manager's mind at a late but crucial stage in the FDI process when all the more functional attributes of the investment have been accounted for.

252   *Peter J. Buckley et al.*

We began this work attempting to get a better understanding of the causal mechanism by which FDI investment choice is made, and to alleviate some of the biases associated with the application of secondary data. What we see is that, just as Dunning (1981) showed that one could not understand trade without understanding the multinational enterprise, it is the case that we cannot understand FDI location choice without understanding the process used to make such choices at the level of the individual manager. Much work remains to get a fuller picture of the process by which these decisions are made and the role that the external environment plays in policing such decisions. Hence we are left with the dubious conclusion that Hypotheses 1 and 2 are both rejected and accepted. At one level our results are a 'ringing endorsement of orthodoxy' – that is, managers make investment choices among a set of investments that are fundamentally driven by market characteristics, firm-specific advantages and return on investment. At another level these results indicate that managers' final investment decisions are highly idiosyncratic, and subject to biases that they might not be aware of themselves when making those decisions.

However, what our results do reveal is that structured experimentation can help to understand the complex decision-making underlying FDI. But this does not mean there are no limitations to what we have done. DCM and BW experiments are based upon random utility theoretic thinking, and suffer from all the limitations to that approach. Hence, if there are serious biases in the models used by managers – for example, if managers suffer from overconfidence bias (Camerer and Lovallo, 1999) – or are using decision models that we have not designed the experiment to investigate – such as elimination by aspects (Tversky, 1972; Manrai and Sinha, 1989) – our findings may have less predictive validity than we would hope (although, as McFadden (2001) notes, the models are remarkably predictive in the aggregate even in this case). Also, although our designs allow us to test interaction effects, our sample size restricts the analysis to mostly main effects. Hence, if managers are erroneously assuming related interactive structures (e.g., wanting to go only into countries with high growth *and* high ROI *and* in the same line of business, but not being able to do so with the options they are given in the experiments) we would not be able to discern this with the data available here. Similarly, we have not embedded our experiments in an environment that accounts for the managers' fiduciary responsibilities. We have no way of knowing, based upon this study, how the managers' choices seen here would translate into a firm's final decision in reality, where all the complexity of ego, bonuses, financial analyst reports, institutional investment pressures and boards of directors comes into play.

Finally, our results have less than positive implications for the set of empirical findings seen in Appendix A. An examination of this research, plus much more that we could have included, shows significant sample domain issues.

Most of the research examines country-out or country-in investment (e.g., Taiwanese inward investment in China, or outward investment from Japan or the USA), in limited numbers of industries (e.g., R&D or semiconductors), with specific rationales that may be idiosyncratic to the circumstances being investigated. Although one can argue that 'revealed preference' data are more relevant because they represent real investment choices, they are also biased in that they may not be predictive in the sense of 'stated preference' data because they do not span the domain of possible investment options. Hence developing a generalisable theory of FDI location choice may have been slowed by our failure to understand the extent to which we have restricted the domain of both our independent and dependent variables. However, we do not know the degree to which this is true until we attempt to re-test our findings in domains specifically structured to deal with this issue.

Future research implications

This paper examined only one set of decisions – FDI location choice by managers. However, it also was an attempt to bring into international business an alternative approach to testing theory. In doing so, we feel there are some implications for other areas of international business research from this work. We can speculate about a few of these.

The first and most obvious implication is that other areas of firm choice behaviour can be investigated in a manner similar to what we have done. For example, the approach here can be modified to study not only entry mode type – e.g., greenfield, joint venture, exporting – but also the facets of the choice of joint venture partner and the nature of the contracts with those partners. Hence we would argue that any area of location and mode choice could be studied experimentally. Furthermore, following from Roth and Kostova (2003), who argued quite elegantly that the MNE is an underutilised domain in which to study many new and interesting management phenomena, we believe that the domain of the management decision-maker is an underutilised domain in which to discover, validate and test existing and new international business theories and phenomena. However, unlike Roth and Kostova, we believe this potentially requires new theorising and new methodologies. In this regard, we are undoubtedly in line with Sullivan's (1998) call for a broader vision and more 'comprehensiveness, connectedness and complexity' (and we would add creativity) in international business research.

Second, it is clear that context matters considerably to decision-making, and this is no different and perhaps even more important in international business decisions. Indeed, the more research that is conducted, the more it is realised that simple economic rationalist *vs* behavioural internationalisation distinctions fall by the wayside. However, experimental approaches are sufficiently robust to allow for consideration of different contexts. In our

254   *Peter J. Buckley et al.*

experiments we examined simple issues of political stability and investment level. However, many experiments now utilise what are known as information acceleration approaches (e.g., Urban *et al.*, 1997) that directly vary the context in which complex decisions are made. Although these have to date been used only in the case of technology products, there is no reason to believe that they cannot be used in more direct business contexts. Hence experiments can be conducted that look at the effects of coups, currency devaluations, and other socio-political scenarios.

Third, because experimental approaches can be designed to address issues of scale inequivalence, they are in general going to be more effective at studying cross-cultural phenomena than simple surveys. Indeed, any survey can be rewritten in a manner that mimics our BW approach, implying that one can theoretically remove all scale inequivalence from a survey instrument. For example, it would not be difficult to redevelop the Hofstede dimensions or any similar scale using this approach, theoretically generating purer measures than Likert-scale approaches alone (Hofstede, 2001).

Fourth, and most controversially, international business research has generally been limited in the approaches it has brought to bear on the phenomena under investigation. We have, to date, borrowed heavily from economics, sociology, social psychology and management but little from cognitive psychology or the rising field of experimental economics. This has limited the field in many ways, but most clearly in the study of the role of the individual decision-maker (manager, regulator, consumer). Our application shows that there are opportunities to utilise new and different methods to add insight to 'old' questions.

Acknowledgements

The authors would like to thank the three anonymous reviewers, the editor of *JIBS*, Arie Lewin, and the co-guest editors, Thomas Hutzschenreuter, Henk Volberda and Torben Pederson, for their comments and helpful suggestions. We would also like to thank participants at the 2004 JIBS Frontiers Conference, the 2005 AIB Conference and the 2006 Berlin ACCS Conference and the various universities where earlier versions of this work were presented. Kristina Simkute and Natia Adamia were instrumental in the data collection effort, and their efforts are gratefully acknowledged.

Appendix A

See Table A1.

Table A1   Recent literature on FDI location decisions

Author(s)	Method	Data and sample	Key variable(s)	Major results
Davidson (1980)	Survey	Foreign operations of 180 US multinationals from inception to 1975. Over 13,000 FDIs (70% of FDI by US MNEs at the time).	Entry frequencies explained by market size, corporate experience, prior presence.	Corporate experience affects location decisions in two ways: (1) firms prefer nations in which they are active to those in which they are not, and (2) firms with extensive experience exhibit less preference for near, similar and familiar markets. Markets that others might perceive as less attractive because of high uncertainty levels are given increased priority as the firms experience rises. *As firms gain experience, the location of foreign activity will increasingly represent an efficient response to global economic opportunities and conditions.*
Woodward and Rolfe (1993)	Panel	187 manufacturing investments of US companies in the Caribbean 1984–1987.	Location of export-oriented US manufacturing FDI determinants.	FDI location positively influenced by: per capita GNP, exchange rate devaluation, length of income tax holidays, size of free trade zones, and manufacturing concentration. Negative effects from wage rate, inflation rate, transport costs and restrictions on profit repatriation.

Continued

Table A1 Continued

Author(s)	Method	Data and sample	Key variable(s)	Major results
Barkema *et al.* (1996)	Panel Compiled	225 foreign entries of 13 Dutch firms.	Longevity of foreign entry.	Cultural distance is a prominent factor in foreign entry whenever this involves another firm.
Burgel and Murray (2000)	Survey	398 *export* decisions of 246 UK technology-based start-ups.	*Entry* mode of export.	Direct export or selling through intermediaries. Choice is a trade-off between resources available and support requirements of the customer.
Mudambi (1998)	Survey	MNEs in West Midlands of UK: 70 valid responses.	Length of duration of operation at a particular location (after accounting for portfolio risk).	Firms with a longer tenure of operations are significantly more likely to invest in any given period.
Brush *et al.* (1999)	Survey	209 responses from plant managers of US MNEs.	Contrast of manufacturing strategy: integrated or independent plant versus international strategy: locate home or abroad.	Manufacturing choices benefit from international issues more than vice versa. Managers rank determinants associated with manufacturing strategy higher than those associated with IB.
Kuemmerle (1999)	Survey	FDI in R&D 32 large MNEs in 4 countries.	Motives for FDI in R&D.	FDI in R&D both to augment knowledge basis and to exploit it. R&D investment at home in multiple sites before venturing abroad.
Chandprapalert (2000)	Survey	100 US companies with FDI in Thailand.	Determinants of FDI in Thailand.	Firm size, market potential, investment risk key variables.
Henisz (2000)	Panel	Sample of 3389 overseas manufacturing operations of 461 firms in 112 countries.	Political and contractual hazards in host countries.	Joint ventures preferred where hazards highest. Host institutions matter.

Continued

Table A1 Continued

Author(s)	Method	Data and sample	Key variable(s)	Major results
Chung (2001)	Panel	US manufacturing 1987–1991 at 4-digit SIC level.	Technology transfer, competition, productivity.	FDI may both transfer and access technology in the host country.
Feinberg and Keane (2001)	Panel	US individual foreign affiliate level data from the US Bureau of Economic Analysis.	Tariff reductions (US–Canada).	Canadian affiliate sales to US negatively correlated with Canadian tariffs, but US parent sales to Canadian affiliates have little association with Canadian tariffs. Substantial heterogeneity to tariff changes within narrowly defined manufacturing industries.
Chung and Alcacer (2002)	Panel	1784 FDI transactions entering US 1987–1993 from OECD countries. International Trade Administration reports	Knowledge seeking (access technical capabilities in host).	Location within USA – greater market size, lower factor costs, better access to surrounding station *and* knowledge seeking limited to firms in research-intensive industries – manufacturing firms may seek this not only through laboratories but also through manufacturing facilities.
Mitra and Golder (2002)	Panel Compiled	19 MNEs with 722 entry operations.	Operations in similar markets on subsequent entry decisions.	Cultural distance from domestic market is *not* a significant factor. 'Near-market knowledge' and economic knowledge have significant effects.
Zhou *et al.* (2002)	Panel	2933 Japanese investments in 27 provinces of China.	Influence of special economic zones and opening coastal cities on inward FDI.	SEZs and OCCs have exerted periodic influences on location of Japanese FDI in China.

Continued

258   *Peter J. Buckley et al.*

Table A1   Continued

Author(s)	Method	Data and sample	Key variable(s)	Major results
MacCarthy and Attirawong (2003)	Survey Delphi	Academics, consultants and government officials.	Motivations of firms to invest in manufacturing.	Top five influences: costs, infrastructure, labour characteristics, government and political factors and economic factors.
Henisz and Macher (2004)	Panel	44 semiconductor firms making 69 foreign investments in new manufacturing plants. (1994–2002).	Explanation of foreign investment in new manufacturing facility.	Firms with more advanced technological capabilities more likely to invest in countries with greater technological sophistication but not in politically hazardous countries. Less advanced technology firms more willing to trade off political hazards and technological sophistication. Firms also trade off other own versus other firms' experience as sources of critical knowledge on foreign investment environments.
Pedersen and Petersen (2004)	Survey	485 firms: 201 Denmark; 168 Sweden; 116 New Zealand.	Familiarity with local markets development over time.	'Shock effect' of foreign market entry develops overtime (lowest level of market familiarity 8 years after entry), supports 'psychic distance paradox' that adjacent countries provide high levels of shock.
Ambos (2005)	Survey	HQ R&D managers. Establishment of laboratory sites of 49 German MNEs survey.	Internationalisation motives of R&D.	Resource seeking rather than market seeking is predominant. Mission affects location.

Continued

Table A1 Continued

Author(s)	Method	Data and sample	Key variable(s)	Major results
Enright (2005)	Survey	1100 MNE managers in Asia Pacific.	Regional strategies and establishment of regional management centres.	Regional structures are important in Asia-Pacific.
Nachum and Zaheer (2005)	Panel	US inward and outward FDI 1990–1998 from the US Bureau of Economic Analysis.	Cost of distance differentially affects investment motivation across industries.	Industries with different levels of information intensity are driven by different investment motivations: knowledge and efficiency seeking at high levels; market seeking at low levels.
Cheng (2006)	Survey	466 Taiwanese investors in China.	FDI mode choice (includes brownfield ventures).	FDI mode choice influenced by resources owned by investor, resources specific to host firm and risk. Incorporates brownfield investment as a choice.

Appendix B

A simple model for BW judgements

Best–worst scaling (hereafter, BWS) is a fairly general scaling method that extends Thurstone's (1927) random utility theory-based model for paired comparison judgements to judgements of the largest/smallest, best/worst, most/least, etc., items, objects or cues in a set of three or more multiple items. Specifically, BWS assumes that there is some underlying subjective dimension, such as 'degree of importance', 'degree of concern', 'degree of interest', etc., and the researcher wishes to measure the location or position of some set of objects, items, etc., on that underlying dimension. We refer to the process of assigning numerical values that reflect the positions of the items on the underlying scale as 'scaling'. The BWS approach is based on the view that such measurement arises from theory, and that theory and associated measurement are inseparable. Thus the scale values derived from BWS are those that best satisfy a theory about the way in which individuals make BW judgements.

260 *Peter J. Buckley et al.*

To begin, we assume that there is a master set of K items to be scaled, $\{I_1, I_2, ..., I_K\}$. The items are to be placed in C subsets, $\{i_1\}, \{i_2\}, ..., \{i_C\}$, and some sample of individuals of interest is asked to identify, respectively, the best and worst items in each of the subsets (or in each of some subset of the subsets). If there are K total items to be scaled, then the total number of subsets that could be presented to the individuals is 2^K, minus all subsets that are null (1), singles (K) or pairs ($K(K-1)/2$), which grows exponentially with K. Thus one needs some systematic way to pick the subsets that makes sense and, as noted by Finn and Louviere (1992), constructing the sets from a 2^K orthogonal main effects design or some higher-resolution design in the 2^K family of designs is a good approach, and one that coincides nicely with previous design theory for the case of only 'best' choices (Louviere and Woodworth, 1983). There are other ways to construct appropriate sets, such as balanced incomplete block designs (BIBDs), and we illustrate the use of such designs in this paper.

Thus BWS assumes that there is some underlying dimension of interest, and one wants to assign scale values to the K items on that single underlying dimension. It assumes that the choice of a pair of items from any subset is an indicator of that pair of items in that subset that are the farthest apart on the underlying dimension. That is, in any subset, say the cth subset, if there are P items, then there are $P(P-1)/2$ pairs of items that could be chosen best and worst, and an additional $P(P-1)/2$ pairs of items that could be chosen worst and best. Thus, for any given subset presented to an individual like the cth subset, the individual implicitly chooses from $2 \times P-1(P-1)/2$ pairs. Let us denote the quantity $2 \times P(P-1)/2$ as M, and for ease of exposition (and because it reflects the case in this paper) we assume that P is constant in every subset (e.g., balanced incomplete block designs lead to subsets of fixed size, M). Now, we can formulate this choice process as a random utility model as follows:

$$D_{ij} = \delta_{ij} + \varepsilon_{ij} \tag{B.1}$$

where D_{ij} is the latent or unobservable true difference in items i and j on the underlying dimension; δ_{ij} is an observable component of the latent difference that can be observed and measured; and ε_{ij} is an error component associated with each ij pair.

Because of the presence of the ε_{ij} component, the choice process of any individual is stochastic when viewed by the researcher, because we cannot know what the individual is thinking. Thus we can formulate the model as a probability model to capture the probability that the individual chooses the ij pair in each subset:

$$P(ij \mid C) = P\left[\left(\delta_{ij} + \varepsilon_{ij}\right) > \text{all other } M - 1\left(\delta_{ij} + \varepsilon_{ij}\right) \text{pairs}\right] \tag{B.2}$$

where all terms are as previously defined. This problem can be solved by making assumptions about the distribution and properties of ε_{ij}. A simple assumption that leads to a tractable model form that has seen many applications in the social and business sciences is that ε_{ij} is distributed independently and identically as an extreme value type 1 random variate (equivalently, as a Gumbel, Weibull or double exponential). It is well known that these assumptions lead to the multinomial logit (MNL) model, which is the form of analysis used in this paper. That is, the choice probabilities can be expressed as

$$P(ij \mid C) = \frac{\exp(\delta_{ij})}{\sum_{ik} \exp(\delta_{ik})} \quad \text{for all } M \, \delta_{ik} \text{ in } i_C \tag{B.3}$$

We can express δ_{ij} as a difference in two scale values, say s_i and s_j, or $s_i{-}s_j$. Hence we can rewrite the model as

$$P(ij \mid C) = \frac{\exp(s_i - s_j)}{\sum_{ik} \exp(s_i - s_k)} \quad \text{for all } M \, \{s_i, s_k\} \text{ pairs in } i_C \tag{B.4}$$

Thus the scale values of interest are s_i and s_j, which reflect the location of each item on the underlying scale.

If the subsets are constructed in such a way that the joint probability of choosing items i and j across all subsets can be estimated independently of the marginal probabilities (e.g., by using a 2^k orthogonal main effects design + its foldover, or a BIBD + its complement), then the model implied by Eq. (B.4) can be estimated directly from the observed counts associated with each best–worst, worst–best pair summed over all subsets in the experiment. If the experiment does not allow one to calculate the total choices of all implied best–worst, worst–best pairs across the subsets (e.g., if one uses only the orthogonal main effects design or only the BIBD, as discussed by Finn and Louviere, 1992), one can approximate the desired scale values by taking differences in the marginal best and worst counts for each item. That is, the simple score $\delta(b_i w_i) =$ total best i – total worst i approximates the unknown difference $s_i{-}s_j$ for each individual or subset of individuals who exhibit the same underlying ordering of the items (apart from judgemental errors). We state this without proof, but note that one can easily see that this must be true by constructing an experiment that permits the joint choice probabilities for all the implied pairs to be estimated independently of the marginal probabilities, assuming an ordering of the items in that experiment, and simulating choices of the items with the highest and lowest rank in the order in each subset. It is easy to show that the total choices over all subsets for the implied pairs will be consistent with MNL, and once one obtains the MNL estimates, one can easily see that the best$_i$–worst$_i$ differences are perfectly proportional to the MNL estimates.

References

Aharoni, Y. (1966) *The Foreign Investment Decision Process*, Harvard University Press: Boston, MA.

Ambos, B. (2005) 'Foreign direct investment in industrial research and development: a study of German MNCs', *Research Policy* **34**(4): 395–410.

Aldrich, J. and Nelson, F. (1984) *Linear Probability, Logit and Probit Models*, Sage Publications: Newbury Park, CA.

Andersen, O. (1993) 'On the internationalization process of firms: a critical analysis', *Journal of International Business Studies* **24**(2): 209–231.

Barkema, H.G., Bell, J.H.J. and Pennings, J.M. (1996) 'Foreign entry, cultural barriers and learning', *Strategic Management Journal* **17**(2): 151–166.

Baumgartner, H. and Steenkamp, J. (2001) 'Response styles in marketing research: a cross-national investigation', *Journal of Marketing Research* **38**(2): 143–156.

Brush, T.H., Maritan, C.A. and Karnani, A. (1999) 'The plant location decision in multinational manufacturing firms: an empirical analysis of international business and manufacturing strategy perspectives', *Production and Operations Management* **8**(2): 109–132.

Buckley, P. (2004) 'The role of China in the global strategy of multinational enterprises', *Journal of Chinese Economic and Business Studies* **2**(1): 1–25.

Buckley, P. and Casson, M. (1976) *The Future of the Multinational Enterprise*, Macmillan: London.

Buckley, P., Newbould, G. and Thurwell, J. (1988) *Foreign Direct Investment by Smaller UK Firms*, Macmillan: London.

Burgel, O. and Murray, G.C. (2000) 'The international market entry choices of start-up companies in high-technology industries', *Journal of International Marketing* **8**(2): 33–62.

Camerer, C. and Lovallo, D. (1999) 'Overconfidence and excess entry: an experimental approach', *American Economic Review* **89**(1): 306–318.

Chandprapalert, A. (2000) 'The determinants of US direct investment in Thailand: a survey of managerial perceptions', *Multinational Business Review* **8**(2): 82–88.

Chen, C., Lee, S. and Stevenson, H. (1995) 'Response styles and cross-cultural comparisons of rating scales among East Asian and North American students', *Psychological Science* **6**(3): 170–175.

Cheng, J. and Hitt, M. (eds.) (2004) 'Part I: Research Forum', in *Managing Multinationals in a Knowledge Economy*, Advances in International Management, Vol. **15**, Elsevier: Oxford, pp: 1–72.

Cheng, Y.-M. (2006) 'Determinants of FDI mode choice: acquisition, brownfield and greenfield entry in foreign markets', *Canadian Journal of Administrative Sciences* **23**(3): 202–220.

Chetty, S. and Blankenburg Holm, D. (2000) 'Internationalization of small to medium-sized manufacturing firms: a network approach', *International Business Review* **9**(8): 77–93.

Chung, W. (2001) 'Identifying technology transfer in foreign direct investment: influence of industry conditions and investing firm motives', *Journal of International Business Studies* **32**(2): 211–229.

Chung, W. and Alcacer, J. (2002) 'Knowledge seeking and location choice of foreign direct investment in the United States', *Management Science* **48**(12): 1534–1554.

Cohen, S. (2003) *Maximum Difference Scaling: Improved Measures of Importance and Preference for Segmentation*, Sawtooth Software: Sequim, WA.

Cohen, S. and Neira, L. (2003) 'Measuring preference for product benefits across countries: overcoming scale usage bias with maximum difference scaling', Esomar 2003 Latin American Conference Proceedings, Amsterdam: ESOMAR, pp: 1–22.

Davidson, W.H. (1980) 'The location of foreign direct investment activity: country characteristics and experience effects', *Journal of International Business Studies* **11**(1): 9–22.

Devinney, T., Midgley, D. and Venaik, S. (2003) 'Managerial Beliefs, Market Contestability and Dominant Strategic Orientation in the Eclectic Paradigm', in R. Narula and J. Cantwell (eds.) *International Business and the Eclectic Paradigm*, Routledge: London, pp: 152–173.

Dunning, J. (1981) *International Production and the Multinational Enterprise*, Allen & Unwin: London.

Enright, M.J. (2005) 'Regional management centres in the Asia-Pacific', *Management International Review* **45**(1): 59–82.

Eriksson, K., Johanson, J., Majkgård, A. and Sharma, D. (1997) 'Experiential knowledge and cost in the internationalization process', *Journal of International Business Studies* **28**(2): 337–360.

Feinberg, S.E. and Keane, M.P. (2001) 'US-Canada trade liberalization and MNC production location', *The Review of Economics and Statistics* **83**(1): 118–132.

Fina, E. and Rugman, A.M. (1996) 'A test of internalization theory and internationalization theory: the Upjohn company', *Management International Review* **36**(3): 199–213.

Finn, A. and Louviere, J. (1992) 'Determining the appropriate response to evidence of public concern: the case of food safety', *Journal of Public Policy and Marketing* **11**(2): 12–25.

Henisz, W.J. (2000) 'The institutional environment for multinational investment', *Journal of Law, Economics and Organization* **16**(2): 334–364.

Henisz, W.J. and Macher, J.T. (2004) 'Firm and country level trade-offs and contingencies in the evaluation of foreign investment: the semiconductor industry, 1994–2002', *Organization Science* **15**(5): 537–554.

Hensher, D., Louviere, J. and Swait, J. (2000) *Stated Preference Modelling: Theory, Methods and Applications*, Cambridge University Press: Cambridge, UK.

Hofstede, G. (2001) *Culture's Consequences: Comparing Values, Behaviors, Institutions, and Organizations Across Nations*, 2nd edn, Sage: Thousand Oaks, CA.

Hymer, S. (1960) *The International Operations of National Firms: A Study of Direct Foreign Investment*, MIT Press: Cambridge, MA (Published 1976).

Johanson, J. and Vahlne, J. - E. (1977) 'The internationalization process of the firm: a model of knowledge development and increasing foreign market commitments', *Journal of International Business Studies* **8**(1): 12–24.

Johanson, J. and Vahlne, J.-E. (1990) 'The mechanism of internationalization', *International Marketing Review* **7**(4): 12–24.

Kuemmerle, W. (1999) 'Foreign direct investment in industrial research in the pharmaceutical and electronics industries: results from a survey of multinational firms', *Research Policy* **28**(2–3): 179–193.

Louviere, J. and Woodworth, G. (1983) 'Design and analysis of simulated consumer choice or allocation experiments: an approach based on aggregate data', *Journal of Marketing Research* **20**(4): 350–367.

Luo, Y. and Peng, M. (1999) 'Learning to compete in a transition economy: experience, environment, and performance', *Journal of International Business Studies* **30**(2): 269–295.

MacCarthy, B.L. and Atthirawong, W. (2003) 'Factors affecting location decisions in international operations: a Delphi study', *International Journal of Operations and Production Management* 23(7): 794–818.

McIntosh, E. and Louviere, J. (2003) 'Separating weight and scale value: an exploration of best-attribute scaling in health economics', Paper presented at Odense University, Denmark.

Manrai, A. and Sinha, P. (1989) 'Elimination-by-cutoffs', *Marketing Science* 8(2): 133–152.

Marley, A. and Louviere, J. (2005) 'Some probabilistic models of best, and best–worst choices', *Journal of Mathematical Psychology* 49(6): 464–480.

McFadden, D. (2001) 'Economic choices', *American Economic Review* 91(3): 351–378.

Melin, L. (1992) 'Internationalization as a strategy process', *Strategic Management Journal* 13(99): 99–118.

Mitra, D. and Golder, P.N. (2002) 'Whose culture matters? Near-market knowledge and its impact on foreign market entry timing', *Journal of Marketing Research* 39(3): 350–365.

Mucchielli, J.-L. and Mayer, T. (eds.) (2004) *Multinational Firms' Location and the New Economic Geography*, Edward Elgar: Cheltenham.

Mudambi, R. (1998) 'The role of duration in multinational investment strategies', *Journal of International Business Studies* 29(2): 239–262.

Mudambi, R. and Navarra, P. (2003) 'Political tradition, political risk and foreign direct investment in Italy', *Management International Review* 43(3): 247–265.

Nachum, L. and Zaheer, S. (2005) 'The persistence of distance? The impact of technology on MNE motivations for foreign investment', *Strategic Management Journal* 26(8): 747–767.

Paulhus, D. (1991) 'Measurement and Control of Response Bias', in J.P. Robinson, P.R. Shaver and L.S. Wrightsman (eds.) *Measures of Personality and Social Psychological Attitudes*, Vol. 1, Academic Press: New York, pp: 17–59.

Pedersen, T. and Petersen, B. (2004) 'Learning about foreign markets: are entrant firms exposed to a "shock effect"?' *Journal of International Marketing* 12(1): 103–123.

Roth, K. and Kostova, T. (2003) 'The use of the multinational corporation as a research context', *Journal of Management* 29(6): 883–902.

Sarkar, M., Cavusgil, S.T. and Aulakh, P. (1999) 'International expansion of telecommunication carriers: the influence of market structure, network characteristics, and entry imperfections', *Journal of International Business Studies* 30(2): 361–381.

Steenkamp, J. and Baumgartner, H. (1998) 'Assessing measurement invariance in cross–national consumer research', *Journal of Consumer Research* 25(1): 78–90.

Steenkamp, J. and Ter Hofstede, F. (2002) 'International market segmentation: issues and perspectives', *International Journal of Research in Marketing* 19(3): 185–213.

Sullivan, D. (1998) 'Cognitive tendencies in international business research: implications of a "narrow vision" ', *Journal of International Business Studies* 29(4): 837–862.

Sullivan, D. and Bauerschmidt, A. (1990) 'Incremental internationalization: a test of Johanson and Vahlne's thesis', *Management International Review* 30(1): 19–30.

Thurstone, L. (1927) 'A law of comparative judgment', *Psychological Review* 34: 273–286.

Train, K. (2003) *Discrete Choice Methods with Simulation*, Cambridge University Press: Cambridge, UK.

Tversky, A. (1972) 'Elimination by aspects: a theory of choice', *Psychological Review* 79(4): 281–299.

Urban, G., Hauser, J., Qualls, W., Weinburg, B., Bohlmann, J. and Chicos, R. (1997) 'Information acceleration: validation and lessons from the field', *Journal of Marketing Research* **34**(1): 143–153.

Wei, Y., Liu, B. and Liu, X. (2005) 'Entry modes of foreign direct investment in China: a multinomial logit approach', *Journal of Business Research* **58**(11): 1495–1505.

Woodward, D.P. and Rolfe, R.J. (1993) 'The location of export-oriented foreign direct investment in the Caribbean basin', *Journal of International Business Studies* **24**(1): 121–144.

Zhou, C., Delios, A. and Yang, J.Y. (2002) 'Locational determinants of Japanese foreign direct investment in China', *Asia Pacific Journal of Management* **19**(1): 63–86.

12
The Role of Headquarters in the Global Factory

1. Introduction

The notion of the global factory was introduced in Buckley (2004) and developed in Buckley and Ghauri (2004). The key idea is that multinational enterprises (MNEs) are becoming much more like differentiated networks. They choose location and ownership policies so as to maximise profits but this does not necessarily involve internalising their activities. Indeed, they have set a trend by outsourcing or offshoring their activities. Outsourcing involves utilising 'buy' rather than make in the Coasean 'externalise or internalise' decision (Coase 1937). Offshoring involves both the externalisation option together with the 'make abroad' location decision (Buckley and Casson 1976). MNEs have developed the ability to 'fine slice' their activities on an even more precise calculus and are increasingly able to alter location and internalisation decisions for activities which were previously locationally bound by being tied to other activities and which could only be controlled by internal management fiat.

This chapter examines the role of headquarters in the global factory. Section 2 explains the meaning of the global factory and the constructs that constitute it. The crucial strategic decisions are ownership and location and these are discussed as issues in the coordination of activities in the global factory in Section 3. Section 4 discusses the power of the global factory and Section 5 analyses flexibility – a key attribute of the global factory. Strategic change over time is analysed in an example in Section 6. Section 7 examines headquarters as a spatial market-making decision taker. Section 8 concludes by summarising the role of headquarters.

William Egelhoff (2007) identified four tasks where 'hierarchical structures with a corporate HQ are superior to network structures in providing the necessary coordination' (p. 2).

1. Accountability to shareholders.
2. Designing and implementing tight synchronisation among subsidiaries.

3. Identifying and implementing economies of scale and scope.
4. Identifying and addressing issues involving significant innovation.

It is my contention that the global factory structure achieves these objectives by combining central control with network systems.

2. Elements of the global factory

The opening up of the global factory has provided new opportunities for new locations to enter international business. Emerging countries such as India and China are subcontracting production and service activities from the brand-owning MNEs. The use of the market by MNEs enables new firms to compete for business against the internalised activities of the MNE. This not only subjects every internalised activity to 'the market test', it also results in a differentiated network (as presented in Figure 12.1) which we term 'the global factory'.

Components of the global factory

The global supply chain is divided into three parts. The original equipment manufacturers (OEMs) control the brand and undertake design, engineering and R&D for the product (although these may be outsourced; see Figure 12.1). They are customers for contract manufacturers (CMs) who perform manufacturing (and perhaps logistics) services for OEMs. In this so-called modular production network, CMs need to possess capabilities such as mix, product

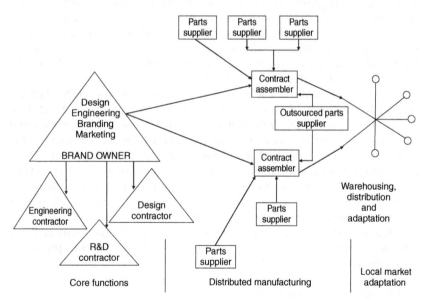

Figure 12.1 The global factory

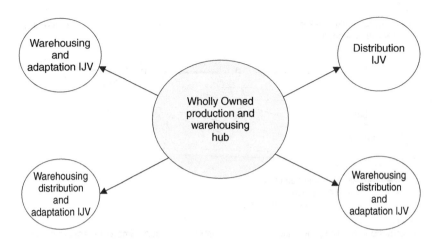

Figure 12.2 'Hub and spoke' strategies: an example

and new product flexibilities while at the same time carrying out manufacturing activities at low costs with mass production processes. Flexibility is necessary to fulfil consumers' product differentiation needs (local requirements) and low cost for global efficiency imperatives (see Wilson and Guzman 2005). The third part of the chain is warehousing, distribution and adaptation carried out on a 'hub and spoke' principle in order to achieve local market adaptation through a mix of ownership and location policies. As Figure 12.2 shows, ownership strategies are used to involve local firms with marketing skills and local market intelligence in international joint ventures (IJVs) whilst location strategies are used to differentiate the wholly owned 'hub' (centrally located) from the jointly owned 'spokes'.

The information structure of the global factory

Casson (1997) highlights the importance of information costs in the structure of business organisation. He sees the brand owner as essentially a specialist in the search and specification functions (for customers and products respectively). 'The brand owner, by intermediating between the producer and the retailer, coordinates the entire distribution channel linking the worker to the final customer' (Casson 1997, p. 159). This intermediation by the brand owner/market maker is intermediation of information, not production. The information structure of the global factory is shown schematically in Figure 12.3. This shows that the brand owner is the information hub of the global factory. The brand owner organises the market process itself. The organisation of production is conventionally within firms but the organisation of the whole production and trade sequence is intermediated by the market making global factory. In many industries, particularly service industries such as banking and insurance, the essence of competitiveness is the processing of information.

The Role of Headquarters in the Global Factory 269

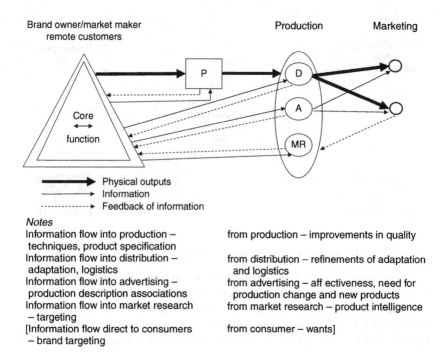

Figure 12.3 The information structure of the global factory

Interfaces

Key interfaces in the global factory are between the core activities of the brand owner (△) and the distributed manufacturing and service centres (□), and between the latter and the distribution functions of warehousing, distribution and adaptation (○).

Secondary interfaces are between outsourced core functions (including possibly design, engineering and R&D), between first tier assemblers and parts suppliers and the interface with logistics, transport and distribution contractors.

The marketing and branding functions are invisible in the diagram but they are the crucial glue together with control mechanisms that holds the global factory system together.

Interface competence

There are a number of key skills on the external integration process. These can be listed as follows and they are outlined in Figure 12.4

1. Identification The task of finding an external source to fulfil an organisational need.

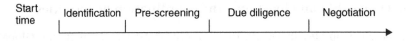

Figure 12.4 Phases of the external integration process

2. Pre-screening Preliminary investigation of supplier and facility to meet the need.
3. Due diligence Full-scale investigation involving all aspects of supply.
4. Negotiation4 Pursuit of final agreement with the supplier.

Governance costs are likely to be large in dispersed networks and as Benito and Tomassen (2007) point out they may be underestimated and even overlooked in the rush to reduce costs.

Stocks and flows in the global factory

Strategies used in the global factory require a rethink of our notion of the stock of investment. Focal firms have decreased their ownership of productive capacity and increased their stocks of intangible assets. Thus production is outsourced to firms who specialise in maintaining and expanding production capacity. Focal firms invest in intangible assets such as:

1. brand equity;
2. management skills;
3. innovative capacity (R&D labs, design facilities);
4. distribution networks.

These assets are embedded within the firm. They are difficult to disentangle and disengage from the firm as a whole and they have an element of non-substitutability. It is difficult for other firms to copy or to replicate these intangible assets. Particular types of intangible assets that have achieved salience and value in the global factory are brand image, embedded supply chain management, design and new product development facilities, distribution networks with local adaptation capabilities and the ability of the management team to achieve customer lock-in.

Casson (2006) notes that networks typically involve stocks and flows. The stock components comprise network *infrastructure*, whilst the flow constitutes *traffic*. The stock components of the global factory are assets, such as production units, R&D laboratories, design centres and offices. The flows generated are of goods, semi-finished products and knowledge. Physical networks are important in sustaining trade whilst social networks are important in sustaining technology transfer, marketing and managerial communications (Casson 2006, pp. 6–7). The global factory is an amalgam of a physical and social network, uniquely fitted to combine support for trade, technology and knowledge flows.

3. Ownership and location – the coordination of activities

Although Complex in Detail, the Key Analytical Decisions in the Global Factory Are Very Simple – Control and Location. the Manager of the Global Factory Has to Ask Two Very Straightforward Questions of Each Activity in the Global Network. Where Should This Activity Be Located? How Should This Activity Be Controlled?

The first question of the optimum location for each activity is of course complicated by managing the interrelationships between activities. The relocation of one piece of the global network will have profound effects on many others, as the links in Figure 12.1 illustrate, but the principles of least cost location are paramount.

The second question concerns the means of control. Should the activity be managed by the market via a contract and price relationship or should it be internalised and controlled by management? There are of course important mixed methods such as joint ventures which have elements of market relationships and elements of management fiat.

It is of course essential to realise that these decisions are taken in a volatile, risky and dynamic situation, that the decision-making process is information-intensive and the environment and competitive pressures are constantly changing. These decisions have to be revisited on a continuing basis. However the principles should never be overwhelmed by detail. As this book goes on to show, the need for flexibility, for judicious collection and use of information and for a knowledge management strategy are complements to the key decisions of location and control.

4. The power of the global factory

What then gives the global factory its power? Why should the global factory be able to hire the contract manufactures, sales outlets, design houses, logistics companies, advertising consultants and research laboratories rather than the other way round? How can global factories exercise this power without ownership?

The answer, as always, is a combination of factors. These factors are entrepreneurship, control and selection of information (Figure 12.3), finance and innovation (Figure 12.5). They are combined within the enabling institutions of the home country which nurture and foster the exercise of entrepreneurship and encourage risk taking and experimentation. This may be also considered as 'second order entrepreneurship' which allows units within the global factor to exercise their abilities to take entrepreneurial decisions.

One such crucial factor is the role of finance. Access to capital markets is a crucial advantage for (the headquarters of) global factories (Buckley and Casson 1976, p. 33). Internal capital markets become less important as access to (more perfect) external markets improves. Thus global factories

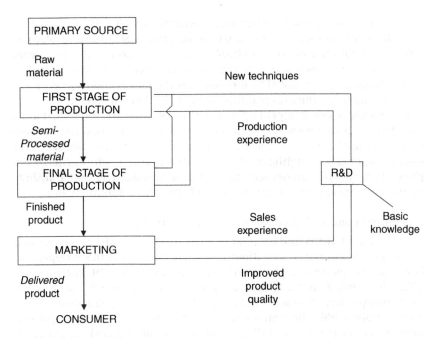

Figure 12.5 Information flows in the multinational firm

headquartered in home countries with more perfect finance markets can generate much better leverage than can, say, a Chinese manufacturer (Aulakh and Mudambi 2005; Buckley et al. 2007). The external capital market also impinges more strongly on global factories in advanced countries. Until recently the share register of major companies rarely moved. Now (2008) hedge funds, private equity investors and Sovereign Wealth Funds move in and out of ownership of leading companies on a regular basis. This discipline of the market impels better operational management.

The power of the global factory arises not only from its brand and its control of information and finance but also to its decision-making skill (entrepreneurship) and its dynamic which derives from R&D in all senses – technical, marketing and process innovation. To be long lasting, brands have to receive constant re-investment. Quality has to be maintained and improved. Advertising promotion and distribution need to be coordinated so as to reinforce the brand. This process of entrepreneurial direction is referred to by Hymer (1968) as 'encephalisation' – putting a brain on the firm.

The brain may be a distributed one – not all its functions will be located at headquarters. The case of 'Frecknall' below shows the transfer over time of brain functions from headquarters to foreign units. There remains, however, a sense of overall control of the global factory centrally even if not all its activities are owned – 'You don't have to own a facility to control it'.

The Role of Headquarters in the Global Factory 273

Control without ownership has been identified as a key feature of modern capitalism by amongst others Nolan et al. (2002), Strange and Newton (2006) and Yamin and Ghauri (2007). Nolan et al. point out the control exercised by 'systems integrators' over first-tier suppliers and the extent to which being part of a global factory involves the sacrifice of independence in, for example, production planning, design, R&D and delivery.

There is also severe competition within the global factory. Individual units are often set up to compete for contracts or for resources. Pedersen and Petersen (2007) identify 'centres of excellence' as winners and pure sales subsidiaries as losers. Hatani (2009) highlights the extreme competition within the Toyota global factory. This strengthens the hand of headquarters and transmits market pressure as well as a 'tournament' philosophy to subsidiary units.

Dynamics: contracting costs and entrepreneurship

Why do entrepreneurs hire assets rather than asset owners hire entrepreneurs? The answer lies in non-contractibility. The key function of the entrepreneur is to exercise judgement in the face of uncertainty (Knight 1921; Casson 1982). Incomplete contracts have a positive effect on the exercise of entrepreneurship – they allow sequential adaptation to changing circumstances in an uncertain world. The firm is thus the agency by which the entrepreneur (whose services are the most difficult to measure or evaluate) combines his assets (judgement) with physical assets. The firm enables previously segmented areas of judgement and skills to be blended together and thus individual entrepreneurship becomes collective organisation. Individuals with entrepreneurial judgement can thus coalesce within the organisation and combine their skills. Because of the non-contractibility (or rather the extremely high costs of contracting) of these skills, this coalition becomes embedded in the firm, thus giving a transactions cost rationale for 'competencies' residing for a finite period of time in certain companies. 'Sticky capabilities' thus emerge.

Transaction costs are, of course, not the whole story (again) but they are an indispensable part of the whole story.

5. Flexibility

Flexible boundaries of the firm: networks and joint ventures

The typical US MNE of the 'golden age' was a vertically, as well as horizontally, integrated firm (Buckley and Casson 1998). In consequence, each division of the firm was locked into linkages with other divisions of the same firm. As Asian competition intensified, there was growing recognition of the costs of integration of this kind.

Commitment to a particular source of supply or demand is relatively low-cost in a high-growth scenario, since it is unlikely that any investment will need to be reversed. It is much more costly in a low-growth scenario, where

274   *Peter J. Buckley*

production may need to be switched to a cheaper source of supply, or sales diverted away from a depressed market. The desire for flexibility therefore discourages vertical integration – whether it is backward integration into production, or forward integration into distribution. It is better to subcontract production and to franchise sales instead. The subcontracting of production is similar in principle to the 'putting out' arrangement described above, but differs in the sense that that subcontractor is now a firm rather than just a single worker.

Disintegration was also encouraged by a low-trust atmosphere that developed in many firms. Fear of internal monopoly became rife, as explained above. Production managers faced with falling demand wished that they did not have to sell all their output through a single sales manager. Sales managers resented the fact that they had to obtain all their supplies from the same small set of plants. Each manager doubted the competence of the others, and ascribed loss of corporate competitiveness to selfishness and inefficiency elsewhere in the firm. Divisions aspired to be spun off so that they could deal with other business units instead. On the other hand, managers were wary of the risks that would be involved if they severed their links with other divisions altogether.

A natural way to restore confidence is to allow each division to deal with external business units, as well as internal ones. In terms of internalisation theory, internal markets become 'open' rather than 'closed' (Casson 1990, p. 37). This provides divisional managers with an opportunity to bypass weak or incompetent sections of the company. It also provides a competitive discipline on internal transfer prices, preventing their manipulation for internal political ends, and bringing them more into line with external prices. There are other advantages too. Opening up internal markets severs the link between the capacities operated at adjacent stages of production. The resulting opportunity to supply other firms facilitates the exploitation of scale economies because it permits the capacity of any individual plant to exceed internal demand. Conversely, it encourages the firm to buy in supplies from other firms that have installed capacity in excess of their own needs.

The alignment of internal prices with external prices increases the objectivity of profit measurement at the divisional level. This allows divisional managers to be rewarded by profit-related pay based on divisional profit rather than firm-wide profit. Management may even buy out part of the company. Alternatively, the firm may restructure by buying in a part of an independent firm. The net effect is the same in both cases. The firm becomes the hub of a network of inter-locking joint ventures (Buckley and Casson 1988, 1996). Each joint venture partner is responsible for the day-to-day-management of the venture. The headquarters of the firm co-ordinates the links between the ventures. Internal trade is diverted away from the weaker ventures towards the stronger ones, thereby providing price and

The Role of Headquarters in the Global Factory   275

profit signals to which the weaker partners need to respond. Unlike a pure external market situation, the partners are able to draw upon expertise at headquarters, which can in turn tap into expertise in other parts of the group.

A network does not have to be built around a single firm, of course. A network may consist of a group of independent firms instead. Sometimes these firms are neighbours, as in the regional industrial clusters described by Best (1990), Porter (1990) and Rugman et al. (1995). Industrial districts such as 'Toyota city', have been hailed as an Asian innovation in flexible management, although the practice has been common in Europe for centuries (Marshall 1919). As tariffs and transport costs have fallen, networks have become more international. This is demonstrated by the dramatic growth in intermediate product trade under long-term contracts. For example, an international trading company may operate a network of independent suppliers in different countries, substituting different sources of supply in response to both short-term exchange rate movements and long-term shifts in comparative advantages.

Flexibility is also needed in R&D. A firm cannot afford to become over-committed to the refinement of any one technology in case innovation elsewhere should render the entire technology obsolete. As technology has diffused in the post-war period, the range of countries with the competence to innovate has significantly increased. The pace of innovation has consequently risen, and the threat of rapid obsolescence is therefore higher as a result. The natural response for firms is to diversify their research portfolios. But the costs of maintaining a range of R&D projects are prohibitive, given the enormous fixed costs involved. The costs of basic R&D have escalated because of the increased range of specialist skills involved, while the costs of applied R&D have risen because of the need to develop global products which meet increasing stringent consumer protection laws. Joint ventures are an appropriate solution once again. By establishing a network of joint ventures covering alternative technological trajectories, the firm can spread its costs whilst retaining a measure of proprietary control over new technologies.

The advantage of joint ventures is further reinforced by technological convergence, for example, the integration of computer, telecommunications and photography. This favours the creation of networks of joint ventures based on complementary technologies, rather than on the substitute technologies described above (Cantwell 1995).

Joint ventures are important because they afford a number of real options (Trigeorgis 1996) which can be taken up or dropped depending upon how the project turns out. The early phase of a joint venture provides important information which could not be obtained through investigation before the venture began. It affords an opportunity which is not available to those who have not taken any stake. It therefore provides greater flexibility than does either outright ownership or an alternative involving no equity stake.

276 Peter J. Buckley

Flexibility and internal organisation

In this very volatile environment the level of uncertainty is likely to be high. Uncertainty can be reduced, however, by collecting information. Flexibility was defined above in terms of the ability to respond to change. The costs of response tend to be smaller when the period of adjustment is long. One way of 'buying time' to adjust is to forecast change. While no one can foresee the future perfectly, information on the present and the recent past may well improve forecasts by diagnosing underlying long-term trends. Collecting, storing and analysing information therefore enhances flexibility because, by improving forecasts, it reduces the costs of change.

Another way of buying time is to recognise change as early as possible. In this respect, continuous monitoring of the business environment is better than intermittent monitoring because the potential lag before a change is recognised is eliminated. Continuous monitoring is more expensive than intermittent monitoring, though, because more management time is tied up.

Investments in better forecasts and speedier recognition highlight the trade-off between information cost and adjustment cost. This trade-off is particularly crucial when volatility is high. High volatility implies that more information should be collected to improve flexibility, which in turn implies that more managers need to be employed. This is reverse of the usual recommendation to downsize management in order to reduce overhead costs.

To improve flexibility whilst downsizing management, the trade-off between information cost and adjustment cost must be improved. There are two main ways of doing this. The first is to reduce the cost of information processing through new information technology (IT). The second is to reduce adjustment costs by building flexibility into plant and equipment, both through its design and its location. A combination of IT investment and flexible plant can reconcile greater flexibility with lower management overheads in the manner to which many MNEs aspire.

The information required for strategic decision-making is likely to be distributed throughout the organisation. It is no longer reasonable to assume that all the key information can be handled by a single chief executive, or even by the entire headquarters management team. It is difficult to know in advance where the really crucial information is likely to be found. Every manager therefore needs to have the competence to process information effectively. Managers need to be able to recognise the significance of strategic information that they acquire by chance, and to have the power of access to senior executives in order to pass it on. In other words, ordinary managers need to become internal entrepreneurs.

Few entrepreneurs have sufficient information to make a good decision without consulting other people, however. In a traditional hierarchical firm, the right to consult is the prerogative of top management. If ordinary

The Role of Headquarters in the Global Factory 277

managers are to have the power to initiate consultation, and act upon the results, then channels of communication with the firm need to be increased. Horizontal communication, as well as vertical communication, must be easy, so that lower level managers can readily consult with their peers.

A natural response is to 'flatten' the organisation and encourage managers to 'network' with each other. This improves the trade-off between local responsiveness and strategic cohesion (Bartlett and Ghoshal 1987; Hedlund 1993). Unfortunately, though, there has been some confusion over whether flatter organisations remain hierarchies at all. However, as Casson (1994) shows, the efficient managerial processing of information normally requires a hierarchical structure of some kind. They key point is that the more diverse are the sources of volatility, the greater are the advantages of widespread consultation. The less predictable is the principal source of volatility on any given occasion, the greater is the incentive to allow consultation to be initiated anywhere in the organisation. In practice this means that an increased demand for flexibility is best accommodated by flattening the organisation, whilst maintaining basic elements of hierarchy.

The costs of flexibility: engineering trust

If flexibility were costless, then all organisations could build in unlimited flexibility at the outset. In practice, the greater is flexibility, the higher transactions costs become. For example, the flexibility to switch between different sources of supply and demand (described above) means that relations with customers and suppliers become more transitory than before. Cheating becomes more likely, because the prospect of further transactions between the same two parties is more remote. Direct appeals to the other party's loyalty lose their credibility too.

The same effect occurs when internal entrepreneurship is promoted. Internal entrepreneurs are given more discretion to act upon information that they have collected for themselves, and this increases their opportunity to cheat.

Giving managers a direct stake in the business activities they help to build is one solution. The firm incubates new business units in which particular managers, or groups of managers, have equity stakes. An alternative approach is to appeal to the integrity of managers instead. They are treated well, and in return are expected to be open and honest about what they know.

It is one of the ironies of the 1970s that at a time when personal integrity needed to be high in order to support more flexible organisation, it had been allowed to fall very low. The decline of traditional religion, the intellectual cynicism created by two world wars, and the rise of mass consumerism have all been blamed for this state of affairs. Communitarians argue correctly that moral values like integrity are most efficiently engineered at the societal level, through family, church and school. But when these institutions fail, they must be engineered to support specific economic relations instead

278　*Peter J. Buckley*

(Fukuyama 1996). Firms must engineer these values amongst their employees at their own expense instead (Kotter 1996). Greater flexibility therefore implies greater costs in promoting a corporate culture that reinforces moral values.

Interaction of firm flexibility and location flexibility

The desire for flexibility may encourage the firm to produce the same product in several locations so that it can switch production between them as circumstances change. Multiple internal sourcing may therefore be pursued even where some sacrifice of economies of scale is involved. DeMeza and Van der Ploeg (1987), Capel (1992) and Kogut and Kulatilaka (1994) have all emphasised that firms can switch production between alternative locations in response to real exchange rate shocks. The basic idea is that MNEs can combine their superior information on foreign cost conditions with their ability, as owners of plants, to plan rather than negotiate output levels, to switch production more quickly than can independent firms.

This strategy requires, however, that the firm should commit in advance to the locations where it believes it will wish to produce. If it is difficult to foresee where the best locations may lie, then flexibility may be enhanced by sub-contracting arrangements instead. Speed of response may be slower, but the range of potential locations is greater. Rangan's (1998) study of production flexibility of manufacturing firms in response to exchange rate changes found that firms did operate flexibly. However the extent of this flexibility was relatively modest and was constrained by past strategies and actions. We can read into this that inertia, possibly from headquarters, was a factor limiting flexibility. Where short-run volatility predominates, multi-national integration may well enhance the value of the firm (Allen and Pantzalis, 1996), but long-run volatility may favour the disintegration of the firm instead.

If a firm is seeking flexibility at one stage of production, then it will experience a derived demand for flexibility at adjacent stages of production. This flexibility is conferred by ease of transport to and from all the locations employed at the adjacent stage. Some locations are inherently more flexible in this respect than others, because they are at nodal points on transport networks. They therefore have low transport costs to a wide range of different destinations. For example, if production is dispersed, then warehousing of the finished product should be at an appropriate hub. Greater demand for flexibility concentrates demand for warehousing at such hubs – for example, Singapore (for South-East Asia) and Lille (for North-West Europe).

An MNE that is seeking flexibility in its sources of supply will wish to choose a location where government policy is *laissez faire*, so that there are no import restrictions. It may be seeing flexibility in the range of products if products too. This encourages it to seek out locations with a versatile labour force. Flexibility is also conferred by supplier networks that operate

The Role of Headquarters in the Global Factory 279

with a high degree of trust. Local production needs to be embedded in an impartial legal system and in strong social networks to ensure that trust is high. An 'invisible infrastructure' of mediating institutions, or equivalently, a large endowment of 'social capital', is therefore a feature of the locations that MNEs committed to flexibility are likely to seek out. Flexibility is not just an element of corporate strategy, but a component of location advantage too. Such location advantage depends crucially on the nature of local institutions and local culture (see Khanna and Palepu 1999 and Ricart et al. 2004).

Flexibility and firm-specific competitive advantage

Flexibility also has implications for firm-specific competitive advantage. Skill in recruiting imaginative employees becomes a competitive advantage when internal entrepreneurship is required. Charismatic leadership by the chief executive may promote loyalty and integrity amongst key staff. A tradition of informal and consultative management will facilitate the sharing of information amongst employees. One way of expressing this is in terms of the 'capabilities' or 'competencies' of managers, or the human resources controlled by the firm (Richardson 1960; Loasby 1999). In a volatile environment where flexibility is crucial, the key resources of the firm are those that promote internal entrepreneurship. The firm consists not of a single autocratic entrepreneur, but a team of entrepreneurs (Wu 1989) co-ordinated by a leader who promotes high-trust communication between them.

It is worth noting that the need for flexibility does not necessarily support the idea of a 'learning organisation'. To be more exact, flexibility has important implications for what people in a learning organisation actually need to learn. According to Nelson and Winter (1982) learning supports the refinement of existing routines. This is misleading. It suggests that the firm operates in a basically stable environment, and merely learns how to do even better what it already does very well. In a volatile environment, however, much of what has been 'learned' from past experience quickly obsolesces. The truly durable knowledge that needs to be learned in a volatile environment consists of techniques for handling volatility. These techniques include forgetting transitory information about past conditions which are unlikely to recur. But while 'unlearning' or 'forgetting' is important, it is often difficult to do. The difficulty of 'unlearning' helps to explain why so many 'downsizing' and 'de-layering' exercises have identified middle-aged middle managers as targets for redundancy or early retirement. Such people are believed to find it too hard to forget. The knowledge they acquired as junior managers was very relevant during the 'golden age', but has since become obsolete. Some managers have proved sufficiently flexible to be retained, but others have not. Those who were too inflexible to benefit from retaining have been required to leave because their knowledge had become a liability instead of an asset in the more volatile situation of today.

6. An example of strategic change in the global factory: 'frecknall'

This example concerns the transfer of commercial expertise to new affiliates in emerging markets (Buckley and Carter 2002). The company, which we will refer to as Frecknall, is a US-owned research-based ethical pharmaceutical manufacturer. During the 1980s and 1990s, the company established new subsidiaries in developing markets throughout the world. By the late 1990s, it had established a four-stage process, which was in use in Eastern Europe and in Africa. The developments in these territories were administered through the UK/Europe subsidiary rather than directly from the US parent. The discussion here will examine both the knowledge transfer to the new subsidiaries and the organisation of this process from the US parent and the UK/European regional HQ.

Frecknall conceives the stages of establishing a new subsidiary in terms of a sequence of four 'affiliate business models' (Figure 12.6). The transfer of expertise takes place over an extended period, and each phase represents an increase in the degree and scope of local control and responsibility. These become possible as the number of individuals with appropriate expertise becomes larger over time, as the depth of knowledge grows and as local operations become more established and aligned both with local conditions and market requirements and with the strategic direction established by the corporation.

In the earliest stage, the subsidiary is directed and monitored in a directive hierarchical relationship by specialists in the regional headquarters. By the final stage, the subsidiary is integrated into Frecknall's matrix form of organisation in which geographical reporting is combined with reporting in the product-based 'global business units'. The organisational and knowledge-process characteristics of each stage can be briefly summarised as follows.

Dependence

In the first stage that a local company is established, these activities are limited to the sales and distribution of Frecknall products. Management of this business is the responsibility of an experienced Frecknall manager, who is therefore almost always an expatriate from the US or Europe. The subsidiary manager reports to the unit in regional headquarters, which is responsible for developing markets within its designated region. This unit is responsible for the marketing strategy for all products handled by the 'dependent' subsidiary and is accountable for its profit. Registration of medicines for sale in the new market is carried out by staff at the regional headquarters

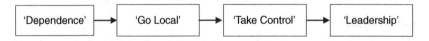

Figure 12.6 Frecknall's sequential affiliate business models

The Role of Headquarters in the Global Factory 281

with the subsidiary manager and staff in the developing markets unit acting as mediators with the regulatory authority and healthcare providers in the target country. The subsidiary manager recruits sales personnel and sets up a distribution network typically by contracting with an established local business. He or she, and the staff recruited for sales, are the main channel through which the developing market unit in HQ acquires knowledge of local market conditions and requirements.

At this stage, the principal requirements for knowledge transfer into the target country are product knowledge, selling experience and good distribution practice concerning the control of medicines. This knowledge is provided through training courses, provided both locally by division staff visiting the subsidiary and centrally by subsidiary staff visiting regional headquarters and where appropriate through monitoring visit audits by staff from regional headquarters.

Go local

This stage is structurally and operationally similar to the previous one, and characterised by the appointment of *local* managers to carry the day-to-day responsibility of the business rather than expatriate managers. Marketing decisions continue to be the responsibility of the development market unit in regional headquarters, which is also still the profit centre for the operation. During this phase, it is also possible that local managers may take over the direct responsibility for product registration and medical liaison with the country authorities and health providers. The individuals who take these senior positions in the developing market has usually benefited from 'switch programme' training, in which they are relocated to an established Frecknall subsidiary for a period to gain operating experience and improve their understanding of and 'alignment' with Frecknall custom and practice. An important mechanism for raising local awareness of Frecknall's corporate perspectives and aims is linking the subsidiary into the company intranet. This provides ready access to technical information, information about market developments and perspectives on corporate priorities and strategy. It not only provides information but also enhances the degree to which local managers identify with the corporation and not simply their own subsidiary, for example, through receiving regular statements directly from the chairman. At this stage, there continues to be close supervision from staff at regional headquarters, who are likely to visit the subsidiary frequently. Headquarters staff must still approve many aspects of local activity. For example, they may wish to ensure that low price decisions are not inconsistent with global pricing policy across the corporation.

Take control

This is the stage in which the subsidiary becomes a profit centre and local management take over formal responsibility for product registration,

282　*Peter J. Buckley*

marketing and sales. Operationally, there continue to be 'dotted line' links to functional managers for each activity in the regional headquarters. Headquarters staff continue to pay regular visits to audit both financial and medicinal good practice. They will also review major contracts.

Coherence with corporate aims is further developed through the subsidiary's participation in the corporate planning process. Two annual meetings consider three-year strategic business plans and one-year operating plans. These meetings bring together subsidiary and corporate managers from several levels of organisation. The forum promotes alignment by the subsidiary with the corporation practice and permits dialogue and exchange of understanding in both directions. The subsidiary continues to be accountable to the regional headquarters for its activities and control of the subsidiary is centralised in unitary form through functional managers reporting to the subsidiary CEO.

Leadership

The final stage brings about a significant structural change. The organisation switches from a functional basis in which the CEO provides central control of the subsidiary to a more decentralised product-based organisation. Product strategies are determined by specialists who now communicate directly with product-based global business units in the US parent. The subsidiary managers continue to oversee sales and distribution and may now be permitted to establish local manufacturing if this is the most cost-effective means to supply the local market. This form of organisation, with a network of communication channels between product and functional specialisations globally and operational managers locally, is the normal structure adopted by Frecknall for operating in mature country markets.

The stages outlined briefly here indicate several ways in which the company overcomes knowledge combination barriers of the kind discussed earlier. For example, the responsibility for new market development is given to a specialist group. This group is located in Europe, a regional headquarters where there is plenty of mature experience, but from where travel to and communication with the new market is easier than it would be for the US parent. The development from 'dependence' to 'go local' to 'take control' illustrates the gradual transfer of expertise into the subsidiary – 'unsticking' the expertise. While the expertise is located mainly in the regional headquarters, profit responsibility lies there, but it is transferred as the knowledge is progressively transferred. In the final mature form or organisation, corporate expertise and practices are sufficiently diffused within the subsidiary that it is possible to decentralise the combination of local and global knowledge from its focus in the subsidiary CEO and the development unit of the regional HQ to separate product managers and global business units. This sequence of changes is indicated in Figure 12.6. In terms of the literature on the strategy-active subsidiary, we can see a temporal sequence of

The Role of Headquarters in the Global Factory 283

transferring to the subsidiary the rightsand abilities to set its own strategic parameters. In examining issues of the spatial location of decision making, we should not neglect temporal factors. Examining the subsidiary in its 'leadership' phase gives a very different picture than that of 'dependence'. Analysts who have identified the strategy-active subsidiary may be focusing on a particular phase in the development of global knowledge management practices as they evolve over time.

A complementary study is that of Delany (2000) who examines the strategic development of subsidiaries of MNEs in Ireland. He produces an eight-stage composite development model of subsidiaries but, it should be emphasised, this is not within a single firm and the cases are compiled into a linear model that is not followed throughout by a single firm. Delany further suggests that the headquarters may be hostile to initiatives taken by subsidiaries or at best 'compliant' with them. In Delany's model, the headquarters management is relatively passive and accepts (or hinders) initiatives at subsidiary level. This is not the case with Frecknall where subsidiary initiatives are encouraged and indeed anticipated (planned for) by headquarters.

Views of entrepreneurial activity in subsidiaries differ greatly in the literature. Studies such as Delany's are often conducted solely at the level of the subsidiary. When interviewed, subsidiary managers are likely to attribute wide decision-making powers and initiatives to themselves and for this reason it is good practice to conduct dyadic interviews at both parent and subsidiary. Much of the real entrepreneurship is conducted at headquarters where judgement is exercised as to when and where to allow subsidiary autonomy and over what areas of decision-making subsidiary autonomy is best fostered (Casson 1982).

7. Headquarters as a spatial market-making decision taker

Fragmentation of the production chain can be accompanied by spatial dissaggregation if

(a) there are technological discontinuities between different stages,
(b) the stages are characterised by different factor intensities, and
(c) the costs of coordination and transport are sufficiently low to make the process economic (Deardorff 2001).

Each of these elements has a technical, a managerial and a political dimension. Strategies of 'fine-slicing' the production chain have combined with technological change, notably the development of the internet and other communications technologies to allow control at a distance (and without ownership) to become more feasible even for elements of the chain requiring fine control. The opening up of China (and now India) creates access to cheap, well disciplined labour and the development of logistics practice

284 *Peter J. Buckley*

reduces costs. Products with standard manufacturing interfaces and services with standard processes are ideal for outsourcing. A lack of interaction of the offshored facility with other functions enables a clean interface to be created and a 'fine-slicing' cut to be made. Products which should not be outsourced include those where protection of intellectual property is crucial, those with extreme logistics requirements, with high technology content or performance requirements, and those where consumers are highly sensitive to the location of production (Boston Consulting Group 2004). Issues of corporate responsibility, compliance and adherence to quality standards (especially in view of the 'lead paint in toys' 2007 issue in China) should be added to this list.

Casson (1999, pp. 84–5) describes the personal computing (PC) industry as an example of the activities of market-making firms. It can be seen as an early example of the operation of the global factory.

> Some of the most successful firms buy in almost all their key components, and do little more themselves than assemble and warehouse the product. In a few cases they merely badge an almost fully assembled product and configure it for its destination by adding pre-loaded software and operating manuals in the appropriate language. An important competitive advantage of the well-established firms lies in the brand, which assures the customers of component quality and after-sales service. But the relative ease of entry shows that brands alone are not enough. Effective management of the distribution channel is the really crucial factor. Distribution of PCs is an information-intensive activity. Tele-sales departments handle large volumes of credit card sales, which are converted promptly into requisitions of particular specifications of product. Inventories have to be kept low, not only because of high interest charges but also because of the continual risk of technological obsolescence. These firms are simply an unusually pure form of the market-making intermediator. The fact that they outsource all their major technological requirements indicates that technology is not the key to their success. Their success resides in the fact that they recognise the logistical imperatives of mass distribution and possess organisational procedures that are well adapted to the information processing needs of the distribution channel.

8. Conclusion: the role of headquarters in the global factory

It is something of an irony that the spatial distribution strategies – ownership and location – make the role of headquarters *more* important in global factories than in conventional vertically and horizontally integrated firms. The authority and choice of headquarters has expanded. The development of 'fine-slicing' means that the determination of ownership and control of each specialised sliver of activity expands headquarters' area of choice. Evidence of the increased power of headquarters might be the level of salaries there compared to elsewhere (even in other units in the home country). Remuneration in headquarters is also likely to increase over time relative to other locations. The control of information in global factories is crucial and the mechanisms determining strategy are more subtle. The doctrine that 'you don't have to own an activity to control it' requires new skills of headquarters functions in global factories. There are important dynamics in this process as headquarters learn how to manage spatially dispersed and organisationally diffuse units within the global factory. This is not a one-way process. Units within the global factory also learn how to manage headquarters (Buckley et al. 2002). The management style that new configurations require is vastly different from conventional 'command and control' methods and the full implications of this are yet to be explored. Headquarters as a 'controlling intelligence' or orchestrator of activities emerge as the best metaphors for their role in the global factory.

In emphasising extra degrees of autonomy given to subsidiaries and other units within the global factory, we should not forget the big picture. The key issue is competition to be the marketing and distribution platform of the big products of the future. That is the key question for headquarters. Other units must operate within this framework set by headquarters; while they may well have crucial areas of decision making and discretion given to them, it is within this overall paradigm that they operate.

References

Allen, L. and C. Pantzalis (1996), 'Valuation of the operating flexibility of multinational corporations', *Journal of International Business Studies*, **27** (4), 633–53.
Aulakh P.S. and R. Mudambi (2005), 'Financial resource flows in multinational enterprises: the role of external capital markets', *Management International Review*, **45**.
Bartlett, C.A. and S. Ghoshal (1987), 'Managing across borders: new strategic requirements', *Sloan Management Review*, **Summer**, 6–17.
Benito, G.R.G. and S. Tomassen (2007), 'The headquarters–subsidiary relationship: an exploration of the costs of governance in multinational companies', Headquarters role in the contemporary MNC, Workshop, Uppsala University, 14–15 September.
Best, M.H. (1990), *The New Competition: Institutions of Industrial Restructuring*, Oxford: Polity Press
Birkinshaw, J., H. Bresman and L. Hakanson (2000), 'Managing the post acquisition integration process: how the human integration and task integration processes interact to foster value creation', *Journal of Management Studies*, **37** (3), 369–87.
Boston Consulting Group (2004), *Capturing Global Advantage*, Boston, MA: Boston Consulting Group.
Buckley, P.J. (2004a), 'The role of China in the global strategy of multinational enterprises', *Journal of Chinese Economic and Business Studies*, **2** (1), 1–25.
Buckley, P.J and M. Carter (2002), 'Process and structure in knowledge management practices of British and US multinational enterprises', *Journal of International Management*, **8** (1), 29–48.

286   *Peter J. Buckley*

Buckley, P.J. and M. Casson (1976), *The Future of the Multinational Enterprise*, London: Macmillan.

Buckley, P.J. and M. Casson (1988), 'A theory of cooperation in international business', in F. Contractor and P. Lorange (eds), *Cooperative Strategies in International Business*, Lexington, MA: Lexington Books.

Buckley, P.J. and M. Casson (1996), 'An economic model of international joint ventures', *Journal of International Business Studies*, **27** (5), 849–76.

Buckley, P.J and M. Casson (1998), 'Models of the multinational enterprise', *Journal of International Business Studies*, **29** (1), 21–44.

Buckley, P.J. and P.N. Ghauri (2004), 'Globalisation, economic geography and the strategy of multinational enterprises', *Journal of International Business Studies*, **35** (2), 81–98.

Buckley, P.J., J. Clegg, A. Cross, P. Zheng, H. Voss and X. Liu (2007), 'The determinants of Chinese outward foreign direct investment', *Journal of International Business Studies*, **38** (4), 499–518.

Buckley, P.J., K.W. Glaister and R. Husan (2002), 'International joint ventures: partnering skills and cross-cultural issues', *Long Range Planning*, **35**, 113–34.

Cantwell, J. (ed.) (1995), *Multinational Enterprises and Innovatory Activities: Towards a New Evolutionary Approach*, Chur: Harwood Academic Publishers.

Capel, J. (1992), 'How to service a foreign market under uncertainty: a real option approach', *European Journal of Political Economy*, **8**, 455–75.

Casson, M. (1982), *The Entrepreneur: An Economic theory*, Oxford: Martin Robinson.

Casson, M. (1990), *Enterprise and Competitiveness*, Oxford: Clarendon Press.

Casson, M. (1994), 'Why are firms hierarchical?', *International Journal of the Economics of Business*, **1** (1), 3–40.

Casson, M. (1997), *Information and Organisation: A New Perspective on the Theory of the Firm*, Oxford: Clarendon Press.

Casson, M. (1999), 'The organisation and evolution of the multinational enterprise', *Management International Review*, **39** (1), 77–121.

Casson, M. (2006), 'Networks: A New Paradigm in International Business History?', UK Academy of International Business Conference, Manchester, April 2006.

Coase, R.H. (1937), 'The nature of the firm', *Economica* (n.s.), **4**, 386–405.

Deardorff, A. (2001), 'Fragmentation across cones', in S. Ardnt and H. Kierzkowski (eds), *Fragmentation: New Production Patterns in the World Economy*, Oxford: Oxford University Press.

Delany, E. (2000), 'Strategic development of the multinational subsidiary through subsidiary initiative-taking', *Long Range Planning*, **33** (2), 220–44.

DeMeza, D. and F. Van Der Ploeg (1987), 'Production flexibility as a motive for multinationality', *Journal of Industrial Economics*, **35** (3), 343–51.

Egelhoff, W.G. (2007), 'Evaluating the role of parent headquarters in a contemporary MNC', Headquarters role in the contemporary MNC, Workshop, Uppsala University, 14–15 September.

Fukuyama, F. (1996), *Trust – The Social Virtues and the Creation of Prosperity*, Harmondsworth: Penguin.

Hatani, F. (2008), 'Power use for network learning: the case of Toyota corporate strategies in the New Asia', International Workshop, Hochschule, Bremen, 1–2 February.

Hatani, F. (2009), 'Pre-clusterization in emerging markets: the Toyota group's entry process in China', *Asia Pacific Business Review*, **15** (3), 369–87.

Hedlund, G. (1993), 'Assumptions of hierarchy and heterarchy: an application to the multinational corporation', in S. Ghoshal and E. Westney (eds), *Organization Theory and the Multinational Corporation*, London: Macmillan.

The Role of Headquarters in the Global Factory 287

Hymer, S. (1968), 'La grande corporation multinationale: analyse de certaines raisons qui poussent àl'intégration internationale des affaires', *Revue Economique*, **14** (b), 949–73.

Khanna, T. and K. Palepu (1999), 'Policy shocks, market intermediaries, and corporate strategy: evidence from Chile and India', *Journal of Economics and Management Strategy*, **8** (2), 271–310.

Knight, F. (1921), *Risk, Uncertainty and Profit*, (edited George J. Stigler), Chicago: University of Chicago Press (1971).

Kogut, B. and N. Kulatilaka (1994), 'Operating flexibility, global manufacturing and the option value of a multinational network', *Management Science*, **40** (1), 123–39.

Kotter, J. (1996), *Leading Change*, Cambridge, MA: Harvard Business School Press.

Loasby, B.J. (1999), *Knowledge Institutions and Evolution in Economics*, London, UK: Routledge.

Marshall, A. (1919), *Industry and Trade*, London: Macmillan.

Nelson, R.R. and S. Winter (1982), *An Evolutionary Theory of Economic Change*, Cambridge, MA: Harvard University Press.

Nolan, P., D. Sutherland and J. Zhang (2002), 'The challenge of the global business revolution', *Contributions to Political Economy*, **21**, 91–110.

Pedersen, T. and B. Petersen (2007), 'Headquarters role in the MNC globalisation process', Headquarters role in the contemporary MNE, Workshop, Uppsala University, 14–15 September.

Porter, M.E. (1990), *The Competitive Advantage of Nations*, London: Macmillan.

Rangan, S. (1998), 'Do multinationals operate flexibly? Theory and evidence', *Journal of International Business Studies*, **29**, 217–37.

Ricart, J.E., M.J. Enright, P. Ghemawat, S.L. Hart and T. Khanna (2004), 'New frontiers in international strategy', *Journal of International Business Studies*, **35** (3), 175–200.

Richardson, G.B. (1960), *Information and Investment*, Oxford: Oxford University Press.

Rugman, A.M., J.R. D' Cruz and A. Verbeke (1995), 'Internalisation and de-internalisation: will business networks replace multinationals?', in G. Boyd (ed.), *Competitive and Cooperative Macromanagement: The Challenge of Structural Interdependence*, Aldershot, UK and Brookfield, US: Edward Elgar.

Strange, R. and J. Newton (2006), 'Stephen Hymer and the externalisation of production', *International Business Review*, **15** (2), 180–93.

Trigeorgis, L. (1996), *Real Options*, Cambridge, MA: MIT Press.

Wilson, J. and G.A.C. Guzman (2005), 'Organisational knowledge transfer in modular production networks: the case of Brazil', Paper presented to AIB World conference, Quebec, July.

Wu, S.-Y. (1989), *Production, Entrepreneurship and Profits*, Oxford: Basil Blackwell.

Yamin, M. and P.N. Ghauri (2007), 'The business network theory of MNCs: what do headquarters do?', Headquarters role in the contemporary MNC, Workshop, Uppsala University, 14–15 September.

Part III
Cultural Distance and Asian Business

13
Close Neighbours and Distant Friends – Perceptions of Cultural Distance

Co-authored with Malcolm Chapman,
Hanna Gajewska-De Mattos, and Jeremy Clegg

1. Introduction

The core argument in this paper is that simple and static measures of cultural distance, which have been predominant in the international business literature, are not sufficient to fully understand this complex concept. We propose that 'objective' measures of culture need to be supplemented by careful and contextual studies of national cultural meetings at the managerial level. We argue that cultural distance should be considered as relative and not absolute, and that it should be treated on a bilateral basis. This approach contributes to a better understanding of when cultural distance, as measured by objective measures, matters. We argue that this can be achieved by using relative measures as supplementary to objective ones, which have been predominant in cross-cultural management literature.

In this paper, we are discussing two pairs of countries – Germany/Poland and the UK/Poland. We first give a brief account of the historical interactions between these two pairs of countries. We do this because we believe that these historical interactions, as they were experienced and as they are remembered, have major consequences for present day interactions at the level of individual managerial experience. Thus the experiences of nations can be reflected in the attitudes of individuals. From a structural anthropological perspective it is to be expected that dualities with resonance at the national scale, will also appear at other levels. We are taking a holistic view here, which is characteristic of both economics and social anthropology.

Therefore, cultural distance is both constructed and interpreted by the perceivers, and it is influenced by experience and history. Our analysis of Hofstede's work below suggests that we can supplement his indices by a more nuanced and contextualised analysis. This leads us to develop a more sensitive approach to cultural distance as suggested by Leung, Bhagat, Buchan, Erez and Gibson (2005).

292 *Malcolm Chapman et al.*

In this article we examine the German/Polish, and the UK/Polish contrast at the level of individual manager. We examine how managers living within these contrasts create and interpret frameworks within which they can understand one another, and also explain their failures of understanding. We argue that differences which are understood, are differences which can be managed.

2. The concept of cultural distance

In this paper we discuss the structuring and interpretation of cultural distance by managers from Germany, the UK and Poland. We are particularly interested in two contrasts – the German/Polish contrast, and the UK/Polish contrast.

Shenkar (2001, p. 519) noted 'few constructs have gained broader acceptance in the international business literature than cultural distance'. The 'cultural distance' to which Shenkar refers is primarily inspired by the work of Geert Hofstede, which is widely cited in literature relating to international business and international management (see Hofstede, 1980, 1991, 2001). Hofstede's 'dimensions of culture' have provided researchers with a way of conceptualising culture, and also with index scores for countries which have been treated as indicators of 'cultural distance'. Hofstede's dimensions are already (as Hofstede himself admits) simplications of complex issues. Hofstede's work has itself been further 'simplified', however, in a much-cited article by Kogut and Singh (1988), where the four dimensions are boiled down into one index of 'cultural distance'. Hofstede's dimensions, and the Kogut and Singh *reductio* of these, have been very widely used by the business academic community (see Bakacsi, Sándor, András & Viktor, 2002; Kirkman, Lowe & Gibson, 2006); we must generally conclude that this community has decided that the advantages of simplification in this area are worth the price. The point is arguable, and has been argued (see Hofstede, 2002; Hoppe, 2004; McSweeney, 2002a, 2002b; Smith, 2002; Triandis, 2004; Williamson, 2002).

Recent summaries of the field have acknowledged the major influence of Hofstede (Leung et al., 2005, p. 357), and the way in which the 'cultural distance' concept has come to dominate research (Tihanyi, Griffith & Russell, 2005, p. 270). Leung et al. (2005, p. 374) say:

> Much of previous research on culture and IB has adopted what we view as a simplistic view of culture, which tends to examine the static influence of a few cultural elements in isolation from other cultural elements and contextual variables. For instance, much of the research inspired by the Hofstede dimensions falls into this category, which, in our view, was instrumental in kickstarting the field.

Having acknowledged previous work, and the seminal contribution of Hofstede, they go on to call for 'multi-layer, multi-facet, contextual, and systems views of culture' (Leung et al., 2005). They also say that

A major challenge for the field is to develop mid-range, dynamic frameworks of culture that are sensitive to their nuances in different contexts (p. 374).

We agree with this summary of the state of play, and hope in this paper to provide some of the complexity, context and mid-range dynamism that are called for.

Shenkar (2001, pp. 520–521) notes that the concept of cultural distance has been used to research such things as the launch/sequence of foreign investment, entry mode and affiliate performance. He then discusses some conceptual reservations about this work, under a number of headings, among them the 'illusion of symmetry', the 'illusion of linearity', the 'illusion of stability' and the 'illusion of causality'. We fully support Shenkar's argument about these illusions, and argue that our own work amplifies and illustrates his criticisms. This issue will be fully addressed in a discussion section of this paper.

The concepts of 'cultural distance' and of 'psychic distance' have often been used interchangeably. In some early and influential studies of cultural effects on firm behaviour, 'psychic distance' was the preferred formulation (see Johanson & Vahlne, 1977; Johanson & Wiedersheim-Paul, 1975). Sousa and Bradley (2006, p. 63) argue that, while the two concepts are certainly related, they also need to be distinguished. They summarise:

Cultural distance reflects a difference in cultural values among countries that should be assessed at the cultural or country level. Psychic distance is based on the individual's perception and should be assessed at the individual level. (p. 63)

There are a number of important unresolved arguments opening up here, and we do not intend to pursue these at length. A stark contrast is drawn here between 'culture' and the 'individual', and the relationship between 'cultural values' and 'individual perceptions', as if these did not interact and as if they could be separately assessed. These distinctions are among the great dilemmas of social science, ever since Durkheim, and in our own material we see constant mutual interaction of 'values' and 'perceptions', and of 'culture' and the 'individual'. We do, however, warmly agree with the importance that Sousa and Bradley (2006) attach to 'perception'. Our study is ethnographic in character, and 'perceptions' are the main focus (for other ethnographic studies see D'Iribarne, Segal, Chevrier & Globokar, 1998; Salk, 1996–7).

294   *Malcolm Chapman et al.*

We are, therefore, providing an ethnographic account of cultural difference which is, as Leung et al. call for, 'multi-layer, multi-facet and contextual', which provides 'mid-range, dynamic frameworks', and which is 'sensitive to nuance in different contexts' (see Leung et al., 2005, p. 374, cited above). We are providing here material that allows us to see into the complexities of the 'illusions' which Shenkar (2001) invokes – of symmetry, linearity, stability and causality. We propose to add another illusion to his list, that of 'neutrality'. And we make 'perceptions' the focus of our study, within the complex interactions between society and individual, and ideas and action.

3. Close neighbours and distant friends – a contrast of contrasts

When Poland looks to its neighbours, it looks primarily east, to Russia, and west, to Germany. Poland has a long history of understanding itself through contrast to these two countries, these two ethnicities. Poland is Christian and Catholic (like parts of Germany, unlike Orthodox Russia.) Poland was heavily influenced by the reformation, and by the counter-reformation. Poland was part of the European Renaissance and Enlightenment, and shone in the Baroque age. Poland is 'European', not 'Asian'. Poland is 'civilised', not 'uncivilised'. Poland has been shut away from its rightful historical place in Europe, by half a century of Communism. (These, it should be stressed, are major themes of Polishness as commonly expressed by Poles themselves; they are not our assertions). Polish identity is not *only* about not being Russian, not being German. Many of these other themes, however (Orthodox or Catholic, Asian or European, 'Enlightened' or otherwise, civilised or not) are locally most likely to be expressed in a context which involves thinking about Russia and Germany. It is the relationship with Germany which is our prime concern here.

Just as Poland has Germany on its mind, Germany, similarly, has Poland on its mind. Germany's geopolitics has found European expression, in recent centuries, on a scale much more ambitious than that of Poland. It has been the immediate neighbours, however, who have posed the first problems, given the first pause for thought. Again, the problem is a complex one, and Germany is not homogeneous, not to be summed up in a few phrases. Nevertheless, when Germany is thinking about itself, then comparisons to East and to West are paramount; they are paramount in thought, and have of course been paramount in action.

The relationship between Poland and Germany is close, intense and highly charged. It has also been an asymmetric power relationship. Historically, Germany has often occupied a position of political and/or economic dominance over its eastern neighbour. Investment patterns in Europe in the twentieth century have reflected this. Poland, during its brief period of independence between the First and Second world wars, found itself apparently 'invaded' by foreign investment (with Germany as a prominent source) (Landau & Tomaszewski, 1964, 1985; Wellisz, 1938). Foreign capital was generally not an issue during the communist period. After 1989, however, Poland was once again open for business, and once again it was Germany companies leading. German ownership of Polish assets, and potentially of Polish land, raised many sensitivities about invasion, occupation, forced emigration, dating back to the violent redrawing of Central European boundaries in the period immediately after 1945. Our research concerns Polish firms that have been acquired by, or at least brought strongly under the influence of, German and UK firms. There are some Polish firms that have made acquisitions in Germany, but the number is very modest compared with the much larger inward capital flows.

By contrast to the Germans, when the British look around the world for exemplars of what they are not, Poland hardly comes into the frame. The British look to France, to Germany, to the Celtic Fringe, to the USA, to the erstwhile Empire and modern Commonwealth. Poland emerged briefly into the British consciousness during diplomatic attempts to contain the increasingly threatening activities of Nazi Germany. It was the German invasion of Poland that drew the UK into the Second World War. This was a defining conflict for the modern world, and it left its traces in the British collective imagination. When the British think about Poland, the earliest event most people have access to is the Second World War, Britain's alliance with Poland, the participation of Polish fighter pilots in the Royal Air Force during the Battle of Britain in 1940, and some experience of Polish emigres living in the UK.

After the war, the Polish communities in the UK remained and prospered, but Poland itself slipped from the news. The 'Iron Curtain' fell, with Poland behind it. Communism and Capitalism, for the duration of the 'Cold War', trod their separate paths. Poland re-emerged into the western European, and British, consciousness, with the rise of 'Solidarity' in the early 1980s. When confidence in the communist systems collapsed in late 1989, Poland re-emerged as a country aspiring to implement a capitalist economic system. It also emerged as a country re-assuming membership of Europe (in the sense, wealthy, modern, civilised, sharing a history with neighbouring nation-states) and aspiring to and achieving membership of the European Union. This transition from communism to capitalism, for the generations that grew to adulthood during the 'Cold War', was dramatic, striking, unexpected and welcome. The result is that for many people in the UK, the most important thing about Poland is that it was communist, and now is not. So when the UK looks at Poland, it sees distant friends in a post-communist economy. The close and tense relationship, which exists between Germany and Poland, is not there between the UK and Poland. These issues are clearly illustrated by our empirical data, as it will be discussed in more detail later on in this paper.

296　*Malcolm Chapman et al.*

The relationships between the pairs of countries that we are talking about here are manifold – they have literary and theoretical elaborations, but they are also relationships which have been *lived*. Poles and Germans have lived in the same towns and villages. They have named the same landscapes with different names. They have fought one another, driven one another out and called one another names. They have intermarried. The German/Polish national difference has multi-dimensional empirical substance behind it. The perceptions of difference, emerging from our analysis, are not cloudy fragments of thought, but bits of life – observations from street and market place, farmyard and town centre, school and family, factory and office. It is not surprising, then, that the means for expression of a Polish/German difference should be readily available to the executives under study. The Polish/German difference (along with its not-quite-mirror image, the German/ Polish difference), has been thought about, worked upon, argued over, many times expressed – we might even say it has been polished.

The UK/Polish relationship has been lived as well, but through different experiences, and with far less intensity. The UK/Poland contrast has some similarities to the German/Polish contrast, but also some very important differences. Like Germany, the UK has been powerful, wealthy and expansive. It has written its own histories. But it has no experience of long-term contiguity with Poland. In this paper, we will show that this has important implications for how Polish and British managers understand their relationship, and their interactions with one another. In what follows we will first discuss the research method of this study and we will then proceed to the empirical part of the paper.

4. Research method

This study adopts a qualitative, interpretive methodological approach and treats managerial perceptions as a focus of analysis. One of the reasons why this method is appropriate for the current study is the fact that it is exploratory in nature. It aims to identify the Polish perceptions of German managers for which no suitable secondary data exist. Quantitative, questionnaire based research could not be used in this case as the categories of this study are not known. Furthermore, the qualitative, interpretive approach is argued to offer a more certain and precise understanding of the societies under investigation, from the point of view of those who are under study (Iribarne, 1996/97; Miles & Huberman, 1994; Yin, 1994).

The main objective of the study is to discover the thoughts and opinions of German, British and Polish managers involved in cross-border business activities. We did not, in the classic hypothetico-deductive manner, try to determine in advance what questions needed answering. We wanted the managers' views and opinions, expressed in their own terms, and expressing their own priorities. This is in line with the dominant research concern in social anthropology, and has been expressed as a concern to research 'native categories' (see Buckley & Chapman, 1997; Harris, 2000, 2003).

This study was conducted in 12 companies in Germany, the UK and Poland,[1] through 63 face-to-face in depth interviews with managers in these companies. The respondents selected for interview were general managers from the foreign-affiliated Polish companies, and area directors responsible for Eastern Europe in German and British parent companies. The purpose of this selection was to identify respondents with extensive relevant knowledge of the topic, who were to some degree comparable between firms (biographical data collected during the interviews confirmed that all interviews had direct and often substantial personal experience of the relevant countries). All Polish respondents came from affiliate companies and all German and British ones came from the parent companies. Interviews were held initially with a general manager from each of the companies, and then typically with the deputy general manager. Further respondents were identified by the first interviewees, employing a 'snowballing' technique (Marschan, 1996).

The interviews were conducted in an unstructured way as the respondents would allow (Chapman, 2001). An interview guide (see Appendix A) was prepared to provide a framework for the researcher if the interviewees ran out of narrative, and it is available from the authors on request. The guide was there to serve the larger purpose, which was to encourage managers to share their view of the world, and specifically of their immediate business situation. Every interview had the potential to develop in different ways, which the researchers tried to encourage, aiming to impose minimum constraints on potential topics of interest (Iribarne, 1996/97; Miles & Huberman, 1994; Vaara, 2002; Yin, 1994). Some of the classic questions of international business were pursued (motives for market entry, motives for specific market entry mode, problems, organisational and national cultural issues), but the time given to these was determined by the interviewees. Several techniques of constructing questions were applied in the interviews (e.g., 'grand tour', 'proactive', 'contrast' and 'category' questions) (McCracken, 1988). It was anticipated that there might be interesting material concerning national cultural issues, and interviewees were to some extent provoked to discuss these if they felt they were of interest. After this, however, the issues were allowed to surface as and when they would, and given the time and importance which the interviewees wished to accord them.

Chapman, Clegg and Gajewska-De Mattos (2004), Chapman, Gajewska-De Mattos and Antoniou (2004) pointed out that *who* and *what* you are as a qualitative researcher 'matters to what you are readily able to discover and to understand' (p. 292). In the current study, the issue of language and nationality is of relevance in this context.

The role of language in cross-cultural interviewing has been addressed in the literature (e.g., Chapman, Clegg et al., 2004; Chapman, Gajewska-De

298   *Malcolm Chapman et al.*

Mattos et al., 2004; Marschan-Piekkari & Reis, 2004; Zalan & Lewis, 2004). In the current study, the language in which the interviews were conducted varied depending on the country. In Poland all the interviews were carried out in Polish, as it was the first language of both the interviewer and the interviewees. In Germany and the UK the language of communication was English. Not operating in one's mother tongue during an interview could potentially restrict the momentum of the responses of the interviewees (Chapman, Clegg et al., 2004; Chapman, Gajewska-De Mattos et al., 2004). It is worth pointing out, however, that all the German executives were quite fluent English speakers, and expressing themselves in English did not seem to be a difficulty.

The impact of the nationality of the interviewer (i.e., Polish) on the richness of the material coming from the interviews also needs to be addressed here. This is potentially important in the context of a very close and intense relationship between Poland and Germany, in contrast to the more distant relationship between Poland and England. This research was concerned with how the Germans and the British viewed the Poles, and how the Poles viewed the Germans and the British. Speaking about this to Poles, meant the interviewer and interviewee shared a common background, however, speaking about this to Germans, meant speaking to people that had every reason to be highly sensitive about the legitimacy of their opinions. Every effort was made, however, to create an atmosphere of cooperation with the interviewees to encourage them to answer truthfully the questions of the study (e.g., by assuring their confidentiality and anonymity).

The interviews were transcribed, and read and re-read. Written up data were compared across interviews and across the companies, and analysed for common themes, stories and issues. This was achieved by multiple readings of the transcripts. The interviews were then colour coded and a list of the main topics, themes and stories were developed. The texts from the interviews were then sorted according to these themes. The main themes were the issues repeatedly mentioned by the interviewees, discussed by many of them, or pointed out by executives as important. The attention of researchers was also directed to 'important absences', and the reasons behind them. There are specialist software packages available on the market (e.g., QSR Nud*ist), but these do not support data in more than one language, which was the case in the current study. Presented with this difficulty the authors used Microsoft Word features for managing long documents to organise data. The interview transcripts were scrutinised for patterns. The most consistent generator of differences and commonalities between the transcripts, was provided by the nationality of the interviewees. This was not imposed upon the transcripts by analysis (except in as much as the interviewees were chosen by nationality), but rather one which they offered up voluntarily.

There are several considerations, within the present work, which might serve to assure its validity and reliability. Firstly, a clear rationale for using qualitative enquiry has been adopted (Parkhe, 1997), and data collection, analysis and interpretation procedures have been clarified (Brewer, 2001; Brouthers & Bamossy, 1997; Festing, 1997; O'Grady & Lane, 1996; Teigland, Fey & Birkinshaw, 2000; Tsang, 2001), as detailed in the beginning of this section. Secondly, one of the principles of data collection is using multiple sources of evidence in order to achieve triangulation (Yin, 1994); in the current study primary data were complemented by various other sources (e.g., annual reports and leaflets of companies, press cuttings, internet sources, historical sources). A summary is contained in the section 'Close Neighbours and Distant Friends – A contrast of contrasts'. This approach allowed the inclusion of new facts and ideas, and increased the opportunity for checking interpretations and identifying patterns. Thirdly, the narratives were supported with the verbatim responses of the executives under investigation, to support claims being made in the paper and to offer the reader the opportunity of drawing their own conclusions (Beechler & Yang, 1994; Marschan, 1996). Fourthly, the findings were cross-tabulated with the data on the characteristics of the respondents (e.g., age, education, length of experience in the company, international exposure, etc.), types of the companies (e.g., M&As, greenfield or equity JVs), and different industries. This provided some useful insights, and helped to build the internal validity of the study (Eisenhardt, 1989). And finally, the findings of the study were compared with conflicting and similar literature, which as Eisenhardt (1989, p. 533) put it 'builds internal validity, raises theoretical level, and sharpens construct definitions'.

5. Empirical evidence

In this section, we present empirical evidence from research into perceptions of German and Polish managers and British and Polish managers working inside situations of business interaction.

5.1. German Polish and British Polish contrast

The German managers, in discussing why Poles were as they were, did not refer to the legacy of communism, but referred to a much more distant past. The sense of German/Polish difference, as expressed by both the Germans and the Poles, seemed to draw on deep roots, and to have less facility for change than the UK/Polish difference. German interviewees saw the Poles as their familiar Eastern neighbour, unchanged either by communism or subsequent 'superficial' reforms:

> I think people don't change a lot. They have the same feeling, but the time changed completely. (D3_GE)[2]

300 *Malcolm Chapman et al.*

The British respondents, by contrast, sought explanation of their Polish counterparts in the legacy of communism. Here is a British manager on the centralised nature of older Polish organisational structures:

> In our company in Warsaw, where everyone has e-mail, fax, it's very easy to communicate with everyone from the senior management to the shop floor. In the old state owned company there was only one fax in the office of the managing director, and everything had to go through him. We were trying to show that if it works well in 'Company I–Poland' it could also work there [in Poznan]. (I1_UK)

The British, like the Germans, tended to see themselves as embodying a set of virtues, which the Poles might be encouraged to imitate. The British, however, were uniform in interpreting Polish shortcomings as a result of the previous system of central planning. For example:

> But that's the characteristics of all the former COMECON economies, whenever there is much tougher competition they say that's too difficult. (H2_UK)
>
> [...]We were late, we thought we were looking at a ready made facility, but it was lacking in international safety standards, it was run in the old communist way. (H4_UK)

The British perceived the Poles to be in a process of rapid mental transformation, as the shadows of central planning disappeared.

> [...] [Poles] are moving from 'write me a rule' people, from one type of society to another. (K1_UK)

British managers also tended to see Poland features that were shared with all post-communist societies: they spoke of 'typical post communists', of 'transforming society', of a 'young generation not affected by communism'. And for the British managers, the trauma of communism was responsible for making the Poles different; now that it was over, then the British expectation was that the Poles would become like the British – undramatically normal.

The British interviewees also tended to describe Poles and Poland as 'unfamiliar':

> English people don't know much about it [Poland]. [...] In the UK you have to get on the plane to come to Poland and Germans are next door. (K3_UK)
>
> The British presence in Poland is weak, perhaps because of the image of this country, where people are queuing for bread for example. I wouldn't

have believed myself that there are bank machines there, big blocks of flats. (K2_UK)

It was also pointed out by the Polish managers that Poland is not very well known to The Polish managers echoed this, in their assessment of how much the British knew about Poland:

> [...] In many countries Poland is associated with a place where white bears are walking on the streets. The knowledge of our country abroad is very limited. (F2_PL)
>
> People from the West do not know us. I know it because I have travelled abroad a lot. Our owners did not have a clue about Poland. They only got to know the country through our company. (J1_PL)

The only instance of familiarity between the Poles and the British, as expressed by the Polish managers, was their participation as allies in the Second World War.

In what follows, we look at the contrast of contrasts, the differences between the German/Polish opposition and the UK/Polish opposition and their origins in the different German and UK experiences of Poland.

5.2. Cultural distance – German and Polish interpretation

Both German and Polish managers agreed that there were differences between them, and there are interesting similarities between their expressions of these differences. We begin with two quotations, one from a German and one from a Pole:

> First, start to think in Polish. Their way of thinking is different from ours. This is based in a history, and we must be aware of it. You have to be aware of the history in the contact with Polish people, as our relations over the centuries have been very specific. (C2_GE)
>
> [...] It's very difficult to work together with Polish people because there is another knowledge, another way to work. (D3_GE)
>
> One has to point out that there are very big differences in mentality, different law, customs and habits [...]. (J1_PL)
>
> It is simply a different mentality of the nation [...].(G2_PL)

It is worth highlighting the assertion that 'our relations over the centuries have been very specific'. The interviewee here probably means 'very painful and difficult'. This makes an important point: whatever the objective cultural differences between Germany and Poland (if indeed there are any), they demand to be understood in their own binary historical context, and relationships between them must be put in this context as well. We are trying to act out the admonitions of this first quotation.

302   *Malcolm Chapman et al.*

The Polish and German managers agreed, therefore, that they were different. This trend was emphasised by all age groups of the interviewees, and from all types of the companies. It is important to mention here that nearly all the German respondents had visited Poland (some of them had lived there for a limited period of time), and that they were all generally well travelled.

In Figure. 13.1 below we present a summary of German interpretation of German–Polish cultural distance.

Expressions without diacritics are those used by interviewees; expressions in inverted commas are those where the phrase was in some way highlighted as slightly unusual by the interviewee. Expressions in parentheses are adjectives, which are implied by opposition, but not explicitly stated; thus, if, for example, a German manager, in discussion of German and Polish qualities, makes the point that Poles are 'lazy', then we have felt able to infer that there was an unspoken assertion to the effect that Germans are 'diligent' (or at least, 'more diligent'). We do not do this lightly. It is an important part of our argument that the system of oppositions referred to above has strong interconnections within it; it is an instrument where, if one string is plucked, the entire structure seems to resonate. There are also contexts

Germans	:	Poles
responsible	:	evade responsibility
disciplined	:	(undisciplined)
'do the coaching'	:	need authority
set the rules	:	need rules and hierarchy
(work individually)	:	work in a networking system
(tolerant)	:	nationalistic
(diligent)	:	lazy
(altruistic)	:	materialistic
(controlled)	:	warm and hospitable

Figure 13.1   German–Polish cultural distance, as perceived by the Germans

Perceptions of Cultural Distance 303

where the implied oppositional adjective remains unexpressed because it is blatantly offensive or self-demeaning.

German and Polish managers made many references to attitudes to authority and responsibility. In the context of the firm, German managers saw Poles as individuals lacking in relevant educational and work skills, and so accustomed to authoritarian management that they were unable or unwilling to take responsibility for problems themselves:

> The problem is taking over the responsibility. We [in Germany] have this problem too, but if someone is responsible in for certain area they take care of it. In Poland it takes a long time to find a person with relevant education and skills. (E5_GE)
>
> The self-control [of Polish employees], awareness, positive approach to work, and identification with the company leaves a lot to be desired. (E4_GE)
>
> One does everything with these people [...], because the Pole is capable, but one has to manage them, show them a new way. (E4_GE)

These Polish national qualities were contrasted to Germany, and presented as a development over time, with Poland behind Germany:

> [...] Polish employees work like Germans 15 years ago. What the boss says is the truth, and they do it, they follow. In Germany this is not the case. They question the boss a lot. (C2_GE)

German managers also pointed out that Poles operated in a networking system, and that it was very important to have the right connections in Poland in order to conduct any business activity there. Corruption in Poland was also mentioned in this context.

> [...] You have to know the right people. The people really taking the decision. And something like a bribe doesn't... well it's helpful. (P_B1_GE)

The 1999 Transparency International 'Corruption Perception Index' ranks countries from 10 to 0, according to the level of corruption perceived to be prevalent in them (10 is not at all corrupt, 0 is most corrupt). In 1999, Poland scored 4.2, which put it about half-way between the most corrupt country, Cameroon, and the least corrupt, Denmark. Germany was 14th on the list of 99 countries, with a score of 8.0.

The German managers (e.g., E5_GE) also made reference to Polish nationalism, which they had experienced while doing business in Poland. This mainly emerged as a feature of the Polish government, which according

304 *Malcolm Chapman et al.*

to the informants, usually acted in favour of domestic Polish companies. Consider the following quotes:

> It can be also bad luck. We have placed an offer, but the Polish government gave it to the Polish applicant. There is a little bit of chauvinism there. (G3_GE)
> [...] We were surprised about the laws they had in Poland concerning the production, the construction of a company. They had laws that were even stricter than the German ones, and we didn't find any Polish producer meeting those standards. We got the impression that the standards are only made for foreign investors, as a kind of protection as well. [...] For example, concerning hygienic topics, we had to meet very strict standards and none of the Polish producers could meet that [them]. We are sure. I've seen 30 of them. (P_B1_GE)

Germans	:	**Poles**
'cybernetic' society	:	imaginative
lack spontaneity and poetics	:	spontaneous
perform routine tasks	:	creative
limited	:	versatile
disciplined	:	need authority
down to earth	:	romantic
cold and reserved	:	warm and open
presumptuous	:	(modest)
uninspired	:	intelligent
credulous	:	smart
responsible	:	evade responsibility
well organised	:	chaotic
diligent	:	(lazy)
clean and tidy	:	(dirty and untidy)

Figure 13.2 German–Polish cultural distance, as perceived by the Poles

Perceptions of Cultural Distance 305

German managers also referred to a rather undesirable form of materialism on the Polish side (e.g. P_B1_GE, D3_GE, G3_GE). Although in their view Poles were very committed to their jobs and they were able to work long hours, they would not do it unless paid accordingly (D3_GE, G3_GE). Some of the executives would even call Poles lazy, as they do not want to work if they do not get a lot of money for it (D3_GE). They are always looking for a good compensation for their work, which can be in a form of money, car or other benefits. 'When they have a goal, they [will] do everything to achieve it' (G3_GE).

The positive features of Poles mentioned unanimously by executives were Polish hospitality and warmth (e.g., D3_GE, D2_GE).

Polish perceptions of themselves, and of German managers, are presented in Figure 13.2 above. The Polish managers described their German colleagues as 'cybernetic' (or 'robotic'), good at routines, but not good at improvising:

> Germans are a society of a higher level of social organisation [...]. A social and cybernetic [organisation], and everyone taken out of the context of their organisation, falls into oblivion of our manager, who is much more versatile. He can react much better in a crisis situation, and has much better knowledge and preparation. [...] A specialist [from Germany] for example from the construction business is trained very well in his subject and virtually leaves no room for discussion. However when one tries to go beyond his narrowly specialised knowledge one totally loses contact with this person, and one is not able to continue conversation. (C1_PL)
>
> [...] If you look at a German fellow for example, let's call him Helmut, who is an employee, and who is to perform a task in a certain way, [you will see] that he will be doing only this task and not thinking of anything else. (A2_PL)

This implies that there is orderliness, but orderliness to the point of disfunction, and machine-like inhumanity. According to Polish managers, Germany had a long tradition of a state of order, where the above-mentioned 'cybernetic structure' of the society functioned without interruptions and where the basic needs of the society were fulfilled. Poland, by contrast was a 'young democracy', where these characteristics were scarcely developed; this has forced Poles 'to manage as one can'.

However, Polish managers did not see this as a defect. On the contrary, although they admitted the need to be coached by their foreign partners, they insisted on being treated as equal partners by German investors (e.g. A2_PL, E3_PL, E1_PL, G2_PL), and contrasted the German capacity for routine with their own creativity and imagination:

> Yes, definitely they are different, and I am saying it is an advantage of our [Polish] employees. In my opinion our [Polish] employees are more open [...]. And if we now go back to Poles [a Pole with the same task as 'Helmut'

306 *Malcolm Chapman et al.*

from a previous quote], he will be thinking, he will be trying to make his work easier, and he will display greater vivacity and sharpness than an average German. (A2_PL)

Polish managers saw themselves as much more dynamic, imaginative, versatile and spontaneous than the Germans. In their view foreign capital encouraged the development of an ambitious workforce, which was able to think economically, and was entrepreneurial (E1_PL). As was pointed out several times by the interviewees, Poles were talented and had considerable potential for development. When compared with their foreign counterparts, Polish staffs were more educated, but lacked the relevant experience (D1_PL).

Germans were also described as being down to earth, cold and reserved, presumptuous and inclined to assume superiority:

They [Germans] are a nation which does not like to admit their mistakes. According to my own observations they do not hesitate to show their intellectual superiority, it changes however after some time. A German person needs some time to understand that Poznan, Poland is a country of educated people, who can be easily partners even for Germans. Moreover, they are disciplined, presumptuous and cold, the latter meaning that it is difficult to get through to a deeper layer of their personality. (A2_PL)

In general we get along very well here. However they [Germans] have this little vice, that whatever they invented here, what they propose is the best, and there is nothing better. One has to be very intelligent and smart, to do what one wants to do without going against their opinion, and without explaining that this [what they propose] is not the best. (C1_PL)

Again, Poles compared the orderly discipline of the Germans (with its assumption of superiority) with their own more creative ability to be 'intelligent and smart' in dealing with the Germans.

Polish managers were generally prepared to accord to the Germans the virtues of being responsible, well organised, disciplined, diligent and clean. They were less inclined to accept as self-characterisations of being irresponsible, disorganised, indisciplined, lazy and dirty. When the Polish managers characterised themselves, they generally wished to cast themselves in a flattering light.

5.3. Cultural distance – British and Polish interpretation

The British and the Poles, like the Germans and the Poles, agreed that they differed.

There was also a cultural issue, as what is common in the UK is unusual in Poland. [...] Poland and Czech Republic are very similar, but for example Poland and UK aren't. They are very different. (K4_UK)

The difficulties were in overcoming the mentality of people, even that of ourselves. We had to switch to another way of thinking. (F4_PL)

One has to point out here that there are big differences in mentality, different law, customs and habits [in England]. We are required to posses a great knowledge about the market. And of course, if we do something well they would even praise us, [...] but they would not implement this solution on their own ground. (J1_PL)

Some of the differences that the British and the Poles found between themselves were similar to those that the Germans and Poles employed. The degree and variety of contrast was, however, generally perceived to be less strongly marked, less strongly insisted upon, less complex, which is consistent with our argument. The British companies in Poland are in a very similar business position, in relation to their Polish partners, as the German companies, which would imply identical tellings of the nature of their business relationship. This was not what we found.

British perceptions of themselves and their Polish colleague are summarised in Figure 13.3.

The British appear as the source of order and rule, which the Poles accept or evade. According to the British managers, Poles function well in hierarchical structures:

They can be a bit, Polish people still like rules, they like a clear hierarchy, they are very sensitive about 'he is my boss' for example. They are very formal. That's not our style. But it evolves over time. When I go to Poland and talk to bankers I have different relationships with staff in Warsaw than in Lodz for example. They treat me, they think this guy must be important, that he comes from the UK, but it doesn't affect our relationship. They have opportunities to ask questions, and people react very well to it (K1_UK).

British	:	Poles
'do the coaching'	:	need authority
set the rules	:	need rules and hierarchy
decentralised	:	with centralised structures
responsible	:	evade responsibility
(controlled)	:	warm and hospitable

Figure 13.3 British–Polish cultural distance, as perceived by the British

308   *Malcolm Chapman et al.*

British	:	**Poles**
need a list of tasks to work	:	creative and imaginative
take a long time to decide	:	spontaneous
phlegmatic and patient	:	chaotic
cold and reserved	:	warm and open
professional	:	evade responsibility
relaxed and informal	:	need authority
work comes first	:	family comes first

Figure 13.4   British–Polish cultural distance, as perceived by the Poles

This need for authority was linked by British interviewees to a Polish tendency to evade responsibility, or to pass responsibility upwards:

> The difficult part are the cultural traditions of way of working, formed in the past, under a different system, changing attitude, style of work, top down hierarchy, no individual responsibility, reluctance to take decisions, and take the responsibility. That's the communist legacy, the legacy of central planning. (I2_UK)

The positive features of Poles mentioned by the executives were Polish hospitality and warmth (e.g., K2_UK).

Polish perceptions of themselves and their British colleagues are shown in Figure 13.4.

There are some similarities between the Polish perception of the British, and the Polish perception of the Germans. The British were seen as a cold and phlegmatic people, who took a long time to decide things, and who needed a list of tasks in order to be able to work:

> Englishmen are bureaucratic. What only counts for them is meeting, minutes and action plan. And on top of that, they divide a hair into four, as the saying goes. (J2_PL)

The British are perceived to be a source of order and rules. This was contrasted with the Poles who saw themselves as warm, spontaneous and full of imagination.

Congruent with this, the Poles emphasised British professionalism:

> [...] British employees are much more professional. [...] They concentrate on their work, on what they are to do, and do it separately from their

Perceptions of Cultural Distance 309

personality, from themselves, and this may be the reason why they might come across as perhaps less friendly but more professional. (H2_PL)

I think they [British] were surprised by Polish hospitality, approach to people, to guests, openness. (I1_PL)

They also spoke of their own need for authority and tendency to evade responsibility. This last characteristic they also tended to blame on the communist system.

Several interviewees observed that their British colleagues were very reserved. Polish interviewees also pointed out the British ability to keep their professional lives separate from the private one. Just to quote one of the executives:

We [Poles] have different habits – strong links with the family. They [British] are detached from the family, they can sit here for long hours, and we would like to go home. (J1_PL)

As in the Polish/German contrast, the Polish managers were prepared to acknowledge the virtue of the calculating orderliness, which the British managers seemed to bring, and to aspire to imitate certain aspects. They also, however, found virtue in their own differences from the British – in Polish warmth, spontaneity and imagination. However, the ideas were less frequently and less intensely invoked, than the Polish/German contrast.

6. Discussion

If we return to Shenkar's (2001) paper, our study addresses four of the main illusions, and adds a fifth, that of 'neutrality'. We have shown that 'small cultural distances', where they are intensely observed, theorised and acted upon, can be far more important than 'large cultural distances' which are not. The social psychologists might say that this is explained by the fact that the differences were 'salient' or 'not salient'; with Pinker (1997, p. 85) we agree that this, and terms like it, are scams, merely redescribing what they purport to explain. We hope that we have taken some valuable steps into explanation, rather than mere redescription.

If we look at the different conceptualisations of difference as between Poland and Germany, on the one hand, and Poland and the UK, on the other, we find some issues arising that might reasonably be related to Hofstede's dimensions.

Where there are issues of relative order and disorder, as there are in German/Polish discussion of mutual characteristics, then we might want to relate these to Uncertainty Avoidance. Following Chapman, Clegg et al. (2004); Chapman, Gajewska-De Mattos et al. (2004), where there are issues pertaining to need for, and exercise of, authority, we might want to relate

310   *Malcolm Chapman et al.*

Table 13.1   Summary of Hofstede's culture scores for Germany, UK and Poland

	PD	I/C	M/F	UA	LTO
Germany	35	67	66	65	31
UK	35	89	66	35	25
Poland	68	60	64	93	32

Based on: Hofstede (1980, 2001) and Nasierowski and Mikula (1998).

these to both Power Distance and Uncertainty Avoidance. We would then want to rank Poland, the UK and Germany, on these dimensions, and explain the differences expressed by the managers, as arising from experience of cultural distance so defined. Poland was not in the original IBM study which gave rise to Hofstede's work, which already presents a difficulty in the use of linear measures of cultural distance. We could, however, make some limited sense of our data using such measures. A summary of Hofstede's scores for Germany, UK and Poland is presented in Table 13.1 below.

If the only attribute at stake were 'cultural distance', then we might say that Germany and the UK were similar (scoring relatively closely, for example, on three of Hofstede's dimensions), and that we would therefore expect their 'cultural distance' from Poland to be similar as well. What we find is dramatically different from this expectation. The 'Poland' that the German managers experience, is not the same as the 'Poland' that the UK managers experience.

The German managers interact with their Polish counterparts in the context of a long and intimate cross-national relationship, which has been extensively lived and theorised – theorised, that is, by ordinary people in ordinary situations. That German managers construct and interpret their experience with Poles has been supported by the secondary historical data and the primary empirical data.

The UK managers are perhaps not so different from the German managers (in Hofstede's terms), but their experience and interpretation of their Polish counterparts was different. The relationship between the UK and Poland has not been as extensively lived and theorised.

If the perceptions and interpretations constructed by the managers were the product of immediate experience, then we might expect the German and UK managers to interpret and express their differences from the Poles similarly and with the same vehemence. We do not find this.

If the perceptions and interpretations of managers were in some way independent of experience (if they were, for example, 'purely historical', or 'mere stereotypes'), then we might expect them to vary randomly between examples, and to show little conceptual coherence. We do not find this either.

Perceptions of Cultural Distance   311

What we are dealing with are ideas deeply ingrained in peoples' minds which are carefully built upon past experiences, and which are also available for the structuring and construal of immediate and current experience. Where the past experiences are similar, then perceptions accord with this. And the same is true for experiences that are different, i.e., they are expressed differently and expressed with varying force. The perceptions are built upon experience, but they also feed into and help to create experience. They are not immutable, but they are not given to rapid change either.

In this context the question of 'objective cultural distance' as between the protagonists, therefore, becomes highly problematic. Relatively minor cultural differences, in situations of intimate contact and long-term interpretation, can become the basis of well-organised structures of living and interpretation. This is a reasonable description of the Polish–German relationship. Greater cultural differences, if these are not rendered important by existing experience and interpretation, can pass by relatively unnoticed. This is a reasonable description of the Polish–UK relationship.

In relation Shenkar's (2001) 'illusion of symmetry', we can argue that UK/Polish difference and German/ Polish difference demand to be understood in their own historical and specific context. There is a 'symmetry' in the perceptions and interpretations we present here, but it is complex and subtle. Cultural distance looks importantly different from each side of these national pairings, and is constructed and acted upon differently as a result. This is in spite of the fact that, conventionally, the cultural distance between (say) Poland and Germany is by definition the same as the cultural distance between Germany and Poland.

In relation to the 'illusion of causality', we can argue that 'small cultural distances', where they are intensely observed, theorised and acted upon, can cause far greater problems than 'large cultural distances' which are not. This is related to the issues explored by Brouthers and Brouthers (2001), where the argument is made that small cultural distance, where it is not anticipated, can have more disruptive effects that large cultural distance for which there is forewarning. This argument is given further application in Fenwick, Edwards and Buckley (2003).

We could perhaps extend the list of 'illusions' surrounding the 'cultural distance' concept, by adding the 'illusion of neutrality': the illusion, that is, that a given 'cultural distance' will always have the same effects upon the action and interpretation of those experiencing it. This 'illusion' is addressed, to some degree, by the illusions of linearity and symmetry. Nevertheless, it probably deserves its own listing. Where countries have been involved in long and bitter political dispute, and perhaps warfare, then small differences matter; where countries have no conflicting interests, then large differences can be ignored or benignly tolerated. Intense confrontations like those between, for example, Japan and South Korea, the USA and Mexico,

312 *Malcolm Chapman et al.*

and Germany and Poland, require recognition that any 'differences', whatever they might be, will not be 'neutrally' viewed.

In relation to the 'illusion of linearity', we can assert that the 'contrast of contrasts' that we have outlined, would tell us very little about (for example) UK/German difference. If the distribution of cultural differences *were* symmetrical, then if we knew that Poland scored 80 on some hypothetical dimension, Germany 50, and the UK 10, we would know that the cultural distance between Germany and Poland was 30. No such comfort emerges from our argument (see Chapman, Clegg et al., 2004; Chapman, Gajewska-De Mattos et al., 2004, for further discussion of this).

In relation to the 'illusion of stability', we can agree with Shenkar (2001) that it is perfectly possible for objective measures to change over time. However, the qualitative approach to cultural distance in which experiences are construed and interpreted, does not involve the measurement of objective features by an impartial observer from year to year. As Tihanyi et al. (2005, p. 374) put it: 'some cultural elements are stable, whereas others are dynamic and changing'. The relative positions of the Germans and the Poles, of Germany and Poland, have been constantly changing at many levels, while at the same time sustaining a kind of consistency of interpretation on another, even as Poland went in and out of sovereign existence, as religions came and went, as horses gave way to motor cars, and as communism gave way to capitalism.

7. Conclusions

In this study, we presented routine expressions of managerial experience from Germany, the UK and Poland in specific situations of the meeting of different cultures. We have argued that Germany and Poland have a close and tense relationship, and that the UK and Poland have a relatively distant and easy relationship. In this context, they are 'close neighbours' and 'distant friends'.

We argue that the dominant concept of cultural distance in international business studies gives us an incomplete understanding of this complex issue. This is because cultural distance is constructed and interpreted by the perceivers, and this construction and interpretation is influenced by experience and history. The approach proposed in this paper sheds some light on how individuals from countries close to one another in terms of Hofstede's dimensions, can actually perceive the distance between them to be great. We have also shown that countries that are distant on the dimensions can, in the context of history and experience, perceive themselves as close, or indeed perceive one another with indifference.

This study shows the need for further research. There is clearly a need to improve and refine the objective measures that are typically used. Our main recommendation, however, would not be concerned with improving existing objective measures, but rather would suggest the need to complement these with deep, dynamic and contextual data. Ethnographic research is one way of doing this.

In other words, by focusing on the qualitative data we can derive dimensional complexities related to the construct of cultural distance that can provide a research framework to advance our understanding of the topic. This approach to conceptualising cultural distance finds ready application in international business contexts. In particular, the findings of this study could be useful for better understanding the interactions between different perceptions the partners (might) have within international mergers and acquisitions and joint ventures. This should facilitate an ability to predict the success or failure of international collaboration processes, and developing useful advice for mergers and acquisitions/JVs executives (i.e., it should not be expected that any one one-size- fits-all solution is available). The ideas presented here are readily transferable to other international business contexts with analogous characteristics (e.g., the US/Mexican contrast, the Japanese/Korean contrast, the Northern European/Southern European contrast and generally core/periphery relationships). We also hope that our approach may allow international business managers, in situations like this, to understand the hostility of others, without being wounded by it (an endorsement of our approach can be found in the Economist Global Executive, 2004).

Appendix A

A.1. Interview guide – Germany and the United Kingdom

Introduction

Note the time (beginning and end).
 Confirm confidentiality.
 Explain the objective and relevance of the research.
 Biographical Data Questionnaire.
 Starting question: Can you tell me a few words about your company?/ What has happened in the company since we last met?

Guiding questions

What is your role in the company?
 How did your firm get where it is internationally? (first international activity, when, how, main markets).
 Could you tell me a few words about your activities on the Polish market? (why Poland, were other possibilities in the region considered, first contact, main difficulties, legal system, main competitors, exceptional events since entering the market, advice to other foreign investors).
 What do you associate Poland with?

314 *Malcolm Chapman et al.*

Do you perceive Poles as a uniform nation? (description of main characteristics at national and company level, comparison with Germans/British).

A.2. Interview guide – Poland.

Introduction

Note the time (beginning and end).
  Confirm confidentiality.
  Explain the objective and relevance of the research.
  Biographical Data Questionnaire.
  Starting question: Can you tell me a few words about your company?/ What has happened in the company since we last met?

Guiding questions

What is your role in the company?
  Could you tell me a few words about your cooperation with a foreign partner? (motives, were other possibilities considered, previous experiences, first contact, length of cooperation, main difficulties, legal system, main competitors, exceptional events since entering cooperation, advice to other Polish companies).
  Could you tell me a few words about working in a foreign owned company in Poland? (previous experiences, differences with Polish owned companies, main advantages, main difficulties, exceptional events, legal system, competition).
  What do you associate Germany/UK with?
  Do you perceive Germans/British as a uniform nation? (show the picture with stereotypical images of Germans/British) (description of main characteristics at national and company level, comparison with Poles).

Notes

1. Poland is third most populous nation in the area of Central and Eastern Europe, and at the time of conducting this research it was a candidate country to the European Union. Since initiating its market reforms, it has experienced a large inflow of foreign direct investment. A considerable amount of this investment came from Germany, and the UK – the existing members of the EU.
2. For reasons of confidentiality the names of companies participating in the study were coded. For example: 'D3_GE' means that it was a 'Company D' originating from Germany.

References

Bakacsi, G., Sándor, T., András, K., & Viktor, I. (2002). Eastern European cluster: Tradition and transition. *Journal of World Business, 37,* 69–80.
Beechler, S., & Yang, J. Z. (1994). 'The transfer of Japanese-style management to American subsidiaries: Contingencies, constraints and competencies'. *Journal of International Business Studies, 25*(3), 467–491.

Brewer, P. (2001). International market selection: Developing a model from Australian case studies. *International Business Review, 10*(2), 155–174.

Brouthers, K., & Bamossy, G. J. (1997). The role of key stakeholder in international joint venture negotiations: Case studies from Eastern Europe. *Journal of International Business Studies, 28*(2), 285–308.

Brouthers, K., & Brouthers, L. (2001). Exploring the national cultural distance paradox. *Journal of International Business Studies, 32*(1), 177–189.

Buckley, P., & Chapman, M. (1997). The use of 'native categories' in management research. *British Journal of Management, 8*(4), 283–299.

Chapman, M. (2001). Social anthropology and business studies: Some considerations of method. In D. Gellner, & E. Hirsch (Eds), *Inside organisations: Anthropologists at work* (pp. 19–33). Oxford: Berg.

Chapman, M., Clegg, J., & Gajewska-De Mattos, H. (2004). Poles and Germans: An international business relationship. *Human Relations, 57*(8), 983–1015.

Chapman, M., Gajewska-De Mattos, H., & Antoniou, Ch. (2004). The ethnographic IB researcher: Misfit or trailblazer? In R. Marschan-Piekkari, & C. Welch (Eds), *Handbook of qualitative research methods for international business*. Cheltenham, UK and Northhampton, MA: Edward Elgar.

D' Iribarne, P., Segal, J.-P., Chevrier, S., & Globokar, T. (1998). *Cultures et Mondialisation: Gérer Par-Delà Les Frontières*. Paris: Seuil.

Economist (2004). What's in the Journals, August 2004, *The Economist Global Executive*, August 27th.

Eisenhardt, K. M. (1989). Building theories from case study research. *Academy of Management Review, 14*(4), 532–550.

Fenwick, M., Edwards, R., & Buckley, P. J. (2003). Is Cultural similarity misleading? The experience of australian manufacturers in Britain. *International Business Review, 12*, 297–309.

Festing, M. (1997). International human resource management strategies in multinational corporations: Theoretical assumptions and empirical evidence from German firms. *Management International Review, 37*(10), 43–63.

Harris, S. (2000). Reconciling positive and interpretative international management research: A native category approach. *International Business Review, 9*(6), 755–770.

Harris, S., (2003). National values and strategy formation by business leaders. Ph.D. Thesis, University of Leeds.

Hofstede, G. (1980). *Culture's consequences: International differences in work related values*. Beverly Hills: Sage Publications.

Hofstede, G. (1991). *Cultures and organisations: Software of the mind*. London: McGraw-Hill.

Hofstede, G. (2001). *Culture's consequences: Comparing values, behaviours, institutions and organisations across nations* (2nd ed.). Thousand Oaks CA: Sage.

Hofstede, G. (2002). Dimensions do not exist: A reply to brendan mcsweeney. *Human Relations, 55*(11), 1355.

Hoppe, M. (2004). An interview with geert hofstede. *Academy of Management Executive, 18*(1), 75–79.

Iribarne, P. d ' (1996/97). The usefulness of ethnographic approach to international comparison of organisations. *International Studies of Management and Organisation, 26*(4), 30–47.

Johanson, J., & Vahlne, J.-E. (1977). The internationalization process of the firm: A model of knowledge development and increasing foreign market commitments. *Journal of International Business Studies, 8*(1), 23–32.

316 *Malcolm Chapman et al.*

Johanson, J., & Wiedersheim-Paul, F. (1975). The internationalization of the firm: Four Swedish cases. *Journal of Management Studies, 12*(3), 305–322.

Kirkman, B., Lowe, K., & Gibson, C. (2006). A quarter century of culture's consequences: A review of empirical research incorporating Hofstede's cultural values framework. *Journal of International Business Studies, 37*, 285–320.

Kogut, B., & Singh, H. (1988). The effect of national culture on the choice of entry mode. *Journal of International Business Studies, 19*(3), 411–432.

Landau, Z., & Tomaszewski, J. (1964). Kapitaly obce w polsce 1918–1939. *Warsaw.*

Landau, Z., & Tomaszewski, J. (1985). *The Polish economy in the twentieth century.* London: Croom Helm.

Leung, K., Bhagat, R., Buchan, N., Erez, M., & Gibson, C. (2005). Culture and international business: Recent advances and their implications for future research. *Journal of International Business Studies, 36*, 357–378.

Marschan, R. (1996). *New structural forms and inter-unit communication in multinationals. The case of Kone elevators.* Ph.D. Thesis. Helsinki: Helsinki School of Economics and Business Administration.

Marschan-Piekkari, R., & Reis, C. (2004). Language and languages in cross-cultural interviewing. In R. Marschan-Piekkari, & C. Welch (Eds), *Handbook of qualitative research methods for international business.* Cheltenham, UK and Northhampton, MA: Edward Elgar.

McCracken, G. (1988). *The long interview. Qualitative research methods series*, vol. 13. Beverly Hills: Sage Publications.

McSweeney, B. (2002a). Hofstede's model of national cultural differences and their consequences: A triumph of faith-a failure of analysis. *Human Relations, 55*(1), 89.

McSweeney, B. (2002b). The essentials of scholarship: A reply to geert hofstede. *Human Relations, 55*(11), 1363.

Miles, M. B., & Huberman, A. M. (1994). *Qualitative data analysis. An expanded sourcebook* (2nd ed.). Beverly Hills: Sage Publications.

Nasierowski, W., & Mikula, B. (1998). Culture dimensions of polish manages: Hofstede's indices. *Organisation Studies, 19*(3), 495–509.

O' Grady, S., & Lane, H. W. (1996). The psychic distance paradox. *Journal of International Business Studies, 27*(20), 309–334.

Parkhe, A. (1997). 'Messy' research, methodological predispositions and theory development in international joint ventures. *Academy of Management Review, 18*(2), 227–268.

Pinker, S. (1997). *How the mind works.* Harmondsworth: Penguin.

Salk, J. (1996–7). Partners and other strangers: Cultural boundaries and cross-cultural encounters in international joint venture teams. *International Studies of Management and Organisation, 26*(4), 48–72.

Shenkar, O. (2001). Cultural distance revisited: Towards a more rigorous conceptualization and measurement of cultural differences. *Journal of International Business Studies, 32*(3), 519–535 third quarter.

Smith, P. (2002). Culture's consequences: Something old and something new. *Human Relations, 55*(1), 119.

Sousa, C., & Bradley, F. (2006). Cultural distance and psychic distance: Two peas in a pod?. *Journal of International Marketing, 14*(1), 49–70.

Teigland, R., Fey, C. F., & Birkinshaw, J. (2000). Knowledge dissemination in global electronics industry. *Management International Review, 40*(1), 49–77.

Tihanyi, L., Griffith, D., & Russell, C. (2005). The effect of cultural distance on entry mode choice, international diversification, and MNE performance: A meta-analysis. *Journal of International Business Studies, 36*, 270–283.

Triandis, H. (2004). The many dimensions of culture. *Academy of Management Executive, 18*(1), 88–93.

Tsang, E. W. K. (2001). Managerial learning in foreign-invested enterprises of China. *Management International Review, 41*(1), 29–51.

Vaara, E. (2002). On the discursive construction of success/failure in narratives of post-merger integration. *Organization Studies, 23*(2), 211–248.

Wellisz, L. (1938). *Foreign capital in Poland.* London: Allen and Unwin.

Williamson, D. (2002). Forward from a critique of Hofstede's model of national culture. *Human Relations, 55*(11), 1373.

Yin, R. (1994). *Case study research. Design and methods. Applied social research methods series* (2nd ed.). Beverly Hills: Sage Publications.

Zalan, T., & Lewis, G. (2004). Writing about methods in qualitative research: Towards a more transparent approach. In R. Marschan-Piekkari, & C. Welch (Eds), *Handbook of qualitative research methods for international business.* Cheltenham, UK and Northhampton, MA: Edward Elgar.

14
Doing Business in Developing and Transitional Countries: An Empirical Example of the Dominant Logic and Its Alternative

Co-authored with Malcolm Chapman, Jeremy Clegg, and Hanna Gajewska-De Mattos

This article applies a social anthropological approach to the understanding of cultural difference. It uses an approach with analogies in structural linguistics, which is strongly supported in social anthropological literature on ethnicity, national identity, and definition and self-definition of peoples (see Ardener 1972; Chapman 1989, 1992; McDonald 1990; Saussure 1916; Whorf 1956).The aim of the research is to understand respondents' perceptions of others and of themselves in the Wielkopolska region of Poland. Moreover, it aims to identify how perceptions were expressed and how they were understood. Qualitative research of this kind does not begin with a research question but builds the object of interest from the findings themselves. What we gain from this study is an understanding of a significant subnational identity issue of a kind that is rarely addressed in the international business and management literature. We examine how regional rationalities are constructed in opposition to, and in relationship with, rationalities at national or global levels. We argue that detailed bilateral comparisons of cultures should supplement the existing standard approaches to studying cultural differences in international business research. This article provides an empirical example of how a dominant national logic and an alternative regional logic are construed and constructed. It uses examples from the Germanic/Slavonic contrast. In particular, we draw on material from the Wielkopolska district of Poland, including a detailed analysis of the mentality of people in this region as they perceive themselves and others.International business academia has concentrated on national cultural characteristics in an attempt to explain interactions between people and companies from different countries. Hofstede's (1980, 1991, 2001) work has been influential in this sphere, giving international business researchers an intelligent and popular picture of what national cultures are like. The local/global issue has commonly been treated as if it were congruent with the national/global issue. When companies are told to "think globally, act locally," the iconography used to express this injunction often reveals this. So, "global" is commonly used to mean operating competently at the level of the entire world – the biggest social, geographic, and demographic unit that we know – and "local" is commonly used to mean operating competently at the level of the nation-state – the dominant subglobal sociopolitical institution.From a social anthropological perspective, within a structuralist framework, many conceptual items are not susceptible to definition in themselves but, rather, are defined in opposition to other things, in systems of contrast. From within the same perspective, it is often found that numerous opposing pairs, although they are not identical, line up with one another in congruent systems. So the opposition global/local can be applied at a number of different levels, and its exact definition cannot be separated from the particular application (e.g., it could be used to mean "world/country" or "world/village"). Similarly, oppositions related to development in time (e.g., "modern/traditional") can readily assume congruence with oppositions related to differences in space or scale (e.g., "global/local"). These structural features of classification and definition by opposition are strongly supported in the social anthropological literature. They do not, however, mix well with positivist calls for exact definition, and it would be a mistake to try to mix the structuralist and positivist paradigms in this regard.There is, of course, room for endless argument and discussion about whether nation-states and cultures can be usefully regarded as congruent and coextensive or as culturally homogeneous. It is probably fair to say that no nation-state is culturally homogeneous in the strictest definition and probably equally fair to say that all nation-states have some cultural characteristics that can be used to make a claim of homogeneity of some kind. Many people, in their normal lives, cope with great complexity and variety in these matters, locally, regionally, nationally, and internationally; as academics, we perhaps struggle to conceptualize these things so fluently. It is not difficult to argue that the nation-state is a fundamentally inappropriate unit around which to conceptualize cultural difference; for example, see McSweeney (2002a), who took issue with Hofstede on this (1980, 1991, 2001). Recent management researchers, however, have invested heavily in Hofstede's ideas (for the scale of this, see Kirkman et al. 2006) and by so doing have assumed the utility (however limited or qualified) of regarding nation-states as cultures, which are culturally internally homogeneous in coherent ways and culturally intelligibly different from one another (for some relevant texts, see, among many, Bakacsi et al. 2002; Hofstede 2002; Hoppe 2004; Kogut and Singh 1988; Leung et al. 2005; McSweeney 2002a, 2002b; Smith 2002; Tihanyi et al. 2005; Triandis 2004; Williamson 2002).This article does not engage further with these arguments at a theoretical level but, rather, addresses them through the

320 *Peter J. Buckley et al.*

particular examples discussed in the first paragraph. By focusing on Poland and Germany, we are looking at identities that, at least in part, are conceptualized as national by those living within those countries. In this sense, our attention to national identities is consistent with the long-standing social anthropological commitment to native categories, that is, to categories of understanding that are generated within the society (or societies) under study and not imposed by the social scientific observer. We are also looking at subnational or regional refractions of these national identities when we focus our attention on the Wielkopolska region of Poland.This article uses the theoretical lens of structural anthropology (Lévi-Strauss 1963; Saussure 1916) to highlight the importance of local rationalities. It examines a particular two-country contrast, that between Germany and Poland. The unit of analysis throughout the article is the manager. We then analyze a local, subnational version of an analogous cultural contrast and show that, although it is constructed out of the same metaphors and ideas, it inverts the more generally accepted national cultural contrast.

Theory and ethnic oppositions

The discussion of the theme of this issue of *International Studies of Management and Organization* contains the following:

> Nations in their early stages of economic development have their dominant rationality based on tradition, human, community, clan and social perspectives. But as the nation develops economically, the dominant rationality becomes less tradition based and more global, and more likely to define human value in economic terms, rather than in traditional terms. Today, in the developed OECD countries, the global economic rationality dominates, and the traditional human and spiritual values are less central. The developing and transitional countries, while valuing economic development, often find the emphasis on pure economic objectives at odds with a more traditional local rationality, where more basic human, community, clan and social objectives receive heavier weight. (Molz and Farashahi 2011)

We cite this at length because it bears very directly upon the cultural differences discussed in this article, as these are expressed by the people under research. The dominant and the alternative logics of business are expressed as oppositions. In particular, our attention is drawn to oppositions between global rationalities, which are "purely economic," and local rationalities, which are "traditional, basic human, social, community, [and] clan." These oppositions are a modern version of metaphors of difference, which have ancient origins and which have indeed an element of human universality (Chapman 1992).

Business in Developing and Transitional Countries 321

This article gives life to the oppositions referred to above by using a structural anthropological view of the construction of national and regional cultural differences. We use the idea of structural opposition, which is derived from structural linguistics and structural anthropology and is particularly associated with the work of Saussure (1916) and LéviStrauss (1963). There is a broad range of literature that has drawn on these ideas (Berger and Luckmann 1967; Pike 1954; Sapir 1921; Trier 1931; Ullmann 1951; Wartburg 1943; Whorf 1956). Bourdieu (1986) provided one of the standard expressions of the ideas in the most general sense. Ardener and his students have particularly applied these ideas to the classification of people (Ardener 1967, 1972, 1974, 1989; Chapman 1989; Hastrup 1998; McDonald 1990). Within this work, the many terms that might be used to describe groups of people, such as populations, tribes, ethnicities, peoples, and nations, were treated as parts of systems of classification in which those making the classification were the people themselves, classifying themselves and others. Systems of classification, from domains other than demographic, had been shown to have characteristic organizing principles – opposition (often binary), arbitrariness, structuring, and restructuring. These same principles were applied to the study of the classification (and self-classification) of peoples to show how ethnic groups define themselves in opposition to others around them, using a range of metaphors that seemed to have some universality.

This section draws upon an extensive analysis of the Anglo-Saxon/ Celtic opposition and its cognate forms back to antiquity (see Chapman 1992). Aspects of the German/Polish contrast can be understood in the light of the Anglo-Saxon/Celtic opposition. The ideas are presented here in an abbreviated form, and the reader should be aware of the wider context presented elsewhere.

Chapman (1992) argues that all peoples have a strong tendency to characterize themselves as orderly, civilized, and properly human and to regard other surrounding peoples as failing to achieve these virtues (Ardener 1989; Lévi-Strauss 1963, 1966). Any cultural differences can be used as material for the construction of differences of this kind, but issues relating to diet, dress, sexuality, kinship, and conventions of nonverbal communication are often prominent. There is, however, commonly an imbalance in presentations of cultural differences in that the historiographical record is often biased toward one series of accounts rather than the other. The historiographical record is biased, that is, in the moral favor of those who do the writing. Thus, the Greeks wrote about the barbarians, the Romans wrote about the Germans and the Gauls, the Norman-English wrote about the Welsh and the Irish, the English wrote about the Celts, and the Germans wrote about the Slavs.

This article is particularly informed by the Roman/Celtic and English/ Celtic oppositions and by the German/Slavonic cognates of these. In Greek/ barbarian, Roman/Gaul, and English/Celtic recensions of these oppositions,

322 *Peter J. Buckley et al.*

we find a picture of the self and the other constructed as follows (Chapman 1992, 210–211):

Self/Other: The Basic Oppositions

Self	vs.	Other
Rule	vs.	Unruly (absence of rule)
Order	vs.	Disorder
Culture	vs.	Nature
Human	vs.	Animal
Controlled	vs.	Uncontrolled
Lawful	vs.	Lawless
Clean	vs.	Dirty
Reason	vs.	Unreason
Intellect	vs.	Emotion
Constant	vs.	Inconstant
Modern	vs.	Backward

The self, who is constructing the picture described through these oppositions, is the one whose picture is recorded. The picture of the other constructed through this series of oppositions is almost entirely negative. It is the picture of the other that self-consciously so-called civilized peoples have left in their accounts. It is important to stress that every people is self-consciously portrayed as civilized. There is probably an element of human universality in the oppositions listed above. History is written by the winners, however. Those peoples that have left the dominant records, the central characters, have characterized themselves to the left of the oppositions and have characterized their alter ties and protagonists to the right of the oppositions. It is easy to see that this system of oppositions between the self and the other has congruence with the oppositions between modern global and human traditional, as these are articulated in contemporary discourse about economic and social development, and about the dominant economic logic and its alternatives.

The oppositions listed above are not politically correct in the modern sense. They are a system of derogation of the other. They can assume a more benign form, however. Chapman argues that with the appearance of romanticism in the eighteenth century and later, the above set of oppositions underwent a metamorphosis. Although the self and the other (or, as it might be called, the center and the periphery) remained the same, the balance of virtue was shifted to the right (Chapman 1992, 212). The result of this is:

Self/Other: The Romantic Reappraisal

Self	vs.	Other
Constraint (rule)	vs.	Freedom (unruly, absence of rule)

Predictable (order)	vs.	Unpredictable (disorder)
Artificial (human)	vs.	Natural (animal)
Urban (culture)	vs.	Rural (nature)
Reserved (controlled)	vs.	Impulsive (uncontrolled)
Formal (controlled)	vs.	Informal (uncontrolled)
Conventional (lawful)	vs.	Unconventional (lawless)
Sterile (clean)	vs.	Fertile (dirty)
Calculation (reason)	vs.	Imagination (unreason)
Measurement (intellect)	vs.	Passion (emotion)
Dull (constant)	vs.	Exciting (inconstant)

This second list, with glosses derived from the romantic reappraisal of primitive naturalness, allows an entirely desirable picture to be drawn from the images of the other and casts an undesirable and dreary pall over the self. It is important to note, however, that the other, while desirable, is still somebody else's construction; the self, dull or not, is still in the metaphorical driving seat.

The Anglo-Saxon/Celtic contrast has many similar features to the German/Polish contrast. In both pairs, the first element, Anglo-Saxon (or English) and German, is and has been more powerful and more expansive, in recent centuries, than the second. Also, in both pairs, the making and recording of events has been more active for the first element than for the second. In both pairs, there has been long-term contiguity on a sometimes troubled geographical frontier. This is why the structural oppositions, which make sense of the Anglo-Saxon/Celtic opposition, turn out to be clearly palpable in the German/Polish relationship (Chapman et al. 2004).

The modern/traditional relationship, as it is articulated in this issue of *International Studies of Management and Organization*, is made of the same stuff. This relates directly to the German/Polish opposition and to the Wielkopolska local variation of this. Germany is, in this context, the modern/global and Poland is, in this context, the traditional/local. Germany, in this context, is rational while Poland, in this context, is something other than rational; what that is can be derived from the oppositions above with both bad and good interpretations. The distinction between rationality, as a cold economic abstraction, and humanity, as a local familial relationship-based quality, connects the theme of this issue of *International Studies of Management and Organization* and the empirical example on which we are reporting.

In this article, we argue that the German/Polish contrast, as expressed by the managers whom we have researched and listened to, can be understood in terms of the oppositions listed above. We also argue, therefore, that the German/Polish contrast can be used as a particular illustration of the more general opposition between modern/traditional and global/ local as these are commonly perceived and expressed. We also take the example

324   *Peter J. Buckley et al.*

of a particular region of Poland, Wielkopolska, and show that the German/Polish oppositions are used in this region to construct an opposition between this region and the rest of Poland as a means by which managers in Wielkopolska put themselves on the modern/global side of the oppositions in contrast to the traditional/local in the rest of Poland. This provides a powerful illustration of the importance, vitality, and versatility of these images and metaphors.

The German/Slavonic contrast

This article is primarily about the relationship between Polish and German managers, as seen from the German and Polish perspective. Many of the ideas that we discuss, however, do not only make sense in the modern context but can be made intelligible through reference to the deep historical links between Germany and Poland. Poland and Germany – and their predecessor states and polities, and the people that live and have lived in them – have a mixed and often difficult history of conflict and cooperation. Chapman summarized the situation as follows:

> The confrontation of German and Slav has had a long sometimes bitter history (see Burleigh 1988; Czubinski and Pajewski 1987; Sugar and Lederer 1969); it is a confrontation which has been strongly economically marked for most of the last two hundred years – by relative prosperity, through differential political rights, by occupational differences, by the Capitalist – Communist divide, and now by the frontier of the European Community, with its tacit line between the "haves" and the "have-nots." (1994, 244)

In discussing the history of Polish-German interaction, one can go back to the founding mythologies of the Polish statehood. The Germans took Christianity to the Slavs; this was, indeed, one of the founding events of Polish nationhood. Christianity, a formal system of rectitude, written and recorded, has always been a force giving powers of definition to those that wielded it, and from the first, the Germans were, in a sense, a step ahead of the Slavs.

Popular thought in central Europe often produces images of civilization in the West (where Germany is the West), which progressively dissipates toward the east. The idea is arguably as old as the Roman empire, trying to find stable eastern boundaries where the line could be drawn between the empire and the barbarian. Christianity moved from south and west to north and east, and those that were incorporated into Christendom, with its renewed scholarship, writing, recording, and legitimating of authority and order, were happy to embrace the idea of themselves as civilized, in contrast to their as-yet-unincorporated neighbors. In German historiography of the sixteenth and seventeenth centuries, German travelers to Poland tended to consider the Vistula river as a border of Europe, and anything located farther east was described by them as a foreign and a less developed civilization (Krzeminski 2002).

There are centuries of vivid history between the evangelization of central Europe and the modern day, but it is worth noting straightaway that the idea of some kind of civilization decline, from west to east, is still potent in central and eastern Europe, and indeed within Poland itself. A person in Poznań in the west, for example, looks down upon people in Bialystok in the east, and people in Bialystok in the east are glad that, at least, they are not in Belarus.

One element of civilization that has given substance to this idea is modern technology. In general, technology transfer in central and eastern Europe has been from west to east and has often been visibly slow and difficult, to the frustration of policymakers and observers (see Wandycz 1974; for a wealth of examples, see also Landes 1998).

Breyer (1955) describes the differences between the Germanizing tendencies of Prussia and the indigenous Polish population, speaking of "the vices, commoner among the Polish than the German residents, of drunkenness, lack of industry, and a tendency towards indolence and vagabondage" (Hagen 1980, 60, citing Breyer 1955). The king of Prussia, Frederick William II, touring South Prussia in 1793, said that it "has been much neglected by bad cultivation and Polish economy ('economie polonèse' [sic])" (Hagen 1980, 52). The phrases "Polish economy" and "economie polonèse" are both translations of the vernacular German *Polnische wirtschaft*, which Hagen describes as "a heavily ironical phrase" (1980, 29).

Wandycz, in his contribution to *A History of East Central Europe*, summarizes the attempt of Poles from Poznania (a predominantly Polish-speaking area incorporated into the Prussian empire under Bismarck) to compete with the dominant German and German-speaking community. He says:

> The Prussian Pole developed characteristics that distinguished him from his countryman under Austria or Russia. He was better educated; he was disciplined, hard working, and enjoyed a higher standard of living; he could compete on nearly equal terms with the Germans. An article written in 1872 well expressed the Poznanian concept of "organic work": "If you are a shoemaker make better shoes, if you are a blacksmith do a better job on the cart...if you are a Polish housewife, make better and cleaner butter, have better vegetables, linen, fruits, and poultry than the Germans have. In this way you will save yourself and Poland....Learning, work, order, and thrift, these are our new weapons." (1974, 229)

Ideas like this are continuous throughout the nineteenth and the first half of the twentieth centuries in the articulation of Polish/German relations

326   *Peter J. Buckley et al.*

(Burleigh 1988, 3–6). The problem is complicated by the partitions of Poland, which meant that Poland did not exist as a state for the entire nineteenth century. During this period, Poland was divided between Prussian, Russian, and Austrian sectors. The opposition between Poles and Germans was realized within the Prussian-governed areas where the Poles were the ethnic majority. The opposition between Poles and Germans, and more largely between Slavs and Germans, was realized and articulated also through the difference between Prussian and Russian Poland – a difference that in 2002 was still palpable.

The extent to which these old and well-established ideas still exist in the world of today is controversial and problematic. The problem is a sensitive one because the ethnic characterizations of popular discourse grew, in the twentieth century and in Germany, into racial and would-be scientific characterizations whose basis and intent became, for the postwar world, something like the quintessence of evil. Nazi Germany put into operation the idea that the Slavonic peoples (as well as others, of course) were less than human and could be treated accordingly. The results were disastrous for central Europe, for Russia, and for Germany itself. In very sincere reparation, Germany since 1945 has made a sustained and profound attempt to renounce the Nazi past and to recreate itself as a model member of the community of nations. It is potentially controversial, therefore, even perhaps wounding, to seem to argue that there is, in terms of interethnic perception, any continuity between the Germany of the 1930s and the Germany of the early twenty-first century. We can make some suggestion of continuity of opinions, however, even if they are not expressed with the same confidence and vigor.

In the immediate postwar period, the frontiers of Poland were shifted westward as parts of what had been Germany became Poland and parts of what had been Poland became Russian (or Ukrainian or Belarusian). This involved large-scale displacement of people, refugee-creation, and misery. Some of the inhabitants of what had been rural eastern Poland were relocated in the ethnically cleansed urban infrastructure of what had been Germany and was now western Poland. This involved putting disaffected rural refugees of Slavonic ethnicity in an urban infrastructure with which they had no experience and which had been built by Germans for whom they had no love. As a film set for illustrating the traditional Prussian view of German/Polish relations, for exemplifying *Polnische wirtschaft*, nothing better could have been devised. The episode is fully described by Mach, who says:

> Even today many people remember the first days after arrival and find pleasure and satisfaction in telling stories about the amount and variety of goods the Germans had left; how the newcomers were smashing pottery and glass, damaging books and breaking windows. Everything

of unknown value was valueless and everything which was German, which was practically everything, was ownerless and could be taken or destroyed. (1989, 168)

The Polish housewives of Poznania, trying to make cleaner butter than their German neighbors, would have been shocked. The Germans would perhaps only have thought that this was *Polnische wirtschaft* as they had been taught to expect it.

Some of the structures of opposition can be built into the very different postwar experiences of (West) Germany and Poland. Germany experienced the postwar miracle, a period of spectacular economic growth and restoration of prosperity and civil society. Poland, by contrast, experienced forty-five years of central planning, with the gradual revelation of the inherent weaknesses of this vast experiment. The economy of Poland, the entire consumer and industrial fabric, grew in many obvious respects increasingly ramshackle over this period. A well-dressed German, in the early 1990s, might well have looked over the border at the Polish neighbors and found metaphors from a much earlier period still appropriate to what he saw.

The ideas take vernacular rather than official form in the most recent period. According to Krzeminski (2002), for example, Polish-German prejudices are most visible in humor and caricatures. These reflect long-standing symbols and patterns, with wealthy Germans opposed to impoverished Poles, powerful Germany opposed to weak Poland, and so on. There is a pattern of opposition of images, where the one is opposed to the other, does not share in the other, and is permanently different from the other.

Research method

This exploratory study adopts a qualitative, interpretive methodological approach and treats managerial perceptions as a focus of analysis. The qualitative, interpretive approach is argued to offer a more certain and precise understanding of the societies under investigation from the point of view of those who are being studied (D'Iribarne 1996–97; Miles and Huberman 1994; Yin 1994).

This study aims to identify the Polish perceptions of German managers, and of themselves, as well as the German perceptions of Polish managers, and of themselves. Therefore we did not try to determine in advance which questions needed answering. We wanted the managers' views and opinions expressed in their own terms and expressing their own priorities. This is in line with the dominant research concern in social anthropology and has been expressed as a concern to research "native categories" (Buckley and Chapman 1997; Harris 2000, 2003).

The study was conducted through fifty-one face-to-face in-depth interviews with managers in eleven companies in different sectors in Germany

328 *Peter J. Buckley et al.*

Table 14.1 Characteristics of the respondents

Respondents[a]	Gender	Age bracket	Experience at a company	Living abroad	International travel[b]
A2_PL	Male	31–35	2 years	No	6
C1_PL	Male	46–50	8 years	Yes	15
C2_GE	Male	41–45	1.5 years	Yes	Most
C2_PL	Male	41–45	1 year	No	7
C3_PL	Male	36–40	15 years	No	7
D1_PL	Male	46–50	6 years	Yes	20
D2_GE	Male	31–35	7 years	No	20
D2_PL	Male	46–50	2.5 years	No	10
D3_GE	Male	31–35	1.5 years	Yes	More than 20
D3_PL	Female	46–50	4 years	No	10
E1_PL	Male	31–35	7 years	No	1
E2_GE	Male	36–40	8 years	No	13
E2_PL	Female	36–40	2 years	Yes	5
E3_GE	Male	26–30	2 months	No	8
E3_PL	Male	31–35	4 years	No	10
E4_GE	Male	41–45	6 years	Yes	30–40
E5_GE	Male	56–60	10 years	Yes	20–30
E6_GE	Male	26–30	19 months	No	15
F2_PL	Female	31–35	2 years	Yes	20
F3_PL	Male	41–45	5 years	No	5
F4_PL	Male	41–45	6 years	No	5
F5_PL	Male	31–35	5 years	Yes	10
G1_PL	Male	51–55	20 years	No	8
G2_GE	Male	36–40	13 years	No	15
G2_PL	Male	31–35	6 years	Yes	10
G3_GE	Male	41–45	12 years	No	10
G3_PL	Male	46–50	7 years	No	3
G4_GE	Male	56–60	30 years	Yes	10
H2_PL	Male	36–40	1 year	No	20
H3_PL	Female	36–40	1 year	No	6
H4_PL	Male	51–55	23 years	No	5
I1_PL	Male	51–55	28 years	Yes	Most
I2_PL	Male	36–40	4 years	No	10
J1_PL	Female	41–45	25 years	No	Not many
J2_PL	Male	51–55	7 years	Yes	Many
P_A1_GE	Male	41–45	15 years	No	8–9
P_A1_PL	Female	41–45	10 years	No	5–6
P_B1_GE	Male	46–50	18 years	No	14
P_B1_PL	Male	31–35	8 years	No	5
P_C1_GE	Male	46–50	20 years	Yes	25
P_C1_PL	Male	46–50	8 years	Yes	15
P_D1_GE	Male	31–35	5 years	Yes	12–15
P_D1_PL	Male	36–40	15 years	No	8
P_E1_GE	Male	36–40	5 years	No	18
P_E1_PL	Male	31–35	7 years	No	1

Continued

Business in Developing and Transitional Countries   329

Table 14.1   Continued

Respondents[a]	Gender	Age bracket	Experience at a company	Living abroad	International travel[b]
P_F1_PL	Female	31–35	3 years	No	3
P_F2_PL	Female	31–35	5 years	No	7
P_G1_GE	Male	51–55	20 years	Yes	Many
P_H1_PL	Male	31–35	4 years	No	Many
P_M1_PL	Male	36–40	15 years	No	7

[a]. Respondents were designated as German (GE) and Polish (PL).
[b]. Number of countries visited for business or leisure.

and Poland. The respondents selected for the interviews were general managers from the German-affiliated Polish companies and area directors responsible for eastern Europe in German parent companies (see Table 14.1 for further characteristics of the respondents). The purpose of this selection was to identify respondents with extensive relevant knowledge of the topic. Interviews were held initially with a general manager from each of the companies, and then typically with the deputy general manager. Further respondents were identified by the first interviewees, employing a snowballing technique (Marschan 1996).

All the interviews were conducted by the same researcher in as unstructured a way as the respondents would allow (Chapman 2001). An interview guide (Appendix 1) was prepared to provide a framework for the researcher if the interviewees ran out of narrative. The guide was there to serve the larger purpose, which was to encourage managers to share their view of the world, specifically of their immediate business situation. Every interview had the potential to develop in different ways, which the researcher tried to encourage, aiming to impose minimum constraints on potential topics of interest (D'Iribarne 1996–97; Miles and Huberman 1994; Vaara 2002; Yin 1994). It was anticipated that there might be interesting material concerning national cultural issues, and interviewees were to some extent provoked to discuss these if they found them of interest. After this, however, the issues were allowed to surface as and when they would and were given the time and importance the interviewees wished to accord them.

The process of analysis of qualitative data is one of the most demanding and least examined aspects of qualitative research methods. Moreover,

> The exact manner in which the investigator will travel the path from data to observations, conclusions, and scholarly assertion cannot and should not be fully specified. Different problems will require different strategies. Many solutions will be ad hoc ones. (McCracken 1988, 41)

330 *Peter J. Buckley et al.*

In the current study, the interviews were transcribed, read, and reread. Written-up data were compared across interviews and across the companies and analyzed for common themes, stories, and issues. This was achieved by multiple readings of the transcripts. The interview transcripts were sample-coded by the authors and then verified by three other colleagues. The three reviewers of the interviews were instructed to work separately. The results of their coding were discussed during several meetings and through correspondence. The final themes were agreed as a result of a discussion during those meetings.

The data were organized by using Microsoft Word features for managing long documents. Sections of the interviews were then color coded according to similarity of content and theme. An extensive activity of this kind has yielded a short list of main themes to subsume the main areas of interest in the data. The main themes were (1) the worker who could not decide for himself, (2) close neighbors and distant friends, (3) motives for market entry, (4) motives for M&As (merger and acquisitions), (5) barriers to M&As, and (6) level of competition in the industry. The texts from the interviews were then sorted according to these themes.

The main themes were the issues repeatedly mentioned by the interviewees, discussed by many of them, or pointed out by executives as important. The attention of the researchers was also directed to important absences and the reasons behind them. The most consistent generator of differences and commonalities between the transcripts was provided by the nationality of the interviewees. This was not imposed upon the transcripts by the analysis (except in as much as the interviewees were chosen by nationality) but, rather, was one that emerged from the interviewees' accounts. This implicit, or explicit, national resonance in the themes gave rise to recurrent oppositions used in constructing pictures of nationality and pictures of self and other. Using recurrent oppositions of this kind is a technique derived from structural anthropology and structural linguistics.

This research has a number of limitations. First, the current study adopted a qualitative, interpretive approach with a relatively small number of interviews. Although qualitative research does not aim to generalize the findings but, rather, to form a unique interpretation of events (Creswell 1994), some limited generalizability of this study was ensured by using an interview guide during data collection. Second, using only one researcher to collect the data could be seen as a potential source of bias in data interpretation. The risk of this was, however, reduced by the use of multiple sources of information (e.g., press cuttings, corporate information) and verification of the identified themes by colleagues. Third, the focus of the study was narrowed down to only one region of Poland. Fourth, companies approached in the study were from different industries; this was a concession made in order to meet all the remaining selections criteria. Ideally intraindustry case research, of one or several industries, might be preferred to reduce the impact of industry-specific effects.

Business in Developing and Transitional Countries 331

Several considerations within the present work might serve to assure its validity and reliability. First, a clear rationale for using qualitative inquiry has been adopted (Parkhe 1997), and data collection, analysis, and interpretation procedures have been clarified (Brewer 2001; Brouthers and Bamossy 1997; Festing 1997; O'Grady and Lane 1996; Tsang 2001), as detailed at the beginning of this section. Second, one of the principles of data collection is the use of multiple sources of evidence in order to achieve triangulation (Yin 1994); in the current study, primary data were complemented by various other sources (e.g., annual reports and leaflets of companies, press cuttings, internet sources, historical sources). This approach allowed the inclusion of new facts and ideas and increased the opportunity for checking interpretations and identifying patterns. Third, the narratives were accompanied by the verbatim responses of the executives under investigation to support claims being made in the article and to offer the reader the opportunity of drawing their own conclusions (Beechler and Yang 1994; Marschan 1996). Fourth, the findings were crossed-tabulated with the characteristics of the respondents (e.g., age, length of experience in the company, international exposure), types of the companies (e.g., M&As, greenfield, or equity joint ventures), and different industries. This provided some useful insights and helped to build the internal validity of the study (Eisenhardt 1989). Fifth, the findings of the study were compared with conflicting and similar literature, which as Eisenhardt put it, "builds internal validity, raises theoretical level, and sharpens construct definitions" (1989, 533).

Empirical evidence from Germany

The images of civilization in the West, which progressively disperse toward the East, find support in our data. This was discussed by the German executives in the context of the safety of the Polish market. Quite interestingly, it received much more attention from the interviewees than economic indicators of their target markets, such as good economic growth and a low rate of inflation (e.g., P_B1_GE, D2_GE).

It is important to note that the interviewees would always refer to the issue of risk (political, financial, country, etc.) in the Polish market in relative terms. The German executives, representing all age groups, often compared it with Russia or Ukraine and concluded that Poland was much safer than those markets (but still less safe than the West). The analysis of the qualitative data showed that the Germans saw a negative relation between safety and eastern Europe. In short, it could be described as "the closer to the East, the less safe it gets."

German managers made many references to attitudes toward authority and responsibility. In the context of the firm, German managers saw Poles as individuals lacking in relevant educational and work skills and

332 *Peter J. Buckley et al.*

so accustomed to authoritarian management that they were unable or unwilling to take responsibility for problems themselves:

> The problem is taking over the responsibility. We [in Germany] have this problem, too, but if someone is responsible for certain area they take care of it. (E5_GE)
>
> One does everything with these people..., because the Pole is capable, but one has to manage them, show them a new way. (E4_GE)

These Polish national qualities were contrasted with those in Germany and presented as a development over time, with Poland lagging behind Germany:

> Polish employees work like Germans did 15 years ago. What the boss says is the truth, and they do it; they follow. In Germany this is not the case. They question the boss a lot. (C2_GE)

German managers also pointed out that Poles operated in a networking system and that it was very important to have the right connections in Poland in order to conduct any business activity there. Corruption in Poland was also mentioned in this context.

> You have to know the right people. The people really taking the decision. And something like a bribe doesn't...well it's helpful. (P_B1_GE)

The German managers (e.g., E5_GE) also made reference to Polish nationalism, which they had experienced while doing business in Poland. This mainly emerged as a feature of the Polish government, which, according to the informants, usually acted in favor of domestic Polish companies. Consider,

> It can be also bad luck. We have placed an offer, but the Polish government gave it to the Polish applicant. There is a little bit of chauvinism there. (G3_GE)

German managers also referred to a rather undesirable form of materialism on the Polish side (e.g., P_B1_GE, D3_GE, G3_GE). Although in their view Poles were very committed to their jobs and were able to work long hours, they would not do it unless they were paid accordingly (D3_GE, G3_GE). Some of the executives would even call Poles lazy because they do not want to work if they are not paid a lot of money for it (D3_GE). They were always looking for good compensation for their work, which can be in a form of money, cars, or other benefits: "When they have a goal, they [will] do everything to achieve it" (G3_GE). The positive features of Poles mentioned

Business in Developing and Transitional Countries   333

Table 14.2 Summary of the German characterization of the German/Polish Oppositions

Germans	Poles
Do the coaching	Need authority
Set the rules	Need rules and hierarchy
Responsible	Evade responsibility
Honest	Corrupted
Fair	Set higher standards for foreigners
Safe	Safer than in Russia
(Tolerant)[a]	Nationalistic
Orderly	(Disorderly)
Disciplined	(Undisciplined)
Diligent	Lazy
(Controlled)	Warm and hospitable
(Can work individually)	Work in a networking system
(Altruistic)	Materialistic
Long tradition of law	(Lawless)

[a] Items in parenthesis were not explicitly articulated by interviewees. They were inserted into the above table, however, because they were implied by the executives. They are oppositions to the characteristics attributed by the Germans to the Poles and themselves.

unanimously by executives were Polish hospitality and warmth (e.g., D2_GE, D3_GE). A summary of the German characterization of the German/Polish opposition is presented in Table 14.2.

Empirical evidence from Poland

The analysis of the qualitative data has shown that Polish executives strongly emphasized that their German colleagues were very different from them. Polish managers believe that they possess a "Polish mentality," which is distinctive from the German one (e.g., P_D1_PL, D2_PL, G3_PL). In this context, the Polish managers described their German colleagues as "cybernetic" (or "robotic") and good at routines but not good at improvising.

Furthermore, according to Polish managers, Germany had a long tradition of a state of order, where the above-mentioned cybernetic structure of the society functioned without interruptions and where the basic needs of the society were fulfilled. Poland, by contrast, was a "young democracy" in which these characteristics were scarcely developed; this has forced Poles "to manage as one can."

However, Polish managers did not see this as a defect. On the contrary, although they admitted the need to be coached by their foreign partners, they insisted on being treated as equal partners by German investors (e.g.,

334 *Peter J. Buckley et al.*

A2_PL, E1_PL, E3_PL, G2_PL) and contrasted the German capacity for routine with their own creativity, imagination, versatility and spontaneity.

Germans were also described as being down to earth, cold, reserved, presumptuous, and inclined to assume superiority. Again, Poles compared the orderly discipline of the Germans (with its assumption of superiority) with their own more creative ability to be "intelligent and smart" in dealing with the Germans.

Polish managers were generally prepared to accord Germans the virtues of being responsible, well organized, disciplined, diligent, and clean. They were less inclined to accept being characterized as irresponsible, disorganized, undisciplined, lazy, and dirty. When the Polish managers characterized themselves, they generally wished to cast themselves in a flattering light. A summary of the Polish characterization of the German/ Polish opposition is presented in Table 14.3. It is clear that the German/ Polish contrast, as attested immediately above, has congruence with the basic self/other oppositions and with the romantic reappraisal self/other oppositions as these were presented earlier.

We now move on to a local reinterpretation of these oppositions. Wielkopolska is a region in western Poland, with the city of Poznań (which the Germans called Posen) as its center. This is a part of Poland that, during the nineteenth-century partition of Poland, was within the Prussian/German

Table 14.3 Summary of the Polish characterization of the German/Polish oppositions

Germans	Poles
Cybernetic society	Imaginative
Lack spontaneity and poetics	Spontaneous
Perform routine tasks	Creative
Down to earth	Romantic
Limited	Versatile
Cold and reserved	Warm and open
Uninspired	Intelligent
Credulous	Smart
Show their superiority	Privileged to work for Germans
Presumptuous	(Modest)[a]
Responsible	Evade responsibility
Well organized	Chaotic
Disciplined	Need authority
Very wealthy	(Poor)
Clean and tidy	(Dirty and untidy)
Diligent	(Lazy)

a. Items in parenthesis were not explicitly articulated by interviewees. They were inserted into the above table, however, because they were implied by the executives. They are oppositions to the characteristics attributed by the Poles to the Germans and themselves.

Business in Developing and Transitional Countries 335

sphere of influence. It is a source of pride to the inhabitants of Wielkopolska, including the managers themselves, that they have a Wielkopolanin mentality. This was widely discussed by the executives representing two age groups, namely 31–35 and 46–50, who traveled moderately and who never lived abroad. This region has been described by one of the interviewees as: "There is no other genuine region like it in Poland" (E3_PL).

It is also located centrally, between the east and the west, and Poznań, its capital, is an axis city between north and southern Poland (E1_PL). It is believed that this region is inhabited by people with Wielkopolanin mentality, which was not very much affected by the communist era in Poland:

> In [Wielkopolanin] mentality the communist system did not cause a lot of damage; it pays. (E3_PL)

To the people of Wielkopolska, the Wielkopolanin mentality "is very different from the mentality, personality of an average inhabitant of Siedlce, Warsaw, Rzeszow, or Bialystok" (A2_PL).

Residents of Wielkopolska, called Wielkopolanie, are conscientious and value their work. As described by one of the interviewees:

> Regional differences are quite visible in politics, you know. We Wielkopolanie enter 'the game' as the last ones, but once we have done it we simply go for it. I can see significant [regional] differences, for example [in Poznań] when one drinks one drinks, and when one works one works. One cannot see it in other regions. We do not wait for someone to give us something, we are not waiting for subsidies. When you compare Warsaw and Poznań, it is really scary. The mess is getting on our nerves. (F3_PL)

The Wielkopolanin mentality was shaped by numerous historical events connected with Germany, not least the partitions of Poland, when Wielkopolska fell into the German sphere. This was expressed as follows by one of the executives:

> Poland is divided into Poland A, B, and C. "Poland A" is a former Prussian partition, "B" – Austrian, and "C" – all the rest. This influences the present order of matters, for example Prussian-diligence, Austrian-order, and I won't mention the rest. Poznań is located in the center of Poland A. This area of Poland has certain [good] economic habits. ... Poland A has got a well-prepared workforce, with habits of the ethic of work. (E1_PL)

This suggests a perceived positive Prussian influence on the work habits of Wielkopolanie discernible in their interactions with foreign investors. An example of this might be the German idea of "continuity of change," by which is meant the continuous search for improvement in processes and production. This need for continuity of improvement, when introduced by German investors into Polish reality, was said by Poles from Wielkopolska to cause confusion and upset the Poles from other parts of Poland, who were used to a stable working environment as well as relatively low expectations of their work performance. The Wielkopolanie, however, believe that they can cope quite well with these challenges. This is because they have the ability to adjust to these new conditions "in their genes" as the remnants of *dryl pruski* (i.e., "Prussian knack" or "Prussian discipline"). It is interesting that German executives, when presented with this idea, opposed it strongly (e.g., G4_GE), and so did the executives originating from other parts of Poland (e.g., D1_PL). The internal diversity within Poland, which the Wielkopolanie were prepared to perceive and to manipulate to their own credit, was less visible from outside Poland. According to Chapman et al. (2004), this is the common fate of strongly held regional perceptions of diversity.

From what we have seen so far, the Wielkopolska mentality is pulled in two ways in relation to the images and oppositions that we have discussed. It has German features, by contrast to the rest of Poland, but it has Polish features in German eyes. In the ethnographic situation that we investigated, in which the models for business and management activity come from outside, particularly from Germany, we would expect such tensions. The same executives emphasize that the Polish mentality is different from the German one, and, at the same time, they claim to possess German-like features. The passage from one of the interviewees can perhaps shed some light on it:

> It seems to me that these are historical implications, because still the longest war of modern Europe did affect us here. We did fight economically during the times of Prussian partition. There were many economic innovations created at that time, which exist in one form or another up to the present. I also think that these initiatives, which were instilled into the nation at that time, result in the existence of many small and medium sized firms, which are developing. (D3_PL)

It is arguable that these characteristics were generated through Prussian (German) influence, not only through external influence during the Polish partitions but also through self-comparison and competition by the Poles themselves. Davies supports this view, describing the Polish movement in Posnania as follows:

> The temper and the possibilities of the Poles in Prussia were far better suited to conciliation than to revolution. ... It [the Polish movement in Posnania] was very staid and bourgeois, and in many ways was an avid

imitator of German virtues. The Poles of Posen were consciously striving to outdo their German neighbors at their own game. (1981, 122)

This view can be supported by Wandycz (1974) quoted earlier in the context of the Polish movement in Posnania.

Conclusions

We have argued that we can make sense of the German/Polish contrast and the analogous Wielkopolska/Poland contrast using concepts derived from structural anthropology. We have illustrated this argument using both historical material and empirical data from recent interviews with managers.

Our argument is that detailed two-country contrasts are an important complement to the standard approaches to cultural difference in international business research and that social anthropological ideas about classification, structural opposition, and definition of the self and the other are fertile sources of insight for understanding such two-country contrasts. We have also argued that local versions of nationally accepted constructions of difference can use the same ideas and metaphors but come to dramatically different conclusions. The case of Wielkopolanin managers in Poland is a vivid demonstration of this.

We argue that there are compelling structural analogies between the global/local contrast, the German/Polish contrast, and the Wielkopolska/ Poland contrast. Three conclusions can be drawn from this. First, the structures of opposition to which we have drawn attention are important and versatile. Second, relativism, in understanding global/national, cross-national, and national/regional differences, is more important than attempting absolute characterizations. Third is the hypothesis that the oppositions we have outlined seem to be universal features of human perception and identity construction.

There is a degree of congruence between the cultural differences that we are discussing and Hofstede's dimensions (see also Chapman 1996–97, 18–19; Chapman and Antoniou 1998; D'Iribarne 1996–97; Nasierowski and Mikula 1998). This is important and interesting, and elsewhere we have discussed this, particularly in relation to power distance and uncertainty avoidance (Chapman et al. 2004, 2008). There is an important difference between Hofstede's approach (and the approach of those that have followed him) and our own. In Hofstede's paradigm, a culture is a national shared set of values – a quasi objective reality – that can be measured and observed. We approach culture as something interpreted and imagined by those within it. There is no conflict between the two approaches but, rather, interesting and fruitful complementarities.

Several issues arise from this research that deserve further attention. First, as multinational corporations continue to expand into areas of the world

338 *Peter J. Buckley et al.*

that were previously out of bounds, the oppositional framework applied in this study might find further applications in other international business contexts. Further research could encompass a comparison of North European versus South European perceptions in a business context or, indeed, further comparison of Germanic and Slavic perceptions using other east European countries (e.g., Russia, Ukraine, Czech Republic, or Slovakia). It would also be interesting to look at the original Anglo-Saxon and Celtic contrast from Chapman's (1992) framework in a business context (e.g., England versus Ireland). Second, with the fall of communism, the opening up of the economy, and Polish accession to the European Union, the presence of foreign investors is increasing in Poland. Polish managers as well as foreign investors currently have much more experience working together than was the case when this research was started. Therefore, it would be interesting to follow up this study with a second round of interviews with the same respondents to see to what extent the experience of working together has influenced their attitudes. It would be particularly exciting to see how Polish attitudes toward foreign investors have changed, especially because in the current research, the Poles demonstrated dual, sometimes contradictory, views of working with their foreign colleagues.

Third, with respect to management theory and its debate on the issue of convergence or divergence of managers' behavior (Tayeb 1994), it would be interesting to see whether Polish managers from Wielkopolska became more like German managers or maintained their differences. The perceptions discussed in the current study are of long standing, and one might not expect them to change significantly. Hofstede provides support for this hypothesis by maintaining that in his IBM study "there was no international convergence of cultural values over time, except toward increased individualism for countries having become richer" (2001, 454). The authors further predict that the phenomenon of cultural divergence will hold for the next few hundred years.

Appendix 1. Interview guide – Germany/Poland

Introduction:

Note the time (beginning and end)
> Confirm confidentiality
> Explain the objective and relevance of the research
> Biographical data questionnaire
> Starting question: Can you tell me a few words about your company?
What has happened in the company since we last met?

Guiding questions:

What is your role in the company?

How did your firm get where it is internationally? (First international activity, when, how, main markets)

Could you tell me in a few words about your activities in the Polish/German market? (Why Poland/Germany? Were other possibilities in the region considered? First contact, main difficulties, legal system, main competitors, exceptional events since entering the market, advice to other foreign investors)

What do you associate Poland/Germany with?

Do you perceive Poles/Germans as a uniform nation? (Description of main characteristics at national and company level, comparison with Germans/Poles)

References

Ardener, E. 1967. "The Nature of the Reunification of Cameroon." In *African Integration and Disintegration*, ed. A. Hazelwood. Oxford: Oxford University Press.

——. 1972. "Language, Ethnicity and Population." *Journal of the Anthropological Society of Oxford* 3 (3): 125–132.

——. 1974. "Social Anthropology and Population." In *Population and Its Problems*, ed. H.B. Parry, 25–50. Oxford: Clarendon Press.

——. 1989. *The Voice of Prophecy and Other Essays*. Oxford: Blackwell.

Bakacsi, G., T. Sándor, K. András, and I. Viktor. 2002. "Eastern European Cluster: Tradition and Transition." *Journal of World Business* 37 (1): 69–80.

Beechler, S., and J.Z. Yang. 1994. "The Transfer of Japanese-Style Management to American Subsidiaries: Contingencies, Constraints and Competencies." *Journal of International Business Studies* 25 (3): 467–491.

Berger, P., and T. Luckmann. 1967. *The Social Construction of Reality: A Treatise in the Sociology of Knowledge*. London: Anchor Books.

Bourdieu, P. 1986. *Distinction: A Social Critique of the Judgment of Taste*. London: Routledge.

Brewer, P. 2001. "International Market Selection: Developing a Model from Australian Case Studies." *International Business Review* 10 (2): 155–174.

Breyer, R. 1955. "Die südpreussischen Beamten und die Polenfrage." *Zeitschrift für Ostforschung* 4 (4).

Brouthers, K., and G.J. Bamossy. 1997. "The Role of Key Stakeholder in International Joint Venture Negotiations: Case Studies from Eastern Europe." *Journal of International Business Studies* 28 (2): 285–308.

Buckley, P.J., and M. Chapman. 1997. "The Use of 'Native Categories' in Management Research." *British Journal of Management* 8 (3): 283–299.

Burleigh, M. 1988. *Germany Turns Eastwards – A Study of Ostforschung in the Third Reich*. Cambridge: Cambridge University Press.

Chapman, M. 1989. "History and Ethnicity – Introduction." In *History and Ethnicity*, ed. E. Tonkin, M. McDonald, and M. Chapman, iv–xxii. London: Routledge.

——. 1992. *The Celts: The Construction of a Myth*. London: Macmillan.

——. 1994. "The Commercial Realization of the Community Boundary." In *The Anthropology of Europe: Identity and Boundaries in Conflict*, ed. V.A. Goddard, J.R., Llobera, and C. Shore, 227–254. Oxford/Providence: Berg.

340   *Peter J. Buckley et al.*

——. 1996–97. "Social Anthropology, Business Studies, and Cultural Issues." *International Studies of Management and Organization* 26 (4): 30–47.

——. 2001. "Social Anthropology and Business Studies: Some Considerations of Method." In *Inside Organizations: Anthropologists at Work,* ed. D. Gellner and E. Hirsch, pt. 1 (1), 19–33. Oxford: Berg.

Chapman, M., and C. Antoniou. 1998. "Uncertainty Avoidance in Greece: An Ethnographic Illustration." In *The Strategy and Organization of International Business,* ed. P. Buckley, F. Burton, and H. Mirza. London: Macmillan.

Chapman, M. ; J. Clegg ; and H. Gajewska-De Mattos. 2004. "Poles and Germans: An International Business Relationship." *Human Relations* 57 (8): 983–1015.

Chapman, M., H. Gajewska-De Mattos, J. Clegg, and P. Buckley. 2008. "Close Neighbors and Distant Friends – Perceptions of Cultural Distance." *International Business Review* 17 (3): 217–234.

Czubinski, A., and J. Pajewski. 1987. *Polacy i Niemcy: Dziesiec wiekow sasiedztwa* (Poland and Germany: Ten Centuries as Neighbors). Warsaw: Wydawnictwo Naukowe.

Davies, N. 1981. *God's Playground: The History of Poland, 1795 to the Present,* vol. 2. Oxford: Clarendon Press.

D ' Iribarne, P. 1996–97. "The Usefulness of Ethnographic Approach to International Comparison of Organizations." *International Studies of Management and Organization* 26 (4): 30–47.

Eisenhardt, K.M. 1989. "Building Theories from Case Study Research." *Academy of Management Review* 14 (4): 532–550.

Festing, M. 1997. "International Human Resource Management Strategies in Multinational Corporations: Theoretical Assumptions and Empirical Evidence from German Firms." *Management International Review* 37 (10): 43–63.

Hagen, W. 1980. *Germans, Poles and Jews: The Nationality Conflict in the Prussian East, 1772–1914.* Chicago: University of Chicago Press.

Harris, S. 2000. "Reconciling Positive and Interpretative International Management Research: A Native Category Approach." *International Business Review* 9 (6): 755–770.

——. 2003. "National Values and Strategy Formation by Business Leaders." Ph.D. dissertation, University of Leeds.

Hastrup, K. 1998. *A Place Apart: An Anthropological Study of the Icelandic World.* Oxford: Oxford University Press.

Hofstede, G. 1980. *Culture's Consequences: International Differences in Work Related Values.* Beverly Hills, CA: Sage.

——. 1991. *Cultures and Organizations: Software of the Mind.* London: McGraw-Hill.

——. 2001. *Culture's Consequences: Comparing Values, Behaviors, Institutions and Organizations Across Nations,* 2d ed. London: Sage.

——. 2002. "Dimensions Do Not Exist: A Reply to Brendan McSweeney." *Human Relations,* 55 (11): 1355.

Hoppe, M. 2004. "An Interview with Geert Hofstede." *Academy of Management Executive* 18 (1): 75–79.

Kirkman, B., K. Lowe, and C. Gibson. 2006. "A Quarter Century of Culture's Consequences: A Review of Empirical Research Incorporating Hofstede's Cultural Values Framework." *Journal of International Business Studies* 37 (3): 285–320.

Kogut, B., and H. Singh. 1988. "The Effect of National Culture on the Choice of Entry Mode." *Journal of International Business Studies* 19 (3): 411–432.

Krzeminski, A. 2002. "Wszystokrady i najezdzcy" (Thieves and Invaders). *Polityka* 4: 2333.

Landes, D. 1998. *The Wealth and Poverty of Nations.* London: Little, Brown.

Leung, K., R. Bhagat, N. Buchan, M. Erez, and C. Gibson. 2005. "Culture and International Business: Recent Advances and Their Implications for Future Research." *Journal of International Business Studies* 36 (4): 357–378.

Lévi-Strauss, C. 1963. *La pensée sauvage*. Paris: Plon.

———. 1966. *The Savage Mind*. London: Weidenfeld and Nicolson.

Mach, Z. 1989. *Symbols, Conflict and Identity*. Krakow: Jagiellonian University.

Marschan, R. 1996. "New Structural Forms and Inter-Unit Communication in Multinationals. The Case of Kone Elevators." Ph.D. dissertation, Helsinki School of Economics and Business Administration.

McCracken, G. 1988. *The Long Interview*. London: Sage.

McDonald, M. 1990. *We Are Not French*. London: Routledge.

McSweeney, B. 2002a. "Hofstede's Model of National Cultural Differences and Their Consequences: A Triumph of Faith – A Failure of Analysis." *Human Relations* 55 (1): 89–118.

———. 2002b. "The Essentials of Scholarship: A Reply to Geert Hofstede." *Human Relations* 55 (11): 1363–1372.

Miles, M.B., and A.M. Huberman. 1994. *Qualitative Data Analysis: An Expanded Sourcebook*, 2d ed. London: Sage.

Molz, R., and M. Farashahi. 2011. "Doing Business in Emerging, Developing, and Transitional Economies: A Heterodox Interpretation." *International Studies of Management and Organization* 41 (1): 3–11.

Nasierowski, W., and B. Mikula. 1998. "Culture Dimensions of Polish Managers: Hofstede's Indices." *Organization Studies* 19 (3): 495–509.

O ' Grady, S., and H.W. Lane. 1996. "The Psychic Distance Paradox." *Journal of International Business Studies* 27 (20): 309–334.

Parkhe, A. 1997. " 'Messy' Research, Methodological Predispositions and Theory Development in International Joint Ventures." *Academy of Management Review* 18 (2): 227–268.

Pike, K. 1954. *Language in Relation to a Unified Theory of the Structure of Human Behavior*. Glendale, CA: Summer Institute of Linguistics.

Sapir, E. 1921. *Language: An Introduction to the Study of Speech*. New York: Harcourt.

Saussure, F. de. 1916. *Cours de linguistique générale*. Paris: Payot.

Smith, P. 2002. "Culture's Consequences: Something Old and Something New." *Human Relations* 55 (1): 119–135.

Sugar, P., and I. Lederer. 1969. *Nationalism in Eastern Europe*. Seattle and London: University of Washington Press.

Tayeb, M.H. 1994. "Organizations and National Culture: Methodology Considered." *Organization Studies* 15 (3): 429–446.

Tihanyi, L., D. Griffith, and C. Russell. 2005. "The Effect of Cultural Distance on Entry Mode Choice, International Diversification, and MNE Performance: A Meta-Analysis." *Journal of International Business Studies* 36 (3): 270–283.

Triandis, H. 2004. "The Many Dimensions of Culture." *Academy of Management Executive* 18 (1): 88–93.

Trier, J. Von. 1931. *Der Deutsche Wortschatz im Sinnbezirk des Verstandes*. Heidelberg: Carl Winter.

Tsang, E.W.K. 2001. "Managerial Learning in Foreign-Invested Enterprises of China." *Management International Review* 41 (1): 29–51.

Ullmann, S. 1951. *The Principles of Semantics*. Glasgow: Jackson.

Vaara, E. 2002. "On the Discursive Construction of Success/Failure in Narratives of Post-Merger Integration." *Organization Studies* 23 (2): 211–248.

342 *Peter J. Buckley et al.*

Wandycz, P.S. 1974. "The Lands of Partitioned Poland, 1795–1918." In *A History of East Central Europe*, vol. 7, ed. P.F. Sugar and D.W. Treadgold. Seattle: University of Washington Press.

Wartburg, W. Von. 1943. *Einführung in Problematik und Methodik der Sprachwissenschaft*. Tübingen: Max Niemeyer.

Whorf, B. 1956. *Language, Thought and Reality*. Cambridge: MIT Press.

Williamson, D. 2002. "Foreword from a Critique of Hofstede's Model of National Culture." *Human Relations* 55 (11): 1373–1395.

Yin, R.K. 1994. *Case Study Research: Design and Methods*, 2d ed. London: Sage.

15
The Rise of the Japanese Multinational Enterprise: Then and Now

Introduction

This examination of Japanese multinational enterprises (MNEs) compares 'then' and 'now'. 'Now' is easily defined – 2008. 'Then' is a concept that tries to pin down the heyday of Japanese firms and therefore of the Japanese economy – or rather the point at which critics and commentators felt that the Japanese economy was at its height. An arbitrary date of 1985 might be used. During the craze for 'Japanese management', Japanese MNEs were felt to hold the answers to many of the key problems of Western economies – harmony (between capital and labour); efficiency in the use of resources; a widely networked economy (Gerlach and Lincoln 2004) based on long-term relationships (Liker *et al.* 1995, Dyer 2000); adaptability of the firm to changing economic locations and of products to local needs and, of course, constant innovation (Aoki 1984, 1990, Imai 1986). 'Now' (2008) looks different. The Japanese economy has an ageing population, rigidities in its domestic structure (very few mergers and acquisitions for instance) and inefficient services, including the vital area of financial services (Hoshi and Kashyap 2004). Japanese management no longer seems the panacea many once thought it to be and Japanese MNEs no longer seem so dominant, even so prevalent and certainly they are less salient.

This study sets out to show that the record of Japanese firms and Japanese management was never so good as it was claimed to be in its heyday, and that Japanese MNEs and their associated management styles are not so irrelevant as they are currently thought to be.

Literature review

Japanese style management and the Japanese economy

In 1985, the author co-wrote a paper on 'The Wit and Wisdom of Japanese Management' that set out to show that too much was being claimed for

344   *Peter J. Buckley*

Japanese management and that no one unified style of management existed in Japanese firms (Buckley and Mirza 1985). Further, much of the success of Japanese management was due to long-standing factors in the Japanese economy. Overnight success it was not! The then paradigmatic elements of 'Japanese management' were: lifetime employment, the seniority system and the enterprise union (Chen 2004). This was to conveniently ignore the fact that these elements applied only in a small subset of the Japanese economy. Non-core employees were not subject to these elements and there were key deficiencies in the management of intellectual property and in innovation. *The Economist* reports that although Japan:

> spends far above the OECD average on research and development (R&D) as a share of GDP, this money is not always put to good use. The Science Council of Japan estimates that Japan's R&D is only about half as efficient as Europe's and America's. Entrepreneurial start-ups account for only around 4 percent of firms in Japan, compared with 10 percent in Europe and over 14 percent in America, and Japan comes bottom in several rankings of entrepreneurship. (*The Economist* 2007, p. 3)

The Japanese economy

Then (in the 1980s) Japanese firms enjoyed high growth and market share, had high bank borrowing levels and achieved high levels of investments (the capital efficiency of this was largely ignored) (Abegglen and Stalk 1985, Imai 1986). Following high asset inflation and the subsequent bursting of the bubble, direct financing through bonds and equity is replacing bank financing, there is a focus on cash flow and the redesign of the Kaisha (Japanese corporations) is underway (Abegglen 2006).

However, there is continuity. Despite the increasing attention to corporate governance in Japan, Japanese firms still do not give excessive attention to the share price (protected as they are from predators by cultural and institutional barriers) (Kishi 2003, Chen 2004).

Has the world passed Japanese multinationals by? First, we must explore the modern (Western) multinational firm – the global factory – and then ask how far Japanese firms fit the model and how far Japanese exceptionalism exists. The 'global factory' is an ideal type of modern flexible multinational firms. It has been applied to Western multinational firms (Buckley 2007) and contrasted with older vertically and horizontally integrated multinationals. The analysis has not, so far, been applied to Japanese firms and there is a great opportunity to do so.

The global factory

Elements of the global factory

The notion of the global factory was introduced in Buckley (2004) and developed in Buckley and Ghauri (2004). The key idea is that MNEs are becoming much more like differentiated networks. They choose location and ownership policies so as to maximize profits but this does not necessarily involve internalizing their activities. Indeed, they have set a trend by outsourcing or offshoring their activities. Outsourcing involves utilizing 'buy' rather than 'make' in the Coasean 'externalize or internalize' decision (Coase 1937). Offshoring involves both the externalization option together with the 'make abroad' location decision (Buckley and Casson 1976). MNEs have developed the ability to 'fine slice' their activities on an even more precise calculus, and are increasingly able to alter location and internalization decisions for activities that were previously locationally bound by being tied to other activities and which could only be controlled by internal management fiat (Buckley 2004, 2007, Buckley and Ghauri 2004).

The opening up of the global factory has provided new opportunities for new locations to enter international business. Emerging countries such as India and China are subcontracting production and service activities from the brand-owning MNEs (Sturgeon and Lester 2003). The use of the market by MNEs enables new firms to compete for business against the internalized activities of the MNEs. This not only subjects every internalized activity to 'the market test', it also results in a differentiated network (Figure 15.1), which we term 'the global factory'.

Components of the global factory

The global supply chain is divided into three parts. The Original Equipment Manufacturers (OEMs) control the brand and undertake design, engineering

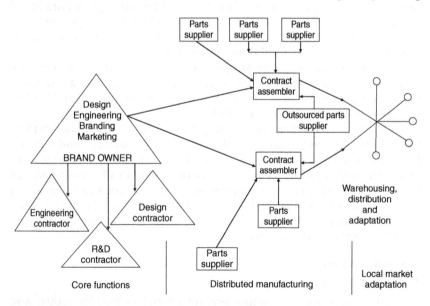

Figure 15.1 Globally distributed production: 'the global factory'
Source: Buckley (2004).

and R&D for the product (Shenkar 2005), although these may be outsourced (see Figure 15.1). They are customers for contract manufacturers (CMs) who perform manufacturing (and perhaps logistics) services for OEMs. In this so-called modular production network, CMs need to possess capabilities such as mix, product and new product flexibilities, while at the same time carrying out manufacturing activities at low costs with mass production processes (Sturgeon and Lester 2003). Flexibility is necessary to fulfil consumers' product differentiation needs (local requirements) and low cost for global efficiency imperatives (Wilson and Guzman 2005). The third part of the chain is warehousing, distribution and adaptation carried out on a 'hub and spoke' principle, in order to achieve local market adaptation through a mix of ownership and location policies. As Figure 15.2 shows, ownership strategies are used to involve local firms with marketing skills and local market intelligence in international joint ventures (IJVs), whilst location strategies are used to differentiate the wholly owned 'hub' (centrally located) from the jointly owned 'spokes'.

The information structure of the global factory

Casson (1997) highlights the importance of information costs in the structure of business organisation. He sees the brand owner as essentially a specialist in the search and specification functions (for customers and products respectively). 'The brand owner, by intermediating between the producer and the retailer, coordinates the entire distribution channel linking the worker to the final customer' (Casson 1997, p. 159). This intermediation by the brand owner/market maker is intermediation of information, not production. The information structure of the global factory is shown schematically in Figure 15.3. This shows that the brand owner is the information

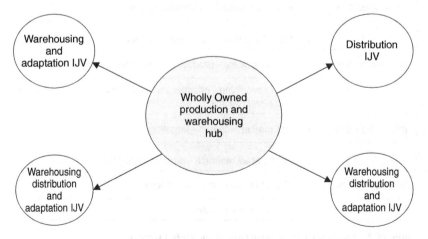

Figure 15.2 'Hub and spoke' strategies: an example
Source: Buckley and Ghauri (2004).

hub of the global factory. The brand owner organizes the market process itself. The organisation of production is conventionally within firms but the organisation of the whole production and trade sequence is intermediated by the market-making global factory. In many industries, particularly service industries, such as banking and insurance, the essence of competitiveness is the processing of information (Casson 1997, Buckley and Carter 2002).

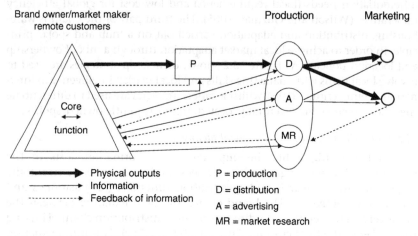

Information flow	into production – techniques, product specification
	from production – improvements in quality
Information flow	into distribution – adaptation, logistics
	from distribution – refinements of adaptation and logistics
Information flow	into advertising – production description associations
	from advertising – effectiveness, need for production change and new products
Information flow	into market research – targeting
	from market research – product intelligence
Information flow	direct to consumers – brand targeting
	from consumer – wants

Figure 15.3 The information structure of the global factory
Source: Buckley (2007).

348 *Peter J. Buckley*

Quasi-internalization

The global factory structure means that the operational boundaries and the accounting boundaries of the MNE do not coincide. The move to being a global supply chain coordinator means that influence, not ownership, is the global factory's ruling principle.

Research questions: ownership, location and the coordination of activities

Although complex in detail, the key analytical decisions in the global factory are very simple – control and location. The manager of the global factory has to ask two very straightforward questions of each activity in the global network. Where should this activity be located? How should this activity be controlled?

The first question of the optimum location for each activity is of course complicated by managing the interrelationships between activities. The relocation of one piece of the global network will have profound effects on many others (as the links in Figure 15.1 illustrate) but the principles of least cost location are paramount.

The second question concerns the means of control. Should the activity be managed by the market via a contract and price relationship, or should it be internalized and controlled by management? There are of course important mixed methods, such as joint ventures, which have elements of market relationships and elements of management fiat (Rangan 1998).

It is of course essential to realize that these decisions are taken in a volatile, risky and dynamic situation, that the decision making process is information intensive and the environment and competitive pressures are constantly changing. These decisions have to be revisited on a continuing basis. However, the principles should never be overwhelmed by detail. The need for flexibility, for judicious collection and use of information and for a knowledge management strategy are complements to the key decisions of location and control (Capel 1992, Kogut and Kulatilaka 1994, Allen and Pantzalis 1996).

The role of MNEs has always been to combine internationally mobile resources (such as knowledge), with locationally fixed ones (labour, natural resources, markets). The notion of the MNE as a network, moving around intangibles whilst locationally anchored at given fixed points by key inputs has been around for a long time (Buckley and Casson 1976). What has changed within the global factory is the degree to which management has the ability to 'fine slice' activities, to locate these in their optimal positions globally and to combine these dispersed activities through coordinating mechanisms that rely decreasingly on ownership. The global factory has perfected control, even at a huge distance, without ownership.

The key problems of the global factory are external. They arise from the existence of unpriced external effects and from the remoteness of much value adding activity from shareholders (and from customers) (Khanna and Palepu 1999). The first set of effects include environmental effects (including pollution), social effects and negative impacts on local firms. The second means that it is difficult for the owners to control the dispersed and disparate activities of the global factory. These two effects can interact making it difficult for shareholders to oversee, and to correct, negative externalities (Nolan *et al.* 2002).

The management effects of this can be serious. Expatriate managers can be absent from their own peer groups for extended periods of time and can be very exposed unless properly supported. Local managers may not manage facilities in the way that (foreign) shareholders might wish. The operation of manufacturing and service facilities in outsourced, offshore locations often do not conform to the standards of the headquarters (HQ) of the global factory. Accusations of running 'sweat shops' and poor conditions within call centres may be diffused by distance ('out of sight, out of mind'). However, it is no longer acceptable for HQ of global factories to pronounce that 'they are not our factories because we do not own them'. Global factories have to recognize that they are responsible for the whole of their supply chains and take social responsibility for their operations. Compliance to standards can be enforced internally (conference calls, video-conferencing, inspections, reports) or can itself be outsourced to specialist companies and non-governmental organizations (NGOs) that monitor social and environmental conditions in low-cost labour conditions.

There remain, however, clashes between local cultures and the world culture of the global factory. At the limit, were global factories to pay advanced country wages in cheap labour countries, this would negate their locational cost advantage and would deter global factories from placing facilities there. It is generally the case that work in global factories is better paid than outside them, particularly when the alternative is low productivity agriculture. Criticism of exploitation of cheap labour is a major cause for concern for global factories. The rise of the 'ethical consumer' and 'Fair trade' products are a sign that at least a segment of consumers are willing to pay higher prices for products made under more humane conditions with better ethical and environmental outcomes.

The extent to which factories and service facilities in cheap labour countries can be upgraded over time is a key issue in examining the impact of the global factory on development. It is also critical that spillovers should be positive in terms of upgrading the workforce through training and education, encouraging local entrepreneurship and fostering indigenous suppliers. Negative spillovers, such as pollution and harmful serial effects, need to be monitored and eliminated if the global factory is to achieve global legitimacy.

350   *Peter J. Buckley*

Findings: Japanese multinationals – hybrids in two senses

Then, as now, Japanese firms remain a special case in organization, philosophy and structure. However, we should note that the industry structure of Japanese firms is peculiar. Table 15.1 shows that the nine Japanese firms in the world's top 100 non-financial firms in 2004 were three motor vehicles firms, three trading firms and three electronics firms. The transnationality index of these firms is 52.2 – exactly the same as Germany, but less than France and far less than the UK (Table 15.2). This is partly a very large economy effect because the USA is lower at 48.8. The role of the financial

Table 15.1 Japanese multinationals in world's top 100 non-financial transnational corporations 2004

			Rank by		
			Foreign assets	TNI	II
1	Toyota Motor Corporation	Motor vehicles	(8)	62	91
2	Honda Motor Co. Ltd	Motor vehicles	21	(29)	87
3	Nissan Motor Co. Ltd	Motor vehicles	28	41	90
4	Mitsubishi Corporation	Wholesale trade	32	87	68
5	Sony Corporation	Electrical and electronics equipment	41	47	(17)
6	Mitsui & Co. Ltd	Wholesale trade	42	71	69
7	Matsushita Electric Industrial Co. Ltd	Electrical and electronics equipment	68	64	27
8	Hitachi Ltd	Electrical and electronics equipment	81	96	77
9	Marubeni Corporation	Wholesale trade	83	91	76

Notes: TNI: Transnationality index – average of foreign assets to total assets, foreign sales to total sales, foreign employment to total employment.
II: Internationalization index – number of foreign majority-owned affiliates to total majority-owned affiliates. The top Japanese firm in each category is bracketed.
Source: UNCTAD (2006), pp. 280–282.

Table 15.2 Japanese non-financial transnational corporations 2004

	TNI	No. of entries
Top 100 largest TNCs	56.8	100
USA	48.2	25
France	59.5	15
Germany	52.2	13
UK	69.2	11
Japan	52.2	9

Note: Observe the comparison with Germany (Kudo 2006).
Source: UNCTAD (2006), p. 33.

market in Japan is highlighted by Table 15.3, which shows that only three Japanese firms figure in the 50 largest financial transnational corporations in 2004 and that they had a relatively low spread index, illustrating their domestic bias (a range of 25.7 to 27.8 against GE Capital Services' index of 64.7). The relative domestic focus of financial services in Japan is reflected in the internationalization of its MNEs which, being more reliant on the domestic capital market, are thus more insular (Kishi 2003). Hoshi and Kashyap (2004) show that Japanese firms are provided with insurance via domestic banks. This contrasts with more entrepreneurial risk taking firms. Ahearne and Shinada (2005) claim that many 'zombie' firms exist in the non-traded goods sector of Japan. The highly inefficient, debt ridden zombie firms are supported by finance from the banks exacerbating a declining productivity performance. It is against this unpromising domestic background that we must evaluate Japanese multinational firms.

Today, a growing number of Japanese firms are alleged to be 'hybrids' between Western and stereotypically 'Japanese' firms (see *The Economist* 2007). *The Economist* sees Japan developing 'a new hybrid model of capitalism that brings together aspects of the old Japanese model, which ran into trouble in the early 1990s, with carefully chosen elements of the more dynamic American or Anglo-Saxon variety of capitalism'. We may query the 'carefully chosen' element of this – again it implies top-down planning and great foresight on the part of unidentified powers in the Japanese economy – but 'hybridity' (or, more accurately, business culture borrowings) seems to be a reasonable description of modern Japanese business (Abo 1994). However, there is a second sense in which they can be said to be hybrids. If we examine Table 15.4, three distinct types of MNE can be outlined.

The first is an 'international' firm where the source country headquarters are dominant and where foreign affiliates are treated as merely subcontractors or sales units. The firm uses internalization rather than contracting, outsourcing or licensing and this reinforces control, centralization and hierarchy. The key focus of the international structure is to support exports from the source country.

Table 15.3 Japanese firms in top 50 financial transnational corporations 2004

	Rank	Spread index
Mitsubishi Tokyo Financial Group	33	27.8
Mizuho Financial Group	36	26.0
Sunutomo Mitsui Financial Group	37	25.7
[NB G.E. Capital Services	1	64.7]

Notes: The Spread Index is the square root of the Internationalisation Index (II) multiplied by the number of host countries. The II is the number of foreign majority-owned affiliates divided by the total number of foreign owned affiliates.

Source: UNCTAD (2006), p. 287.

352 *Peter J. Buckley*

Table 15.4 Models of multinational firms

1. *'International'*
- Headquarters (HQ) dominant
- Subsidiaries treated as (preferential?) subcontractors
- Increase in internalization for control
- Often support for exports from source country

2. *'Multinational'*
- HQ delegates functions to subsidiaries
- 'Clone' model as extreme case
- Finance, branding (research & development) retained in centre
- Core functions internalized

3. *'Global factory'* (network model)
- HQ retains branding and associated functions
- All activities located in optimum locations
- Shift to externalization of functions (offshoring, outsourcing)

Table 15.5 The global factory and the hybrid Japanese ideal type

	Global factory and Japanese hybrid	
	Similar	**Different**
Information system	✓	
Supply chain	✓	
Team working	✓	
Labour market		?
Innovation system		?
Hierarchy		?
Openness to foreigners [at top level]		X
Capital market relationships		X

The second archetype is the 'multinational' firm in which functions are delegated to foreign affiliates and the extreme case is the 'clone' model where 'miniature replicas' of the parent firm are located in key markets. Production and marketing are separated and located in the locations most suitable for these operations. Finance, branding and other core functions such as R&D are retained in the source country HQ and core functions are internalized.

The third form is the 'global factory', as described above, where HQ retains only branding and its associated functions (including financing). All the firm's activities are 'fine-sliced' and are located in the places that give optimum cost conditions for the supply chain as a whole. There is a major and profound shift to the externalization of functions through outsourcing and offshoring.

Japanese firms may be said to be hybrids of types 1 and 3. There has been a long-standing externalization of functions within large (and medium-sized)

The Rise of the Japanese Multinational Enterprise 353

Japanese companies with a definite strategy of the relocation of activities (particularly production) to low-cost locations, largely in Asia (Makino *et al.* 2004). Indeed, Japanese firms were leaders in the offshoring movement and led the opening up of China as a low-cost production source. However, this is combined with a dominant HQ and the philosophy that the foreign units of the 'hybrid Japanese global factory' are more akin to subcontractors than to network partners.

This can be summarized in Table 15.5, which compares 'the global factory' with 'the hybrid Japanese ideal type'. Both use global information systems, sophisticated, integrated supply chain management and team working. However, the innovation systems in Japanese firms are less open than in true global factories, the internal labour markets of Japanese firms are less permeable to outside market forces and there remains more hierarchy in Japanese firms (Chen 2004). A good example that links the last two points is that far fewer non-Japanese rise to senior management and board-level positions in Japanese companies, than non-nationals do in European or American companies. The capital market relationships of Japanese companies are also less open than in the normal case of the global factory (Aulakh and Mudambi 2005). There remain close links between individual companies and banks, and Japanese companies are less open to receiving foreign finance (equity and debt) than other MNEs (Kishi 2003).

Some of this has an evolutionary explanation. For instance, Ozawa (2002) posited four stages of Japanese FDI:

(1) Labour – intensive industrialization and 'elementary stage' of overseas investment.
(2) Heavy and chemical industrialization and the 'resource seeking' stage of multinationalism.
(3) Subcontracting – dependent, assembly based industrialization and the 'assembly transplant' stage of multinationalism.
(4) Flexible manufacturing and the 'strategic localisation' stage of global operations.

It is possible to argue that these stages also describe the past development of US and European investment and that a time-dependent model is far more appropriate than a nationality of ownership explanation. What Ozawa (2002) has described is the changing patterns of relative location costs as the source country develops and its interaction with types of external markets that are most easily internalized (markets in cheap labour and low technology intermediate goods, in relatively unprocessed inputs in a vertically integrated operation, in market-seeking operations and finally, in high technology inputs, sophisticated labour and information). None of this requires specifically 'Japanese' explanatory variables. The retreat of internalization and the shift to outsourcing and offshoring has been the most

354 *Peter J. Buckley*

recent stage in the development of MNEs as we have seen. Again, this has been the policy of both 'Western' and Japanese multinationals and it is even being utilized by the 'new' emerging country multinationals. In many ways, Japanese MNEs were ahead of the trend in offshoring as the literature on hollowing-out shows (see Tejima 2000).

Discussion

The rise and continued success of Japanese MNEs is not a conventional or uniform story. It is important to contrast Japan's most internationalized companies versus the rest, and Japanese small and medium enterprises (SMEs) have suffered more than proportionately from the impact of hollowing-out, the credit crunch and the aforementioned lack of entrepreneurial start-ups (Kikkawa 2006). Japanese MNEs, like all MNEs, vary by sector, by firm and by their administrative heritage (history). The principles governing their operations are the same as for 'Western MNEs' and their evolution and strategy has much in common with their Western counterparts.

There are special issues, however, in examining Japanese MNEs. Their financial integration with world capital markets still remains less than 'normal' MNEs and their insularity in financing reflects this, although financing remains available at attractive rates (Suzuki 1987). Knowledge management policies seem to differ between Japanese and Western MNEs. Japanese firms are less open and their innovation systems are less internationally networked. Japanese MNEs are facing demands to increase their flexibility and openness – hence the 'hybrid' state frequently alluded to in the financial press.

As always, internationalization issues are closely linked to the structure and institutions of the domestic economy. Japanese MNEs reflect the capital market, the innovation system and the business culture of the home economy (Buckley and Casson 1976, Collinson and Rugman 2008). These institutional and cultural factors have led to 'capitalism with Japanese characteristics' and therefore to MNEs that reflect this. Japan has always retained local competition rather than encouraging the creation of a single 'national champion'. This has had the benefit of several Japanese MNEs being able to run foreign experiments and to use different global strategies. However, Japanese MNEs have persisted with licensing rather than foreign investment (Okimoto 1989, Anchordoguy 1990) and the consequent loss of control of the global platform has not served them well. In addition, 'catching-up' has proved easier than taking global leadership (Murtha *et al.* 2001, Hoetker 2006). Globalisation requires new strategies. It also requires new domestic policies and structures to support Japanese global firms and the global factory system. Although the Japanese government has taken steps to promote corporate change, the full impact of these policies on firm performance is as yet unclear. Japan has not yet fully adapted to the new

The Rise of the Japanese Multinational Enterprise 355

system of global competition in which the head office orchestrates a global factory based on a flexible and resilient international network (Buckley 2009).

Conclusions

From 'then' to 'now', the world has changed. The rise of India and China make global competition much more aggressive. There are far more suitable locations for cost-based competition. The integration of markets and the wider pool of economies drawn in to a modern globalization process means that the world economy is far more volatile (Buckley and Casson 1998). A key response of MNEs to volatility is to be increasingly flexible. Japanese firms have responded to this by developing 'global factory' like strategies in outsourcing, offshoring, relocating and fine-slicing their global activities, especially to locations in East and Southeast Asia and Eastern Europe. However, they have not yet fully responded in opening up their internal capital markets to external influences and their top-level labour markets to foreign executives. Headquarters control and high levels of internal integration of activities that leading Western MNEs have outsourced has led to the idea that Japanese MNEs remain 'hybrids' between 'international' firms and fully global firms in their strategies. An implication to be drawn from this conclusion is that deeper understanding is needed of whether this 'hybridity' represents a new *status quo* or merely reflects a stage of transition to new organizational forms.

References

Abegglen, J.C., 2006. *21st century Japanese management*. Basingstoke: Palgrave Macmillan.

Abegglen, J.C. and Stalk, G., 1985. *Kaisha, the Japanese corporation*. New York: Basic Books.

Abo, T., ed., 1994. *Hybrid factory: the Japanese production system in the United States*. New York: Oxford University Press.

Ahearne, A.G. and Shinada, N., 2005. Zombie firms and economic stagnation in Japan. *International economics and economic policy*, 2 (4), 363–381.

Allen, L. and Pantzalis, C., 1996. Valuation of the operating flexibility of multinational corporations. *Journal of international business studies*, 27 (4), 633–653.

Anchordoguy, M., 1990. *Computers Inc.* Cambridge, MA: Harvard University Press.

Aoki, M., 1984. Aspects of the Japanese firm. *In*: M. Aoki, ed. *The economic analysis of the Japanese firm*. Dordrecht: North Holland, 3–43.

Aoki, M., 1990. Towards an economic model of the Japanese firm. *Journal of economic literature*, 28 (1), 1–27.

Aulakh, P.S. and Mudambi, R., 2005. Financial resource flows in multinational enterprises: the role of external capital markets. *Management international review*, 45 (3), 307–326.

Buckley, P.J., 2004. The role of China in the global strategy of multinational enterprises. *Journal of Chinese economic and business studies*, 2 (1), 1–25.

356   *Peter J. Buckley*

Buckley, P.J., 2007. *The global factory: manufacturing and services in the new global economy.* Vienna: UNIDO.

Buckley, P.J., 2009. The role of headquarters in the global factory. *In*: V. Holm and V. Andersson, eds. *Headquarters role in the contemporary MNE.* Cheltenham: Edward Elgar.

Buckley, P.J. and Carter, M., 2002. Process and structure in knowledge management practices of British and US multinational enterprises. *Journal of international management*, 8 (1), 29–48.

Buckley, P.J. and Casson, M., 1976. *The future of the multinational enterprise.* Basingstoke: Palgrave Macmillan.

Buckley, P.J. and Casson, M., 1998. Models of the multinational enterprise. *Journal of international business studies*, 29 (1), 21–44.

Buckley, P.J. and Ghauri, P.N., 2004. Globalisation, economic geography and the strategy of multinational enterprises. *Journal of international business studies*, 35 (2), 81–98.

Buckley, P.J. and Mirza, H., 1985. The wit and wisdom of Japanese management: an iconoclastic analysis. *Management international review*, 25 (3), 16–32.

Capel, J., 1992. How to service a foreign market under uncertainty: a real option approach. *European journal of political economy*, 8 (3), 455–475.

Casson, M., 1997. *Information and organisation: a new perspective on the theory of the firm.* Oxford: Clarendon Press.

Chen, M., 2004. *Asian management systems.* London: Thomson Learning.

Coase, R.H., 1937. The nature of the firm. *Economica*, 4 (n.s), 386–405.

Collinson, S. and Rugman, A.M., 2008. The regional nature of Japanese multinational business. *Journal of international business studies*, 39 (2), 215–230.

Dyer, J., 2000. *Collaborative advantage: winning through extended enterprise networks.* Oxford: Oxford University Press.

Gerlach, M. and Lincoln, J., 2004. *Japan's network economy.* Cambridge: Cambridge University Press.

Hoetker, G., 2006. Do modular products lead to modular organization? *Strategic management journal*, 27 (6), 501–518.

Hoshi, T. and Kashyap, A., 2004. *Corporate financing and governance in Japan: the road to the future.* Cambridge, MA: MIT Press.

Imai, M., 1986. *The key to Japan's competitive success.* New York: McGraw Hill.

Khanna, T. and Palepu, K., 1999. Policy shocks, market intermediaries, and corporate strategy: evidence from Chile and India. *Journal of economics and management strategy*, 8 (2), 271–310.

Kikkawa, T., 2006. Reorganisation of enterprises in Japan: the response of Keiretsu and small companies. *In*: G.D. Hook and H. Hasegawa, eds. *Japanese responses to globalization.* Basingstoke: Palgrave Macmillan, 184–202.

Kishi, M., 2003. Foreign direct investment by Japanese firms and corporate governance: in relation to the monetary policies of China, Korea and Japan. *Journal of Asian economies*, 13 (6), 731–748.

Kogut, B. and Kulatilaka, N., 1994. Operating flexibility, global manufacturing and the option value of a multinational network. *Management science*, 40 (1), 123–139.

Kudo, A., 2006. The response of Japanese capitalism to globalization: a comparison with the German case. *In*: G.D. Hook and H. Hasegawa, eds. *Japanese responses to globalization.* Basingstoke: Palgrave Macmillan, 131–150.

Liker, J.K., Ettie, J.K., and Campbell, J.C., 1995. *Engineered in Japan: Japanese technology – management practices.* Oxford: Oxford University Press.

The Rise of the Japanese Multinational Enterprise 357

Makino, S., Beamish, P.W., and Zhao, N.B., 2004. The characteristics and performance of Japanese FDI in less developed and developed countries. *Journal of world business*, 39, 377–392.

Murtha, T.P., Hart, J.A., and Lenway, S.A., 2001. *Managing new industry creation: global knowledge formation and entrepreneurship in high technology.* Stanford, CA: Stanford University Press.

Nolan, P., Sutherland, D., and Zhang, J., 2002. The challenge of the global business revolution. *Contributions to political economy*, 21 (1), 91–110.

Okimoto, D.I., 1989. *Between MITI and the Morbeet.* Stanford, CA: Stanford University Press.

Ozawa, T., 2002. *Pax-Americana led macro-clustering and flying-geese style catch-up in East Asia: mechanisms of regionalised endogenous growth.* Columbia University Centre on Japanese Economy and Business working paper series.

Rangan, S., 1998. Do multinationals operate flexibly? Theory and evidence. *Journal of international business studies*, 29, 217–237.

Shenkar, O., 2005. *The Chinese century.* Upper Saddle River, NJ: Wharton School Publishing.

Sturgeon, T.J. and Lester, R.K., 2003. The new global supply-base: new challenges for local suppliers in East Asia. Industrial Performance Centre (IPC) working paper, MIT-IPC-03–006. Cambridge, MA: Massachusetts Institute of Technology.

Suzuki, Y., 1987. *The Japanese financial system.* Oxford: Clarendon Press.

Tejima, S., 2000. Japanese FDI, the implications of 'hollowing out' on the technological development of host countries. *International business review*, 9 (5), 555–570.

The Economist, 2007. Going hybrid. *The Economist*, 1 December, p. 3.

UNCTAD, 2006. *World investment report 2006.* Geneva: UNCTAD.

Wilson, J. and Guzman, G.A.C., 2005. Organisational knowledge transfer in modular production networks: the case of Brazil. *Proceedings of the Academy of International Business annual conference*, July, Quebec.

16
Japanese Multinational Enterprises in China: Successful Adaptation of Marketing Strategies

Co-authored with Sierk A. Horn

Introduction

This paper examines three case studies of Japanese multinational enterprises (MNEs) in China (ItôYôkadô, Shiseidô and Toyota). The case studies are of three iconic companies. They are from different sectors (retailing, consumer goods and automobiles) and all have had to adapt their business models to Chinese conditions. The paper examines the direction, extent and nature of adaptation of the Japanese firms' business models in China and seeks to explore the changes in terms of conventional 'Japanese' international marketing behaviour as portrayed in extant literature. It examines the Chinese context and consumer behaviour in China to show the influence of the host country on adaptation to foreign market conditions. With a view to the change in quality and quantity of Japanese investment in China, the case studies were deliberately chosen to show the spectrum and extent of adaptation efforts.

The rise of the Chinese consumer market offers unique insights into the extension and adaptation of home market strategies. Foreign firms, including Japanese MNEs, have entered the market approximately at the same time, and face a new and often adverse environment. They need to learn the local rules of engagement. China puts ethnocentric extensions of home market strategies to the test. Stereotypical views of 'Japanese', 'Western' and 'Asian' management styles must be challenged,[1] and this study explores the applicability of received theory to Japanese firms' operations in China. The best way to do this is to provide empirical evidence of what firms actually do. The case studies analyse Japanese management in China and provide a litmus test of the degree to which a 'Japanese' management system is adapted to a 'Chinese' ('Asian') environment. The paper challenges the traditional portrayal of the globalisation path of Japanese firms, which are commonly thought to follow geocentric strategies (in contrast to the polycentric approaches of European MNEs).

Using Rugman's (2008) classification: Itô-Yôkadô is bi-regional (Asia and North America), Shiseidô is home-region orientated and Toyota is close to being a global company. Our three case studies thus encapsulate the spectrum of international and internationalising companies. Our paper therefore offers answers, at firm level, to three key questions:

1. To what extent does the international marketing behaviour of Japanese firms differ from that in the past?
2. How far have Japanese firms overcome their ethnocentricity by successfully implementing local marketing flexibility?
3. To what extent are Japanese home market idiosyncratic strengths transplanted into the Chinese market?

Research framework

Historically, much has been made of the Japanese international marketing approach. In Western literature it has been widely described as superior to[2] and more efficient than that of Western competitors.[3] Numerous studies have attempted to portray Japanese marketing methods. As shown in Table 16.1, conventional theory indicates that Japanese competitive advantages derive from organisational abilities, information processing capabilities, product-segment fit, identification of customer needs and wants, long-term orientation and aggressive growth strategies (market share). Most findings, however, relate to the heyday of Japanese management and largely ignore the widely documented (at least in the Japanese literature) problems of Japanese firms in adapting to local market environments.[4] Contrary to Western understanding, extant Japanese literature classifies the international marketing approaches of Japanese firms as 'simple-global', with a strong emphasis on product standardisation and an omnipotent Japanese headquarters.[5] If we assume that global strategies are a product of specific management vistas, this ethnocentric heritage (as opposed to the polycentric globalisation paths of many European firms)[6] becomes a barrier to success – particularly in view of the increasing heterogeneity of world markets. New consumers in emerging markets and the increasing atomisation of consumer behaviour in developed markets force firms to find a balance between integration advantages and differentiation needs. The presumed strength of Japanese marketing may then indeed be an inherent weakness. Recent studies reveal that the centrally orchestrated global marketing management of Japanese firms is giving way to decentralised decision processes. These show that Japanese firms are in the process of outsourcing key functions such as production, human resources, R&D, finances and marketing to their subsidiaries.[7] Consequently, this means that this 'forced' decentralisation strategy is evolving into one of subsidiary leadership.[8]

Japanese firms and the international market environment have evolved dramatically, but accurate descriptions of contemporary Japanese international

360 *Peter J. Buckley and Sierk A. Horn*

Table 16. 1 Japanese marketing as portrayed in the extant literature

Product Product differentiation, product design, rapid product line extensions, superior product quality, continuous improvement, group work, consensus-orientation, time-intensive decision process, quick and efficient implementation	Doyle et al. (1988); Czinkota and Kotabe (1990); Delios and Beamish (1999), Nakane (1970); Tanouchi (1983); Abbeglen and Stalk (1985); Saunders et al. (1987)
Focus and targeting Orientation towards (potential) high-growth segments	Genestre and Herbig (1995)
Market orientation Long-term strategy, positioning in high-growth segments, aggressive market share orientation, domination strategy	Doyle et al. (1987); Wong et al. (1987); Kotabe and Okoroafo (1990); Johanson and Yip (1994); Siddhartan (1998)
Management High flexibility and pragmatism, reliance on local staff, consultative and indicative government assistance, global innovation and local adaptation, high control/high risk orientation, importance of prior experience	Wong et al. (1987); Anand and Delios (1996); Fongsuwan (1999); Papanastassiou and Pearce (1994); Iwasa and Odagiri (2004); Kumar (2001); Taylor et al. (2000); Somlev and Hoshino (2005); Sakakibara and Serwin (2000); Delios and Henisz (2000)
Communication Focus on advertising less than on personal services, importance of brand name	Genestre and Herbig (1995); Delios and Beamish (1999)
Market research Advanced research capability, clear view of customer and competitor, stringent data monitoring	Saunders et al. (1987); Wong et al. (1987); Johanson and Nonaka (1987)
Pricing Cost reduction, efficient large-scale manufacturing, pricing ('dumping') as a tool to gain rapid market share	Doyle et al. (1987); Langlois (1997)
International orientation Little adaptation of marketing mix to local market, geocentric market approach	Kotabe and Okoroafo (1990); Meffert and Bolz (1998); Johanson and Yip (1994); Yip (1996); Horn (2000)

marketing behaviour are largely absent. A substantial body of research has recorded the international approach of Japanese firms amid recent rapid economic integration and increased economic linkages between China and the rest of Asia, including Japan. The thrust of this research concentrates on internationalisation motives and strategies.[9] Within this literature there are a number of studies that investigate the activities of Japanese firms in emerging economies, most notably China. As most of these studies are based on quantitative and econometric analysis,[10] their explanatory value for the international marketing behaviour of Japanese firms remains somewhat limited.

Several interrelated factors are responsible for this myopia: (1) Japanese firms have been reluctant to introduce modern marketing techniques in their home market, making the international findings look arbitrary. Changes in Japanese consumption patterns and the arrival of foreign firms have, however, led to intensified competition, and serving individual consumer needs has become paramount.[11] The effect of this on international strategy is unexplored. (2) The literature is mainly geared towards Japanese firms' behaviour in developed markets (with the notable exception of Fongsuwan 1999).[12] The shift towards emerging economies, particularly in East Asia,[13] suggests the need for careful scrutiny. Japanese strategies here seem to have changed dramatically. (3) In the wake of the bursting of the bubble economy and the longest recession Japan has experienced in the post-war era, Japanese firms were forced to adapt their organisation and management, including 'Japanese-style' marketing.[14] Today the Japanese marketing environment is characterised by saturation, hyper-ageing and mass-customisation. In this 'pressure cooker' environment, Japanese firms have had to develop new home market strengths.[15] These form the basis of their international strategy.[16] If marketing orientation has become *the* key determinant of Japanese management in the home market, strategic behaviour outside Japan may evolve accordingly.

The question thus arises: to what extent is the international marketing behaviour of Japanese firms today different from the past? A further central dimension of exploration is whether Japanese firms have overcome their inherent simple-global management style by successfully implementing local marketing flexibility. The Chinese market is an excellent environment in which to assess the international marketing profile of Japanese firms. First, China has emerged as prime destination of Japanese foreign direct investment (FDI) in Asia, and Japan's premier trade partner.[17] Second, China's economic growth policies, market liberalisation and market opening to foreign business[18] have given rise to a high degree of Sino-Japanese economic interdependency. Third, following China's accession to the World Trade Organisation (WTO) in December 2001, Japanese firms have started to reconfigure China's position as a FDI destination. Investments for domestic sales have overtaken export-orientated motives,[19] signalling a shift towards China as both a prime production location and a key market. Fourth, amid this shift from production-orientation to market-orientation, Japanese corporations need to adapt to the new rules of engagement.[20] Nascent Chinese consumerism and intense local competition challenge Japanese international marketing expertise.

Comparative case studies help to focus on micro details of the operation of Japanese companies in China and facilitate a fresh and more realistic look at the localisation of marketing *à la Japonaise*. The three case study firms have key challenges to face in reaching Chinese customers, and in adapting their products and business models to Chinese conditions. Our initial focus

362   Peter J. Buckley and Sierk A. Horn

is on success factors for the Japanese firms in China. This enables us to identify continuity and change in Japanese marketing strategies in China, and to identify the extent to which the success factors arise from Japanese home market idiosyncratic skills. We are also able to identify intercultural awareness and successful adaptation to Chinese conditions.

Itô-Yôkadô in China

While the entry modes of Western retailers into Asian markets are well known, little research has been done on the internationalisation of Japanese retailers.[21] This section offers insights into how Itô-Yôkadô, one of Japan's premier retailers, entered the Chinese market, reacted to past and current barriers to competition and tailored its marketing to Chinese consumer behaviour (location, store layout, communication).

Seven&I Holdings is a key player in Japan, one of the world's most advanced retail environments. Established in 2005, and following the purchase of the former US-based parent company (2005) and the merger with Millennium Retailing (2006), it has become the largest distribution/retailing operation in Japan. Its retail formats include department stores (Sogo, Seibu, Robinson), convenience stores (7-Eleven), general merchandise stores (Itô-Yôkadô, Marudai), supermarkets (York Benimaru, York Mart), food services (Denny's, Poppo), speciality stores (Mary Ann, Akachan Honpo), financial (Nanaco) and IT services (7-Dream.com).

The general merchandise store arm of the Seven&I Holdings, Itô-Yôkadô Co Ltd, is central to this retail conglomerate. The primary business model is that of dominance (*Dominanto Senryaku*), i.e. location decisions follow the sole logic of area dominance. Instead of developing a loose nationwide network, Itô-Yôkadô has developed high-density operations concentrated in key areas of Japan. This means high efficiency in terms of customer reach (two thirds of its stores are located in the highly populated Kantô region, which comprises more than a third of Japan's overall population), but also in logistics, advertising and brand awareness.[22] Regional concentration is also inherent in its commitment to tailoring its operations to local consumption patterns.[23] This ranges from regional adaptation of store formats to one-to-one marketing as part of the customer relationship strategy. Store planning, layout and product assortments vary geographically in accordance with local lifestyle profiles in the trading area. Local grounding is achieved by the integration of local produce or ingredients. Individual consumer preferences are carefully monitored (using POS/database/store cards). Based on this information, stores can react flexibly to changes in consumption patterns and new needs.

Success factors

Local partnerships. Itô-Yôkadô has only recently begun to test international waters. After approval was given for the first foreign-capital owned

Japanese Multinational Enterprises in China 363

countrywide chain store by the Chinese government, Itô-Yôkadô opened its first GM supermarket outside Japan in 1997. Through a majority joint venture (JV) with local retailer Chengdu, Itô-Yôkadô was established in Sichuan province. In the following year Itô-Yôkadô established the Beijing-based Huan Tang Yôkadô group via a minority JV.[24] Itô-Yôkadô expanded its China operations step-by-step. Today, the firm operates six GM supermarkets in Beijing and two in Chengdu.

In addition to the expansion plans of Itô-Yôkadô in Beijing (four further GM superstores in 2008, followed by the establishment of a distribution centre and further store expansion), Seven&I Holdings has intensified its involvement in China. In 2004 7-Eleven (Beijing) Co Ltd was established, and by May 2007 the group had developed a network of 53 convenience stores in Beijing. The group expanded to 350 stores.[25] Further to this, the group formed a JV with Wangfujing Department Store Co in 2005,[26] planning a chain of 20 stand-alone supermarkets in the Beijing area by 2008 (as majority shareholder: 40 per cent held by the Chinese partner and a combined 60 per cent by Itô-Yôkadô and subsidiary York Benimaru). These investment activities highlight the importance of the Chinese market to the group.[27] While current operating income is comparatively low,[28] the group is firmly establishing itself as local/regional key player.

Location strategy. A key aspect of Seven&I's expansion in the Chinese market is local concentration. General merchandising and convenience stores, as well as the supermarkets, are geographically focussed on the Chinese capital. With the exception of the retail brands Sogo and Seibu (arising from the merger with Millennium Retailing), all operations are located in Beijing and Chengdu. Plans to extend the operations to Tianjin, Chongqing, Shenyang and Dalian have been put on hold.[29] This is in stark contrast to the activities of Western retail chains and at first sight seems somewhat surprising.

China's retail fragmentation may justify a localised concentration; however, the economic divide between metropolitan/coastal regions and the largely underdeveloped hinterland forces retailers to re-visit their expansion strategies. The French retailer Carrefour and US retailer Walmart Stores have found different answers to retail developments in China. The geographic profile of these retailers is distinct from the Japanese strategies,[30] as they pursue what might be called a 'sprinkler strategy'. Due to the competitive environment, maturation effects[31] of metropolitan retail markets and expected growth in the hinterland, these retailers are simultaneously expanding their operations across China. The inherent business model of geographic dominance outlined above throws a different light on Itô-Yôkadô's China activities. The home-market approach of selective/regional dominance seems to be replicated and extended in the Chinese market. Vertical 'deep integration' synergies as in Japan (streamlining distribution, logistics and brand awareness) are drivers of this concerted multi-format expansion.

364　*Peter J. Buckley and Sierk A. Horn*

The initial strategy of central locations was replaced by an extension to city peripheries, without forfeiting the idea of deep integration.[32] While further store operations continued to follow strategic market entry criteria (target group, catchment area, competition), a more flexible route was taken to new store selection. Abandoning the minimum location preconditions,[33] the speed of store openings accelerated from 2003. Itô-Yôkadô's most recent GM store in Chaoyang district, opened in 2007, exemplifies the shift towards integration into new urban developments (greenfield developments with combined living, shopping and working).[34] However, it also signals intensification of competition for prime retail locations.

Consumer focus. Adapting to local consumption patterns is at the very centre of Seven&I's business model. In the first twelve months of its China operations it was confronted not only with the obvious and anticipated divergences in Sino-Japanese consumption patterns, but also with vast regional differences[35] in style, colour and brand preferences and physical attributes between Chengdu and Beijing.[36] These experiences reconfirmed the company's strategic path of localisation. Prior to the launch of the Chengdu store, a task force of Japanese managers lived for a prolonged period in China to get first-hand experience of daily life and local lifestyles. The management was aware that western-style supermarkets, and their inherent aspects around self-service and central check-out, were at this time a completely new concept to Chinese consumers. Itô-Yôkadô identified cleanliness, safety and freshness as differentiators from local competition – on top of status as a window to modernity ('foreign', 'exciting'). The bundling of offers in one place was put forward as a unique selling proposition (USP).[37] Differences and changes in lifestyles are constantly monitored, enabling the firm to react to marketing variations and build up local expertise.

Shiseidô in China

Shiseidô is a Japanese success story in China and serves as an example of how Japanese MNEs primarily target luxury segments.[38] It also shows that Japanese firms have a remarkable and so far under-explored ability to fine-tune and fine-slice their marketing activities to the local environment.[39] Not only has the toiletry manufacturer for the first time in its corporate history developed brands specifically/solely for a foreign target market (Aupres, Za) in contrast to other markets, but it has also successfully integrated both localised and globalised facets of its approach.

Shiseidô is one of the world's biggest manufacturers of cosmetics. While characterised as 'homehost oriented',[40] firm level data reveals that the firm is able to draw from substantial international experiences. The first regional steps were taken as early as the 1950s (with exports to Taiwan, Singapore and Hong Kong), followed by an expansion to North America, Europe and

South Pacific in the 1960s. In 2007, Shiseidô was active in 67 countries, with 12 manufacturing (50 in Asia) and eight R&D (mainly in Europe, North America) overseas facilities.

Foreign MNEs are key players in the Chinese cosmetics and toiletry market. Japanese cosmetic firms were among the first to arrive in China. While domestic manufacturers serve the lower to medium end of this developing mass market, foreign brands, skilfully entering with massive marketing budgets and fine-tuned advertising, have become icons of modern lifestyle. Foreign manufacturers dominate this market, with Procter&Gamble, L'Oreal and Unilever leading the retail sales table.[41] Shiseidô is ranked seventh overall, and dominates among Japanese cosmetic corporations in terms of retail sales followed by Kao (in 15th place overall). Shiseidô possesses a nuanced brand profile, close to the market leaders Procter&Gamble and L'Oreal in key dimensions of consumer evaluation.[42]

Success factors

Localisation of R&D. Early on, Shiseidô identified the Chinese market as a cornerstone of the firm's international expansion strategy. As early as 1980 the cosmetic manufacturer exported products[43] to China. With the motto 'high quality, high service, high image,' skin products were available in Beijing.[44] Here the firm benefited from increased fashion awareness, brought about by the influx of Western-style fashion shows. By 1990 cosmetic markets were rapidly growing and Shiseidô set up a majority JV with the Beijing Liyuan Cosmetics group. The objective of this undertaking was to use the Japanese firm's technology to develop cosmetics for the local market.[45] After the establishment of production facilities in Beijing, joint research on Chinese skin, hair and consumer behaviour (i.e. cosmetic awareness/consciousness) was conducted for over two years.

After the market introduction of the Shiseidô mainline (imported from Japan in 1993), the brand 'Aupres' was launched in 1994. From 1998 the Shiseidô group extended its production facilities. New facilities were added to the Beijing operations and in Shanghai a second plant[46] was opened. Again the cosmetic manufacturer opted for a majority JV and split production between these two operations. While in the Shanghai plant 'Za' and 'Pure & Mild' are produced, premium brands are produced and/or assembled in Beijing. The newly formed Shanghai Zotoc Citic Cosmetics Co therefore signals a strategy shift to include middle income earners in the customer portfolio. In 2002 the firm added a research centre to its China activities, where adaptation requirements and potential (e.g. exploration of Chinese medicine) are explored.

Branding and communication. Shiseidô's brand architecture and socio-economic segmentation strategy in China[47] has been innovative. On the one hand, the orientation towards premium brands is evident. While import brand positioning is clustered towards the high end, locally produced Za and Pure & Mild address the middle-price segments. By 2010 the main target groups will be households with a minimum income of US$33,000. The Aupres brand was developed solely for the Chinese market and is not sold in Japan. It was first launched in Shanghai (Pacific Mall) in 1994.[48] With its exclusive (European) yet localised appeal (in advertising, only Chinese models were used and its exclusive development for Chinese skin was highlighted),[49] it struck a chord with Chinese consumers. With a core target group of 20–40 year old female professionals[50] and its high quality/ medium price range positioning,[51] Aupres became an instant success story in China. Key factors include a relationship of trust between the company and the local government, the technological expertise of the JV partner and the fine-tuning of the Aupres products to local needs.[52]

Despite fierce price competition, Shiseidô has achieved stability since the initial market launch. The line-up was carefully extended and today sales of Aupres exceed those of combined Shiseidô brands; in addition, more retail space is allocated to it. The firm has localised its brand hierarchy, so that Aupres acts as an umbrella for the Shiseidô brand name. This turns the usual patterns of Japanese brand management upside down, because in Japan the firm name acts as the umbrella brand. Competitors such as Procter&Gamble and L'Oreal have tried to follow the route of localised development, but Shiseidô still has an edge as the firm is perceived to have a better understanding of 'Asianness'. This image is strengthened by the retail staff and their focus on individualised consulting services.

Meticulous market research[53] detected an increased market potential for top-of-the range cosmetics in China[54] – triggering not only the influx of Shiseidô's top brand (Cle de Peau) but also the extension of existing brands. The new Aupres brand (Supreme Aupres) is targeted at an increasingly affluent clientele (higher price, superior image).[55] Hence a dual brand strategy can be deducted. On the one hand the firm extends its brand portfolio downwards (for example Za, Pure & Mild) to reach a bigger customer base. On the other, it strengthens its position in the premium segments either by new brand introductions[56] or careful up-scaling of existing brands.

Retail outlet selection and adaptation. Deregulation opened the path to the expansion of retail channels in 2003. The selection of retail outlets is key to the success of Shiseidô, which attaches great importance to fine-tuning its retail marketing mix. Shiseidô started to add chain stores to its department store retail channels in Beijing, Shanghai and Hangzhou. A further advance was the establishment of Shiseidô (China) Holdings in 2004. The nation-wide roll-out of speciality stores is coordinated from Shanghai. These investments mirror the importance that Shiseidô attaches to this market. China with its huge market potential is crucial to the strategy of the cosmetic group. Shiseidô's profits in China outpace those of other regions. Beauty counsellors[57] are extensively trained (centralised in Beijing) to meet the needs of the customers.

Toyota in China

Toyota has overtaken the recently bankrupted GM to become the world's leading car manufacturer. In this light it is surprising that this prominent Japanese firm struggles to gain a strong foothold in China. Even though it has been in the vanguard of Japanese investment in China, it has traditionally lagged significantly behind competitors such as Volkswagen (which had almost three times Toyota's unit sales in China in 2004), but is currently closing this gap in terms of unit sales.[58] The case study will scrutinise the historic development of Toyota's operations with particular attention to barriers for Japanese companies in China.

With global sales in more than 170 countries, manufacturing facilities in 26 countries, and eight R&D sites outside Japan, Toyota is a good example of a global firm. While industrialised markets remain a strong source of revenues (the majority of Toyota's income is generated here, and Japan continues to be the firm's key market), the manufacturer is in the process of restructuring its global sales architecture. A key ingredient of its strategic vision 'global 15' – which aims to establish Toyota as the world's No 1 car manufacturer with a world market share of 15 per cent by 2020 – is the firm's success in emerging markets. From a volume perspective it is anticipated that the BRIC markets (Brazil, Russia, India, China) will grow in prominence. Within these four growth markets, China is a critical element, contributing more than half of overall market sales. Despite its latecomer status, Toyota envisions a market share of 10 per cent. This equates to sales of one million cars. With more than 200 local and foreign automakers, the Chinese car market is, however, a prime example of 'mega-competition'.

Success factors

Network creation and leveraging partnerships. Notwithstanding a 40 year history in China, it was not until 1988 that Toyota collaboratively manufactured the one-box car (Hi Ace) under license to Shenyang-based Jinbei Corp. Realising the growing importance of the Chinese market, Toyota intended to extend its operations in China. However, the firm failed in its bid to secure a JV agreement with Shanghai-based Automotive Industry Corp (SAIC). As the Chinese government declared a five-year moratorium for further car manufacturing/assembly, Toyota lost first-mover ground to its main competitors VW (1984) and General Motors (a beneficiary of Toyota's failed bid). Technology transfer tie-ups were used as beachheads. In 1996 a co-operative venture with Tianjin-based Fengjin Corp was agreed, to form Tianjin Toyota Motor Engine Co Ltd. In 1998 these activities in Tianjin were extended with the establishment of Toyota-affiliated suppliers. In what has been termed 'pre-clusterisation',[59] Toyota developed partnerships and built up a substantial local supplier network. Following government approval in 2000, Sichuan Toyota Motor Co Ltd was founded, and in a 50:50 JV with

368 *Peter J. Buckley and Sierk A. Horn*

the First Automotive Works (FAW) group the minibus model Coaster was produced. Tailored to the Chinese market, this was the first fully locally manufactured product under the Toyota brand. In 2002 Toyota deepened its partnership with the FAW group to establish the Tianjin FAW Toyota Motor Co Ltd. The Vios model was developed in Japan, jointly manufactured in China and targeted at South East Asian markets.[60] The sports recreation vehicle models (SRV) Land Cruiser (manufactured in Jilin) and Prado debuted in 2003, and Toyota's world bestseller Corolla was introduced in 2004. 2005 saw the geographical expansion towards Guangzhou, where Guangzhou Toyota Motor Co Ltd was established; from 2006 the new Camry model was produced here. In the same year the Crown was relaunched and Toyota's middle-class model Reiz introduced (it was subsequently rebranded the Mark X model). The introduction of the Lexus brand completed Toyota's line-up. In contrast to the other models, this luxury brand is not manufactured locally, but is imported from Japan.[61] The geographical expansion of production facilities is related to consecutive model launches and widening coverage of target markets.

Product introduction. The evolution of model introductions followed an upward segment pattern, reflecting the socio-economic shifts in Chinese society. In the case of passenger vehicles, the Japanese manufacturer carefully developed its local product line-up by consecutive moves into higher price segments. This pattern was followed with its SRVs and special vehicle models. The Lexus brand is a spin-off from the Toyota brand umbrella.[62] It is positioned as a standalone, top-of-the-range brand with only loose associations to its manufacturing origin.

Lexus is distinct because the top model was introduced first, followed by a trickling down to the 'lower' price segments (which are of course still higher than for the Toyota models). In this way the entry-level models benefit from halo effects. All models are produced in China with Toyota's latest technology. The firm is trying to close the three month-market introduction gap between launches in Japan and China. This simultaneous launching of product models reinforces the influence of home-country marketing activities.

While Toyota is extending its production bases in China, it is also consolidating its sales, marking a shift towards market-seeking investments. Toyota has consequently been developing a strong foothold in the Chinese market – compensating for its latecomer disadvantages. In the area of passenger cars it ranked third with a market share of 8.2 per cent (September 2007). This success was the result of the re-launch of the Camry and the introduction of the Corolla – both of which are in the top 10 of best-selling cars in China.[63] It also highlights the successful market strategy of the Japanese automaker: the smaller car classes are left to local competitors, while Toyota focuses on the middle to upper-class segments (and in the case of Lexus on the top luxury class).[64] Within China, the metropolitan areas of Shanghai, Guangdong and Beijing are the most important sales areas.

Speed. In the competitive Chinese car market Toyota has identified speed as a key enabler for successful operations. In this respect, Toyota follows a localised marketing approach, in that the local subsidiary is given room to manoeuvre, in order not only to reflect Chinese consumer needs but also to react speedily and flexibly to changes in the market environment.

Within the Toyota group, product promotion follows the motto: 'where products are different, they must be differently explained'. This localisation of communication goes beyond the adaptation of advertising copy. The media mix is carefully chosen and focuses on the diffusion speed of information. Next to word-of-mouth communication, Chinese consumers collect information primarily via the internet. Toyota's webpage has therefore become the key source of successful marketing communication. This contrasts with the firm's strategy in the home market, where emphasis is put on diverse media including TV commercials and magazine advertisements.

A comparative analysis of the cases

The case study scenarios of Itô-Yôkadô, Shiseidô and Toyota in China help to re-assess Japanese marketing in foreign markets in general and the dynamics in developing markets in particular. The first question posed above was the extent to which Japanese international marketing practices had evolved. Based on our three case studies, the answer is – substantially. In terms of product, focus and targeting, market orientation, management and market research, there has been considerable evolution. This is less true in communication and not confirmed in institutional support and pricing. Pertaining to our second research question, on whether Japanese firms have successfully implemented local marketing flexibility, our three sample firms have all shown a high degree of cultural awareness and willingness to adapt the marketing mix locally. Geocentric attributions of the international orientation of Japanese firms seem in this light oversimplified. Table 16.2 represents our expanded understanding of Japanese marketing in China. Commonalities in success factors occur in the emphasis on quality, consistently high service provision and selection of distribution and communications networks. All three firms are sensitive to intercultural differences between Japan and China, and additionally to regional differences within China. The focus on research and development and the careful monitoring of consumer behaviour are keys to the firms' flexibility and customer responsiveness. Based on extensive market intelligence, they have successfully tailored their products/services towards growing medium to premium market segments.

Product/service

All three firms emphasise a high degree of product awareness, with a fundamental belief in offering superior quality. Product launches are rapid, almost

370   *Peter J. Buckley and Sierk A. Horn*

Table 16.2 Comparative analysis of case studies

	Retailer Itô-Yôkadô	Consumer goods manufacturer Shiseidô	High value consumer goods Toyota
Product/Service	– Initial concentrated location choice – Rapid extension of retail outlets in affluent metropolitan areas – Focus on retail experience and quality – Business development as product of consumption patterns monitoring	– Careful selection along product-country fit – Diverging brand architecture – Focus on high quality, service and brand recognition – Retail outlet selection	– Rapid product introduction – Speed/small time gap between China and home market – Use of latest technology – Focus on high brand recognition
Focus and targeting	– Supermarkets positioned as 'windows to modernity' – Middle-income group as main target	– Aspirational brand development – Affluent middle class and high-end earners as main target	– Status symbol brand – Metropolitan concentration – Target luxury segment
Market orientation	– Growing importance of Chinese market within company network – Market entry simultaneously with Western competitors – Deep integration (forward and backward)	– Key market for group growth – Market entry prior to most Western competitors	– Initially cautious approach, now important market for global growth targets – Latecomer due to government restrictions
Management	– Mainly Majority JVs, concentrated – Reliance on local employees – Centralised R&D – Flexible and pragmatic reaction to changes in market environment (store concept characteristics)	– Majority JVs, concentrated – Close liaison with headquarters, but high management flexibility – Strong focus on local R&D, JV partner selection (technological expertise) – Local citizenship	– Mainly 50:50 JVs – Majority JV at supplier level – Location choice dispersed due to two partners – Focus on local R&D, technology transfer

Continued

Japanese Multinational Enterprises in China 371

Table 16.2 Continued

	Retailer Itô-Yôkadô	Consumer goods manufacturer Shiseidô	High value consumer goods Toyota
Communication	– 'Localised' adaptation of advertising – Importance of brand recognition – Consistency in high quality service	– Service focus – Fit of retail, advertising, product – Multi-channel communication – Focus on brand management	– Media-mix focus on internet – Experiential services – Focus of dealership network metropolitan areas (product fit)
Market research	– Data base marketing (POS system) – Substantial a *priori* planning – Awareness of substantial regional differences in customer base (learning curve)	– Substantial a *priori* planning – Monitoring of socio-demographic consumer differences – External and internal market research	– External and internal data collection, qualitative and quantitative – Awareness of information diffusion patterns – Appreciation of regional differences
Pricing	– Pricing concomitant to target segment – Determined by location choice	– Pricing concomitant to non-mass market target segment (medium price range for toiletries) – Upward and downward pricing, related to product positioning	– Price variations across segments, with focus on middle to premium class – Upward and downward market development
International orientation	– Extension and replication of basic business model – Built in marketing flexibility	– Adaptation of basic business model – Coordination between HQ and local management (including JV partner)	– Maintenance of basic business model – Little to no product adaptation, but corridor to fine-tuning marketing mix

372 Peter J. Buckley and Sierk A. Horn

staccato-like (particularly in the case of Toyota), and with a clear focus on developing products to local needs (particularly Shiseidô). The latter case is interesting as it first established a strong localised platform (the Aupres brand) and developed a good understanding of the local market environment, and then introduced Japanese brands and retailing techniques. In this sense the case studies show that Japanese firms are highly adaptive, developing products continuously along the trajectory of sub-regional consumer needs and changes over time. The Itô-Yôkadô case shows a very pragmatic approach to the Chinese market, basically extending its business model to China (domination) but at the same time showing a high degree of cultural awareness. Services are adapted to local consumer behaviour, and in many cases Itô-Yôkadô monitors and 'educates' consumers to learn new skills, e.g. store cards, in a process of continuous improvement.

Focus and targeting

In contrast to their experience in developed markets, all three firms have successfully addressed the rise of affluent, middle-class consumers in China. Thus, they are not competing with local firms but with other top-of-the-line marketers and brands. While this focus on up-market segments may be a distinct feature of Japanese marketing behaviour in emerging markets, it contradicts the over-generalised and maybe outdated understanding that Japanese firms are positioning their products as mass-market, value-for-money brands. Nevertheless, the anticipated focus on high-growth segments can be maintained, as the presence of Japanese firms in China itself mirrors the fact that that they follow emerging consumer clusters. By adequately developing new segments, our cases not only underline a highly nuanced understanding of Chinese consumer shifts, but also highlight the fact that Japanese firms are capable of taking the lead in defining and addressing emerging segments. As they are developing these segments both upward and downward (with the beachhead brand as platform), they also show finely nuanced and to date unreported positioning skills. Japanese firms have always struggled to develop a premium image for their products, which to some extent has to do with their brand heritage as low-cost competitors, but this hurdle seems to have been overcome in the case of the Chinese market, where this initial positioning gives more room for brand manoeuvring (e.g Toyota's experiences with Lexus).

Market orientation

All three firms have identified China as a cornerstone to secure long-term growth. Their activities are stringently market-orientated with a clear eye on the consumer. They are all carving out specific market niches that they then attempt to dominate, particularly by establishing a leadership position in that specific product segment. In this respect all three firms can be shown to follow an aggressive market share strategy. For the retailer

Itô-Yôkadô this is evidenced by the local focus (domination strategy), while Toyota explicitly aims at reaching a specific market share in China. In order to achieve this, they also prefer to concentrate their operations geographically, even when this policy is constrained by (two) JV partners (Toyota). However, both Shiseidô and Toyota have begun to diffuse their operational network. This reflects a pragmatic expansion strategy, particularly as the firms entered China with no existing customer base. It is also a reflection of expanding circles of affluence in China, as the middle class grows and emerges in non-metropolitan areas.

Management

Key aspects of Japanese marketing behaviour derived from the home market (our third question) continue to thrive, including the firms' long-term orientation and commitment. On the one hand, this is evidenced by the ownership strategies where majority JV is the preferred entry mode, providing high levels of control. On the other hand, the importance and reliance on local staff has been reconfirmed across all three case studies. Even if key functions are filled with expatriate staff, the evidence suggests a high level of intercultural awareness, including Chinese language competence.[65] While no significant institutional support by the Japanese government has been detected, the identification of local partners has been the key to the successful market presence of all three firms. Japanese firms are sensitive to the local environment. This may take the form of a delegate responsible for government relations or simply shared ownership (JV) with local representatives. Via JVs they have gained access to the Chinese market expertise, including management, human resources and marketing. These partnerships have also enabled joint R&D, and with it the tailoring of products and services to local consumer needs. The managements have shown great flexibility, foresight and pragmatism in setting up their businesses in China.

Communication

With a focus on brand recognition, all three firms have taken great care in communicating the values of their brands to Chinese consumers. Experiments with the brand hierarchy have been captured by the case studies. The traditional umbrella brand orientation of Japanese firms has been supplemented by more flexible approaches with looser links to the corporate brand, including even Western-style single brand strategies. Shiseidô has been hugely successful in reversing its brand hierarchy with the company brand 'added on' to the single-brand Aupres. Similarly, Toyota has introduced its stand-alone brand Lexus, while at the same time being forced to deviate from its mega-brand due to local partnerships (Jinbei-Toyota etc) or potential new government regulations that foresee the use of Chinese characters instead of English characters. Itô-Yôkadô was forced to adapt its branding strategy to local market needs: it used a shop-in-shop

374 *Peter J. Buckley and Sierk A. Horn*

system for anchor brands to overcome branding problems of the Itô-Yôkadô brand. In addition to flexibility of brand management this also reflects current Japanese marketing thinking. All three cases underline the significance of longstanding brand-building, in contrast to the traditionally short product life-cycles prevalent in Western markets. Contrary to horizontal brand extension, the case study evidence highlights a trend towards vertical product introduction and therefore segmentation. This new aspect of international marketing can be interpreted as a direct outcome of developments in Japan itself, where similar strategies towards streamlining the product line-up have been implemented. The rapidity of product introductions, particularly in the case of Toyota, is notable. Potentially the result of Toyota's latecomer position, it nevertheless portrays the Japanese firm's flexibility, pragmatism and, most importantly, uncompromising commitment. As an outcome of this evolving brand management and an awareness of the importance of word-of-mouth communication in China, all firms have tailored their communication-mix to the local environment. Diverse communication channels are therefore complemented by individually tailored communication (narrow-casting using the internet or mobile phones). A further facet, so far under-explored in extant literature, is the importance of personal services. All three firms go to great lengths to train service personnel and to secure coherency in customer experiences, thereby adding a new facet to the debate on Japanese marketing approaches.

Market research

All three firms take great care in collecting information about consumers and consuming trends. Substantial planning and monitoring prior to the market entry/product launch, plus tapping into the expertise of local partners, have helped to develop a profound understanding of the Chinese market environment. In contrast to the earlier focus on 'hard' data (i.e. the importance of market share, as opposed to soft data in the form of in-store observations by product managers),[66] the firms now actively engage in collecting first-hand consumer insights. All three firms use multiple channels that may range from 'soft' in-house data collection (point-of-contact information collection by sales representatives, use of help-line information etc.) to 'hard' data methods such as most advanced POS systems. The firms interviewed also use external market research agencies or omnibus studies. Across all firms we found that local partners are a vital form of gaining and fine-tuning consumer insights. These multi-method designs enable Japanese firms to anticipate and to react to changes in Chinese consumer behaviour. Beyond the understanding of substantial differences in Sino-Japanese customer bases, the commitment to market research has lead to the awareness (and appreciation) of substantial regional and socio-demographic differences. Through stringent data monitoring, the firms also have a clear view of competitors. Features of the traditional market research focus are therefore complemented by modern, customer-orientated, quantitative and qualitative data collection methods. The case studies confirmed the importance and centrality of market research in foreign markets. Instead of a linear extension of 'hit products' from the home to the world market, as conventionally and conveniently reported, full or partial product adaptation based on extensive market research becomes paramount. Products are even developed solely for the Chinese market, underpinning a high degree of adaptation competence. Important aspects of this marketing localisation are the establishment of R&D facilities and the stringent integration of marketing research in product development processes, indicating new strengths in Japanese marketing behaviour not reported in extant literature to date.[67]

Pricing

Contrary to the common profile of Japanese pricing strategies and concomitant to the positioning strategies, our case studies reveal that they are by no means addressing the lower, price-conscious segments of markets. Their commitment to quality dictates an orientation towards middle to high-end consumer clusters. Leaving the low-price brackets to local competition or specialised retailers, this brings them into direct competition with Western manufacturers. After the initial targeting of high(er)-end consumers (equating to high prices), they are currently in the process of extending their market presence. With its full product line-up Toyota is addressing medium to premium price segments. Equally, Shiseidô has extended its presence both upward and downward.

Japanese international marketing

This research adds to our knowledge about Japanese international marketing behaviour and answers the questions relating to adaptation in local marketing flexibility and utilising Japanese home market strengths. In reviewing the case studies it is apparent that Japanese firms have substantially extended their marketing repertoire. Generalised attributions of geocentric orientation cannot be maintained. The reality shows much more nuanced approaches than have been reported to date. Japanese firms are entirely capable of customising their marketing mix to the local environment. In the case of China, the findings support and extend numerous facets of Japanese corporate behaviour.

International orientation

All three firms base their success on the transplant of idiosyncratic strengths into the Chinese market. At the same time, however, intercultural sensitivity

376 *Peter J. Buckley and Sierk A. Horn*

is prevalent across all three cases and has led to different responses in terms of their business models. Itô-Yôkadô emphasises the decentralisation of decisions, Shiseidô focuses on coordination between the HQ and the local management, especially relations with the JV partner, while Toyota essentially keeps central control because of quality and speed concerns. These differences reflect not only sectoral issues (retailing versus consumer goods and cars) but also differing philosophies and administrative heritages. The retailer (Itô-Yôkadô) emphasises flexibility and customer responsiveness whereas the other two firms, needing more control of product specification and brand protection, are more conservative. However, the emphasis on speed of introduction of new models is also a feature demanding head office control in the case of Toyota. Consequently, we can describe Itô-Yôkadô as extending the basic philosophy of its business model 'dominance' by introducing built-in flexibility, largely determined by adaptation to indigenous Chinese consumerism. Shiseidô adapts its basic business model. A divergent brand architecture, brand extensions, distribution channel development and, overall, careful attention to specific issues of the Chinese market have added specifically 'local' elements to its global strategy. Toyota, however, has continued its basic business model. There are few product adaptations and the marketing mix is merely 'fine-tuned'. A similar brand architecture to the home market is deployed, and although some innovations have taken place in service provision, these are customer-dictated. The three firms have thus responded differently to China in terms of their business models.

The response of Japanese firms is not uniform and the formula that Japanese firms follow a simple-global approach appears outdated. They rather are in a transition phase of increasingly developing a corridor that allows for a built-in flexibility to tailor marketing to the local environment (in the case of China). Within this general inclination to adapt to local needs, we found a high variation among our limited sample of three firms, which we perceive as a warning not to fall into the traditional trap of over-generalising JMNE findings. We characterise Itô-Yôkadô as *extending* its business model, Shiseidô as *adapting* and Toyota as *maintaining* its model from Japan to China. This is further enhanced by Itô-Yôkadô's model of decentralising decision-making to and within China, Shiseidô's of emphasising coordination of decisions across borders and Toyota's of centralising control to enhance quality and speed of new model introduction. It is shown that generalisations across sectors and firms are dangerous, and that forensic micro-studies are necessary to pick up important nuances of international strategy.

Summary

Japanese international marketing has evolved. While some aspects of success (organisational abilities, long-term orientation, aggressive growth strategies, ownership, R&D) have been diffused from developed to emerging markets, others have been extended (identification of customer needs and wants, information-processing capabilities). Segmentation and positioning are fine-tuned and are significantly different from Japanese strategies in developed markets. The relatively short timeframe of foreign firms' market presence in China enables Japanese brands to address upmarket consumer clusters in parallel with Western brands. The case study approach underlines the necessity of testing received knowledge with the new realities of the international business environment. At the same time it sends out a clear warning not to over-generalise. Japanese MNEs adapt to the Chinese market in multifarious ways. It would be a mistake to characterise a 'Japanese' strategy for the Chinese market, as no single approach predominates. Even within our sample of three case studies, strategies vary between the three firms and within each firm they vary over time. In all three cases, the Japanese MNEs are very conscious of consumer needs in China and the dynamics of these needs. It is a fallacy to believe that because China is a poor nation the strategies have to be aimed at low-cost products. The luxury segment is large, growing, lucrative and identifiable. Each of our three firms pays great attention to the appearance, growth and sustainability of this sector and targets it precisely. Because of rapid changes in Chinese demand patterns and consumer behaviour, it is essential for firms to keep in touch with its development. However, Japanese investors in China are not just responsive to demand patterns – they are prepared to lead them. This involves taking risks with standard business formats and with cherished home country practices. This, Japanese firms are prepared to do in China. Thus, Japanese firms balance stability (safe consumer sectors) with innovation (new products). A similar balance can be seen between adaptation to Chinese conditions and the use of standardised products, formats and approaches. The first strategy attracts revenue, the second reduces costs and therefore risks. A flexibility of approach is evident from Japanese MNEs in China – witness the extent to which they are willing to modify strategies over time as conditions change. Overall, we conclude that Japanese MNEs are not 'Western' or 'Japanese' in their approach to the Chinese market, but are flexible, realistic and pragmatic.

Acknowledgement

This research was generously supported by academic research grants from the Universities' China Committee, London. We are grateful for comments on earlier versions by Philip Stiles and Charles Baden-Fuller and two anonymous referees.

378   *Peter J. Buckley and Sierk A. Horn*

Appendix

Methodology

To investigate the realities of Japanese marketing dynamics in developing markets, this study uses a multiple case study approach within a single setting. Qualitative research is a point of departure for innovative ideas, theory genesis and refinement. Case research permits us to explore complex phenomena within a real-life context. This approach is also particularly suitable to provide a rich context for processes that would otherwise be undetected. Following a replication logic, the use of comparative case studies underpin a more robust inductive analysis as the basis for theory refinement.[68]

Comparative case studies were chosen as the research method in order to focus on the micro details of the operation of Japanese companies in China. The three analysed firms all have key challenges to face in reaching Chinese customers and in adapting their products and business models to Chinese conditions. The method of enquiry was open interviews with multiple respondents in each firm, conducted in Japanese. This was backed up by primary source material. The use of open interviewing techniques allowed a respondent-driven agenda to emerge, and our relatively open categorisation of operations in China helped the Japanese managers to focus on the important aspects of their Chinese operations without researcher-induced biases. As will be seen, these techniques enabled us to reach a much more nuanced understanding of the key elements driving Japanese operations in China, and adjustments of their business models.

Retailing, Cosmetics and Automobile are consumer-oriented industries representative of an emerging marketing expertise in Japan. The three cases were selected on the basis of their particular leadership function within the Japanese market in terms of their industry position. Seven&I Holding is Japan's largest retailer, and its convenience store arm ranked number one in terms of retail value or market share for consecutive five years. Equally, with a market share of 16 per cent, Shiseidô is an industry leader of Japanese cosmetics and toiletries. Toyota Motor Corp too is a dominant force in Japan's automotive industry. Excluding its affiliated brands (Lexus, Daihatsu, Hino), Toyota products hold a market share of 30 per cent in Japan.[69] Each firm has built its strong domestic industry position through a commitment to product development and marketing innovation.[70] With a view to the assumed impact of the domestic business model on the design of China operations, home-market strength was a decisive selection criteria. Further to this, all three firms possess substantial international expertise. In the Global Fortune 500 ranking, Seven &I Holdings is the highest ranked Japanese retailer. As of 2008, it was ranked 141 overall (with US$49.7 million in revenue), and globally holds ninth position in its industry. Shiseidô is a global top performer in the cosmetics and toiletries industry. While ranked

Japanese Multinational Enterprises in China 379

1363 in the Global Fortune 2000, it holds sixth place in its specific industry category. Toyota is one of the largest corporations worldwide. As of 2008, it was ranked fifth in the Fortune 200 ranking (with US$15.0 million in revenue), outperforming other global car manufacturers, including the once dominant North American firms GM and Ford. As all three firms follow a strategy of continuous geographic expansion (as outlined in various company reports, available online), they are distinct examples of Japanese MNE internationalisation, and provide a useful lens through which corporate behaviour in China can be investigated. Using Rugman's classification (2008), distinct differences as regards international market orientation are evident. Toyota is bi-regional/global, with 80 per cent of revenues in North America and Asia; however it continues to increase its European activities. Itô-Yôkadô is bi-regional, with 39 per cent of sales in NAFTA. Shiseidô is home-/host-oriented (80 per cent of revenues are regional). In short, the firms are evolving along diverging trajectories, and it is likely that these differences result in diverging international experiences.[71]

Semi-structured expert interviews were conducted in both Japan (for Toyota, using marketing and retail think tanks, advertising agencies) and Beijing, China (for Itô-Yôkadô, Shiseidô and Toyota) in two waves between April and September 2007. All interview partners held a leading marketing or top-management position. The interviews were conducted in Japanese. The number of interviewees totalled 15. To further establish Japanese perceptions, and for triangulation purposes the authors conducted an extensive literature review of original language material (Kokkai Toshokan and Nikkei Telecommunication 21 data base). Each interview lasted at least two hours, in most cases longer (including factory visits). The interviews focused on: (1) company background and marketing orientation in Japan; (2) motivations for the firms' Chinese market entry; and (3) Chinese consumers and the comparative impact on the local marketing design. Information on recent developments in the three firms in China was complemented by follow-up contacts, review of press releases and company material (newsletters, websites etc.). This three-dimensional approach, involving three core firms, marketing experts and literature review, is an effective way not only to analyse Japanese perceptions of marketing activities in China, but also to shed new light on how marketing of Japanese MNEs has evolved since its 1980s heyday. Intercultural sensitivity and language competence must not be underestimated for this undertaking and are essential for a cross-disciplinary research approach.

References

1. P. J. Buckley and H. Mirza, The wit and wisdom of Japanese management: an iconoclastic analysis, *Management International Review* 25(3), 16–32 (1985); P. J. Buckley, Asian network firms – an analytical framework, *Asia-Pacific Business Review* 10(3–4), 254–271 (2004); S. A. Horn, *Interkulturelle Kompetenz im Zugang*

380 *Peter J. Buckley and Sierk A. Horn*

zu Japanischen Konsumenten [Intercultural Competence in Accessing Japanese Consumers]. Deutscher Universitäts-Verlag, Wiesbaden (2005) p. 324.

2. P. Kotler and L. Fahey, The world's champion marketers: the Japanese, *Journal of Business Strategy* 2, 3–13 (1982).

3. P. Doyle, J. Saunders and L. Wright, A comparative study of British, US and Japanese marketing strategies in the British market, *International Journal of Research in Marketing* 5, 171–184 (1988).

4. H. Shigegaki, *Nihon Kigyô no Kokusai Chôsei Mekanisumu* (International Coordination Mechanism of Japanese Firms), Kokusai Keieiron (International Management Theory), Gakubunsha, Tokyo, (1998) p. 236. M. Yoshihara, H. Itagagki and S. Morokami, *Kokusai Keiei* [International Management]. Yuhikaku, Tokyo (2005); H. Yoshihara, *Nihon Kigyô no Kokusai Keiei* [International Management of Japanese Firms], Dôbunkan, Tokyo (1992) p. 324.

5. T. Shimizu, *Gurôbaru Mâketingu* [Global Marketing]. Zeikei, Tokyo (1995) p. 256. and S. Morokami, Gurôbaru Mâketingu no Chôsei to Tôsei [Control and coordination of global marketing]. in S. Morokami and T. Fujizawa (eds.), *Gurôbaru Mâketingu* [Global Marketing], Kôtokusha, Tokyo, 193 (1997).

6. K. Backhaus, J. Bueschken and M. Voeth, *Internationales Marketing* [International Marketing]. Schaeffer-Poeschel, Stuttgart (1996) p. 306.

7. H. Shigegaki (1998) op. cit. at Ref 4.

8. P. Doyle, et al (1988) op. cit. at Ref 3; M. Czinkota and M. Kotabe, Product development the Japanese way, *Journal of Business Strategy* 11(6), 31–36 (1990); A. Delios and P. W. Beamish, Geographic scope, product diversification and the corporate performance of Japanese firms, *Strategic Management Journal* 20(8), 711–727 (1999); C. Nakane, *Japanese Society*, University of California Press, Berkeley (1970) p. 188. K. Tanouchi, *Japanese Style Marketing Based on Sensitivity, Japan: Marketing/Advertising*, Dentsu, Tokyo (1983), pp. 77–81 (1983). J. C. Abegglen and G. Stalk, *Kaisha*, McGraw-Hill, New York (1985) p. 320. J. Saunders, L. Wright and P. Doyle, *A Comparative Study of US and Japanese Marketing Strategies in the British Market*, Loughborough University of Technology Department of Management Studies (1987); A. Genestre, P. Herbig and A. T. Shao, Japanese international marketing strategy, *Marketing Intelligence and Planning* 13(11), 36–46 (1995); V. Wong, J. Saunders and P. Doyle, Japanese marketing strategies in the United Kingdom, *Long Range Planning* 20(6), 54–63 (1987); M. Kotabe and S. C. Okoroafo, A comparative study of European and Japanese multinational firms' marketing strategies and performance in the United States, *Management International Review* 4, 353–370 (1990). J. Johanson and G. S. Yip, Exploiting globalization potential: US and Japanese strategies, *Strategic Management Journal* 15, 579–601 (1994). J. Anand and A. Delios, How Japanese MNCs have matched goals and strategies in India and China, *The Columbia Journal of World Business* 31(3), 50–62 (1996); W. Fongsuwan, A comparative study of international marketing strategies between Japanese, American and European multinational companies: Thailand 1997, *Centre for ASEAN Studies Discussion papers* 25, (1999) – Available under: http://webh01.ua.ac.be/cas/PDF/CAS25.pdf (1999). [Accessed 20 January, 2008]. M. Papanastassiou and R. Pearce, The internationalisation of research and development by Japanese enterprises, *R&D Management* 24(2), 155–165 (1994); T. Iwasa and H. Odagiri, Overseas R&D, knowledge sourcing, and patenting, an empirical study of Japanese R&D investments in the US, *Research Policy* 33, 807–828 (2004); N. Kumar, Determinants of location of overseas R&D activity of multinational enterprises: the case of US and Japanese corporations, *Research Policy* 30, 159–174

(2001); C. R. Taylor, S. Zou and G. E. Osland, Foreign market entry strategies of Japanese MNCs, *International Marketing Review* 17(2), 146–163 (2000) London. I. P. Somlev and Y. Hoshino, Influence of location factors on establishment and ownership of foreign investments: the case of the Japanese manufacturing firms in Europe, *International Business Review* 14, 577–598 (2005); M. Sakakibara and K. Serwin, US distribution entry strategy of Japanese manufacturing firms, *Journal of the Japanese and International Economies* 14, 43–72 (2000); A. Delios and W. J. Henisz, Policy uncertainty and the sequence of entry by Japanese firms 1980–1998, *Journal of International Business Studies* 34, 227–241 (2003); J. Johanson and I. Nonaka, Market research the Japanese way, *Harvard Business Review* 65(3), 16–22 (1987); C. Langlois, For profit or for market share? The pricing strategy of Japanese automakers on the US market, *Journal of the Japanese and International Economies* 11, 55–81 (1997); H. Meffert and J. Bolz, *Internationales Marketing-Management* [International Marketing Management]. Kohlhammer, Stuttgart (1998) p. 280. G. S. Yip, Global strategy as a factor for Japanese success, *The International Executive* 38(1), 145–167 (1996); S. A. Horn, Strategisches Identitätsmanagement Transnationaler Unternehmen [Strategic identity management of transnational corporations], Dissertation Freie Universitaet Berlin, published on microfiche, (2000) p. 441.

9. A. Delios and P. W. Beamish, Regional and global strategies of Japanese firms, *Management International Review* 45, 19–36 (2005); R. Farrell, N. Gaston and J.-E. Sturm, Determinants of Japan's foreign direct investment: an industry and country panel study, 1984–1998, *Journal of Japanese International Economies* 18(2), 161–182 (2004); K. Kiyota and S. Urata, *The role of multinational firms in international trade: the case of Japan, Japan and the World Economy, 560,* Research seminar in international economics, University of Michigan. Available at: http://ideas.repec.org/d/fbyokjp.html (2007). [Accessed 20 January 2008]. S. Makino, P. W. Beamish and N. B. Zhao, The characteristics and performance of Japanese FDI in less developed and developed countries, *Journal of World Business* 39, 377–392 (2004); Y. S. Pak and Y.-R. Park, Characteristics of Japanese FDI in the east and the west: understanding the strategic motives of Japanese investment, *Journal of World Business* 40, 254–266 (2005); N. S. Siddharthan and M. L. Lakhera, Foreign direct investment and location advantages: Japanese perceptions of India compared to China and ASEAN, *Journal of International and Area Studies* 12(1), 99–110 (2005); S. Tejima, Japanese FDI, the implications of 'hollowing out' on the technological development of host countries, *International Business Review* 9, 555–570 (2000); E. Tomiura, Technological capability and FDI in Asia: firm-level relationships among Japanese manufacturers, *Asian Economic Journal* 19(3), 273–289 (2005); Y. Yoshida and H. Ito, How do the Asian economies compete with Japan in the US market? Is China exceptional? A triangular trade approach, *Asia-Pacific Business Review* 12(3), 285–307 (2006).

10. P. W. Beamish and R. Jiang, Investing profitably in China: is it getting harder?, *Long Range Planning* 35, 135–151 (2002); R. Belderbos and M. Carree, The location of Japanese investments in China: agglomeration effects, keiretsu, and firm heterogeneity, *Journal of the Japanese and International Economies* 16, 194–211 (2002); R. Belderbos and L. Sleuwaegen, Japanese firms and the decision to invest abroad: business groups and regional core networks, *Review of Economics and Statistics* 78(2), 214–220 (1996). J. F. Cassidy and B. Andreosso-O'Callaghan, Spatial determinants of Japanese FDI in China, *Japan and the World Economy* 18, 512–527 (2006); S. Cheng, The role of labour costs in the location choices of

382 *Peter J. Buckley and Sierk A. Horn*

Japanese investors in China, *Papers in Regional Science* **85**(1), 121–138 (2006); S. Cheng, Structure of firm location choices: an examination of Japanese greenfield investment in China, *Asian Economic Journal* **21**(1), 47–73 (2007); K. C. Fung, H. Iizaka and A. Siu, Japanese direct investment in China, *China Economic Review* **14**, 304–315 (2003); X. Ma and A. Delios, A new tale of two cities: Japanese FDIs in Shanghai and Beijing, 1979–2003, *International Business Review* **16**, 207–228 (2007); R. Wakasugi, The effects of Chinese regional conditions on the location choices of Japanese affiliates, *The Japanese Economic Review* **56**(4), 390–407 (2005); C. Zhou, A. Delios and J. Y. Yang, Locational determinants of Japanese foreign direct investment in China, *Asia-Pacific Journal of Management* **19**(1), 63–86 (2002).

11. Y. Aoki, *Burando Birudingu no Jidai* [The Era of Brand Building]. Dentsû, Tokyo (1999) p. 325. H. Katahira, *Pawâ Burando no Honshitsu* [The Essence of Powerbrands]. Daiyamondosha, Tokyo (1998) p. 378.

12. W. Fongsuwan (1997) op. cit. at Ref 8.

13. S. Collinson and A. M. Rugman, The regional nature of Japanese multinational business, *Journal of International Business Studies* **39**, 215–230 (2008); JETRO, *White Paper on International Trade and Foreign Direct Investment: Japanese Corporate Activity in New Growth Markets and the Emerging East Asian Free Trade Zone, Tokyo*, Japan External Trade Organisation (2006) p. 38.

14. S. A. Horn (2005) op. cit. at Ref 1.

15. S. A. Horn, Konsumgütermarketing in Japan: entwicklungspotentiale des markenmanagements [Consumer goods marketing in Japan: new potentials in brand management]. *Jahrbuch der Absatz- und Ver-brauchsforschung* **47**(4), 391–405 (2001).

16. M. E. Porter, *Competitive strategy: techniques for analyzing industries and competitors*, The Free Press, New York (1980) p. 396. M. E. Porter, *Competitive advantage of nations*, Palgrave Macmillan, London (1998) p. 896. W. Lazer, S. Murata and H. Kosaka, Japanese marketing: towards a better understanding, *Journal of marketing* **49**, 68–81 (1985).

17. JETRO, *Japanese trade and investment statistics*. Available at: http://www.jetro. go.jp/en/stats/statistics (2007). [Accessed 20 January 2008].

18. R. Herd and S. Dougherty, China's economy: a remarkable transformation, *OECD Observer* **251**, 13–16 (2005).

19. JETRO (2006) op. cit. at Ref 13.

20. T. Matsui, Genchika to Hyôjunka no Hazamade [The gorge between localisation and normation] in Y. Yamashita (ed.), *Burandingu in China* [Branding in China], Tôyô Keizai Hôsha, Tokyo, 75–108 (2006).

21. Exceptions are R. Larke, Expansion of Japanese retailers overseas, in J. Dawson and J.-H. Lee (eds.), *International Retailing Plans and Strategies in Asia*, Haworth Press, Binghamton, 99–120 (2004); J. Gamble, Consumers with Chinese characteristics? Local customers in British and Japanese multinational stores in contemporary Japan, in F. Trentmann (ed.), *The Making of the Consumer*, Berg Publishers, London, 175–198 (2006); T. Yahagi, Itôyôkadô no Chûgoku Genchika Purosesu [Itô-Yôkadô's localisation process in China]. *Keiei Shizai* **41**(4), 71–99 (2005) (Hôsei University).

22. T. Yahagi (2005) op. cit. at Ref 21.

23. S. Sakamoto, Chengdu Itôyôkadô Hanjôki [Success story of Chengdu Itô-Yôkadô]. *JC Economic Journal* 20–23 (February 2005); Anon, 'Kôjô' to 'Shijô' wo Horiokosu [Uncovering workshops and markets]. *Gekiryu Magazine* 64–67 (August 2005).

24. T. Yahagi, (2005) op. cit. at Ref 21; A. Hanawa, Itôyôkadô ga 'Sanbon no ya' de Idomu [Itô-Yôkadô challenges with three arrows], *Decide* 18–27 (April 2005).

Japanese Multinational Enterprises in China   383

25. The establishment of a convenience store chain in China is timely. This retail format signals not only the advent of new urban lifestyles, that place emphasis on convenience (and expression of modernity). As this convenience is compensated by top-up fees of 15–20% of high street supermarket prices, it also signals a diversity of income structures (with an estimated income threshold of US$3,000 as benchmark for convenience store development). Legal changes in China in 2006 now allow for franchise operations, which will fuel the expansion of 7-Eleven outlets.

26. Itô-Yôkadô has positioned itself as a mid-income retailer. The Wangfujing Supermarket chain, however, uses an up-market appeal (Anon., 2005, op. cit. at Ref 23), and halo-effects towards the Itô-Yôkadô brand are to be expected.

27. A. Hanawa (2005) op. cit. at Ref 24. Anon (2005) op. cit. at Ref 23.

28. Seven&I Holdings (2005).

29. Anon (2005) op. cit. at Ref 23.

30. A similar pattern as that of Seven&I can be demonstrated for the Japanese AEON group. While it also expands its operations in China, the stores are mainly located in Guangzhou region.

31. According to M. Friese, CEO of a Beijing-based marketing consulting agency, it becomes increasingly difficult to identify promising locations for retail outlets. One factor is the cost explosion of land (particularly in metropolitan areas such as Beijing or Shanghai), which makes further expansions difficult.

32. A. Hanawa (2005) op. cit. at Ref 24.

33. These initially foresaw a total space of 24,000 sqm, shop floor space of 15,000 sqm with a sales space ratio of over 62%, minimum of 2–3 floors, and the rent payments below a 5% threshold of the expected sales, T. Yahagi (2005) op. cit. at Ref 21.

34. S. Sakamoto (2005) op. cit. at Ref 23.

35. Chinese consumer decision processes differ decidedly from routine purchases such as white T-shirts, because of price and practicability considerations. China's societal and geographical heterogeneity leads to further differentiation: Itô-Yôkadô planned to introduce beige and white polo shirts – traditionally Japanese male summer wear. As well as the price, these items failed due to perception differences. Chinese consumers prefer colours over design aspects on the one hand and the Beijing working population had the perception that light colours get dirty easily (differences in garment washing patterns) on the other. And as they are not washed regularly they are not usually worn by Chinese workers, T. Yahagi (2005) op. cit. at Ref 21.

36. As the retail brand is not well known in China, it initially also faced difficulties in developing an adequate supply base, S. Sakamoto (2005) op. cit. at Ref 23.

37. New employees are undergoing a strict service training. Here customer interaction is exercised using role play and on the job training, Gamble (2006) op. cit. at Ref 21.

38. F. Miyamoto, Chûgoku ni okeru Shiseidô no Burando Mâketingu [Shiseidô brand marketing in China]. Kuoriti Manajimento [Quality Management]. 57(10), 16–23 (October 2006); K. Sham, Chûsan Kaikyô no Taitô de Kyûseichô suru Chûgoku Kôkyû Keshôhin Shijô [Chinese luxury cosmetics market accelerates in the wake of the rise of the middle class], Kokusai Shôgyô [International Commerce Industry]. 46–50 (March 2007).

39. P. J. Buckley, The Strategy of multinational enterprises in the light of the rise of China, Scandinavian Journal of Management 23(2), 107–126 (2007).

384 *Peter J. Buckley and Sierk A. Horn*

40. C. H. Oh and A. Rugman, Regional sales of multinationals in the world cosmetics industry, *European Management Journal* 24(2–3), 163–173 (2006).
41. Euromonitor, *Cosmetics and Toiletry – China, Euromonitor International*, Global market information database, London (2006) p. 24.
42. Nomura Kenkyûjo, *Chûgoku Shijô de no Kigyô Burando Senryaku* [Corporate brand strategies in China]. Searchina Institute, Seiunsha, Tokyo (2007) p. 254.
43. In the early days the firm provided hotels in Beijing with soap and toothpaste.
44. F. Miyamoto (2006) op. cit. at Ref 38.
45. The Chinese market is not only huge but also highly heterogeneous. Class affiliation and income levels vary with regional economic development – and with it consumptive patterns (e.g. the urban–rural split). Access to media and retail outlets (and with it an influx of Western imagery) is territorially incongruent. Moreover, the climate plays a pivotal role in product adoption of cosmetics and toiletries. Cold areas in northern China show very different product preferences (e.g. ageing crèmes) from consumers in the warmer south (lifestyle accessories). Socio-demographic aspects too are important. Because the history of cosmetics in China is very short, consumption patterns are not similar to Western ones. The 'cosmetic role model' of the mother as the blueprint for toiletry use is non-existent (and rather taken over by media/beauty consultants). Accordingly, the majority of consumers – even for premium products that in Western markets are usually reserved for an elder generation (40s/50s) – are in their 20s and 30s. While this younger generation is benefiting most from China's economic rise, elder age clusters lag behind in disposable income. This complex mix makes for an attractive yet fragmented and fluctuating consumer market.
46. Demand fuelled further expansion in the aftermath, with a third extension to the Shanghai plant to be completed by the end of 2007.
47. K. Miyakawa, *Shiseidô's business development in China*. Available at: http://www.investment.gov.cn/2005–10–27/1130425544124.html (2005). [Accessed 20 January 2008].
48. R. Kanayama, Chûgoku Zenshi 5000 Ten no Senmonten wo Mesashu Shiseidô [Shiseidô aims to open 5.000 specialty stores], *Ekonomisuto* [Economist] 94–95 (10 April 2007); Anon, Depâto, Chenstoa no Ryôrin ga Kamiai Chûgoku Shijô wo Sekken [Storming the Chinese market with a dual strategy of department store and chain store]. *Gekiryu Magazine* 32(3), 8–12 (2007).
49. The brand name translates into 'a part of you'.
50. S.A. Horn, Product adoption and innovation diffusion: the case of Japanese marketing to China, *Asia Pacific Business Review* 15(3), 389–409 (July 2009).
51. By producing the Aupres products in China, high import taxes were avoided and the final price is below that of other Shiseidô products.
52. T. Ueda, Shiseidô no Gurôbaru Tenkai ni Okeru Chûgoku de no Seikô [Success in China as part of Shiseidô's global development]. *Japan Marketing Journal* 89, 84–100 (2003).
53. Shiseidô conducts multi-channel market research, both internally and externally (user profiling). The counters in high end department stores and flagship stores (Wangfujing, e.g.) are the eyes and ears of the marketing department. The commitment to regional diversity is met with nationwide research. Moreover, a customer help line is used to collect further information about Chinese consumers.
54. With the influx of international brands consciousness for cosmetics increased. This created more demand and therefore opened the door for more brands.

Japanese Multinational Enterprises in China 385

55. Shiseidô plans to export this brand to other Asian countries, including Japan.
56. Following the Aupres success story the firm further develops localised brands, such as the recently introduced Urara, Asplir and Whitia Y. Kawashima, *ShiseidôBurando* [Shiseidô brand]. Aspekuto, Tokyo (2007) p. 248.
57. More than 80% of Shiseidô employees work as beauty counsellors, underlining the importance the firm attributes to marketing and service.
58. *IHS Global Insight (2007) Auto insight database*. Available at: http://www.globalinsight.com. [Accessed 20th January 2008].
59. F. Hatani, Pre-clusterization in emerging markets: the Toyota group's entry process in China, *Asia Pacific Business Review* 15(3), 369–387 (July 2009).
60. The Vios is also manufactured in Thailand, Indonesia, Singapore, and Malaysia. While originally developed for East Asia the model found its way back to Japan's domestic market in the form of the Belta.
61. The Toyota group's newest success story, the environmental friendly Prius, was only recently introduced into China. With no tax incentives from the Chinese government, prices of the Prius are considerably higher than in Japan and Europe. This model is therefore unattractive for Chinese consumers and sales are symbolic rather than the herald of another success story.
62. This brand spin-off stands in the tradition of recent changes in Japanese brand management. The nature of Japanese business systems (keiretsu and activities in various industries) dictated until recently a concentration on 'umbrella brands'. K. Suyama and H. Umemoto, *Nihongata Burando Yûi Senryaku* [Japanese style brand dominance strategy]. Daiyamondosha, Tokyo (2000) p. 258. Changes in consumer behaviour and corporate restructuring brought an introduction of Western style brand management with a strong focus on the development of single brand profiles.
63. Global Insight, Country report: China (*Automotive*), Waltham, 1–7 (2007).
64. Y. Inaba, *Toyota in China: full speed ahead, Business Week, 6 March*. Available at: http://www.business week.com/globalbiz/content/mar2006/gb20060309_341430.htm. [Accessed 20 January 2008].
65. For example, the case of Suntory in T. Matsui (2006) op. cit. at Ref 20.
66. J. Johanson and I. Nonaka (1987) op. cit. at Ref 8.
67. Cross functional teams, e.g. T. Fujimoto and M. Yasumoto, *Seikô Suru Seihin Kaihatsu* [Successful product development]. Yuhikaku, Tokyo (2005) p. 345.
68. J Bortz and N. Doering, *Forschungsmethoden und Evaluation* [Research methods and evaluation]. Springer, Berlin (2006) p. 897. R. K. Yin, *Case study research: design and methods*, Sage, Beverly Hills (2008) p. 240. R. E. Stake, *Multiple case study analysis*, The Guilford Press, New York (2006) p. 342.
69. JAMA (Japan Automobile Manufacturers Association), *Active matrix database system*. Available online under: http://www.jama-english.jp/statistics/index.html. [Accessed 20 January 2008].
70. M. Shuwa, *Sebun Irebun Sôsui Suzuki Toshifumi* [Seven Eleven's Commander Suzuki Toshifumi]. Shuwa System, Tokyo (2004) p. 94. K. Morita, *Sôha no ryûtsû inobêshon* [Retail Innovation and the Contend for Supremacy]. Keiô Gijuku Daigaku Shuppan, Tokyo (2004) p. 302.
71. A. M. Rugman and S. Girod, Retail multinationals and globalization, *European Management Journal* 21, 24–37 (2003); S. Collinson and A. M. Rugman, (2008), op. cit. at Ref 13. C. H. Oh and A. M. Rugman, (2006) op. cit. at Ref 40; A. M. Rugman and A. Verbeke, A perspective on regional and global strategies of multinational enterprises, *Journal of International Business Studies* 35, 3–18 (2004).

Index

Africa, foreign investment in, 73
agency
  costs, 45
  human, 56
  theory, 103–4
agglomeration effects, 20–1, 134
AMD, 159–60
American industry, 75–8
Anglo-Saxon/Celtic opposition, 321–39
Annales school, 8
assets
  intangible, 1, 12–14, 138–9
  knowledge-based, 95
  tangible, 192

bandwagon effect, 17–18
barriers to entry, 134
BenQ, 146–7
best-worst scaling (BWS), 236–7,
  244–50, 259–61
bounded rationality, 11–12, 97
branding, 133, 143–4, 146, 210, 269, 352
brands, purchase of, 146–8
Buckley, P.J., 1, 11, 15–16, 24–8, 39–47,
  54, 56, 78, 87–8, 95–9, 134
bunching effect, 20
business cultures, 2
business history, 7–9, 28, 30
Byé, Maurice, 85–7

Canada, 75–8
  investment in, 80–4
capital markets, 63, 66, 130, 131, 149,
  271, 354, 355
capital mobility, 62, 79–80, 86
cartels, 63, 75
Casson, Mark, 1, 11, 15–16, 24–8, 39–47,
  51, 54, 56, 63, 78, 87–8, 95–9,
  135–6, 139, 224, 270, 284
Chaebol, 149
Chandler, Alfred, 9, 26
China, 2, 134, 144, 227
  brand purchase by, 146–7
  consumer market in, 358

foreign investment in, 71–3
  global factories in, 146
  Japanese multinational enterprises in,
    358–79
  manufacturing in, 131
  outward FDI, 146, 147–8
China National Offshore Oil
  Corporation (CNOOC), 147
Chinese multinationals, 26
Coase, R.H., 1, 9, 11, 28, 40–1, 63, 87–8,
  94–5, 134, 266, 345
Cobb-Douglas production function,
  192
commodity chains, 137–8
communication, 13, 19, 24, 40, 46, 53,
  74–5, 98–9, 102, 139, 188, 277
communitarians, 277–8
comparative advantage, 17, 109, 114,
  124, 134, 275
comparative studies, 21–3
competition, 16–17, 87
  in global factor, 273
  role of, 171–4, 176
competitive advantage, 18, 19, 107, 200
competitiveness, 66–8, 159
complementary knowledge accession,
  209, 215
complementary knowledge acquisition,
  210–12, 215
computer processor industry, 159–60
conglomerates, 149
consolidation, 40, 148
constant returns to scale (CRS), 192
consultation, 277
consumption, 132
contracting costs, 273
contract manufacturers (CMs), 48, 135,
  267–8, 346
control, 11, 24, 272–3, 280, 281–2, 285,
  348–9
coordination, 53, 188
corporate governance, *see* governance
corporate performance, *see* firm
  performance

388 *Index*

costs
  agency, 45
  contracting, 273
  of flexibility, 277–8
  information, 41, 51–3, 98–9, 135–8
  of innovation, 187
  internal, 45
  of knowledge transfer, 214–15
  production, 96
  transaction, 10–12, 43–5, 53–4, 96–9,
    101, 103, 137, 141–2
cross-border activities, 10, 20
cultural clashes, 349
cultural difference, 318–39
cultural distance, 2, 124, 227, 291–314
culture, 8, 22, 99
  entrepreneurial, 143

degree of internationalization (DOI),
    183, 187, 200
development
  constraints on, 140–1
  FDI and, 71–4
  impact of global factory on, 129–51
  role of the state in, 149–50
disintegration, 41, 274, 278
distribution, 17, 19, 20, 48–51, 55, 68,
    78, 135–6, 138, 140, 143, 147–8,
    267–8
domestic industry, FDI and, 80–4
domestic markets, 132
domestic production, 112–15
Dunning, John, 60, 87, 107, 109, 125,
    224

East India Company, 66
eclectic paradigm, 18, 19, 87, 107–25
e-commerce, 133
economic development, *see*
    development
economic nationalism, 69
economics
  heritage of, 61
  industrial, 62–3
  international, 62
education, 142–3
emerging economies, 46–7, 134, 138,
    143–6
  doing business in, 318–39
  entrepreneurship in, 141–2

multinationals from, 25–6
encephalisation, 272
entrepreneurial culture, 143
entrepreneurs, 109–12, 119–21
entrepreneurship, 43–4, 80, 141–2, 149,
    272
  contracting costs and, 273
  transaction costs and, 141–2
Europe, American industry in, 75
evolutionary theory, 19, 26
exchange of threats hypothesis, 18
expatriate managers, 349
exporting, 15
externalisation, 39, 43
externalities, 139

fine-slicing, 24, 36–7, 46, 50, 54, 55,
    134, 136–7, 283–4, 355
firm
  evolutionary theory of, 19
  growth of, 43–4, 62, 84
  institutional theory of, 28
  knowledge-based view of, 186–7
  resource-based view of, 18–19
firm performance, innovation and,
    183–5, 191–2, 200–1
firm size, 168–71, 175
first mover advantage, 144
flatter organisations, 277
flexibility, 52, 135, 268, 273–9, 346
  competitive advantage and, 279
  costs of, 277–8
  firm, 277–8
  internal organisation and, 276–7
  location, 277–8
  in R&D, 275
flexible specialisation, 27
follow-my-leader theory, 20
foreign direct investment (FDI), 10–18,
    20, 24, 112–13
  concept of, 69–71
  control of domestic industry and,
    80–4
  development and, 71–4
  early theories of, 74–80
  emerging economies, 117–20
  horizontal integration of, 131
  knowledge-asset-seeking, 109, 120–3
  location decisions, 224–61
  modern theories of, 84–7

Index 389

foreign direct investment (FDI)
– *continued*
 motives for, 68–9, 76
 outward, 146, 147–8
 theory of, 63–4
 timing of, 45
 two-way flows of, 78–9
 utility from, 117
foreign firms, 10
foreign markets, involvement in,
 14–15
foreign market servicing, 15, 44, 78
foreign operations, management of,
 68–9

gambler's earnings hypothesis, 84–5
general equilibrium model, 108, 122–3
generalized method of moment (GMM),
 177n3
Germany/Poland interactions, 292,
 294–6, 299–306, 320–39
global factory, 44–53
 assets of, 138–9
 competition within, 273
 components of, 48–51, 267–8,
 345–6
 concept of, 266
 consolidation, 148
 driving factors in, 133–4
 economic development and, 129–51
 elements of, 134–5, 267–70, 344–5
 flexibility of, 273–9
 information structure of, 51–2, 135–8,
 268–9, 346–7
 integration process, 269–70
 interfaces, 269–70
 key elements of, 52–3
 location of, 271
 management of, 54–5
 ownership of, 271
 power of, 140, 271–3
 problems of, 349
 purchasing power of, 140
 role of headquarters in, 266–85, 349
 role of the state, 149–50
 stocks and flows in, 270
 strategic change example, 280–3
globalisation, 27, 129–32
 corporate governance and, 139–40
 driving factors in, 133–4

global supply chain, 48, 131, 135, 136,
 267–8
global value chains, 137–8
glocalisation, 27, 49–50, 69
governance
 attitudes toward risk and, 100–1
 choice of structure, 102
 of global factory, 269–70
 globalisation and, 139–40
 internal transaction costs and, 96–9
 of MNEs, 94–104

headquarters, role of, 55, 266–85,
 349
Heckscher-Ohlin model, 16
Hicks, John, 8
high-tech firms, 169, 175
Hilferding, Rudolf, 65
historical research, 21
history, 7–9
Hobson, C. K., 74–5
Hobson, J. A., 64
home bias, 132
horizontal integration, 12, 131
hub-and-spoke strategies, 48, 135, 136,
 267–8, 346
human agency, 56
Hume, David, 8
Hymer, Stephen, 1, 9–11, 60, 63, 79,
 87–8, 224
Hymer-Kindleberger hypotheses,
 9–10

IBM, 146
imperfect markets, 26
imperialism, 64–6
impersonal forces, 56
India, 131, 134
indigenous firms, 144
industrial economics, 62–3
industrial organisation, 224
industry technology cycle, 14
information and communication
 technologies (ICT), 101, 159
information costs, 41, 51–2, 53, 98–9,
 135–8
information flows, 43, 188, 272
information gathering, 46
information structure, of global factory,
 51–2, 135–8, 268–9, 346–7

390 Index

innovation, 42, 133, 149
  competition and, 171–4
  costs of, 187
  exploitation and appropriability of,
    188–90
  firm performance and, 183–5, 191–2,
    200–1
  role of internationalization in,
    183–201
institutional environment, 102–3
institutionalist economics, 27
institutional theory of the firm, 28
intangible assets, 1, 12–14, 138–9
Intel, 159–60
inter-industry spillovers, 13, 161–2,
  166–8
internal costs, 45
internalisation, 39–56, 119–20
  advantages of, 39–40, 107, 109
  costs of, 40
  spatial element of, 55
internalisation theory, 10–13, 42,
  94–104, 274
internal markets, 274
internal organisation, flexibility and,
  276–7
internal transaction costs, 96–9, 101,
  103
international business, 1, 21–3
international business theory, 9–21
  long-run, 23–7
  managerial relevance of, 88
  modern, 84–7
  pre-Hymer, 60–89
international competitiveness, 66–8
international economics, 62
international-expansion strategy, 201
internationalisation, 14–16, 129–32
  calculative approach to, 228–9
  definition of, 185
  eclectic paradigm and, 107–25
  innovation and, 183–201
  negative effects of, 188
  process issues, 227–8
  process model, 228–9
international joint ventures (IJVs), 48,
  54, 102, 135, 268
international management, 68–9, 87
international marketing, 358–79
international production, 10–11, 18

intra-industry spillovers, 13, 159, 164–6
investment climate, 81
invisible infrastructure, 279
Itô-Yôkadô, 362–4, 369–75

Japan, 2, 21, 149
Japanese economy, 344
Japanese multinational enterprises
  in China, 358–79
  hybrids, 350–4
  management styles, 343–4
  marketing strategies, 358–79
  rise of, 343–55
joint stock companies, 66–7, 74
joint ventures, 48, 54, 213, 224, 268,
  273–5, 348

Keiretsu, 149
Kindleberger, Charles, 9
knowledge, 25, 214
  culture and, 99
  leakage, 188
  scientific, 184, 187–8
  tacit, 99
knowledge accession, 207–10, 214–15,
  219
  complementary, 209, 215
  supplementary, 209–10, 215
  trust and, 216–18
knowledge acquisition, 207, 210–15, 219
  complementary, 210–12, 215
  supplementary, 212–13, 215
  trust and, 216–18
knowledge-asset-seeking FDI, 109,
  120–3
knowledge-based assets, 95
knowledge-based economy, 20
knowledge-based view of the firm,
  186–7
knowledge transfer, 13, 206–20
  cost and, 214–15
  knowledge accession, 208–10
  knowledge acquisition, 210–13
  modes of, 207–8
  trust and, 215–18
Korea, 143–4

labor input, 192
labor productivity, 192
labour exploitation, 349

Index

large multiterritorial unit (LMU), 85-7
Lazonick, 27
leadership, 282-3
learning organisations, 279
least developed countries, 142-3
Lenovo, 146
Lewis, Cleona, 70-1
licensing, 15-16, 63, 112, 115-17, 119, 120, 121-2, 159
localisation, 27, 49
local managers, 13, 349
local market adaptation, 135, 139
location, 45, 49, 271, 348
location advantages, 19-21, 107, 109, 118, 119-20
location decisions, 2, 224-61
  BW experiment, 236-7, 244-50
  calculative vs. process approach to, 228-9
  choice-modelling experiment, 230-6, 237-44
  literature on, 226-8, 255-9
location factors, 132-3
location theory, 88
Lund, Arne, 79-80

Magee, Stephen, 13-14
management, 87
management skills, 54-5
managerial decision-making, 45, 56, 100, 103-4
  location decisions, 2, 224-61
managers
  attitudes toward risk of, 100-1
  competencies of, 19
  expatriate, 349
  international awareness in, 14
  local, 13, 349
  objectives of, 98
manufacturing, 135
  offshoring, 131, 283-4
  production chain and, 135-7
market imperfections, 95
marketing strategies, 358-79
market-making intermediaries, 144
market-stealing effect, 159
Marxism, 65
mass production, 133
monopoly, 45, 144
monoposny, 140

moral values, 277-8
motivation, 53, 99
multinational enterprises (MNEs), 1-2, 10, 79
  see also global factory
  emergence of, 117-20
  from emerging economies, 25-6
  FDI by, 12-14, 15-17
  future of, 40-2
  governance of, 94-104, 139-40
  information flows in, 43, 272
  Japanese, 343-55
  location decisions by, 224-61
  marketing strategies, 358-79
  models of, 351-3
  as network, 348
  research on, 108-9

nations, 132-3
negative spillovers, 159
networks, 51, 273-5
NUMMI, 213

offshoring, 49, 50, 131, 134, 283-4
oligopoly, 17-18, 87
opportunism, 11-12, 99
organizational learning, 214
original brand manufacturer (OBM), 145, 146, 148
original design manufacturer (ODM), 144-5, 148
original equipment manufacturers (OEMs), 48, 135, 144, 148, 267, 345-6
Orwell, George, 9
outsourcing, 49, 134, 137, 138, 283-4, 345
ownership advantages, 10, 18, 80, 107-9, 118-21
ownership strategies, 49

partial equilibrium, 108
Penrose, Edith, 63, 84
Phelps, Dudley Maynard, 68-9
Poland
  doing business in, 318-39
  German interactions, 292, 294-6, 299-306, 320-39
  UK interactions, 292, 294-6, 299-301, 306-13

392 Index

portfolio investment, 80–1
portfolio theory, 9
production activities, 95
production chain, 135–7, 283–4
production costs, 96
productivity, 131, 192
product life cycle, 16–17, 20, 186, 189
profits, 191–2
psychic distance paradox, 227

quantitative research, 21
quasi-internalization, 348

rational action modelling, 41
regional economic integration, 130
Remer, C. F., 71, 72
rentier investments, 73
research and development (R&D), 42,
   143
  firm performance and, 183–5
  flexibility in, 275
  internationalization and, 186–8
  role of competition and, 171–4, 176
  spillovers, 157–77, 187–8
research methods, 21–3
resilience, 52–3
resource-based view, 18–19
risk, attitudes toward, 82, 100–1, 103
risk aversion, 14, 82, 84, 100–1, 103,
   224–5, 228–9, 241
risk diversification theory, 20
rule-driven behaviour, 41

scientific knowledge, 184, 187–8
Scottish Enlightenment, 8
Shanghai Automotive Industry
   Corporation (SAIC), 146
Shiseidô, 364–6, 369–75
Smith, Adam, 66
social capital, 279
South Korea, 149
sovereignty, 132
sovereign wealth funds, 150
spatial distribution strategies, 55, 283–5
spillovers
  inter-industry, 161–2, 166–8
  intra-industry, 164–6
  measurement of, 160–2
  negative, 159
  R&D, 157–77, 187–8

stakeholders, attitudes toward risk of,
   100–1
standardization-differentiation
   continuum, 49–50
state, role of the, 149–50
strategic alliances, knowledge transfer
   in, 206–20
strategic change, 280–3
strategic information, 276
subsidiaries, 55, 76, 84
supplementary knowledge accession,
   209–10, 215
supplementary knowledge acquisition,
   212–13, 215
supply chain
  global, 48, 131, 135, 136, 267–8
  vertical integration, 133

tacit knowledge, 99
Taiwanese companies, 146–7
tangible assets, 192
tariff jumping, 76, 78
TCL, 146–7
technological change, 16, 133
technological opportunities, 168–71,
   175
technology transfer, 12–14, 17
Teece, D.J., 96
textile industry, 148
theory of the growth of the firm, 43–4,
   62, 84
tit-for-tat hypothesis, 18
Toynbee, Arnold, 22
Toyota, 367–75
trade theory, 224
transaction cost analysis, 10–12
transaction costs, 43–5, 53–4, 137
  entrepreneurship and, 141–2
  internal, 96–9, 101, 103
transitional economies, doing business
   in, 318–39
trust, 103, 207
  engineering, 277–8
  knowledge transfer and, 215–18

UK/Poland interactions, 292, 294–6,
   299–301, 306–13
uncertainty, 44, 46, 56, 86
United States, 227
unlearning, 142–3, 279

Index 393

Uppsala model, 26, 224–5
utility, 111–17

value chains, 137–8
Vernon, R., 16–17, 20, 23, 25
Vernon hypothesis, 14
vertical integration, 12, 131, 133

Vico, Giambattista, 8
volatility, 44, 45, 100–1

wages, 140
warehousing, 48–9, 135, 136, 267–8
Wilkins, Mira, 26
Williamson, Oliver, 10–12, 28, 67, 96–7

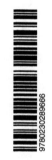